POLITICAL IDEOLOGIES IN CONTEMPORARY RUSSIA

Political Ideologies in Contemporary Russia

ELENA CHEBANKOVA

McGill-Queen's University Press

Montreal & Kingston · London · Chicago

ISBN 978-0-2280-0340-3 (cloth)
ISBN 978-0-2280-0341-0 (paper)
ISBN 978-0-2280-0437-0 (ePDF)
ISBN 978-0-2280-0438-7 (ePUB)

Legal deposit fourth quarter 2020
Bibliothèque nationale du Québec

Printed in Canada on acid-free paper that is 100% ancient forest free
(100% post-consumer recycled), processed chlorine free

Library and Archives Canada Cataloguing in Publication

Title: Political ideologies in contemporary Russia/Elena Chebankova.

Names: Chebankova, Elena A., author.

Description: Includes bibliographical references and index.

Identifiers: Canadiana (print) 20200274651 | Canadiana (ebook)
20200274740 | ISBN 9780228003410 (paper) | ISBN 9780228003403
(cloth) | ISBN 9780228004370 (ePDF) | ISBN 9780228004387 (ePUB)

Subjects: LCSH: Ideology—Russia (Federation) | LCSH: Russia (Federation)—
Politics and government.

Classification: LCC JA84.R9 C54 2020 | DDC 320.50947—dc23

This book was typeset by Marquis Interscript in 10.5/13 Sabon.

For Dennis

Contents

POLITICAL IDEOLOGIES IN CONTEMPORARY RUSSIA

1

Introduction

Ideology has been a matter of academic and political interest since the nineteenth century. It has been studied through various prisms: as a history of ideas, as intellectual thought animating and informing political action, as a system of beliefs, and as a cultural phenomenon establishing parameters of political cultural hegemony. The arrival of Marxism made the study of ideology much more methodological by moving the concept of ideology to the realm of 'superstructure', to be analysed from an historical perspective. Marx and Engels insisted that all ideologies are false, in that they are conditioned by the forces of economic production and therefore reflect the interests of the ruling class. Post-Marxist interpretations redefined the purely economic understanding of ideology and, in the writings of Gramsci, Althusser, Derrida, and others, granted it serious cultural foundations. Post-Marxists argued that living customs covertly 'normalize' social relationships within society and instil an atmosphere of common-sense cultural practices, which persuade the exploited of the benefit of their own exploitation.

The development of the welfare state in the twentieth century ensured a brief and superficial convergence between the interests of working and wealthy classes. Proprietors of the means of production deemed the idea of redistributing some income towards the working class rational – for fear of a potential backlash. This brought about a tenuous period of social harmony. The concept of the 'death of ideology' was invoked in the 1950s, when the gap between left and right was bridged as a result of easing socio-economic conflict. Rising living standards, an emergent welfare state, and ensuing political apathy shifted politics from the realm of economic interest to one of managerialism and consensus.

With the departure of communism at the end of the 1980s, liberalism seemed to be the unequivocal winner of the political and cultural discourse. This allowed the annunciation of yet another 'end' – this time Francis Fukuyama's (1992) 'end of history'. Despite these recurrent 'ends', ideology remained surprisingly resilient and reluctant to leave the political scene. More importantly, the 'end of history' ushered in an era of globalism and introduced new parameters to the global redistribution of wealth and power. With it came a host of new social, political, and cultural issues, which marked the beginning of fresh conflicts with redefined economic and cultural-civilizational ruptures.

Russia was among the leading participants in the debates on these issues. She was at the heart of new ideological battles due to developments in the international economic and geopolitical arena, the establishment of new socio-cultural realities in post-communist countries, the pressures of identity politics in developed states, and Russia's political and economic stabilization during the early 2000s.

Surprisingly, a comprehensive analysis of the ideological context that animates Russia's foreign and domestic policies has not yet been exhaustively articulated. The literature on the Soviet Union devotes significant attention to the study of Marxism-Leninism, as well as Russia's pre-existing philosophical and intellectual texts, which informed the Union's policy conduct at home and abroad. With the dissolution of the Soviet Union, most commentators assumed that Russia would follow 'normal' (read Western) patterns of development, and its new political scene would be legitimized by Western intellectual and ideological models. When such assumptions proved to be erroneous, another claim was adopted: this was the idea that Russia would form a kind of ideational uniformity resulting from Putin's alleged suppression of the opposition.

It would be wrong to assume that, in the Putin era, Russia's political and ideological landscape is uniformly bleak and uninspiring. The past decade has seen an increased interest in Russia's contemporary political ideologies. A number of authors adopted a more nuanced approach to the subject of ideological diversity in contemporary Russia by paying keen attention to various streams of Russian political thought and philosophy. Research articles and books offering a detailed and sophisticated study of Russian nationalism have emerged (Laruelle 2018). Conservatism and its impact on Russia's past and present has been scrutinized (Robinson 2019), links to fascism are being debated (Snyder 2018; Umland 2005; Umland 2008; Motyl 2015), Eurasianism has been seriously examined (Shlapentokh 2007; Laruelle 2008), and ideological aspects of Russian foreign policy have become the focus of academic attention (Morozov and Makarychev 2011; Tsygankov 2016). Serious research has been conducted into Russia's Enlightenment, and it discusses political ideas of that period, from the point of view of their connection with parallel Western thinking, as well as from the premise of Russia's own religious-orthodox base of the process (Hamburg 2016).

At the same time, room remains for an expanded study of Russia's new ideological realties. Key questions need to be asked: Which ideas animate the actions of Russia's ruling elite, opposition, and civil society? What motivates Russia's political actors and how do they convert their goals into ideological rhetoric? Which international and domestic constraints shape Russia's political thinking? How does Russia's new class structure influence Russia's current ideological discourse? Contrary to the view that discursive uniformity reigns in Russia, this book will show that the country is experiencing serious theoretical debates across a wide spectrum of modern ideologies. The fragmented nature of Russia's ideological scene, its multiplicity, and its lack of clear direction informs the living body of Russia's contemporary politics and generates a keen interest in its impact on Russia's future evolution.

RATIONALE OF THE STUDY

People are tempted to explain political actions and situations according to their own standards of rationality. At the same time, philosophical and historical literature argues that the rationality of political actors depends on the context and conventions of their environment. In the majority of cases, agents act within two different intentional streams. First, they can act against the general backdrop of conventional rationality, disputing and disrupting established norms and morality. By doing so, they can change the existing moral outlook of society and establish new parameters of socio-political interaction. Second, actors can merely reiterate existing truths and customary practices and remain within the bounds of these conventions. In this case, they pick and choose available conventions that are deemed rational within their socio-cultural paradigm, without questioning their rationality. For both streams, the existing social context serves as a benchmark and influences the understanding of an agent's actions. Therefore, explaining the rational motivations and intentions of political actors requires an examination of the discursive and contextual scene within which these actors function.

Richard Rorty, Peter Winch, Quentin Skinner, James Tully, Roger Griffin, and other historians of ideas claim that rationality pertains to specific socio-cultural paradigms. Thus, some rational actions within a specific paradigm may seem irrational to an external observer. Alasdair MacIntyre (1971, 9–10) insists that those outside the established consensus would not necessarily find the goals and ideas of those within the consensus rational. Therefore, without grasping the overall environmental context surrounding political actors, we cannot come close to explaining the political institutions that these actors erect or the practices and actions they adopt. Such conventions define the 'general ideological context' of a given society. Tully (1988, 9) argues that this context could be examined via existing 'literary and philosophical works, speeches, rhetorical exercises, public debates, texts, and official speeches, as well as academic writings. All these represent speech acts, and like any other form of social action, these are conventional actions.' Tully (1988, 9) assembles these acts under the rubric of ideology and claims that 'ideology is a language of politics defined by its conventions and employed by a number of writers.'

Ideology, then, becomes a useful frame of reference for the study of the characteristics of a given society. It is informed by action and changing realities, yet it also informs action and channels developing realities in a particular direction. Quentin Skinner notes:

> The problem facing an agent who wishes to legitimate what he is doing at the same time as gaining what he wants cannot simply be the instrumental problem of tailoring his normative language in order to fit his projects. It must in part be the problem of tailoring his projects in order to fit the available normative language (in Tully 1988, 14).

On the one hand, the ideological context often conditions participants to speak within the existing borders of conventions to legitimize actions that could fall beyond the established bounds of prevailing morality. Actors deploy discursive means to appropriate existing language that is universally understandable to promote their desired course of action. Looking at Russia, the Gorbachevian *new thinking* paradigm, which he introduced as an ideological companion to his *perestroika* programme, was a vocal example of such an approach. The language of Marxism-Leninism was deployed to justify the desire of political elites to move away from the existing economic orthodoxy and, partially, to convert their political influence into tangible economic gains. The language of the return to *true Leninism* was adopted, along with the relaxation of the Soviet economic environment and the introduction of private co-operatives that were supposedly in line with Lenin's New Economic Policy. This example reinforces Quentin Skinner's general argument (2002, Vol. 1, 145–8) that ideology often masks intentions and actions that would otherwise be deemed unreasonable or immoral, and so it attempts to break the boundaries of existing conventions to ensure policy change.

On the other hand, ideology is constrained by the realities of the age, and so it depends on how far the existing boundaries can be stretched. Projects must be tailored to come across as realistic within the given conventional context. Martin Seliger (1976, 16) insists that, while ideologies are considered to guide action, this also depends on the circumstances within which policies were conceived. These exigencies affect the structure and nature of ideologies and even political philosophies. Therefore, the development of any society is always accompanied by the development of ideology, the understanding of which could be instrumental to the study of the evolution of political processes. If we seek explanations for political actions from a rational point of view, it becomes essential to ascertain the general ideological context surrounding existing political actors.

If we scrutinize the Russian case, the rationale for studying ideologies in the contemporary context becomes ever more evident. We can easily establish that explanations for political activity are often given from a comparative angle that renders to Russia's political actors some degree of rationality. Many of these explanations are versed in a uniquely Western type of rationality, and some strive to assign normative definitions, according to a Western perspective, to Russia's actions. A number of comparative works have emerged that juxtapose the rationality and motivations of Russia's political actors to those from similarly 'revisionist' or 'authoritarian' states (Levitsky and Way 2002; Ambrosio 2009; Krug and Libman 2015; Lankina, Libman, Obydenkova 2016). It is evident that, for a Western observer, this approach is useful in understanding Russia's political processes. However, this method bears hidden limitations for those wishing to build a more holistic picture. We therefore need to supplement comparative and positivist methods of study with a more qualitative approach to examine Russia's ideational, contextual, and discursive climate. This would enable the explanation of the political intentions and motivations of Russia's actors and of the political processes that take place in Russia.

The Russian case illuminates the importance of studying the discursive arena in general as a venue for anticipating or explaining *potential* and existing political action. One main difficulty in studying ideologies in Russia is that many ideas are part of the general discourse but are not yet reflected by mass or sectoral political movements. Existing ideologies create a specific cultural context, in which political actions could gestate for a prolonged period. Hence, Russia's nascent ideologies could exist in some, but not total, isolation from programmatic political parties. This distinguishes Russia from Western-type states, in which the majority of existing political ideas are accurately reflected in the programmatic rhetoric of various parties – though this is non-linear even in the Western context. Alasdair MacIntyre has suggested that ideologies are lodged in three different realms: political, sociological, and philosophical. To this end, ideology does not belong only to 'particular changes of the changing world which can be investigated only by empirical inquiry' (MacIntyre 1971, 6). In other words, it cannot be measured solely by the empirical existence of programmatic political movements. Ideology is evident in three separate spheres: the sociological sphere, in which we study the nature of people's social existence; in the political sphere, where we examine programmatic political action; and in the realm of metaphysics and philosophy, in which we investigate 'normative statements on the state of the world, as well as the relationship between the truth or falsity of empirically investigable processes and events' (MacIntyre 1971, 6).

Leszek Kolakowski (2005, 10) aptly argues that intellectual trends originate before their programmatic embodiments and have a history of their own; they have 'a prehistory in a range of questions that come to the fore, or a series of isolated answers that are knitted into a single whole by some outstanding mind,' and they are 'thus transformed into a new cultural phenomenon'. Therefore, we could speak of what are, at first glance, paradoxical phenomena, such as 'Cartesianism before

Descartes', 'Marxism before Marx', or 'Christianity before Christ' (Kolakowski 2005, 10). Thinkers, such as Albert Hirschman, Bernard Williams, and Eric Hoffer, concur that internal, psychological, factors are responsible for the launch of civic action. Bernard Williams (2005) argues that exogenous factors alone cannot move us to act, they merely produce knowledge, and simply knowing is insufficient to induce action. Thus, the reasons for action are always internal: a person must feel before he is moved to act.

It follows from this that some ideas, or indeed ideologies, have not been translated into meaningful political action expressed by programmatic parties, but this does not signify that these ideas are not being pondered by political thinkers, intellectuals, the general public, and those with influence over political processes. This holds particularly true in Russia, whose political system ensures the widest possible spectrum of political ideologies and ideas, albeit at the discursive, not partisan, level. The partisan programmatic level remains weak and largely controlled by the state apparatus, which encourages only select parties to make it to this political level. Such a situation means that it is even more important to study the existing political discourse in Russia at various levels, starting from partisan action and ending with nascent or marginal ideas. Politicians, analysts, and students of contemporary Russia need to be aware of existing intellectual trends and ideas circulating in the contemporary Russian landscape. One ought to be alert to the *entire* complex of ideas in order to anticipate and accurately narrate the emergence of potential political action. Scrutinizing the origins of action once it has surfaced condemns an observer to the mammoth task of catching up with, rather than anticipating (or fully understanding), political developments.

Russia can surprise an observer with rapid and unexpected political eruptions, as was the case at least twice during the twentieth century. In 1917, Minister Irakli Tsereteli lamented that no political party in Russia was able to take full responsibility for the country. In response, Vladimir Lenin, at the First All-Russian Congress of Workers' and Soldiers' Deputies on 4 June, allegedly proclaimed, 'Yes, there is such a party!' to confirm the ability of the Bolshevik party to take on this responsibility. It is an anecdotal, light-hearted remark, but once a phrase like this has been uttered, an analyst who searched for programmatic parties at the expense of examining the general discursive environment falls a step behind in scrutinizing this party's genesis, motivations, and ideology. These considerations explain the rationale of this book and the need to study the development of political ideologies in Russia, particularly since the collapse of the Soviet Union.

MAIN THEMES AND PROBLEMS

Ideology represents a part of discourse and the means to legitimize political action. This generates two important and problematized themes. The first concerns the understanding of ideology as an instrument used to legitimize political action and expose ongoing social conflicts. While examining the ideological climate in Russia we must establish which socio-political conflicts these ideologies strive to reflect and which tasks and actions they seek to legitimize. The second theme considers ideology as a part of discourse and is concerned with its evolution. It delves into the history of ideas and could be conditionally detached from the existing institutional and political climate of the age. The key question that arises here is whether we can study ideology with reference to texts that originated elsewhere, in a different age and cultural context? In the case of Russia, the question is whether we can deploy Western ideological texts and historical patterns to understand the uniquely Russian political and ideological context.

Ideology as the Means of Legitimating Action

Skinner (2002, Vol. 2, 157) argues that agents deploy ideology to justify those of their actions that do not fit within the limits of the prevailing morality of their society. Griffin (2006, 81; see also Hamilton 1987) concurs with this position by arguing that ideology is 'aimed at justifying a particular pattern of conduct, which its proponents seek to promote, realize, pursue, or maintain'. The most important element of this construction is that such ideological (or rationalist) activity also reflects shifting power relations within society. Hence, ideologies are usually formulated and reformulated to fit and accommodate these power shifts.(Tully 1988, 23).

These assumptions lead to a host of questions applicable to the Russian case. What is the questionable conduct that contemporary Russian ideology seeks to justify? Which political developments does it reflect? Which challenges does it seek to respond to? Which conflicts and shifts in power relations does it illuminate? In response to these questions it is safe to assume that Russia's contemporary ideological scene reflects the significant shift in power that took place at the end of the twentieth century with the collapse of the Soviet Union. Property relationships have been redefined, resulting in the emergence of a new rich and poor. A new class structure has surfaced, dispensing with the erstwhile egalitarian assumptions of economic equality, however virtual these became towards the end of the Soviet Union's existence. The international environment presented new realities that deprived the Russian Federation of the pre-existing political and military might of the Soviet state. New ethnic cleavages, as well as patterns of ethnic dominance and subordination, have surfaced with the influx of migrants from former Soviet republics – a development that pulled the rug out from under the feet of the old Soviet myth of the 'friendship of peoples'.

Russia's contemporary political climate is beleaguered by various problems of an economic, social, political, and international nature, such as the growing division between poverty and wealth, the struggle for greater social justice, unequal access to economic, political, and legal resources, the fragility of the state apparatus, bitter memories of the 1990s, adverse relationships with the West, scepticism towards cultural pressures of Western neo-liberalism and identity politics, and Russia's growing role in international affairs. In this context, the ideological climate of the age must deal with several key tasks. First, it is geared towards strengthening and consolidating the state as a traditional Russian vehicle of stability, security, and economic growth. Second, it is torn between the need to legitimize new capitalist property relations and unavoidable moral commitments to the ideas of social justice and equality embedded in the perceptions of those who were born and matured in the late USSR. Third, it aims to respond to the growing security threats that, to a majority of Russians, emanate from the West.

First, the turbulent period of the 1990s, and the lessons of the civil war, resulted in the need to consolidate the Russian state. Russia experienced two major national catastrophes in the twentieth century. The first state collapse took place with Russia's entry into the First World War, resulting in the fall of the monarchy, the disintegration of the Russian Empire, and the subsequent Bolshevik revolution that was to change the course of Russia's history in a radical direction for over seventy years. The second major social catastrophe took place with the fall of the Soviet Union. Then the demise of the erstwhile Soviet Empire completed the unfinished disintegration of the Russian Empire, the remains of which the Red Army and the Communist government had managed to reassemble and glue together in the course of the 1918–21 civil war. These two major events contributed to the significant de-alignment of Russian and Soviet societies and involved considerable transformations across societal cleavages, as well as the reconsideration and reassessment of all pre-existing cultural codes and behavioural patterns. Twice in the twentieth century Russia experienced the breakdown of her historic myths and unity, the demoralization of society, decline in interpersonal and institutional trust, as well as a significant drop in individual and civic responsibility. These circumstances obviated the need to consolidate Russia's state power with the view of assuring stable development in the future. A number of Russian scholars agree that the arrival of Vladimir Putin led to a consolidation of the Russian state apparatus. Yet, this process had to be accompanied by some serious forms of ideological justification.

The overall logic has become that once a state power has been consolidated and ensures at least minimal forms of external protection and internal order, citizens are obliged to support it. Dismantling the state would immediately lead to the loss of Russia's defence potential, imminent external invasion based on previous historical patterns, and be tantamount to losing Russia's territorial, cultural, and political integrity. All these events would lead to more ominous consequences for ordinary men than a corrupt and inefficient government at home. Citizens have a duty to submit to the government, because of their common desire for stability, peace, and prosperity. Such obligations only end when the holders of power become incapable of protecting the people from external threats and commotion at home. In many ways, the logic of contemporary pundits of the Russian state is reminiscent of the Hobbesian *de facto* schema: 'political obligation is based not on legitimist principles but on the assumption of a strictly mutual relationship between protection and obedience' (Skinner 2002, Vol. 3, 22). Russia's mainstream ideologies seek to exonerate the extant Russian state, even though its legitimacy could be questioned from the perspective of social justice, the legitimacy of the USSR's dissolution, and glaring inequality in the legal, economic, and social spheres. Differing ideological streams such as conservatism, liberalism, and nationalism obtained state-driven connotations, and, one way or another, focused on a stronger state as a vehicle for stability and economic development. I will be returning to this theme in the chapters devoted to these specific ideologies.

Second, the consolidation of new forms of production and new forms of ownership over the means of production established in the wake of the U S S R's collapse required some serious ideological justifications. The task proved to be more complex than it seemed initially with the launch of *perestroika* and *new thinking*. It is important that a large share of the Russian population is still immersed in a Soviet upbringing that has been transferred to children via family and educational institutions staffed with bearers of the Soviet cultural and political mentality. The normalization of capitalist socio-economic and political relationships, economic inequality, and minimization of the welfare state has become a difficult, yet necessary, task for the new ruling elite. Like early capitalists of the Western European Reformation, Russia's new rich lacked moral support within the impoverished population of the post-Soviet state and had to find some ideological means of legitimizing their behaviour. Rhetorically, glorification and the significant reassessment of the pre-Revolutionary patterns of Russian life, greater socio-political union with the Church, and an emphasis on traditionalism, culture, and history all served to normalize new post-Soviet forms of socio-economic inequality. This inequality has become questionable to many who were born and educated in the spirit of Soviet morality that, at least verbally, professed much greater redistribution of income towards the working class, as well as the general spirit of fraternity and comradeship.

Third, it is the view of many Russian analysts and the public that Western policies towards Russia hinder economic and political stabilization. As a consequence, the external threat has been considered a greater evil than any corrupt power at home. It is important to note that the initial ideology of Russia-Western relations developed throughout the Yeltsin and early-Putin periods and was informed by the economic interests of those holding Russia's new wealth. The newly emerged Russian elites sought to integrate into the liberal world order and join the club of rich states. The size of the stake they sought to obtain within the world-governing institutions has not been fully discussed and was not a prime bargaining issue. Those elites sought to abide by the existing global rules, become part of the global elite, preserve and multiply personal capital obtained since the dissolution of the Soviet Union, and have an occasional say on the matters of cardinal importance to world affairs. These intentions have been animated by the overarching ideology of joining the Western civilization. This ideological stream dominated Russian discourse for a large part of its post-Soviet development. The end goal of this stream was seen in the creation of what Alexander Dugin referred to as 'corporation Russia' – a state fully compliant with Western socio-political patterns and occupying a decent place among rich Western countries – with no disruption to its ideological and economic agendas.

At some point, however, it became clear that such a strategy was not going to bring fruitful results. Global elites anticipated that, due to Russia's size, resources, and economic potential, and its historical propensity towards constructing alternative visions of politics, the country could at some point fall out of their control and strive for larger stakes in international economic institutions. The rift between the expectations of Russian elites and the concerns of their global counterparts has surfaced. As a result, the task of developing and justifying some forms of 'national', 'patriotic', 'state-inspired' forms of capitalism emerged. In this context, the ideas of Russia's civilizational distinctness, driven by some deeply held religious and historical values and the goals of 'saving' Europe from the 'sins' of postmodernism, became instrumental in conducting both foreign and domestic policies.

That being said, a brief disclaimer is needed, as the picture is still rather more nuanced. Forces of cultural preservation have also emerged in Russia with the dissolution of the Soviet Union and against the backdrop of Western liberal triumphalism, which was accompanied for many ordinary Russians by the loss of their pre-existing moral, ethical, and historical frames of reference. These forces of cultural self-preservation engendered a search for Russia's unique epistemology that could match Russia's specific ontology (Dugin 2012c). The challenges of constructing a new post-Soviet identity have become prominent and have invoked metaphysical questions of self-understanding, self-reflection, and a reassessment of the history of Russian ideas and socio-political events. From this perspective, Russia's general rejection of Western postmodernism and value interventionism has cultural-philosophical, as well as political-economic, foundations.

All these wide-ranging problems invoked overarching conservatively inclined thinking across all ideological streams. Hence, the paradigm of state conservatism has emerged as the mainstream form of discourse. In brief, all the main ideologies within this paradigm sought to develop a uniquely Russian state based on a multi-ethnic community that relies on previous periods of Russia's history and the country's idiosyncratic political traditions. This paradigm defends Russia's originality, a multipolar world, traditional Christian values, the idea of Russia as a state-civilization, a nation-state–oriented elite, and the establishment of the Eurasian Union as an institutional bloc capable of promoting independent socio-cultural and economic development of its composite members. This ideological direction was consolidated with the Crimea conflict of 2014. From that point onwards, the construction of 'civilization Russia' (to use Alexander Dugin's 2016 terminology) became its unequivocal final goal. Liberal and left radicalism, in which left and liberal ideology form a unique political symbiosis, emerged as a subordinate counter-discourse, or counter-paradigm, that seeks to subvert the main conservative episteme. Representatives of radical-left and liberal streams deploy almost-identical rhetorical means, refer to similar painful issues, and raise similar socially oriented problems in an attempt to dismantle conservative hegemony. Their final goal seems globally oriented, yet liberals view a Russia merging with the West on the West's terms as an ultimate final destination, while the left harbours goals of reawakening a dormant class consciousness at the world-wide level with open-ended outcomes. As already observed, despite having different goals in the international arena and different visions of Russia's future, both conservative traditionalist and pro-Western liberal paradigms have common economic motivations, seen in the legitimation of economic relations established since the dissolution of the Soviet Union. It is significant that the radical left joined the pro-Western liberal paradigm relatively recently, since the White Ribbon protests of 2011–12. This arrival mars the overall picture of the commonality of economic intentions between the two general paradigms, because the political economic motivations and overall vision on the Russian eschatology of the radical left remains in the shadows.

As a result of this dualism, all ideologies under review in this volume will have this split nature. Each group of ideologies diverges along the two given paradigmatic trajectories and will be Janus-faced, with each face looking in either traditionalist or Western-liberal directions. As mentioned, the main difficulty in examining ideologies in Russia lies in the fact that very few programmatic parties form around specific ideologies. A meaningful discussion of ideology and ideologically driven, programme-based political action in Russia will invariably face the problem of sluggish partisan activity. Ideologies remain mostly as a part of discourse and a part of the public sphere lodged in the intellectual written and public debates, supplemented with marginal forms of civic activity. Yet, if we were to imagine that Russia's ideologies were to form meaningful political parties, we could, perhaps, observe two versions of the liberal, nationalist, conservative, feminist, multiculturalist, and other ideological parties that would reflect the existing political paradigms, traditionalist and liberal.

These paradigms question and interrogate each other, although they could not merge into a single system in that they lack a general commonality of intentions towards Russia's future place in the world order. Russia's ruling elite fosters an open dialogue among those radical alternatives, while subtly marginalizing those that lie outside the dominant conservative traditionalist discourse supported by the state. More importantly, the state does not try to reach a consensus between radical liberals and traditionalists, thus fully embracing and exposing the existing divide within society. Indeed, various ideological alternatives are readily available in various public-sphere outlets, starting with state television and ending with popular Internet TV channels, where a large number of political discussions take place. At the same time, high public awareness of the radical left and liberal paradigmatic cause and its immediate intellectual and political availability (pro-Western liberal parties always take part in the elections at all levels, and this could be the case for the radical left in the future) precludes them from being novel and immediately appealing to the Russian public. This system could be referred to as *paradigmatic pluralism*, which assumes the existence and dialogue between varying paradigms of socio-political thinking. The political system established by Putin during the time he has been leader rests on this unique balancing mechanism, which levels radically different ideological paradigms that reflect problems, conventions, and challenges facing contemporary Russian society. This system of balancing paradigmatically different ideological positions, which then become the hallmark of Russia's extant political system, could be branded as 'Putinism'.[1]

Western Textual References and Historical Parallels

The second theme concerns the links that this work draws between Russia's discourse and the history of Western political ideas and philosophy. Critics might note (and such criticism would chime in well with my previous discussion of the contextual nature of rationality) that Russia's ideological scene should be discussed somewhat in isolation from its Western counterparts due to Russia's idiosyncratic (from a Western observer's perspective) political system (Seliktar 2004;

Shlapentokh 1998). Nevertheless, the book makes abundant references to Western ideological discourse and will discuss the way in which Western ideational models and constructs are deployed to match Russian intellectual realities. How could this be explained? In an attempt to respond to the charge of overlooking the chasm between the cultural, political, and historical evolution of Western and Russian modernity, we can invoke Paul Ricoeur's propositions on the general validity of the texts (speeches, pamphlets, literature) across historical contexts. His ideas, supported and expanded by Jacques Derrida, Stanley Fish, Quentin Skinner, and others, are formulated in the 'reader-response' approach. Ricoeur's general argument is that the history of ideas can be studied with the specific purpose of appropriating ideational constructs and applying them to any given contemporary context. Pre-existing ideas and texts can be deployed in the process of constructing the ideology and discourse of new authors, and in a modified form they can become a significant part of a contemporary narrative. Ricoeur argues that texts may well have precise intended meanings, but over the course of time, texts 'will acquire an autonomous space for meaning which is no longer animated by the intentions of its author' (Ricoeur 1981, 174; see also Skinner 2002, Vol. 3, 92).

Paraphrasing Ricoeur, Skinner (2002, Vol. 1, 92) notes that 'what the text says now matters more than what the author meant to say.' In this way, we recover the validity of the text for the contemporary climate and appropriate it for our own purposes, while interpretation of the text becomes tantamount to finding its lessons for contemporary use. Stanley Fish, as well Jacques Derrida, have also been exponents of the 'reader-response' approach, with Fish (1980) insisting: 'We must look into the consequences of texts for the meaning that we hope to recover; for they are the meanings that we create' (cited in Skinner 2002, Vol. 1, 93). Indeed, as mentioned earlier, we are invariably constrained by the spirit of our age and its prevailing morality. Yet it could also be argued that ideologies often grow out of interpretations of past philosophical texts appropriated to contemporary conditions. Ideologies are not constant; they are living and evolving segments of a discursive arena. As discourse evolves along with political, cultural, contextual conditions, so do ideologies that borrow and reinterpret previous texts to match contemporary realities (Shull 1992, 733). Martin Seliger (1979, 22) invokes Napoleon, who divided ideology on ideas (essentially the belief system) and the philosophical endeavour to explain the formation of ideas. Antonio Gramsci also sought to study ideology first as a science of ideas, searching for their origins in historical texts, and second as the system of ideas that depend on historical-political factors and material context (Filippini 2017).

The frequent reference by Russian intellectuals to Western texts serves the purpose of recovering useful meanings that could be appropriate for contemporary tasks and context. Therefore, despite some visible ontological differences, the dialogical approach to the lessons of Western European history and philosophical literature becomes an instrumental part of the Russian discourse. Moreover, political ideas always develop in a dialogical fashion. The evolution of the Western philosophical tradition, for example, is heavily indebted to Greek and subsequent Roman thought. As Bernard Williams (2005, 3) notes, 'the legacy of Greece to Western philosophy is Western philosophy,' and further observes that Western philosophy 'not only started with Plato but spent most of its life in his company' (2006, 148). By using the same analogy, one could claim that Russian philosophy, though a self-sufficient philosophical stream (Hamburg, 2016), spent a large share of its time in the company of Western philosophy, in a constant dialogue with its main figures. It is in such spirit that this volume will also make a number of historical references to both Russian and Western events of significance in its various chapters. Skinner (2002, Vol. 3, 238) argues that 'ideological arguments are commonly sustained by an appeal to the past, an appeal either to see precedents in history for new claims being advanced, or to see history itself as a development towards the point of view being advocated or denounced.'

One general historical comparison is of interest at this point. Delving into the underlying foundations and rationale of Russian ideological discourse, one could discover, with much surprise, that the kernel of ideology is strikingly similar to the political climate of the English Civil War and the interregnum period of the seventeenth century. English philosophers and pundits of that period also thought to legitimize the *de facto* power of the state after a serious state collapse reflected in the regicide – the first to occur in the modern period. How could those thinkers justify political obligation to the newly formed authorities that redistributed and reshuffled power relations within the country? A quest for political and economic stability emerged that became a priority of public policy. That period, along with its goals and motivations, produced many of the intellectual foundations of the modern European period, epitomized in the political thought of

Thomas Hobbes and John Locke. In many ways, Russia's emerging bourgeois order is motivated by considerations of stability similar to those that motivated John Locke, the ideologue of the English bourgeoisie, after the troubled years of the English Civil War. As John Dunn (1969, 18) notes, 'order, learning, diligence control, a comfortable and well-esteemed place in the world well protected from the storms outside' became the main motivators for Locke's ideas. Instead of the searching for the world 'full of exuberant and emotional indulgence, stability comes to be the main goal'. And with it, 'settlement is the great aim and authority the mode of its attainment' (Dunn 1969, 18).

Another parallel of interest is that the interregnum period was also tasked with linking various periods of British history into one coherent narrative. This narrative should have logically tied up the Norman conquest, which disrupted the power relations of medieval England, the post-conquest period of development and stability, and the potential future trajectory that was to follow the upheaval invoked by the regicide and the revolution. Ideological and rhetorical schema must have been created to instil logic, coherence, and the vindication of power and civic obligation to it on behalf of the general population. Russia's contemporary ideological discourse is similarly tasked with constructing viable links between the three broken periods of Russian history: the pre-Revolutionary imperial era, the Soviet period, and the post-Soviet present. Fitting the erstwhile Soviet discourse into the contemporary building of Russian conservatism becomes the foremost task of Russia's thinkers and ideologues who seek to uphold the existing state while avoiding denunciation of the Soviet period of Russia's past. To these ideologues, those who strive to repudiate the Soviet period of Russian history will invariably face the weakening and even the disintegration of the contemporary Russian state. This is because both eras, contemporary and Soviet, are inextricably linked at the social, political, economic, and cultural levels.

The post-Soviet present flows organically from the Soviet past and is ubiquitously conditioned by it. To ignore those realities would amount to committing a pernicious mistake at the strategic level and reveal extreme intellectual short-sightedness. It is often argued that religious leaders who repudiate the Soviet past and hail the fall of the Soviet state, inadvertently exonerate the disintegration of the post-Soviet space, and with it, an imminent disintegration of the united Russian Orthodox world – a development we witness in the attempts to grant autocephalous status to the Ukrainian Orthodox Church.

The dissolution of the political union led to the dissolution of the union of the Church in just two decades. Politically, disparaging the Soviet past is similar to the rejection of the ideas of social justice and the ideal of human equality – a mistake, catastrophic in the Russian context. Remarkable achievements of the Soviet state in the areas of science, education, the exploration of space, and the dissemination of Russian culture and sports linger in the memories of ordinary people and are deployed by elites. Russia's contemporary military achievements rest on the redevelopment of erstwhile Soviet technologies. Many ideological points that unify contemporary Russians hark back to the middle of the twentieth century. To this end, a meaningful linkage between the past and present becomes paramount to consolidating socio-political stability in Russia. The task resembles the goals of the Soviet historiography that managed to reconcile the ideologically alien periods of pre-Revolutionary Russia with the ideas of the strong state epitomized in the USSR. Then the reigns of strong monarchs such as Ivan IV, Peter I, and Catherine the Great were hailed as some of the finest examples of Russian statehood. This book will look into a number of historical examples invoked in the contemporary Russian ideological discourse as the means of advancing various conservative doctrines that could help to answer Russia's existing political challenges. In particular, historical discourse will figure in the chapters on conservatism, nationalism, and multiculturalism, each of which refers to the modes of formation of the Russian state.

Finally, my historical references to parallel Western experiences perhaps become clearer upon some further reflection. First, Russia entered the period of modernity with a significant historical lag. The Petrine period (1672–1725) could be considered a watershed for Russia. The painful transformation towards modernity had only just been launched, and was met with severe resistance from the reluctant population. The twentieth century was marked by Russia taking a path of 'alternative modernity' embodied in Soviet communism (Havel 1989). Only following the USSR's collapse did Russia fully enter the period of capitalist modernity. This historical feature had some serious implications for Russia's perceptions of the ideas of civic nation, bourgeois morality and the individual liberties that come with it, social justice and equality. Hence, early European debates on modernity could be explicable within Russia's historical and cultural context. Second, as I have already mentioned above, Russia's major political upheavals in the twentieth century are similar in magnitude and consequence to those major political transformations taking place in Europe during the periods of revolution and civil war. From this perspective, the references to Western periods of major transformation cease to be as outlandish as it might first appear.

STRUCTURE OF THE STUDY

The rest of this book will examine the main ideological strands present in Russia that are buttressed by the extant paradigmatic rift. Chapter 2 opens the thematic part of this book with discussion of the two strands of liberalism. The chapter will argue that, much like Western liberalism, Russia's liberalism falls into the two broad categories of monistic-radical and pluralistic-moderate approaches. This is the debate between Kantian and Hobbesian or Rawlsian and Millian views on individual freedom and liberty. It is a question of whether we are headed towards designing one, invariably liberal, framework of social life, or striving to reconcile and balance competing and incommensurable ideas and interests within a given polity. The chapter focuses mainly on the pluralistic trend of Russia's liberalism, as Western academics and policy-makers study Russian liberalism primarily through its monistic prism.

Chapters 3 and 4 focus on differing dimensions of Russian conservatism. Two paradigms enter the scene again. There is a liberal-conservative, or 'reactionary liberal', branch – something that could be classed as Russia's classical conservatism. The statist-conservative branch, which I refer to as fundamental conservatism, represents a more traditionalist wing of conservatism. Both philosophical streams legitimately occupy a rightful place in the family of conservative thought in Russia and cumulatively compose an intellectual tradition of contemporary Russian conservatism.

The liberal or classical dimension of conservatism, which is detailed in Chapter 3, often finds intellectual intersections with contemporary liberal and ethnic nationalisms. In contrast to Russian nationalism, it is averse to revolutionary changes and presses for the gradual development of the Russian state and society, consolidating the experience of the imperial era as well the most critically selected elements of the Soviet past that pertain to universally convincing achievements. This conservatism admires the political evolution of the West and views Russia as part of European civilization, albeit with some serious restrictions. Being on a similar wavelength with nationalism and liberalism, it praises individualism and self-responsibility, believing that Russia could begin her revival and flourish via improvement in the status of each individual.

The statist fundamental dimension of Russian conservatism, which will be detailed in Chapter 4, sets similar historiographical ambitions. It seeks to integrate the various periods of Russia's evolution and ascertain a path for the future that could most accurately reflect the country's past. Yet, it prioritizes values differently. First, it considers a strong and viable state as the epitome of Russian political evolution. Second, it refuses to accept a European legacy for Russia, viewing Russian civilization as a self-sufficient and separate cosmos. It posits that the values of European liberalism are harmful and detrimental to Russia's development and progress. Intellectuals of this tradition pursue a fundamental project, narrating the cardinal features of Russia's alternative modernity. Finally, they constantly search for the condition of world peace and harmony articulated through the idea of culturally and historically embedded human communities engaged in a critical and mutually enriching dialogue in the world arena.

Chapter 5 discusses the spectrum of left-wing ideas in Russia. It argues that a clearly formulated left-wing discourse can disrupt the two-dimensional paradigmatic pluralism of contemporary Russia. Socialist ideas have the potential to challenge the existing ideological landscape and alter the priorities of both traditionalists and liberals. The chapter will also discuss the importance of the Soviet socialist heritage to contemporary Russian politics.

Chapter 6 deals with various dimensions of Russian nationalism, a strand of thought also buttressed by paradigmatic division. Liberal nationalism envisages the path of European nationalism for Russia. It argues that Russia should transform its state, institutions, and regional composition into a mono-ethnic Russian state of a liberal-democratic nature, similar to the mono-ethnic nations of Western Europe. It is the ambition of liberal nationalism to redefine the Russian nation in terms of the European understanding of a nation-state. The distinct value package of such understanding rests on the ideas of liberalism, individualism, and the progressive accumulation of liberal capitalist behavioural patterns. Following J.S. Mill, theoreticians of this type of nationalism remind us that nations require some form of civic maturity that signifies the 'passing of traditional society', the end of barbarity, and the negation of 'nature' by a 'republican order', to deploy Kant's theorizations.

Statist nationalism, on the other hand, shows Russia's imperial and civilizational inclinations. From this point of view, it uses an entirely different type of logic. It dispenses with the idea of ethnic nationalism that has the mature rational nation built at its apex. Rather, this type of nationalism deploys civilizational thinking. In contrast to the rigid rationality of a nation, civilization requires mere *faith* in the natural ability of a civilization's participants to accept their chosen universal order based on the goodness of their chosen epistemology (Mezhuyev 2016). Civilization necessitates a *faith* in the unclear-but-predestined 'end of history' that binds participant ethnic groups in a universal push towards creating perfect order, peace, and happiness. That historic push requires participants to develop a universal logic in the application of political forms within its cultural realm and to exercise a common *Kultur*, to use the Fichtean idea, which expresses true common goals of unity.

Chapter 7 introduces Russia's perspective on the contemporary architecture of international relations. Russia's main view is geared towards the establishment of a multipolar world order in the wake of the *de-facto* dissolution of the Yalta arrangement. The discussion tackles the two competing approaches to the newly emerging world order: globalist universalist, based on the unipolar understanding of contemporary international politics, and multipolar pluralistic, based on the diversity of political, economic, and financial forms and norms. Given that at the official level Russia has become an ardent defender of the multipolar world order, some specific theoretical, philosophical, and methodological approaches to the structure of international relationships have emerged in the Russian discourse.

Chapter 8 examines the particularities of Russia's multiculturalism. It does not come as a surprise that debates within this ideological strand are also buttressed by the traditionalism-liberalism split. The discussion will highlight the already familiar paradigmatic differences through the prism of the Western theory of liberal and communitarian types of multiculturalism.

Chapter 9 deals with the particularities of Russian feminism. It will examine existing debates within this highly contested ideological field in Russia. Issues pondered within this area also centre on the radical liberal and conservative wings of feminism. The chapter touches upon the erstwhile Western division in feminism, of the feminism of equality and the feminism of difference. The first type of feminism, espoused mostly by successful and financially stable middle-class women, seeks to blur the differences between genders and achieve a state of complete equality among men and women within the existing social structure. The second type of feminism, espoused mainly by economically disadvantaged groups, strives to accommodate the existing differences between genders, claiming the sheer physical impossibility of overcoming the rift. They point at the decisive role of men in drafting the existing rules of the game. Hence, the second strand of thought calls for a redefinition of the norms of society with a view to accommodating the distinct experience of women. While the Western context has largely moved on from this crude binary division of feminist thought, it is important to bear in mind that Russia remains, by and large, a traditional country, in which such a division still stands. The chapter discusses how Russia accommodates this theoretical split, highlighting the history of Russia's own feminism from the late-Imperial era to the Soviet and post-Soviet periods. A brief conclusion summarizes the study with some reflections on the future of paradigmatic pluralism in the Russian context and beyond.

POTENTIAL DEBATES AND CRITIQUE

In finalizing this introductory section, I have to point out that I in no way assume my effort to cover Russia's political ideologies has been exhaustive. It is an arduous task to write a good book, let alone a book with the ambitious aim of uniting so many different themes under one umbrella. Hence, I anticipate that readers and colleagues will have various criticisms and suggestions. The most obvious criticism that could be levied is that the volume does not have separate chapters on fascism and, potentially, Eurasianism. Given that space is always an issue, those omissions are intended, for the reasons given below.

Let me begin with fascism. Pinpointing systematic fascism in contemporary Russia could be more difficult than it seems. Fascism is not taken seriously by mainstream political movements and is not immediately present as an openly adopted political doctrine in contemporary discourse. There is no distinct mainstream party that espouses and promotes this ideology unambiguously. Likewise, no particular social movement of significance adopts fascist doctrines and presses for the establishment of a fascist state.[2] One could find marginal networks on the fringes of Russia's political spectrum that would indulge in such political fantasies, but these are usually clandestine and often led by an odious person with a radical and extremist character (Maxim

Martsinkevich is an example). Many such leaders have been convicted of extremism; they either serve custodial sentences or remain on parole for allegations of extremism. Pure fascism, as an inter-war European phenomenon with a clear ideological distinction between Nazism and other more opportunistic variants, has become a contemporary political simulacrum (Dugin 2012c). It is often believed that such fascism was eradicated in the aftermath of the Second World War (Nolte 1965, 401; Trevor-Roper 1968, 18; Weber 1964), while neo-fascism is treated as a related, but distinct, phenomenon (Laqueur 1993).

Nevertheless, while political structures based on fascist principles may be dead, the ideology has not died (Gregor 1969; Sternhell 1978). As a system of thought, it has experienced various declines and rebirths, and the refinement of its foundations, as different brands of fascism, other than those of Mussolini or Hitler, have emerged (Sternhell 1978; Botz, 1987). Therefore, the basic elements of fascism are dispersed within different segments of Russian, as well as Western, societies (Goldberg 2007). Fascistic political styles, behavioural patterns, and ideas spring up intermittently within various groups and political movements. Fascism wanders occasionally into some institutional policies, political goals and ambitions, speeches, and emotions. Its dispersed nature makes it difficult to pinpoint fascism with precision, and the study of fascism becomes a 'daunting and bewildering task' (Preston 1985, 46). At some levels, elements of fascism enter our day-to-day affairs in different ideological guises, hiding behind the facades of 'liberalism', 'good intentions', 'inclusion', 'order', 'values promotion', and 'an upholding of tradition' (Goldberg 2007). At the same time, this process becomes so all-encompassing as to undermine fascism as a meaningful and influential concept. Therefore, for the purpose of this volume, we would struggle to accumulate meaningful and systematic material to justify a separate chapter on the subject.

I am aware that a number of Western observers would hold a different opinion on the matter and claim that Russia has turned into a sort of fascist state (Snyder 2018; Iampolsky 2015; Kasparov 2013; Motyl 2015). It is the view taken in this work that such a position is overly politicized and weakly substantiated. It also dilutes useful analytical instruments currently available to researchers of other important political ideologies in Russia. Some exponents of this stance, such as Garry Kasparov, represent the rhetorical voice of Russia's most-radical political opposition. Having taken this author factor into account, such a stance becomes explicable in the context of political and discursive struggle in Russia. Within these circumstances, the term 'fascist' is used liberally to discredit political opponents or to merely denote authoritarian social trends. Some academic authors (Motyl 2015), while referring to Russia's political system as fascist, do not offer a systematic analysis of fascism from a theoretical point of view, obfuscate the issue, and ignore the historical and social dilemmas of Russian society (see Laruelle 2018 analysis). As Andreas Umland (2008) rightly observed, while Russian state rhetoric may come across as imperialistic and to some extent nationalist, it is far from adopting a revolutionary ultra-nationalist stance, which represents one of the foremost markers of fascism. Furthermore, it is rarely pointed out that fascism is primarily an ideology of inequality – racial, ethnic, social, and political. Russia's society, in contrast, shows consistent historical longings for justice, equality, and truth at the political, social, and cultural level (see Chapter 5 of this volume). Occasionally, those longings are taken to their 'most extreme' and 'absurd' conclusions, as Isaiah Berlin (1994) has rightly observed. It is in this light that Alexei Zudin (1995), who viewed fascist trends in Russia as an alien Western export, should be understood.

The strong position of the Russian leader is another commonplace from which parallels with Hitler and Mussolini are drawn (Kasparov 2013). This argument also dismisses Russia's historical and religious particularities, which point at the traditionally reverent attitude to the state leader throughout the entire period of Russia's history (see Chapter 6, discussion on state patriotic nationalism). Last but not least, Timothy Snyder, in his numerous articles and the book *Road to Unfreedom*, cites Russian twentieth-century philosopher Ivan Ilyin as the ideological founding father of contemporary Russian fascism, or a 'prophet of Russian fascism' to deploy his exact phrase. This point is also highly debatable for a variety of reasons. First, the influence of Ilyin on the contemporary Russian ideological and philosophical landscape is limited, notwithstanding the fact that Putin included him in his list of cited and recommended authors. As French-American historian Marlene Laruelle (2018) rightly notes, Putin's administration is non-ideological 'by design' and 'draws inspiration from a wide variety of figures and themes, offering a multifaceted ideological bricolage in which Ilyin is just one among many, many others.' Second, many contemporary Russian philosophers, such as Boris Mezhuyev, Lyubov Ulyanova, Egor Kholmogorov, and others, choose to describe Ilyin as a liberal or liberal conservative (Berdyaevskiye Chteniya

[Berdyaev Lectures] 2015). Finally, while citing Ilyin, Russian politicians (such as Putin) and public figures (such as Sergey Mikhalkov) refer to the liberal parts of his philosophy, as opposed to its authoritarian facets. Hence, portraying Ilyin as a cornerstone figure of Russia's contemporary fascism does not do justice to all those complexities.[3]

As to Eurasianism, it may be tempting to include this philosophical strand in the study of political ideologies. Yet it is the view adopted in this volume that Eurasianism could be treated more as a philosophical and methodological doctrine, denoting a particular attitude to the geostrategic position of Russia as being located neither in Europe nor in Asia, but representing a separate cultural-civilizational and geopolitical *Eurasian* realm. At this level, Eurasianism is also linked to the idea of culturally based regional integration, as well as to the concept of the plurality of cultures and value systems. Eurasianism also provided important methodology to the philosophical school of structuralism, which will be briefly covered in the thematic chapters devoted to conservatism (see Chapter 4 in particular). Therefore, Eurasianism is considered here as an important methodological context or a base upon which other, ideologically politicized, constructions that legitimize interests and policies could be built. Those constructions represent fundamental (or radical) conservatism, which will be discussed in Chapter 4, state patriotic nationalism (Chapter 6), as well as the multipolar world theory (Chapter 7) advocated and promoted by the Russian officials in the world arena. Therefore, various references will be made to Eurasianism, illuminating the link between its main methodological and philosophical positions and their application in different ideological contexts.

Finally, I must reiterate that this work is an exegetical effort to elucidate living ideologies in contemporary Russia and to shed light on the philosophical connections between the current conventions, history, and intellectual narrative of the contemporary political environment. This task in itself is perhaps unrealistically ambitious, given the breadth of the subject and the avalanche of problems facing contemporary Russian society. Along with this is an effort to demonstrate links between these political ideologies and to pinpoint the ways in which such ideologies address similar problems of geopolitical, cultural, ethical, and political nature. The reader will no doubt discover that many ideological trends crosscut each other at various junctures and in interesting fashions. Those meeting points are flagged in chapters devoted to respective ideologies, while the common tasks and the points of departure are discussed earlier in this opening chapter. At the same time, this work does not intend to build a full institutional or political picture of contemporary Russia – a point which may not seem sufficient to readers who seek to obtain an empirical account on the matter. Having said that, this theoretical study of Russia's ideological foundations will no doubt be instrumental in constructing a subsequent empirical picture that accurately details actors, social movements, and their activities. This could be a matter of a separate volume, undertaken either by this author or colleagues willing to investigate the task.

2

Liberalism

Russian liberalism is often studied, understood, and presented through the prism of the radical-liberal opposition, the views of which may be equally appealing and disturbing to commentators, depending on their political preferences. Yet activists and thinkers of the radical-liberal opposition, though espousing liberal ideas, could not meaningfully claim the right to speak on behalf of Russia's liberal school of thought. This chapter argues that contemporary Russian liberalism must be studied through the prism of two competing trends – moderate pluralist and monistic radical. The discussion will briefly cover some of the main aspects of the monistic tradition but will mainly focus on the pluralist trend of Russian liberalism, as this intellectual current is under-represented in Western media and academic debate. The discussion suggests that, due to political temperance and a nuanced approach to Russia's socio-political realities, this trend of Russia's liberalism is more promising and conducive to the entrenchment of the liberal idea in Russia.

Before going any further, it is important to note that the division of liberalism into different groupings is not unique to Russia. Ideological and tactical disagreements within liberal practice are also significant in the West. Bearing in mind that Russian political thought is derived from its Western counterpart, it seems feasible to discuss the main divisions within the Western liberal trend and then search for an echo of these debates in Russia. This approach will determine the chapter's structure. The first section will discuss the two competing faces of the Western liberal tradition, while the following two sections will examine the nature of ideological discourse within the Russian moderate-pluralist and radical-monistic liberal trends, with a particular emphasis on the pluralist tradition.

LIBERALISM AS A FAMILY OF IDEOLOGIES

It has long been observed that liberalism is not a unified ideology, but rather a family of concepts, debates, values, institutional arrangements, and practices (Weinstock 2007, 244; see also Appiah 2005). John Gray (2000, 44) writes: 'just as liberal regimes cannot be identified by a range of essential properties, so liberal theorists and thinkers are not alike in having common ideas. It is a basic error to search for the essence of something as heterogeneous and discontinuous as *the* liberal tradition.' Hence, we can treat liberalism as a family of metaphysical and practical proposals towards achieving the good life, which shares the common principle of individual liberty and a belief in the existence of competing human interests. From this point, liberalism splits roughly into two separate broad directions that will be consequential to our discussion of Russia. The first direction represents the philosophy of a rational consensus built on the universal primacy of liberty; it defends the possibility of discovering one true way for humans to flourish. The second direction represents the philosophy of value pluralism, which is driven by the recognition of diversity and multiplicity of incommensurable and conflicting models of ethical human life. Pondering the nature of modernity – the socio-political framework within which liberalism was born and flourished – Samuel Eisenstadt (2002) observes that it (modernity) was permeated with two contradicting forces. Some were leaning towards generalizations and universality, while others resisted that universal push, thus recognizing an intricate pattern of different forms of modern socio-political organization. Hence, liberalism, as an ideology and a system of thought, could schematically fall into the monistic and moderate-pluralistic trends.

The first, universalizing liberal 'monistic' (Parekh 2006) tradition was chiefly inaugurated by John Locke and Immanuel Kant, and inspired by Aristotle, who thought that the right answer rests on a correct premise and cannot contain error (MacIntyre 1988, 142). It was developed in the twentieth century by the liberal-consensus politics of John Rawls, Brian Barry, Friedrich Hayek, Western modernity champions led by Talcott Parsons and followed loosely by liberal multiculturalists such as Will Kymlicka (1995) and Joseph Raz (1986). These twentieth-century proponents of the monistic tradition advocated the establishment of a liberal basic framework that could host the diversity of various lifestyles, whose flavour and essence will generally reflect the consensus liberal nature. This line of thought considers liberalism as a general recipe, 'universal in authority and application', and views liberty as the primary value (Gray 2000, 117–21; Parekh 2006, 81–4). The problem of social stability and justice is resolved by 'ensuring equal access to the maximum possible number of liberties to all members of the community and making sure that people act in accordance to their will without interference from others' (Skinner 2002, Vol. 2, 165). It is also often believed that this liberal consensus represents a genuine 'breakthrough' of humanity and has a 'genuine normative-functional superiority' over other forms of political organization (Wagner 2012, 6–7). Hence, it is argued that progress and modernization would invariably place demands of liberty on societies, and, as societies become more modernized, they will move politically towards this rational Euro-American consensus (Diamond and Marks 1992; Lipset 1960, as examples).

The second tradition was partly a legacy of non-liberal thinkers, such as Thomas Hobbes and David Hume, who recognized the multiplicity of competing and conflicting individual lifestyles and searched for a pattern of coexistence among such individuals within a society that is not bound by ideological commitments. It also inherited the ideas of J.S. Mill, who indirectly regretted the universalizing push of his time, arguing for the uniqueness of individual opinions. Therefore, universal philosophy, though possible, must be mediated by a 'philosophy of national character' (Parekh 2006, 42; Gray 1995 and 2000; Berlin 2006). Moreover, this tradition chiefly represents the intellectual outcome of the Enlightenment's critics, led by thinkers such as Vico and Herder. Herder, in particular, replaced the global notion of universal 'civilization' with a particular idea of 'culture' (Clark, 1969; Gray 2000, 47–50; Berlin 2006, 223–36; Parekh 2006, 67–76).

In the twentieth century, pluralist-liberal thought developed and advanced in various directions, often going beyond the strict limits of liberalism, yet retaining its underlying liberal nature. This thought was espoused and promoted by value-pluralist liberals, such as Isaiah Berlin (2006), John Gray (2000), Bikhu Parekh (2006), and Richard Rorty (1983); moral realists, such as Bernard Williams (2005); communitarian liberals (Taylor 1994); numerous historians of modernity and theoreticians of the multiple-modernity thesis (Eisenstadt 2002; Wagner 1994 and 2012; Huntington 1996; Huntington 2006; Hobson

2012; Bauman 2007); as well as post-Marxist champions of radical democracy (Mouffe 1988; Laclàu and Mouffe 1985; Daly 1999). All these thinkers claim, in one form or another, that modern life could flourish in different patterns, sharing a very loose underlying background. This, as Berlin argues, requires a peaceful coexistence among different cultures, not their merging into a universal civilization, as Locke and Kant envisaged earlier (Gray 2000, 52–4; Wagner 2012, 4–5). Hence, liberalism, as these thinkers argue, is preoccupied, alongside other ideologies, with the development of *a* model of ethical life for humanity, and the liberal project is just one of many conflicting and incommensurable paradigms that could suggest a path for achieving such a life (B. Williams 2005, 22–3).

In many ways, these two faces of liberalism echo the dual approach to the concept of freedom advanced by Isaiah Berlin. The positive idea of freedom, according to Berlin, has grown out of the tradition of German idealism represented by Kant, Fichte, and Hegel, which believes in the 'inviolable inner self' and places human beings at the centre of the universe as ultimate authors of their lives. This inevitably results in claims that people are solely responsible for the construction of everyday morals, values, ideas, and the entire structure of the world around them (Berlin 2006, 193; Pinkard 2002). Therefore, this pattern treats freedom, in Spinoza's lexicon, as a *recognized necessity*, which is required for self-authorship and the building of the outer world. It follows that, when the liberating nature of the self-creationist model becomes evident to all, society will be able to form an organic orchestra in which each will play his/her chosen instrument to the best of his/her abilities (see Berlin's critique of Fichte 2006). Therefore, freedom in this particular type of society becomes a 'fact of life' (Raz 1986, 369–70 and 394), a universal condition binding such a society with the principle of personal autonomy.

Another competing interpretation of freedom is a negative one. Here we speak merely of the absence of constraints on the agent, who can choose among meaningful alternatives of the good life (MacCallum 1967; Berlin 2006; Gray 1995; Skinner 2002, Vol. 2). And it is in this idea that the origins of value pluralism lie, in that value pluralism assumes that the fate of humanity is not determined and not bound by the *necessity of freedom* wrapped in a particular narrative of an ideal community. Rather, freedom is the opportunity to make a 'meaningful choice' among conflicting and incommensurable alternatives

(Gray 1995). At times, such a choice may entail opting for a set of alternative social benefits that might be viewed as superior to individual freedom (Gray 1996, 154–5; Huntington 2006) (much like Aristotle claimed that ideal forms of government may change over time, depending on varying circumstances, see Skinner 2002, Vol. 2, 67). Hence, the two competing interpretative forces tear the idea of freedom in two separate directions. The first force stands for personal autonomy and views freedom as a necessary condition that enables humans to achieve their ends. The second advocates a mere non-interference in the process of choice-making.[1]

These competing traditions of liberal thought fuel competing trends within the realms of policy-making, political rhetoric, and activism, as well as political practice. In Russia, these trends split liberal thought into two rival groups: pluralistic-moderate and monistic-radical. Both trends share their commitment to freedom, constitutionalism, the rule of law, and equality of opportunity. Yet one side admits that life can flourish in differing forms that should be taken into account, while the other defends Russia's Euro-centric political path towards freedom as an ultimate destiny. This disagreement, which may come across as minor at a first glance, becomes consequential to their subsequent answers to the host of existential questions that concern Russia's place in history, international relations, pace of reforms, attitude to society, identity, and, finally, tasks for the future.

Monistic-radical liberalism is geared towards a radical reconstruction of the Russian state and society, aiming for the full convergence between Russian and Western political and socio-cultural patterns on the basis of the Western liberal consensus. This goal determines domestic and foreign-policy proposals, as well as accompanying political rhetoric. The pluralistic-moderate group views liberalism as a family of ideologies and, similar to its Western counterpart, claims that the European version of liberalism has no privileged place among other doctrines and paths towards achieving an ethical life. These thinkers argue that, if Russian people were to reject liberalism, it would be 'regrettable' (Pivovarov 2011), but should be countered through discourse, persuasion, and discussion rather than through an 'ideological war on conservatism' (Yanov 2003). Hence, this branch of thought also aims to achieve European liberal values, albeit through accounting for various factors and realities that influence and shape domestic and international debates and not through the radical recasting of

Russia's society. In what follows, I will briefly account for the central aspects of the monistic idea and will move on to a thorough treatment of the pluralist trend with a view to bringing it out of the shadows.

RADICAL-MONISTIC LIBERALISM

Arguably, Russian monistic liberalism originates in the nineteenth-century ideas of Peter Chaadaev (Yanov 2003), who thought that Russia would have no tradition of her own, no past, no future, no history, unless it chose to learn and integrate with Europe (Copleston 1986). Chaadaev also argued, in line with the monistic fashion, that human history represents a single, unified enterprise that has the sole purpose of creating a Kingdom of God on earth. The West, due to its adherence to Catholicism, had already embarked on this project and was on the way towards creating a just society.[2] Thus, Chaadaev warned that Russia's future lay solely and squarely in her movement towards the family of fraternal European peoples and argued that this movement corresponded with Russia's geostrategic interests (Yanov 2003).

Today this trend holds with the view that there is a universal path of societal development, which lies in the Western/Euro/America–centric version of liberal democracy and the market economy, and sooner or later the world will be built on the basis of the Western political system. These thinkers argue that Russia represents a distorted replica of Europe (*Isporchennaya Evropa* Yanov 2003) and that the aim is to overcome this distortion sooner rather than later with the view of altering the course of Russia's history towards full convergence with 'proper' Europe. Many such critics aim to subvert the stable reproduction of the 'Russian matrix' as the historic existential pattern, which, in their view, forbids Russia's convergence with the political paradigm of the West. These authors appeal to the West, who in their minds should not accept Russia patiently 'as it is'. Rather, the task of the West, they argue, is to understand Russia's difference *and* engage it, with the view to helping it along the path of compliance with the political norms adopted and practised in the West (Shevtsova 2008).

In the foreign-policy realm, monistic liberals claim that domestic challenges determine countries' international identity. Since the construction of European liberal society at home remains a priority for these thinkers, they argue that Russia must move away from her traditional geopolitical constraints, as seen in the need to assume responsibility for the large territory occupied by culturally diverse ethnic groups endowed with vast natural resources. Alexandr Yanov (2003) calls on Russia to abandon her extant geostrategic ambitions and look at the example of Europe, which is now composed of smaller states that have long since forgotten their moments of 'geopolitical glory'. Only through revising her place in the world's arena, he argues, can Russia fully merge with Europe and adopt the European course of development, which, in his mind, represents Russia's genuine historic goal.

At this juncture, radical liberalism meets with Russian ethnic nationalism, which also has a monistic-liberal nature. Such an intellectual alliance is not a surprise, given the academic research on theoretical compatibility between nationalism and liberalism (Kymlicka 1997). From this point of view, radical-liberal activists propose to reconsider Russia's territorial integrity for the sake of implementing the model of a 'cozy European home'. They claim that Russia must focus on constructing her European identity, which stands at odds with the culture of the North Caucasian regions, and from that point of view such regions could be sacrificed for the sake of implementing the European choice to the full. These authors appeal to Russian ethnic nationalism, which is opposed to Russian civic patriotism and traditionalist multiculturalism, and hopes to access the European space as a Europeanized, territorially reduced, but 'civilized' region. Konstantin Krylov, the leader of the National Democratic Party, and, with some exceptions, Stanislav Belkovsky are the most notable intellectuals within this wing. We will return to their ideas in Chapter 6 of this book.

Monistic liberals lament the fact that the Russian public consistently rejects their advocacy of the Eurocentric liberal consensus, and forgoes it in favour of the country's traditional thinking, in which Russia's geopolitical constraints determine domestic debates. These thinkers view Russia's conservative traditionalism as an historical dead-end, and, to use harsher language, a 'cancerous tumour on the body of Russia'. Boris Makarenko (in Tretyakov 2011) claims: 'when this cancer becomes metastatic and threatens Russia with imminent death, society calls a liberal doctor to save its life. The doctor does his job and when the patient recovers, it chases the doctor out, accusing him of all mortal sins, including state betrayal.' Popular disappointment with the liberal-remedy projects often fuels the radicalization of the monistic discourse. While some monistic liberals hold on to the production of balanced, intellectual, and logical critique, some resort to ideological reductions, simplifications, explicit self-diminution, and subversive rhetoric.

In such cases, the literature, journalism, and social media of this segment campaign against the norm-giving elements of the Russian political culture and target the 'Russian matrix' from all possible directions. These attacks concern stable collective identities evolving around the ideas of the Russian statehood, Church and religion, attitudes toward the Great Patriotic War, and Russia's historical past. A host of writers, including the late Valeriya Novodvorskaya, with her notorious branding of Russians as a 'cancer of humankind', Alfred Kokh, Artemy Troitsky, Yulia Latynina, Evgeniya Albatz, Bozhena Rynska, Dmitry Bykov, and many others, often act as a radical-subversive force that seeks, through radical public expressions, to target the very heart of Russia's state-forming 'lifeworld'. A few examples might be of interest. Valery Panyushkin (2005) claims: 'it would be easier for everyone if the Russian nation would cease to exist. Even Russians would feel better, if they no longer had to work on their nation-state but rather turned into a small ethnos like avars of khanty.' Olga Romanova (2013), one of Russia's radical liberal journalists, targets war memories by branding the new national cemetery for military veterans as a 'graveyard for pets.' Bozhena Rynska (2013) makes derogatory statements about Russian pensioners, while liberal art and music critic Artemy Troitsky (2010) brands Russian men as a type that 'must become extinct'.

A number of radical-monistic liberals go as far as to partially vindicate the Nazi German invasion of Russia as a 'liberating' effort that attempted to relieve the Soviet Union of communism. Grigory Amnuel, a Russian liberal film director and eminent public figure, defends instances of collaboration with Nazi Germany, vindicating select members of the Bronislaw Kaminsky Lokot administration on the occupied territory of the Soviet Union. The Lokot Republic was a Nazi administrative unit established on the territory of the Bryansk and Oryol regions as an experiment in self-governance by collaborators. The size of the republic's territory was comparable to that of Belgium. Bronislaw Kaminski, who headed the republic, was a particularly merciless SS collaborator, subsequently an SS general (Waffen-SS Brigadeführer), and decorated with Waffen-SS orders received personally from Heinrich Himmler. Kaminski was directly responsible for mass burnings and executions of partisans and civilians on the occupied territory of the Bryansk and Oryol regions. When the German Army was retreating, Kaminsky's SS brigades were forced to relocate accordingly, first to Belorussia and then to Poland. Subsequently, Kaminsky's SS units took part in crushing the 1944 Warsaw uprising. Substantial evidence shows that the Kaminsky brigade had been involved in rape, murder, robbery, looting, and other atrocities. According to the Nuremberg Tribunal materials (Dallin 1972), the German central command, when informed of Kaminsky's actions, tried and executed him for military crimes. Despite the atrocities of the Lokot Republic's leaders, however, Amnuel directed a highly favourable documentary on Roman Redlich, Kaminsky's deputy head of ideology and propaganda. The film remained largely silent on Redlich's Lokot engagements and his personal associations with Bronislaw Kaminsky (Amnuel and Kurginyan 2017). Instead, Redlich was given the chance to state his opinion on the fascist regime in Germany. Curiously, he described the latter as 'silly', 'inefficient', and 'hardly appropriate for Russia', but not much more. Amnuel's apology for Redlich relies on the fact that the latter was not personally responsible for executions, being 'merely' the head of the ideology department in the Kaminsky administration.

Amnuel's position is not unique. Russia's literary, journalistic, and public space of the monistic-liberal persuasion is full of vigorous discussions on the issue of collaborators. Dmitry Bykov, Russia's eminent liberal writer, journalist, and educator, referred to Hitler as a 'liberator of Russia' and stated that his failure to garner support among Russia's intelligentsia was related solely to his 'negative' treatment of Jews (Melman 2019). Nikita Sokolov, liberal deputy director for research of the Eltsin Centre, Aleksandr Minkin, and Evgeny Ikhlov similarly pressed for rehabilitation of General Andrey Vlasov and Hitler collaborators that he led in their various public speeches (Kulikov 2016). It is questionable whether these and other expressions of political nihilism are a temporary trend or a stable identity internalized by Russia's monistic thinkers. Interestingly, many such thinkers have taken a more socially oriented left-leaning stand following the incorporation of Crimea and economic sanctions imposed on Russia by the West in its wake. What is clear, however, is that nihilistic rhetoric has been a stable literary and political style of many monistic liberals since the 1990s, which has been well documented by researchers (Lukin 2000; Garadzha 2006; Khakamada 2008).

MODERATE-PLURALIST LIBERALISM

Why Pluralist?

Now let me turn to the discussion of the moderate-pluralist tradition of Russian liberalism, which will compose the rest of this chapter. Before proceeding to the discussion of the main tenets of this intellectual trend, we must contextualize it within the history of ideas and understand why thinkers of this tradition fall under the entire rubric of liberal-value pluralism. This contemporary liberal thought could be viewed as the intellectual continuation of a wide variety of trends, both Western and Russian. In many ways, representatives of this line could cumulatively reflect the image of a middle-ground Russian liberal intellectual of the nineteenth century, Ivan Turgenev, championed by the historian of ideas Isaiah Berlin. Berlin (1994, 302) colourfully paints this liberal as a 'well-meaning, troubled, self-questioning' moral being, bearing 'witness to the complex truth,' painfully torn between revolutionary radicalism and support of state tyranny and despotism.

Apart from these middle-ground liberal figures, pluralist liberals also to some extent inherit, with some exceptions and exclusions, the tradition of the nineteenth-century *pochvenniki*, who in contrast to much of Russia's radical intellectual scene of that period, studied, admired, and respected Turgenev's texts. The *pochvenniki* group championed a distinct Russian culture and socio-political tradition and were critical of Western consensus rationalism. At the same time, they tried to avoid the idealization of ancient Russia – a trend that was a characteristic of the original Slavophiles – and pressed for 'the development of a Russian culture enriched with what was believed to be of value in Western life and civilisation' (Copleston 1986, 153).

More importantly, most of the nineteenth-century liberal intellectuals echo the German Romantic tradition and thought that claimed there was no predetermined course of history, no stable pattern to life, and no laws of nature that could fully capture and explain the functioning of human society. As Berlin (1994, 295) notes, they saw 'tendencies and political attitudes as functions of human beings, not human beings as function of social tendencies'. This perception would subsequently help many pluralist-liberal thinkers to cast aside the idea of an inevitable arrival of one single model of societal harmony applicable to the entirety of humanity (Inozemtsev 2013, 29; Filatov 2006)

– an idea that appears today in the guise of the global promotion of democracy and an idea that, within the Russian scene, is realized through the push of monistic-radical liberals towards the rigid and fervent compliance with and idolization of all Western norms.

Clearly, this nineteenth-century influence is the forerunner of Russia's contemporary liberal-pluralist idea that Western modernity should serve as a mere procedural framework, which must be filled with Russian cultural substance. Pluralist liberals admit *some* universal significance to the model couched in Western notions of freedom, reason, and unhampered economic activity. Hence, they claim, much in the fashion of their pluralist counterparts in the West, that the world cannot expect a mere diffusion of the Western political and economic model on a global scale without it being enriched with particular cultural, historic, and economic patterns of the host localities. As Igor Bunin (in Tretyakov 2008) observes, 'we cannot deny that Europe will always be a building block of Russia's liberal identity; and therefore, we cannot completely reject the historic experience of European countries. On the other hand, we must understand that Russia is building her own country, her own system, and resolving her own particular problems.'

Thus, if history does not have a rigid predetermined pattern, or if this pattern has only a very loose nature, it is down to individuals and societies to be the authors and creators of their own paths (Inozemtsev 2013, 29; Mezhuyev 2005, in Tretyakov et al.; Prokhorova 2005, in Tretyakov et al.). On this path, such thinkers argue, peoples and nations are entitled to make mistakes, sometimes tragic and unforgettable. Yet, they are also entitled to have the chance to rise, reassess their alternatives, and learn from the past without pathos or abstract rhetoric, without the digression to ideological dogmatism, but in a rational manner of gradualism, education, and critical deliberation. Yuri Pivovarov (2011, in Strizhak et al.), professor of history at the Moscow State University, while rejecting the Soviet experience, states:

[T]his was a mistake made by my people at the turn of the twentieth century. Yet, I believe that many other peoples in the world made analogous mistakes. More importantly, I believe that my people will find the inner strengths to recover from those mistakes, reassess their destructive potential, and find, through rational analysis and discussion, an alternative that could correct the wrongdoing.

This dispassionate debate, in his mind, should consider various aspects of Russia's past and focus on future ways of assuring individual liberty, creating civilized and cultured life devoid of despotism, suffering, injustice, and oppression.

Finally, the ideas of pluralist liberals also intersect, at some points, with contemporary Russian conservatism, which argues that both Russia and Europe represent two streams of one European civilization and share one common cradle. Conservative publicist Natalya Narochnitskaya (2011) writes that both Russian and European traditions

> gave the world glorious examples of Latin and Orthodox spirituality. These remarkable trends expressed two different methods of finding God, as well as the two different forms of apostasy. Goethe's Faust became the epitome of an inquisitive and independent Western mind, which does not tolerate any higher judge above him, while Ivan Karamazov of Dostoyevsky demonstrated a daring challenge of the Russian pride, which does not want to put up with the connivance of evil on earth.

We will discuss particularities of the conservative intellectual trend in the following two chapters. Here, I must just reiterate that the nerve of Russia's moderate contemporary conservatism runs through appeals for a dialogue between the two great cultures, Europe and Russia, their mutual complementarity, and mutual enrichment through argument, debate, and discussion. The fates of both Russia and Europe are entangled and intersected, conservatives argue. Yet, being two parallel sub-civilizations, they must reflect on their common history, and not speak of another universalist project that could push European borders towards the Russian heartland, assimilating her to the new norms and morals, and 'entrusting the Council of Europe to be the judge of Russia's civilizational maturity' (Narochnitskaya 2011).

It is also important, however, that, while echoing some aspects of Russia's conservative thought, the heart of pluralist liberals still lies with those who cherish the values of individual liberty above all else and the West as the forerunner and champion of these values. They ache when the advocacy of Western liberalism takes ugly forms of radicalism, political nihilism, and national self-denial (Lukin 2000), yet they would not explicitly distance themselves from those radicals, in particular if this would mean helping the cause of fundamental conservatism, state tyranny, and bureaucracy (Ryzhkov 2013).[3] They argue passionately that Russia is an integral part of the great European culture (as opposed to being a distinct, albeit sibling, civilization to Europe), they feel European, and they insist that it is with Europe that Russia should march (Prokhorov 2012; Polyakov 2004; Remchukov in Tretyakov 2008; Inozemtsev, full analysis in White 2011, 308; Bunin, in Tretyakov 2008). These thinkers become the proponents of European liberal thought at home, hoping that it can gradually take root and secure a stable and genuine following. They observe with some sadness (Kara-Murza, in Tretyakov 2011; also Pivovarov, in Tretyakov 2011) that Russia has a 'turbulent love affair with Western liberalism', and claim that the goal of Russian society is to make this volatile relationship of extreme passion and ensuing suffering more harmonious and 'stable akin to an old, and perhaps slightly boring, marriage'.

These themes run throughout Russia's pluralistic liberalism. Yet it could be best summarized and investigated through four main propositions of practical and metaphysical nature. First, moderate-pluralistic liberals are convinced that Russian liberalism is a home-grown indigenous phenomenon that has a long history and tradition, and not a distorted copy from the West, which may seem the case to some casual observers. Second, they claim that the main purpose of Russian liberalism is to contain social chaos through limiting both the state and the mob. This determines that the relationship of these liberals with the state has a character of opportunistic co-operation. Third, and partly following from the second, these liberals are focused on the problem of the progressive economic development of Russia. On this basis, they argue (Kara-Murza 2008) that Russian liberalism has a primarily legal, rather than metaphysical or political, character; this partly marks its distinction from Western liberal thought, which is represented by all dimensions of the metaphysical, legal, and political. Fourth, they claim that the idiosyncratic nature of Russian liberalism is also a reflection of the immanent duality of Russia's identity – an identity that is being torn between geopolitical and cultural-normative aspects of being. These proposals deserve further investigation.

The Genesis of Russian Liberalism

One could not fail to notice that Russian liberalism has been derived from and dependent on its Western counterpart and evolved mostly in response to the preceding Western tradition. This, however, is not surprising. Porter and Gleason (1998, 62) observe that the history of

Russia cannot be 'viewed as sui generis, but instead as being in the context of European history'. Martin Malia (1994, 6–10 and 28–30; Kotsonis 1999, 125) also views Russian political thought of all eras through the prism of a European history of ideas. In particular, he analyses Russian communism as a strand of European thought that harks back to Rousseau's radical advocacy of democracy and equality, German idealism, with its faith in dialectic and self-development, and Marxism, which combines these two trends with the idea of progress towards a classless society.

From this follows the confidence of pluralist liberals that, although developing in dialogue with Western thought, the Russian liberal tradition is still a viable, potent, and self-sufficient branch of the liberal family of philosophies and practices. Different thinkers cite relatively recent dates from which Russia could start citing the history of her liberalism. Alexei Kara-Murza (2007), professor of philosophy at the Moscow Institute of Philosophy, names the 1762 coronation of Catherine II as the birth of Russia's liberal tradition. Yurii Pivovarov (2011) claims that Russian liberalism dates to 18 February 1762, when Peter III issued a decree that relieved nobility from compulsory state military service. From this time on, both Kara-Murza and Pivovarov (2011) argue, the liberal idea was on a steady rise in Russian socio-political and cultural life.

Pivovarov, Kara-Murza, Vladimir Pligin, and many other pluralist liberals trace a chain of continuous episodes in Russia's history during which the liberal tradition developed, evolved, and gained ground in both institutional and societal dimensions. Of particular importance were Catherine the Great's consultations with one of Russia's first liberals, Count Nikita Panin, the reliance on liberals during the Patriotic War of 1812 by Alexander I, and the Decembrist revolt of 1825. To continue, liberal reforms under Alexander II (Filatov 2006; Kara-Murza 2011) represented a milestone in the evolution of the liberal practice in Russia, while Peter Stolypin's reforms reflected a time when the demand for liberal reforms had become evident both for the state and society (Pivovarov 2011, in Tretyakov; Kara-Murza 2011, in Tretyakov). Furthermore, in a debate with their Western colleagues (Porter and Gleason 1998; Dahlmann 1998; Starr 1982, 25; Robbins 1987, 16–19; Petro 1995, 44–7), Russian liberals (Kara-Murza 2008) claim that *zemstvo* history contributed a great deal to the theory and practice of Russian liberalism.[4]

Against the backdrop of historic evidence, Pivovarov (2011, in Tretyakov) concludes that 'Russia has very strong traditions of liberalism. She is permeated with liberalism, and the tradition of Russian liberalism is reinforced with people, ideas and institutions.' Liberalism, Pivovarov (2011, in Tretyakov) continues, represents a very strong driving force of Russian history, even though it has been partially defeated by other competing trends. Pivovarov (2011, in Strizhak) laments that liberalism 'experienced an unfortunate setback during the events of the 1917 Revolution and Civil War'. However, he continues, 'it has resurfaced from the 1950s onwards, when the Khrushchev and Brezhnev years witnessed, among other trends, a new resurgence of liberal thought.'

The Soviet era, therefore, was not devoid of the liberal idea (see English 2000 and Timofeev 2004 as examples of Western analysis that sustain similar claims). Moreover, Pivovarov (2011, in Tretyakov; see also Filatov 2006) goes as far as to claim that anything good that has been conducted in Russia during the past three hundred years was initiated, developed, and led by the liberals. Kara-Murza (2008), Bunin (2008), Remchukov (2008), Fadeyev (in Tretyakov 2013b) partly agree with this by arguing that liberals have always been 'on duty for Russia' and have always been needed 'during her darkest days' in order to lead her, through reforms, stabilization, and progressive political-economic remedy, to 'better days and new accomplishments' (Kara-Murza 2008; see also Tretyakov 2008).

Chaos and Alternatives

From this follows that the principal task of pluralist liberalism is seen in the need to achieve societal stability and progressive development and to contain chaos and 'barbarism' (Kara-Murza 2008). Yet, in order to meet such challenges successfully, these thinkers advance a specific liberal recipe that rests on the principles of individual liberty, restriction of power by civil society, justice, and economic development (Kara-Murza 1995, 413). The demands for individual liberty and societal involvement in governance are often in conflict with the need to ensure political order and societal stability (Huntington 1996). Hence, pluralist liberals strive to establish the most suitable way of navigating between the Scylla of statism, personalized and expanded government, hand-managed control of society, selected application of laws, and the suffocating hypocrisy of state propaganda and the

Charybdis of individualistic atomization of society, the loss of historic ground and narrative, territorial disintegration, in which Russia could join Europe only as a set of separate independent liberal region-states, and the self-destruction of the Russian civilization.

Based on these considerations, moderate-pluralist liberals name three main threats to social stability. The first threat is the state, which, through tyranny, elitism, exclusion, and corruption could become a source of social chaos and destabilization. The second enemy is the mob, which is, in their view, easily persuadable, excitable, radically destructive at the height of its dissatisfaction, but deeply conservative at the time of reaction. The last, and by no means least, enemy of stability is radical-monistic liberalism, which may seem surprising to some casual observers, but logical to Russia's pluralist liberals, who hold up this ideological strand as one main cause of defeat of the liberal idea in their country. Talking about these threats, Kara-Murza (1994; 1999; 2007) often draws on the thought of Aristotle, for whom social chaos stems from the unimpeded rule of the majority masses (seen in the Aristotelian political form of *democracy*), as well as from despotism of an elitist and self-seeking state (seen in the Aristotelian political forms of *tyranny* or *oligarchy*).

In both cases, unethical life and chaos occur through the digression of these respective ruling factions towards promotion of various sectional interests, instead of the promotion of the common good (Taylor [C.C.W.] 1995, 243–8; Skinner 2002, Vol. 2, 32–3). These ideas are also found in late-medieval and Renaissance thought, which gave rise to modern republicanism. Machiavelli pondered a similar dilemma and claimed that the threat to peace and stability can emanate from the masses, as well as from the 'powerful individual or faction' within the state that could capture power, reduce community to servitude, and rule in their 'selfish interests instead of promoting the common good' (Skinner 2002, Vol. 2, 129, 200–3, and 143).

In many ways, the appeals of Russia's liberals to classical Western thought to curb chaos are not surprising. The evident oscillation between the state and the crowd as potential sources of social instability runs across much of the Western critique of the modern age. To some, the contradiction that arises between the need to ensure personal autonomy and sustain institutions of social management and control represents the central problem of 'early liberal modernity' (Wagner 1994; Eisenstadt 2002; Foucault 1977; Le Bon 2002; Simmel 1971). This dilemma is well in line with fears of majorities held by early constitutionalists in the United States (Dahl 1956). In a more general tone, Malia (1994, 31) claims that 'democracy has carried a negative charge of mob-rule and anarchy' for much of the history of human thought, and only obtained positive connotations with the introduction of universal suffrage in America and France during the 1820s and 1830s and 1830s and 1840s respectively.

Notwithstanding such historic dilemmas, *contemporary* Western liberalism is increasingly leaning towards deliberative aspects of democracy, advanced by Bruce Ackerman (1998), Jurgen Habermas (1989), and their numerous intellectual allies (Nino 1996; Held 1988; Guttman and Thompson 2004), and the left. The latter gains prominence with the evolution of post-modernist trends and the increasing political significance of new social movements that represent subaltern and disadvantaged segments of societal periphery. This aspect creates a dividing line between Western left-leaning liberalism and the Russian liberal trend that, by following the intellectual chain from Aristotle to the Renaissance and reiterating the fears of early constitutionalists, gravitates towards the right side of the political spectrum. Indeed, many Russian liberals (Pivovarov 2011, in Tretyakov 2011; Kara-Murza 2008, in Tretyakov 2008; 2011, in Tretyakov 2011) admit the conservative overtones of their thought and often include the supposedly conservative early-nineteenth-century Slavophiles movement in Russia's liberal tradition. Pivovarov (2011, in Tretyakov 2011) claims that, while disagreeing with many of its premises, he admires Russian conservatism. Conservatism, in his mind, also has a strong tradition and raises questions of immediate philosophical and political significance to Russia.

In this light, we have to examine the attitudes of Russia's liberals towards both the state and society. To capture the nerve of pluralist thought on society we must turn to the classical modernist idea of progressivism (Giddens 1990; Wagner 1994). The speeches and texts of Russia's pluralist liberals are permeated with echoes of J.S. Mill, who claimed that liberalism, and the Doctrine of Liberty, can only be applied to a culturally mature society – a society where an individual understands that rights come with responsibilities, that liberty can and should be deployed for the purpose of human self-flourishing, for pursuing meaningful goals and tasks, for choosing between varying alternative life-styles, which would help reflect and realize a person's talents to the best possible degree (Gray 1996, 85 and 120; Inozemtsev 2013, 36). This also resembles Huntington's (1996, 5) concern that the 'equality of political participation' must be matched by the 'art of associating together' – that is, that freedom of participation must be practised within a particular institutional context.

Mature communities, Russia's pluralist-liberals (Kara-Murza 1994; Kara-Murza 1995, 415; Kara-Murza 1999) argue, could sustain their stability by deploying the Lockean recipe of state and civil society (Taylor 1995; Keane 1988; Ehrenberg 1999; Cohen and Arato 1992). Here, society is pre-political and it builds up the state from below.[5] Yet they stress that to achieve such a result we must be dealing with a particular *type* of society. Building on the claim that not all societies that merely assure individual autonomy can be called civil, these thinkers argue against the premature imposition of the liberal idea upon a nation which is not ready to embrace this social paradigm. Kara-Murza (1994; see also Inozemtsev 2013, 33) states that 'archaic society built on the principles of normative redistribution does not require liberalism, or democracy and freedom as such.' He proceeds to argue that 'liberalism which was imposed "from outside" of its indigenous and organic context into the context, in which it is not required, could quickly digress to the destructive atomisation of society and the ensuing social chaos.'

Boris Kapustin (1994; 2004a; 2004b; see also critique of Kara-Murza 1994) formulates his vision of the central question of liberalism as 'how to ensure a stable social order if an individual has been let free' – a formulation that invariably raises a question about the nature and maturity of such an individual. This sentiment does not only reflect J.S. Mill but also stretches back to the thoughts of nineteenth-century Russian liberal thinkers, who made a clear distinction between the concepts of freedom (*svoboda*) and volition/whim (*volia*). The former is associated with responsibilities and virtues that must accompany rights and autonomy, and the latter with unrestrained rebellion, which could have devastating consequences, particularly in its Russian interpretation.

These liberals' fear of the mob extends to the fear of an 'individuated' mass consumer – self-focused, preoccupied with abominable interests, gullible, and, what is worse, easily manipulated and radicalized (Durkheim 1972, 115; Dodd 2005, 20–1; Sennet 1978; Lasch 1979; Inozemtsev 2013). To these ends, Kara-Murza (1994), Vadim Mezhuyev (2005), and other liberal thinkers are somewhat apprehensive of postmodern liberal trends that 'leave an individual in the vacuum of stable values and draw him into the mass consumption of popular culture, politics, and norms' (Mezhuyev 2005).[6] Vladislav Inozemtsev (2013, 30–1), a professor at the Higher School of Economics, views the process of individuation as capable of questioning the demand for democracy in contemporary societies. He also ponders the problem of highly segmented multiculturalism that to some extent questions liberalism and democracy in the West. Inozemtsev (2013, 31–2) claims that the future of democracy depends far more on 'the answer to this question than it [does] on the pace of democratic transformations in Niger or on the level of economic success of the liberal autocracies of South-East Asia.'

Kara-Murza (1994) refers to the past and sides with Simeon Frank and Alexander Izgoev, who both claim that the October revolution was the triumph of 'individuation' (Durkheim 1972, 115),[7] and not 'Russia's innate collectivism', as it is usually perceived. This individuation was wrapped in the collectivist rhetoric of bolshevism, which targeted all stable values of the past and promised freedom and prosperity in some brighter future. Yet, when the time came to share power, resources, and influence, those collectivists soon revealed their individuated nature, and social interaction took place much in the Hobbesian fashion of a war of all against all for most of the 1920s until the Leviathan settled the score closer to the 1930s.

The fastidiousness of these liberals towards the type of society they seek could partly explain the gulf that exists between these thinkers and the Russian public at large. As Vitaly Tretyakov (2013b) argues, 'many in Russian society feel that our liberals want to create liberalism and the liberal state only for their own kind' and that 'inherent snobbism, intellectual arrogance, and the genuine dislike of Russia creates a bad reputation for our liberals' (Tretyakov 2011). Yet, pluralist liberals, while talking about the need for constructing liberal values at home, are careful about placing the blame for their absence squarely on society's shortcomings – this is the job they largely leave to the radicals and, when the battle gets too hot, quickly distance themselves from this group. Pluralistic liberals claim that, while society needs to be progressive enough to embrace liberal values, the process of constructing a liberal culture should be incessant and persistent (Khakamada 2008; Ryzhkov 2011). In some ways, they deploy the Kantian model of transcendental reason, and hope that, at some point, the political culture of Russian society can entrench itself in the climate of liberalism; it is at that point that every member of society will realize the necessity of liberty as one main factor in sustaining order and harmony (Kara-Murza, in Tretyakov 2008; Filatov 2006; Fadeyev 2013; Khakamada 2008; *Expert* 2013).

These pluralistic liberals stress that the patient attempts to promote liberal values should never cease and highlight the significance of this task in potential political situations of the future. Kara-Murza (1994) warns that 'if the old order cannot ensure stability and further restrictions do not yield positive results, but the liberal safety net at the same time has not been prepared, this situation could lead to the worst outcome of a "new barbarism".' Yurii Pivovarov (Tretyakov 2005) similarly argues that it could be tragic to overlook the moment in which society can take a leap into liberal politics. In this situation, the consequences could as destructive as bringing liberalism from outside and imposing it in a forceful manner too early. Pluralist liberals argue that Russia was ready to embrace the liberal political system as early as at the end of the nineteenth century, and yet rejected this path due to individuation, chaos, and radicalism that eventually resulted in the step towards bolshevism in 1917 (Tretyakov 2005).

Now, what is their attitude to the state? Historically, Russian liberalism viewed the state as its dialogical partner, and, if managed properly, virtuously, and progressively, the source of social stability. Kara-Murza (in Tretyakov 2008) argues that 'classical Russian liberalism' – by which he assumes its moderate-pluralist wing of the nineteenth century – "has never been an enemy of the state or Russian statehood." He (in Tretyakov 2008) continues, that

> these liberals were awed by the results of the French Revolution, which to their mind stemmed from the degradation of the state. Therefore, Russian liberalism always sought to save the state from slipping into self-seeking destructive policies, whose results may lead to popular protest of that magnitude. When they persisted, they have always succeeded. More importantly, they have always saved Russia, and Russian statehood, from collapse, economic decline, and defeat in the international arena.

Many Western observers also note that the relationship of pluralist liberals with the state has always had, in the words of Harley Balzer (1991), an air of 'reciprocal ambivalence'. Porter and Gleason (1998, 62) claim that in the nineteenth century the liberal class had a 'Janus-like relationship with the regime; that it accepted the legitimacy of the state as the motor force of development while simultaneously seeking to free itself from the government's overweening nature.' Some observers (Porter and Gleason 1998) lament this situation and claim that, due to this predicament, Russia's civil society remained immature and incomplete. Yet these assessments must be qualified in that they depend solely on a theoretical standpoint to civil society adopted by an observer. If we view civil society as an antagonist/negation of the state, much in the Marxian fashion (Seligman 1992, 7–8; Lewis 1992, 1–16; Keane 1988; Cohen and Arato 1992; examples of this approach in Diamond 1996, 236–7; Schmitter 1985, 96–100), then we can sustain this critical charge against Russian liberalism. If we, however, accept civil society as an entity partly coterminous with the state, in either a Hegelian, Lockean, or even Hobbesian understanding, then this claim could come across as somewhat more dubious, because parts of civil society in this trend are actively co-operating with the state in various aspects of social life (Inoguchi 2002; Keane 1988; Lewis 1992; Chebankova 2012) and have the dual goal of curbing the state's influence *and* assisting it in the prevention of social chaos.

It is on that basis that Kara-Murza (in Tretyakov 2008) argues that the main enemy of Russia's contemporary liberalism remains social chaos and, from that point of view, liberals 'do not want to demolish the state. Rather, they want to improve it with the view to ensure harmony, prosperity, and stable development.' Konstantin Remchukov (in Tretyakov 2008) also notes that 'as a liberal, I am not willing to make myself an enemy of Russian statehood. Rather, I merely disagree with some of the policies of the extant government and offer different recipes of doing things in various spheres.' With this in mind, Russian moderate-pluralist liberalism proposes 'reformism from above', which assumes gradualism, opportunism, and co-operation with various social forces, including the state, and systematic distribution of the liberal idea among the general public.

Legalism and Progress

Now when the position of these liberals on the state and society became clear, some issues are still outstanding. Listening to their deliberations on containing societal chaos, one cannot help but wonder where the borders of this chaos are and which particular social conditions could be defined as chaos. Would these thinkers consider the postmodern process of redefining collective identities as chaos? At the end of the day, this process primarily targets the national identity and affiliation with the nation-state, creating in their stead global-local alliances of similar-minded individuals (Tretyakov 2009a; Eisenstadt 2002). Could the new social movements that redefine the borders of state control and the entire process of social interaction be considered as chaos? This dynamic also brings new lifestyles, sometimes shocking, sometimes radical and conflicting, and from that point of view uncontrolled, chaotic, and presenting a challenge to stable identities. In other words, the question one might ask these liberals is how do they define the borders of the political?

It is interesting that, while being aware of this intellectual challenge, Russian pluralist liberals do not give concrete answers to these questions. They will debate some or most of these problems on different occasions, with different conclusions (Tretyakov 2005; Tretyakov 2009a; Tretyakov 2009b; Tretyakov 2011). Yet they avoid providing a systematic definition of chaos. Bearing this omission in mind, they claim that Russian liberalism, as a tradition and practice, has always somewhat ignored the political dimension of social life and focused rather on its legal aspects (Kara-Murza in Tretyakov 2005; Kara-Murza 2007). Boris Chicherin and Peter Struve – the leading liberals of the early-twentieth century – have been lawyers and contributed much to the development of the legal thought and tradition in Russia (Filatov 2006).

Contemporary pluralist liberals, though not professional lawyers, stress the primary significance of reforms within the legal dimensions of the political system. Nikolay Svanidze, Russia's liberal historian, claims that 'first and foremost I want to achieve equality of all citizens before the law. I want to create a situation, in which we will not have first- and second-class citizens, regardless of their religion, political attitudes, and professions' (Shevchenko and Svanidze 2012). Similarly, the leaders of Russia's oldest liberal party, Yabloko, mostly stress the need of judicial reform, for they consider it as the immediate remedy to the social problems facing Russia today. In their view, the rule of law, equality of all before the law, and real independence of the courts are needed before Russia is able to proceed to more-complex questions of defining the borders of the political and determine the interplay between individual freedom and social control, as well as the nature of social chaos.

Another important observation concerns the fact that the legal argument is often geared to defending private-property rights and economic activity. The logic behind this claims that, in the conditions

of fair play, legal economic order will lead to prosperity and the establishment of a solid middle class, and this could fuel the demand for
greater political inclusiveness and be mature enough to foster appropriate institutions of political participation. Valery Fadeyev (2013;
2013b, in Tretyakov et al.), the editor-in-chief of the influential journal
Expert, invokes a classical understanding of liberalism as a 'doctrine
capable of sustaining nation-state capitalism, stable economic growth
and development, as well as an efficient bureaucracy capable of providing an administrative framework to these dynamics.' He also sees
the idea of personal autonomy, in which each individual is free to
pursue a meaningful project of self-development, as vital to the realization of progressive economic needs. To these ends, he is determined
to create a system that protects property rights, in which judicial
decisions will be impartial and balanced and large, medium-sized, and
small businesses will be enabled to develop in a stable manner.

In many ways, the emphasis on the legal dimension of social
life becomes entirely logical if we treat Russia squarely in terms of
European history. Indeed, legal and constitutional order emerged
and entrenched itself in leading European countries well before full-
fledged democracy. Legalism represented the first building block of 'civil
society', which was seen essentially as 'economic society' and called
on to protect economic activity and property rights (Malia 1994).
Development of the 'economic society', in the absence of other social
benefits, involved significant brutality and invoked serious human costs
during the eighteenth to nineteenth centuries (Engels's gripping account
of the conditions in working-class Britain provides revealing evidence).
Nevertheless, this was a gradual process, leading to the formation
of a comprehensive system of rights and freedoms and the more-
inclusive democratic governance with which we are familiar today.
T.H. Marshall's 1949 account of the evolution of rights in Europe
systematizes this sequence of events. Marshall argues that 'civil rights'
first appeared in the eighteenth century to signify the rights to free
economic activity and protection of private property; political rights,
seen in the ability to take part in the political process through voting
and forming political associations, emerged later in the nineteenth
century, while social rights, seen as the entitlement to social benefits,
socio-political equality, and the subsequent ideological empowerment
of societal periphery, accelerated throughout the twentieth century.

Hence, bearing in mind such an historic perspective, the legal economic leniency of Russian pluralist liberalism could be seen more as

a sign of political temperance than philosophic omission. Such thinkers insist that Russia, having eliminated her bourgeois 'economic civil society' throughout the Soviet decades, will invariably require time to resolve this predicament before it is able to develop other aspects of political democratic governance. They also realize that the legal dimension must come first in the sequence of rights evolution, and only when this aspect is implemented in full, can Russia focus on other sectors of her socio-political development. In this light, Kara-Murza (2007, in Tretyakov) claims that any modernization of Russia must begin with the modernization of her legal institutions, which would subsequently enable the harmonious functioning of economic, political, and social sectors of life.

Some Western authors echo this idea from different perspectives. While disagreeing on the causality between economic market and political legal order, many Western authors agree that political democracy must be attempted only after the state has confirmed its capability to effectively govern society and navigate the networks of a market economy through a host of legal institutions. Huntington (2006, 7–9), for example, argues that, in order to achieve a more inclusive and democratic government, societies must first establish a capable legal order that can provide stable governance (2). For him, effective and legitimate institutions serve as a precondition for subsequent development in the economic, political, and social spheres. Huntington (2006, 7–8) claims that we 'can have order without liberty' but we cannot have 'liberty without order'. Malia (1994, 506–8) is more focused on the economy. He claims that the main problem of post-Soviet Russia is to build 'a liberal economic order while simultaneously developing a democratic polity'. Yet he also argues that 'it is a much more arduous task to create the myriad institutions that make a mature market economy than it is to fashion a political democracy' (507) and that 'there are no examples of political democracies *without* a market-driven economy' (508).

One potential caveat is that such emphasis on legality may lead to a situation in which the law is used to defend the interests of the privileged economic class or the state, to neutralize the political activity of society, and subsequently to produce a deficit of legitimacy – a common criticism developed by the Russian left and discussed later in Chapter 5. This problem could be investigated through the Western debate on juridification initiated by Otto Kirchheimer and continued by Jürgen Habermas and Michel Foucault (Teubner 1987, 9–12).

Juridification is understood in terms of the gradual increase of rules, laws, and regulations that, on the one hand, proclaim rights and freedoms and on the other hand strictly define the areas and procedures within which such freedoms can be applied, thereby restricting the lifeworld and depoliticizing social processes.

This somewhat brings us back to the idea that most Western states had established their extant political systems through expanding rights on the one hand, but has to use force to entrench such a system on the other. Habermas (1987), in his *Theory of Communicative Action*, traces these processes through the 'waves of juridification' that began with the establishment of the early absolutist state and ended with the emergence of a global human-rights system, which has both empowering and constraining effects on individuals. If we were to think about the situation in Russia in these terms, we could suggest first that the legal emphasis echoes a distinct path of European civilization, and second that juridification is an ambivalent phenomenon that led overall to the expansion of rights and participation, rather than to their limitation.

The Duality of Russia's International Identity

Moderate-pluralist liberals further reveal their political temperance in the debates around Russia's international identity and its impact on the evolution of values, norms, behavioural patterns, and political goals at home. They argue that, in much the way the interpersonal communication of humans shapes their acts and identity in everyday life, the nature of geopolitical discourse determines states' identities and behaviour in the domestic and foreign arenas. I raised this point earlier when referring to pluralist liberals' distinction from their monistic counterparts, who espouse a slightly different approach, claiming that domestic debate determines foreign identity. From this point of view, pluralist liberals argue, Russia's international standings set the country's goals and commitments and compel her to behave in a certain manner at home and abroad. Following Vladimir Solovyov on the one hand, and Lev Gumilev on the other, these thinkers insist that Russia has both *civilizational* (European) and *geopolitical* (Eurasian) identities (Kara-Murza 1998).

Geopolitical struggles in the Eurasian space, as well as Russia's geographic location on both continents, shape her Eurasian geopolitical identity as a large state with interests in both Europe and Asia.

Peter the Great's partially successful attempts to convert Russia into a modern European power, as well as Russia's medieval battles with Europe for religious and cultural primacy (with Poland and Lithuania representing the most meaningful historical-existential alternatives) shaped Russia's European identity. Hence, Russia's European identity carries civilizational and existential tones, for it was in Europe that Russia's main battles for power and influence took place, and it is with Europe that Russia held most of her cultural lifelong dialogue (Filatov 2006).

This situation fuels the duality of Russia's domestic and international discourse. The European civilizational identity drives domestic debates on liberalization and progress towards European norms and values, as well as sustaining international discourse on Russia's commitments to the ideals of democracy. The Eurasian component fosters arguments on Russia's separate historical path, which, from this geostrategic point of view, stems from a far broader range of factors than the mere failure to modernize the country's economy and technological potential, as some monistic thinkers would claim (Dubin 2004, 305–6 and 316; see also Filatov 2006).

Hence, both European and Eurasian discourses are lodged in the parallel and equally legitimate aspects of Russia's history and both are the rightful occupants of the country's ideological scene. Kara-Murza (1998) observes that the state usually assumes responsibility for the geopolitical Eurasian dimension of Russia's identity and does the job of honouring Russia's commitments in her vast geographic space. The liberal opposition, on the other hand, feels responsible for the civilizational aspect of Russia's identity that is geared towards popularization of European norms and values in the cultural, political, and social spheres. Understanding the inherent duality of the Russian identity, Kara-Murza (1998; 2009) argues, could become a clue to shaping a harmonious approach to Russian politics and society and constructing the civic nation that will be able to transcend the seemingly unbridgeable epistemic division between the traditionalist (Eurasian) and liberal (European) discourse (Gorshkov 2009, 17–18; Gorshkov 2007; Byzov 2006).

Instead of building a *consensus* on either a liberal or Eurasian foundation, the formation of which will invariably involve a zero-sum game for both parties, pluralistic liberalism calls for *coexistence* between these identities. Such coexistence, however, is not seen in merely leaving each competing discourse to its own devices. This would lead to radicalization of both episteme, simplification of the debate, the eventual annihilation of one side by another, and the subsequent reconstruction of the hegemonic discourse, which would take place on the basis of the winning discourse consensus and invariably possess indoctrinating overtones. Instead, Kara-Murza (2009), following Russia's liberal philosophers of the twentieth century Georgy Fedotov, Fedor Stepun, and Vladimir Veidle, calls for the open recognition of Russia's epistemic duality of identities, gradual deconstruction of each competing discourse, determination of the rational ground in each of these strands, elimination of the radical components, and reconstruction of *both* doctrines on the basis of their mutual understanding. Therefore, Kara-Murza (2009) argues that the task of contemporary Russian liberalism is neither a slavish idolization of the state, nor the perpetual mimicking of oppositionist sentiment, or an ardent attempt to uproot the government – and it is certainly not a radicalization of the liberal discourse with the view to imposing liberalism forcefully upon the reluctant population. Rather, this task is seen in resetting (*perezagruzka*) liberalism so that it can occupy a rightful place in the debate that takes place over the construction of Russia's new civic identity.

MAIN ACTORS AND POLITICAL ACTIVITY

We now have to turn to a brief discussion of the political representation of the liberal views discussed above. It is important to note that, in the wake of the 2014 incorporation of Crimea into the Russian Federation, radical liberals lost their general support base. They have thus adopted a more left-wing socialist-oriented platform in order to garner greater public approval. Many of the existing figures and organizations began to gravitate towards the moderate liberal side. Let us discuss the existing monistic-liberal wing and then move to the pluralist strand.

The Party of People's Freedom (*Parnas*), led by Russia's former prime minister Mikhail Kasyanov, is the most vocal party of monistic-liberal leanings. The party takes part in most federal, regional, and local elections, albeit with relatively little success. Despite this minimal electoral success, however, the party is capable of gathering large rallies in support of its ideas. Its leaders formed the kernel of the 2011 White Ribbon protests in Moscow, organized rallies in memory of Boris Nemtsov and against the policies of the Russian government in Ukraine. Russia's radical liberals hold annual congresses in Vilna, Lithuania, which are attended by eminent radical opposition leaders such as Gary Kasparov, Ilya Ponomarev, Evgeniya Chirikova, Dmitry Nekrasov, Dmitry Bykov, and many others. The Open Russia foundation supported by Mikhail Khodorkovsky holds to a similar political platform. The foundation seeks a thorough de-Sovietization of Russian society, with a view to dispensing with Russia's great power ambitions, wresting power from the hands of state conservative elites, consolidating the neo-liberal economic course, and, most importantly, merging with the Euro-Atlantic political, economic, and military space. This could be done at the expense of Russia's partial disintegration (as seen in various statements by radical opposition leaders such as Evgeniya Albats, Alfred Kokh, Konstantin Borovoy, and formerly Arkady Babchenko) and by the revision of the official Second World War narrative established by the Soviet Union and adopted by contemporary Russia.[8]

The pluralist wing, as we have already discussed, seeks to legitimize the post-Soviet political and economic order, consolidate property rights, construct legal and judicial systems on the basis of European standards, and ultimately build a 'corporation Russia' (Dugin 2016) that could join the Western world as a rightful partner (while retaining some of its historical idiosyncrasies). This agenda corresponds to many tasks pursued by the Russian state. This ideological wing has a sizeable political representation within the Russian government and political elites. Vladimir Pligin, a member of the Russian State Duma during four convocations and the leader of the liberal wing of the United Russia party, is a prominent representative of pluralist-liberal views. Alexey Kudrin, Russia's former minister of finance, leading economists of the Russian government, and to some extent Russia's prime minister, Dmitry Medvedev, share pluralist-liberal views. Russia's oldest democratic party, Yabloko, openly sides with the pluralist-liberal platform by arguing that, in contrast to radical liberals, it seeks to reflect a democratic liberal platform and account for the wishes and sentiments of the Russian people at large. Yabloko takes part in regional, federal, and local elections with moderate success in a number of regions. Its representatives are frequent guests of Russia's publicly televized debates, and some of its members, such as Vladimir Lukin, Igor Artemyev, Mikhail Evraev, Aleksandr Kynev, Andrey Babushkin, and Natalya Evdokimova, occupy governmental and senior consulting positions.

Russia's Party of Growth (known as The Right Cause Party until 2016) expresses similar pluralist-liberal views. It is composed of eminent political and media figures from the 1990s (Sergey Stankevich, Irina Khakamada, Oksana Dmitrieva, Evgeny Tarlo, and Leonid Gozman), who still hold significant influence over Russia's political process. The organization is headed by Boris Titov, who is a member of the Presidential Administration, responsible for liaising with Russian businesses. Oksana Dmitrieva, former Yabloko member, heads the St Petersburg regional legislature representing the Party of Growth. Irina Khakamada, a member of the Presidential Council on Human Rights (until 2018), participates in the party's higher political council. Ksenia Sobchak, a renowned political journalist, migrated between radical and pluralist-liberal viewpoints, finally settling on the pluralist version of liberalism during her 2018 presidential electoral campaign. Russia's leading opposition figure (and Internet blogger), Alexey Navalny, led the 2011–12 White Ribbon protests and now heads the public Fund for the Struggle Against Corruption. He often changes his political orientation, migrating between monistic liberals, nationalists, and even left-wingers, but most often remains within the camp of pluralist liberals. In general, pluralist liberals have a large influence over Russia's economic, cultural, and social policies. They also enjoy a significant metaphysical reach within Russian society, representing one of the most important suggested options for the future trajectory of Russia's development.

To conclude, this chapter has argued that Russian liberalism is composed of two main trends, moderate-pluralist and monistic-radical, to reflect the general paradigmatic split within Russian society. Both strands of liberalism represent rightful and essential parts of the country's liberal discourse. The discussion claimed that, while monistic-radical liberalism is geared towards the comprehensive restructuring of Russian society, with a view to achieving its full compliance with European norms, the pluralistic side is focused on resolving the problems of social chaos and order through achieving a particularly stable, liberal, form of governance, which would invariably take into account distinct Russian realities.

3

Conservatism

Many analysts and observers of Russian politics are becoming increasingly interested in the nature of Russia's contemporary conservatism. Western observers mainly remain sceptical, while their Russian colleagues are trying to reach a consensus on the nature and genesis of this ideological trend. This chapter will argue that conservatism has a long, historic tradition within Russia's political life. More importantly, it contributed to the formation of a political consensus within Russian society over the past decade. As we discussed in the introduction, most of Russia's ideologies are buttressed by the paradigmatic split on the liberal and traditionalist wings. This chapter will discuss the 'liberal', or moderate, side of conservatism and its main tenets; an examination of the more 'traditionalist' facet of Russia's conservatism will appear in the next chapter. The discussion will begin with an overview of some overarching features of Russian conservatism and will then proceed to examine some of the particular elements that are applicable to the contemporary political situation in Russia and beyond.

CONSERVATISM: MAIN POSITIONS

At the outset, it seems logical to outline a number of overarching theoretical positions that form the basis of Russia's conservatism and compose a prism through which this ideology's particular features can be examined. We can select the three most important points. First, conservatism, as an ideology, is distinct from other ideologies, in that it represents a standpoint, a position. In contrast to strictly ideational ideologies, such as communism, socialism, liberalism, nationalism, and fascism, conservatism does not have a clearly formulated package of existential values. Neither does it have a meaningfully articulated project for an ideal model of future society (Mannheim 1936, 40). As Huntington (1957, 458) notes, 'no conservative ideal exists to serve as the standard of judgment. No political philosopher has ever described a conservative utopia. In any socio-political system, there may be institutions to be conserved, but there are never conservative institutions.'

However, while such positionism (Mannheim 1936, Huntington 1957) plays a large part in the Russian conservative outlook, it cannot define it fully. Thinkers and ideologues of contemporary Russia (Remizov 2010; Leontyev 2010; Averyanov, in Ilyashenko et al. 2014) seek to qualify the positionist approach by claiming that it deprives conservatism of its developmental dynamic and restricts its future-oriented potential. Hence, the second main characteristic of Russian conservatism is its focus on the future, which divorces it from the positionist past- (or present-)centred frame of mind. From this point of view, this thought is preoccupied with the ways of weaving the eternal concepts and morals into the fabric of a contemporary, future-focused world. In doing so, conservatives divorce the past from the eternal by selecting those transcendental values of previous ages that they wish to take to the future (Leontyev 2010; see also Mezhuyev, in Tretyakov 2013a; Grot 1891). In other words, Russian conservatism seeks to recreate tradition in a new form. Russia's conservative analyst Mikhail Remizov (2010, 15–16) brands this re-actualization of eternal morals within the conditions of postmodern urban society as 'productive revanchism'.

Thus, in contrast to the established Western view that contemporary society is focused on the future (Giddens 1990, 94), Russian conservatism hopes to diffuse its attention between the past, present, *and* future. At the same time, this future-oriented focus of Russian conservatism is rather idiosyncratic. Its most important aspects are of an economic nature. These are largely linked to the socio-political turmoil that the country succumbed to during the twentieth century. The rapid change of ideological paradigms, which inflicted painful wounds on Russian society, gave these thinkers incentives to search for the most stable methods for the *development and modernization* of Russia. This development is seen in building a prosperous country resilient to the repetition of past troubles. Hence, their project is largely a reaction to the deprivation of Soviet times, the impoverishment and moral collapse of the 1990s, and the gradual economic recovery of the 2000s (Remizov 2010, 7–8).

Anthropocentrism is the third overarching feature of contemporary Russian conservatism. Conservative thinkers see humans as the main actors of historic progress. They believe that each stage of socio-political development determines its own model, or narrative, of a Man. They seek to narrate a particular human anthropology that could provide a meaningful alternative to the neo-liberal and left-liberal spirit of the age. These thinkers take modernity as a foundational matrix and strive to integrate its features into the rapidly changing nature of the postmodern world. The Man of modernity, they argue, is a self-developing, progressive being with the Kantian will to Reason and the Nietzschean will to power (power to overcome personal weaknesses) (Dugin 2009; Remizov 2010; Tsymbursky 2008). With the help of these qualities, Men of modernity have produced the finest works of literature and art, as well as a wealth of scientific discoveries and inventions.

Transition to postmodernity, they argue (Tsymbursky 2008; Panarin 2001; Remizov 2010), is intertwined with accelerated globalism, urbanization, growing professionalism, migration, and the rise of multiculturalism, development of segmented identities, and a redefinition of family and gender relations. The uneven fabric of the postmodern society plunges the world into uncertainty by depriving humans of the previously established norms, values, and behavioural patterns that have been formed gradually by faith, religion, and politics of previous centuries. As Anthony Giddens (1990) notes, the Man of postmodernity becomes a creature of 'self-actualization', often seen in the pursuit of hedonistic pleasures, particular personal emotions, and fancy desires. The postmodern atmosphere of uncertainty makes it increasingly difficult to narrate normative parameters that define a contemporary Man. Yet, this problem remains central to the future development of any type of society, for its successful resolution ensures a stable reproduction of socio-political foundations of human civilization (Remizov 2010; Mezhuyev 2012).

Russian conservatism sees the task of narrating the anthropology of contemporary Man as the main challenge of the age (Remizov 2010). This drive is also fuelled by the embitterment that stems from the erosion of pre-existing Soviet paradigms of human behaviour produced by the Soviet *type* of modernity. Hence, conservatives are concerned with building a bridge between some positive norms of the Soviet (and Russian Imperial) modernity and contemporary postmodern Russia. These three intellectual trajectories determine a conservative answer to a host of substantive questions pondered by Russian conservative thought today. What is the role of the state and the societal expectations placed upon it? How should we treat historical myths and apply them to the present? How should Russia's cultural-civilizational distinction, her permanent search for political alternativism, be expressed? How should particular cultures of the world be preserved? What are the ways of development and modernization of Russia? I will discuss these issues in what follows by referring to the anthropocentric and positionist features of conservatism in the first four points and by examining the future focus of this thought in the final subsection of this chapter.

Attitude to the State

The conservative attitude to the state entails two main features: anthropocentric and positionist. The former places a range of unique demands on the state through a particular set of socio-political and ethical values. The latter exhibits support of the strong state that could ensure security, territorial integrity, stable development, and modernization of Russia. In the first case, conservatives diverge from the liberals and socialists, who seek to regulate the state through taxes and surplus value. In this sphere, conservatives stress the idea of intergenerational justice and argue that Russia's large oligarchic capital unjustly enjoys the benefits of former Soviet assets – the land, the wealth of natural resources, the system of large industrial enterprises (Remizov 2010). Thus, they seek to control the state by demanding that it place the brakes on large industrial capital that, in their view, has outstanding intergenerational debts to the ex-Soviet people.

In many ways, these ideas involve a monumental anthropological task of creating a qualitatively new national elite. This elite should, instead of siding with neo-liberal global interests led and directed by the West, create a new existential value package for Russia. This value package could act as a paradigm, a framework within which both society and its large industrial capital would operate. For most conservatives, it is the task of creating a class of national bourgeoisie whose main loyalties would lie at home and whose objectives would coincide with the immediate interests, development, and fate of Russia (Kurginyan 2009; Delyagin 2014b). Russian national capitalists, in this conservative view, must make a clear psychological, emotional, as well as rational economic connection between personal enrichment and their country's future. This capitalist economic elite, conservatives insist, must stop viewing Russia as a mere hunting ground and treat it like a financial and historic home. In many ways, they propose the values of patriotism and loyalty to the nation-state that clash with the postmodern idea of cosmopolitanism and world citizenship.

Mikhail Khazin (2013), one of Russia's left-wing economists, a permanent member of the conservative Izborsky Club, and a member of the higher council of the International Eurasian Movement, claims that, since the very dawn of Russia's capitalism, the country's elite was divided between those who belonged to the so-called national bourgeoisie and those who merely conducted business in Russia, but did not link their personal and financial future with this country. The Russian royal family, he argues, belonged to the second category, which largely precipitated the outcome of the Russian revolution. So, did the late Communist economic and political elite, whose aim was to convert their political power into tangible personal assets and to become part of the global system of capitalism. With the collapse of the USSR, this very elite has privatized resources and turned their extraction to personal advantage, channelling the proceeds abroad.

Yet the financial crisis of 2008, as well as the post-2014 Crimean sanctions, revealed that there are segments of Russia's big business that have stakes in sustaining Russia's national interests and securing the geopolitical strength of the country (Khazin 2013). Representatives of such big business appeal to the Russian state to defend their interests abroad. This created, probably for the first time since the collapse of the Soviet Union, a psychological link between the new industrial elite and the Russian state, invoking (or creating the grounds for invoking) feelings of loyalty desired by conservatives. Wide circles of Russia's conservatives enthusiastically welcomed this tentative emergence of a national bourgeoisie. Sergey Kurginyan, a socialist-conservative and a member of the Izborsky Club, called for the creation of a wide political alliance between the national bourgeoisie and the patriotic forces of the left, while Mikhail Delyagin (2014b; 2013) claimed that 'offshore oligarchs must be neutralized as a political and economic force'.

These sentiments led conservative ideologues to develop a package of measures that aimed to end the situation in which Russia's economic elite channel their profits abroad and claim loyalty to global financial institutions, thus challenging and subverting the Russian state (Shugaev, in Bogdanov 2014; Fursov 2011; Aksyutich 2014; Dugin and Oganesyan 2012; Delyagin 2014a). Putin's 2013 initiatives on expatriating companies from offshore jurisdictions (Ryabukhin, in Bogdanov 2014; Prokhanov 2012; Alexandrov 2013; Delyagin et al. 2012) and legislative bills that banned Russian politicians from opening bank accounts abroad are of particular importance. The law on foreign accounts also prohibited the possession of foreign property. Similar initiatives concerning large infrastructural projects aimed at the development of national capital and industry. Vladimir Yakunin, the former head of Russia's Railroad Corporation and a close associate of Vladimir Putin, called for the radical change of Russia's developmental model. He suggested massive investment in, and development of, Siberian and Far Eastern infrastructure – a project that could place industry, production, and an industrial economy sector at the heart of Russia's development.

From the positionist perspectives, Russian contemporary conservatism is also intrinsically linked to the idea of a strong state that could sustain the country's geostrategic interests in the international arena in order to achieve stable development at home. In many ways, this tenet of conservatism mirrors early republican thought. The early humanist vision of politics assumed that 'the most basic aim of any ruler must always be *mantenero lo stato*', that is, strengthening the state and defending its people (Skinner 2002, Vol. 2, 9 and 121–2). Such ideas are thoroughly positionist, in that there is no recipe or agreement on how to achieve these goals (Skinner 2002, Vol. 2, 22–3 and 121; Huntington 1957, 460). Valery Fadeyev observes the closeness of Russia's conservatism to these early ideas: 'we must return to our historic idea of a strong country, and this should form the emerging consensus in Russia. This consensus has republican connotations, but at the same time, it bears traces of Russia's traditionalism and conservatism.'

It is also important that different varieties of Russia's conservatism that existed throughout the country's history have been united by the goal of preserving *a* model of Russian statehood that is conducive to securing and maintaining Russia's strength in the international arena in order to assure stability at home. While substantive (ideational) means towards meeting such statist targets alter with the change of political eras, the procedural framework has always been in the achievement of Russia's sovereignty and great power status internationally. The breadth and magnitude of this great power status also varied with time. Yet the concept of Russia's ability to pursue her geostrategic interests abroad independently and to defend the inviolability of her natural and political borders remained unchanged.

This position is largely driven by a host of geopolitical and domestic fears that have both theoretical and idiosyncratic explanations specific to Russia. From a theoretical angle, Huntington (1957, 470) aptly notes that 'men are driven to conservatism by the shock of events, by the terrible feeling that a society of institutions which they have approved or taken for granted and with which they have been intimately connected may suddenly cease to exist.' In most cases, such fears are constructed around artificial or real perceptions of rivalry, around the 'fear of the unknown or the obscure', around 'a hasty identification or "naming" in the stark terms of good and evil, divine and demonic' (McCormick 1997, 109; Adorno and Horkheimer 1999; Cassirer 1946; Sorel 1999). Indeed, Russia lives, or at least perceives herself as living, in a permanent state of danger. The struggles for influence over the Eurasian space, for political positions in Europe, and for the architecture of international affairs all test Russia's statehood, territorial integrity, and position in the world arena. The intensity of this battle is matched by Russia's unique geographic position, the vastness of her landmass, and the richness of her natural resources. As Peter Hitchens (2014) notes, Western critics of Russia must understand the realities of Russian history that have always dictated the feelings of threat.

> The country has not natural defensible borders. A street in southern Moscow, *Ulitsa Bolshaya Ordynka* (the street of the Great Horde) commemorates to this day the five-yearly visits to Moscow of the Great Horde, to collect a tribute from that frontier city. We tend to think that the Urals, supposedly mountains but really rather unimpressive hills, form Russia's eastern boundary. But it isn't really true. From every direction, the heart of Russia lies open to invaders. Moscow has been invaded or occupied by Swedes, Poles, Lithuanians, The Golden (or Great) Horde, Crimean Tatars, and Napoleon. No wonder the Russian word for "security" (*byezopasnost*) is a negative construction ("byez" means "without"; "opasnost" means "danger"). The natural state of things is danger (Hitchens 2014).

Thus, from an historic perspective, geopolitical fears, coupled with the fears of domestic unrest induced from abroad, constitute the foundation of Russia's positionist conservative drive to consolidate the state. In modern times, Russian conservatism emerged in response to the horrors of the French Revolution, which shook the foundations of European order and threatened Russia with similar developments at home (Rogger 1966; Berlin 1994). In this light, Russian conservatives have been permanently engaged in the ideological struggle against domestic utopias and liberal radicalism that attempted to undermine the stability of the state. In 1907 Prime Minister Peter Stolypin succinctly described the struggle of Russian conservatism with the liberal and left-wing radicals by saying that 'they are in need of great upheavals. We are in need of a great Russia' (Ascher 2001, 4; Waldorn 2002). Conservatism of the early-nineteenth century stood against the circle of Decembrists who challenged the foundations of the Russian state in 1825, proposed to set Poland (then part of the Russian Empire) free, and planned to diminish the Russian army (Starikov 2011). Later, at the end of the nineteenth century, conservatism countered the radical-socialist revolutionary movement led by intellectuals such as Dobrolyubov and Chernyshevsky. In 1905, conservatives condemned those liberals who sent congratulatory telegrams to the Japanese emperor on his victory over the Russian army in the Russo-Japanese war (and this case seems both topical and indicative for many contemporary conservatives of today, particularly in light of the radical liberal sentiments discussed in Chapter 2; see Mikhalkov 2014).

In the twentieth century, conservatism was in many ways the defensive drive toward securing Russia's achievements in the spheres of economics, science and technology, education, space and Arctic exploration, and many other areas of human achievement. From this point of view, the policies of Soviet Communism had a strong conservative flavour. It could be argued that the Bolsheviks ceased to be globalist-left radicals almost immediately upon assuming office. Their subsequent travails in constructing a world economic, military, technological, and nuclear superpower capable of adequately defending itself were evidence that supported Russia's conservative course. In very recent times, Russia's conservatives have been united by the idea of consolidating a Russian state that could return the country to its former leading position in the spheres of intellectual achievement, science, technology, and economic production. Alexander Prokhanov (2014), a leading member of the conservative Izborsky Club, has always hoped that the Russian state achieves a particular 'spiritual consolidation and strength'. He has called for Russia to 'restore its values and recreate its place in history'. The state, according to Prokhanov, should be capable of 'strategic doings'. It should have the 'economy, [and] industry which can sustain the realization of all strategic plans'.

Interestingly, Western European – and to a large extent North American – conservatism also emerges partly in response to the geopolitical fear of, and rivalry with, Russia. Such fear is driven by differences in value packages, customs, political traditions, and, more significantly, geostrategic considerations. While Russia often feels the need to protect her statehood, civilizational distinctness, and vital military-economic geographic territories from Western assimilation – and this is what fuels Russia's conservatism of all types – Europe has a similar need to consolidate her political will in opposition to the perceived threat from the East. This sentiment is particularly well reflected in the writings of Carl Schmitt and Friedrich Nietzsche, which remain topical to this day. Schmitt claims that Russia stands as a serious counterforce to all consolidated political forces of the West, such as liberalism, socialism, and the Church (McCormick 1997, 94–6). This is due to Russia's extremity 'in its countlessness, in its embrace of the technical', and because it is 'so radical in its rebellion against form of any kind, in its embrace of spiritual anarchy' (cited in McCormick 1997, 95).

Nietzsche (1990, 138), at the same time, was a forerunner of this sentiment by seeing Russia's strength of will as a threat to Europe:

> [T]he strength to will ... is strongest and most amazing by far in that enormous empire ... in Russia. There the strength to will has long been accumulated and stored up and kept in reserve, there the will is waiting menacingly – uncertain whether as a will to negate or a will to affirm – to discharge itself ... It may take more than Indian wars and complications in Asia to rid Europe of its greatest danger.

Nietzsche, in this fear of Russia, proclaims the arrival of grand politics. He predicts the struggle over the 'mastery over the whole earth – the *compulsion* to grand politics' (Nietzsche 1990, 138), and calls on Europe to unite in response to the Russian threat. He invokes it [Europe] 'to become equally threatening, namely to *acquire a single will* by means of a new caste dominating all Europe, a protracted terrible will of its own which could set its objective thousands of years ahead – so that the long-drawn-out comedy of its petty states and the divided will of its dynasties and democracies should finally come to an end' (Nietzsche 1990, 138).

History and Myth

In this light, the creation of various myths – historical, political, and civilizational – represents the *modus vivendi* of Russia's conservative thought. From a theoretical perspective, deployment of myths based on powerful interpretations of events invokes civic consciousness and has both positionist and anthropological objectives. In the former case, myths aid the tasks of civic mobilization and the sense of collective security. As Sorel (1999, 140) claims, human beings 'do nothing great without the help of warmly coloured and sharply defined images which absorb the whole of our attention.' He also insists that not all things can be explained rationally, and that proponents of rationality will never 'understand why an individual, be it a Napoleonic soldier or a striking worker, would perform a selfless and heroic act' (Sorel 1999, xi; see also Mannheim 1936, 120). In the second case, myths help to maintain the sense of belonging to a group of people with a distinct collective identity. In this case, Le Bon (2002) claims that people are guided by unconscious motivations and that those motivations are often formed collectively.

At the same time, the spontaneity of the myth-building process has been questioned, in particular during the age of information and technology. McCormick (1997), following Cassirer (Cassirer 1946, 282) writes:

> [M]yth has always been described as the result of an unconscious activity and as a free product of imagination. But [in the twentieth century] we find myth made according to plan. The new political myths do not grow up freely; they are not wild fruits of an exuberant imagination. They are artificial things fabricated by very skilful artisans. It has been reserved for the twentieth century, our own technological age, to develop a new technique of myth. Henceforth, myths can be manufactured in the same sense and according to the same methods as any other modern weapon – as machine guns or airplanes. That is a new thing – and a thing of crucial importance.

Russia's conservative thought sustains a similar view, claiming that information wars and battles for the dominant interpretation of history and current affairs has become the hallmark of postmodern politics. Margarita Simonyan, the editor-in-chief of RT [Russia Today] TV, admitted that the channel is virtually positioned on the nerve of contemporary politics. It struggles for a sizeable place in the discourse and provides an interpretation alternative that is capable of winning minds in the information wars that take place in today's world. A similar confession came from US officials, when Hillary Clinton (2011) insisted that the '[information] war has been declared' and that the United States must step up its efforts in the struggle against the alternative media that provides an interpretation of events which differs from the US position. In this complex situation, myth meets myth; interpretation meets interpretation, and political narrative meets another political narrative. Hence, truth and reality become segmented and particular, with each segment resting on a set of powerful myths, particular truths, and particular interpretations (Lyotard 1979; Wagner 2012; McCormick 1997; Dugin 2009). Relying on this position, Putin (2013) also claims, quite in tune with the American line, that information campaigns and myth-building represent 'one form of global competition. These are marked by the attempts to influence the world-view and self-perceptions of entire peoples, and to impose alien value systems. This form of the global world competition is very similar to that which takes place in the sphere of natural resources and transportation.'

In this environment, an historic myth becomes the focus of primary attention from Russian conservatism – from both positionist and anthropological angles. These are erected with the view of alleviating the condition of epistemological uncertainty, to position the nation in one stable, geopolitical track, and to form an existential identity that could buttress such a trajectory ideologically. The task of Russian conservatism is to tie up various stages of Russia's history, in the same fashion as France managed to tie up her revolutionary terror and Jacobin dictatorship in her own narrative – a point that we have elaborated in the Introduction. Pondering this task, conservative journalist Mikhail Leontyev (2011) worries that Russian history has been demythologized more than any other history in the world due to its numerous revisions at different periods. Yet he sees a tentative conservative consensus emerging in Russian society – a consensus that is based on the understanding that 'our history belongs to us; that we cannot transplant other experience and someone else's history to our soil; that we have to learn the lessons of our history and take from it what is of particular value to our particular culture and our particular civilization.'

In this light, Putin's policy on the study of history and the creation of a single textbook for schools must be translated as the need to develop an historical myth that will meet such challenges. He claims that 'Russia must create a value-spiritual basis, upon which each person, and in particular young persons, may build their civic consciousness.' Putin (2012) claims that Russia will not be able to 'resurrect her civic self-consciousness unless it understands that the country's history enjoys one thousand years of historic development', and that 'Russia did not begin in 1917 or 1991', as some re-established historic myths of the 1990s claimed. Only by uniting the country around this thousand-year-long myth could Russia develop her strength for future evolution. Interestingly, this approach to history is reminiscent of the German Romantic idea of *Volksgeit* championed by Herder, Shiller, Fichte, Shelling, and their followers in the fields of art, theology, jurisprudence, and international relations. *Volksgeit* describes a metaphysical notion that signifies the spiritual development of people concentrated in the spirit of the group (Berlin 2006, 232). It is understood that there are 'varieties of human experience as the self-expression of the infinitely various spirit of the nation, of the people, or of history, or of the universe' (Berlin 2006, 232–4; Mannheim 1936, 120–1; Bowle 1954, 30–4; Pinkard 2002). This idea relied on collectives of individuals, rather than on single individuals, and emphasized the importance of interconnection between historical and social patterns. It hoped for the 'possibility of connecting representatives from widely different walks of life under the aegis of a common historical spiritual umbrella of the *Volk* and that the presence of those collectives that have a common unconscious "spirit" and common collective memory allows us to treat such collectives as single indivisible units' (Mannheim 1936, 41; Cassirer 1946).

This resonates remarkably with Putin's 2013 idea of 'spiritual clamps', which are called upon to unite Russia around the pattern of her socio-historic development. From this point of view, the emphasis on 'the spirit', spirituality, traditional values, and history are not surprising. In many ways, Putin calls for the revival of Russia's *Volksgeit*, which can serve as a foundation for the new national idea. Hence, he chooses to ignore the cosmopolitan sentiments of Russia's liberal intellectuals, whose views are largely out of step with the dominant segments of Russian society, and sides 'with Russia's moral majority' – in many ways pragmatically, but nevertheless with a view to responding better to Russia's traditional spirit (Lavelle 2013). In his 2013 Valdai speech, he laments that Russia, having suffered the collapse of her statehood twice during the twentieth century, to some extent lost those unifying 'historic codes', or 'spiritual clamps', that could implicitly reflect the national spirit and the internal logic of its historic development (Putin 2013).

Yet, in contrast to Herder, Shiller and other Romantics, contemporary Russian conservatism searches for the conceptual middle ground, in which an individual is not considered as being 'entirely submerged to the single spirit of the whole nation, of which he/she is a small cog and for which he/she is prepared to die if need be' (Berlin 2006), but as an important part of the whole, without which the entire organism cannot function properly. The importance of this particle (atom) is seen in the fact that the whole, while united by common memory and foundation, cannot be considered as completely unified or as having a unique agreement on the idea of the good life that it has formed through the centuries and which it alone understands and cherishes. Rather, there is a clear recognition of the profound divergence of views, of the creative, inventive, and intelligible origin of various intellectual trends that must seek coexistence and dialogue.

Putin (2013) claimed that he hopes for dialogue among those different social and intellectual forces, which have divergent perceptions of Russia's history and future. He calls for an epistemic reconciliation of Russian society by claiming that 'the Westerners, the Slavophiles, the proponents of the strong state and the liberals must work together on drafting our common goals for the future.' In this light, the implicitly embedded value pluralism – in which Russia is not seeking consensus on either a liberal or conservative basis, but instead hopes for the recognition and coexistence between these epistemically different ideas of the good life – becomes the cornerstone of the conservative plan for the future. Russian conservatives believe that traditional Russian values have always been based on tolerance and intercivilizational dialogue. Russia, in their mind, has almost always – with the exception of the Soviet period – managed to avoid the formation of the total concept of ideology, in which one group (the nation) subconsciously shares a particular point of view (Mannheim 1936, 64–5). As Vladimir Medinsky, Russia's minister of culture, argues, 'we never had Crusades. Our tsars have never promoted an idea that Russia is for Russians. We have always relied on inter-cultural, inter-religious, inter-ethnic, and inter-civilizational dialogue.' It becomes clear that Russia's conservatism is searching for ways of critically reconstructing the country's distinct historic-ontological myth, so that *Volksgeit* is able to capture, with some degree of certainty, specific historic moments within which it is located. Achieving this requires 'an episteme, a space, in which the myth of the people could engage the logos of the state.' (Dugin 2009).

Russia as a Political Alternative

Following logically from the above, Russian conservatism also rests on the belief that, in order to secure the country's stable development domestically and internationally Russia must 'be herself', that is, preserve her existential, cultural, and ideological distinctness. This thinking leads to the development of a conservative political idea of Russia's alternativism. This idea of alternativism obtained practical political character and was fed into a century-long praxis, which could be seen in Russia's constant effort to become a political alternative to the West. It was initially visible through the distinct Orthodox religion, which developed an idea of the Third Rome, rivalling the Holy Roman Empire (Hartley 1992, 369–70), was consolidated by a strong claim to European great-power status presented by Peter I and Catherine II, and was finalized with the idiosyncratic inland structure of her empire. This alternativism triumphed during the era of Soviet Communism, when Russia was pursuing an alternative path to Euro-American capitalism (Fursov 2012; Kurginyan, in Tretyakov 2007).

It is important that this lenience towards alternativism departs from the existing geostrategic competition and tension of ideological values and should invoke the concept of the political enemy. At the same time, it is important to remember that, while Russia's political myths are defensive in character and stem from geopolitical fears discussed earlier, the enemy and enmity do not occupy a central significance in their narrative. Rather, despite claiming the right to an alternative, Russian conservative myth calls for a productive dialogue, co-operation, and mutual complementarity between Russia and Europe. From this point of view, Russia's conservatism is similar to the conservatism of Leo Strauss, whose idea of political enmity stops short of the full Schmittian concept of the political seen in the need to define one's identity through enmity and through the potential of a military conflict and civil war. As Meier (1995, 87) observes, the 'friends that Strauss chose for himself tell us much more about his identity.' It is significant, however, that friendship does not imply assimilation and full convergence, just as enmity does not imply a full-scale battle through which one could define an existential inner self. In this light, Russia is permanently balancing the duality of her attitude to Europe. Writing during the Soviet period, Berlin (1994, 181) makes a unique observation on the complexity of Russia's relationship with Europe:

> [T]he peculiar amalgam of love and hate is still intrinsic to Russian feelings about Europe: on the one hand, intellectual respect, envy, admiration, desire to emulate and excel; on the other, emotional hostility, suspicion, and contempt, a sense of being clumsy, *de trop*, of being outsiders; leading as a result, to an alternation between excessive self-prostration before, and aggressive flouting of, western values. No visitor to the Soviet Union can fail to remark something of this phenomenon: a combination of intellectual inadequacy and emotional superiority, a sense of the west as enviably self-restrained, clever, efficient, and successful: but also as being cramped, cold, mean, calculating, and fenced in, without capacity for large views or generous emotion, for feelings which must, at times, rise too high and overflow its banks, for heedless self-abandonment in response to some unique historical challenge, and consequently condemned never to know a rich flowering of life.

From this point of view, Russia's conservatism shows relentless attempts to convert a perceived European enemy into a dialogical partner, and it chooses an aggressive action only in response to the enemy's cultural, value, economic, and geostrategic attacks. One of Russia's leading conservative thinkers, Natalya Narochnitskaya (2011), argues that the great Romano-German and Russian Orthodox cultures share the same Christian roots. She rightly insists that, prior to modern constitutions of all types, we have been united by the ethical norms of 'do not kill', 'do not steal', 'Our Father', and the Sermon of the Mount. Hence, Russia and Europe represent two branches of one ancient civilization, whose aspiration has always been to achieve a genuine dialogue, mutual complementarity, and peace on the continent. Narochnitskaya (2011; see also Kildyushov, in Tretyakov 2009b) is critical of the Schmittian and Nietzschean drive towards animosity and self-definitions through the process of political enmity. The key to the relationship between Russia and Europe, she argues, is not in the creation of new dividing lines. These lines are not novel in that they painfully reflect the essence of the centuries-long rivalry, which culminated in the emergence of the 1941 *Drang nach Osten* idea. A simple assimilation of Russia into the West European ideational and ethical sphere does not serve the purpose. Genuine unity and dialogue, Narochnitskaya (2011) claims, is seen in the *mutual recognition* of the 'validity and equality of our existential experience. It is seen in the understanding that our future lies in the constructive dialogue of historic heritage and creative potential of all ethnic, confessional, and cultural dimensions of Europe: Germanic, Roman, and Slavic, and more precisely in reconciliation between Latin and Orthodox Europe' (see also Polyakov 2004).

This argument has an additional geopolitical dimension. Some conservative thinkers believe that Europe, Russia, and the United States must each become strong poles of international political influence, and the power should be redistributed equally within this triangle. The main idea is the creation of a multipolar world, in which power will be redistributed equally among strong centres of political and economic influence that would include China, India, Latin America, South Africa, Russia, the European Union, and the United States. Hence, the return of Russia as one of the cornerstone elements of international relations could stabilize the European continent, provide it with a new developmental impetus, and return it to its former glory. Narochnitskaya (2011; 2014) claims that, in the current geopolitical climate, Europe is becoming peripheral in the twenty-first century's geopolitical scene; and the further Russia is from Europe, the more the 'old Europe' loses its status of a geopolitical centre of gravity. She argues that the United States seeks to secure control over resources, capital, and transportation produced in the Middle East and Asia. To achieve this, they need full political control over Europe and Eurasia. Hence, the weakening of Russia is not required to increase Europe's independence. Rather, such weakening is intended to fit the 'old Europe' into the Atlantic geostrategic project and turn it into a springboard from which the United States could control Eurasia. Narochnitskaya insists that this is not the game of Europe but of someone else. In this game, the 'old Europe' will invariably become a mere protectorate, stripped of its independent decision-making capabilities.

The anthropocentric (or ideational) angle of this conservative argument on political alternativism claims that Russia must become a centre of the twenty-first-century alternative view on globalization. Alexandr Panarin (2001) talks about the emergence of the so-called fourth realm, which is excluded from the globalist socio-economic consensus. This realm, Panarin argues, is not limited to the excluded of the third (underdeveloped) and second (developing) worlds. Rather, it encompasses the excluded of the entire planet, united by their resistance to arbitrariness, greed, and the rampant nature of global capital. He claims that the globalist open society works as a social-Darwinist environment, in which resources and territories are taken away from those less able and transferred to the hands of those who are more aggressive and technologically equipped. Moreover, the newly obtained riches cannot be fully deployed for the benefit of the rapidly emerging national periphery using the outdated national-sovereignty principle. These resources have now become redistributed in favour of the participants of the new global consensus (Panarin 2001).

Hence, globalist elites break with their own populations, driving them into a new periphery and demanding that they repeat the ideological mantra that could sustain this process (see similar criticism in Lasch 1994; Harvey 2007; Chomsky 1998). In support of this argument, left-wing journalist Maxim Shevchenko (2012b; 2012a) calls the neo-liberal group of multinational corporations that control global investment banks, the International Monetary Fund, and stock exchanges the international 'party of power'. This party, he argues, is at the heart of decisions over multi-billion-dollar contracts, and in this way exerts economic, political, and ideological control over large groups of ordinary people (see also Keane 2003). Geidar Dzhemal (2012b), the late leader of Russia's Islamic Committee, adds that the global international bureaucracy reinforces this 'party of power' and, without being elected, swings key decisions in favour of global corporations that finance these institutions. The contemporary division lines, Dzhemal (2012b) argues, run through the 'party of global capital and international bureaucracy' and the 'party of national elites', who 'still support the nation states' sovereignty and the social periphery of national labour (see also Akopov 2014; Fursov, in Tretyakov 2007; Nagornyi, in Tretyakov 2007). Ordinary people who are repelled by the unfair redistribution of global wealth side with the latter, which often leads to the emergence of radical sentiments (Shevchenko 2012a).

Panarin (2001) is convinced that, due to these developments, the world will become bipolar again, though this new bipolarity will not be of a military kind. Rather, there will be a division of those who consider compassion for the unsuccessful and the excluded to be a key component of their morality and elevate it to a central place in opposition to those who support the ethics of success and practicality. The latter group, Panarin argues, is led by the globalist elite that strives for world domination and constructs the architecture of international relations based on the principles of inequality of its participant actors. Hence, it is the ghetto, domestic and international, that must raise its head and call for a redefinition of the postmodern globalist idea of a Man. This must be a Man of compassion, a Man of social justice, and a Man of social solidarity. Panarin believed that Russia must become the centre around which this alternative morality and the new human narrative would congregate, and writes (2001):

> [T]hose, who have decided that natural selection has done its job and that the impoverished people have no alibi, would gather around the United States – the safe haven of an 'economic man.' Those, who stick to the great tradition of compassion and repel the idea of natural selection and triumph of strong over the weak, will stand by Russia … Resistance to America, as the epitome of the pagan cult of power and success, will not take place in the military-industrial sphere. The role of Russia in this area had passed. Rather, a new standoff will take place in the new ethical sphere. This will be a standoff between "an economic" Man and "a social" Man, between the morality of success and the morality of solidarity. Those who long for the vanity of success will choose America-centrism. Those who cannot agree with the decay of their country, as well as the majority of the world's periphery, will reinvent their morals from a great religious tradition – tradition that is older than modernity and tradition that will survive modernity.

Hence, in the mind of these conservatives, Russia must inspire the world to a fairer redistribution of international power and create a coalition of those who are willing to stand against the spread of morality that claims the civilizational superiority of the West.

This anthropocentric myth also has a strong social-conservative component. This stems from the understanding that globalization is conducted on the basis of the Western neo-liberal value matrix and that this matrix has the potential to modify and challenge distinct socio-cultural narratives of the rest of world (Smirnov 2014; Shevchenko 2008; Ilyashenko et al. 2014; Wagner 2012; Nagornyi, in Tretyakov 2007). Hence, Russian conservatism is trying to construct a myth that resists the pressures of the rapidly globalizing Eurocentric civilization and its distinct progressive-liberal value package, which is actively promoted world-wide. Putin (2013) lamented the fact that many postmodern values of the West, in particular those related to the rapid redefinition of stable identities, such as gender, family, and nation, pose a significant challenge to the largely conservative percep-tions of the Russian majority. Mikhail Veller, a contemporary Russian writer, notes that such challenges to stable traditional morals form a political basis that unites the state and society in Russia. In this light, the postmodern liberalism of the West figures as a serious opponent of Russia's conservatism. In a critique of liberalism, Russia's conser-vatism claims to represent the country's (and even the world's) silent majority, while claiming that both neo-liberalism and left-leaning social liberalism are ideologies that defend minorities. In contrast to this, conservatism defends the wishes of those large segments of the population that are rooted in the ideas of history, nation, tradition, and religion. It is those of this stratum, whose voices are silenced due to the attempts of both strands of liberalism to dominate discourse via the dogmatism of political correctness (Remizov, in Tretyakov 2013a; Mizulina 2013; Narochnitskaya 2014).

This position invokes such Russian conservative ideas as the defence of traditional family, compassion, promotion of patriotism, and reli-gious values based primarily on Russia's traditional Abrahamic reli-gions (Putin 2012; Putin 2013). In most cases, these conservative myths resemble Carl Schmitt's theorizations on political theology that build on 'the opposition of authority to anarchy, of faith in revelation to atheism, of the defence of the theological, of the moral, and of the political idea against the paralysis of "all moral and political decisions in a paradisiacal, secular world of immediate, natural life and unprob-lematic carnality"' (Meier 1995, 76). In this light, various Russian conservatives, such as Mikhail Remizov (2010), Konstantin Malofeyev (in Tretyakov et al. 2010), and others criticized new Western family practices, in which the categories of 'mother' and 'father' have been replaced by the 'parent A' and 'parent B' proxies, practices regarding wearing religious symbols at workplaces, and other policies related to redefining traditional interpersonal relations. Many such delibera-tions resulted in the enactment of a number of social-conservative bills. This particularly concerns the adoption of the law banning propaganda regarding a homosexual lifestyle among minors, as well as the adoption of rhetorical, economic, and political measures to support families.

More importantly, such critique is entangled with scepticism towards global capitalism and the global rich. A large number of Russian conservatives believe that the extant focus of the West on lifestyle and identity politics serves the interests of global capital that seeks to shift the perception of humans as collectives of individuals, united by a common spirit and traditional values, towards a new instrumental approach that views humans merely as labour tools called on to reproduce wealth (Khomyakov, in Tretyakov 2013c; Karabanova, in Tretyakov 2013c; Fursov 2012; Starikov 2013). Pre-existing traditional identities, such as nationality, culture, family, gender, and locality, act as an impediment to the global movement of labour and capital. Hence, the redefinition of these core values aids political justification of the new realities of the global world. In this light, shoehorning people into a multitude of particular cosmopolitan lifestyle identities breaks the bounds of social solidarity and reduces the potential for resistance. Such redefinition is also aimed at producing a highly specialized and mobile post-industrial workforce (Shishova, in Tretyakov 2013c; Khomyakov, in Tretyakov 2013c; Shevchenko 2009; Fursov 2012; Starikov 2013; Tretyakov 2013b). This new workforce should be able to change jobs quickly, follow the capital to different parts of the world, and be generally silent about strenuous conditions of employment. Conservatives believe that in such conditions people part with previously important existential values and turn into the cogs of the global capitalist structure, susceptible to political manipulation and devoid of social solidarity. These are the conditions of a controllable chaos in which control is exerted through the dismemberment of communities entrenched in those previously stable identities.

These sentiments also reflect a general conservative consensus that had formed in the West during the second half of the twentieth century. Western conservative sentiment exposed the moral limitations of contemporary capitalism and argued that it must be built not on a mere *laissez-faire* principle but rather on 'an almost Hegelian sense that the values of community, loyalty and deference must be prized and cultivated above all' (Skinner 1985, 8–9). Among such voices are those who claimed that the positivist ambitions of social science and public-relations campaigns deprived people of moral principles, proclaiming 'end of ideology' explanations to action, and by 'doing so accepted [the] silence of bewildered masses for agreement' (MacIntyre 1971, 3–11). Moreover, such thinkers warned that the hollowing out of the ideological foundations of the political system could result in a subsequent legitimation crisis, because the system, based on political technologies as opposed to a deeper conceptual foundation,[1] will struggle to appeal to its constituents at the time of economic hardship and decline (Habermas 1988, 33–94; see also Tweedy and Hunt 1994, 294–6; Thompson and Held 1982, 4–6; Crossley and Roberts 2004, 5–8; Skinner 1985, 9).

Cultures and Particularity

Theories of cultures and civilizations continue the line of conservative thought. Civilizational thinking rebels against the universalist tendencies of ideational ideologies, liberal or socialist, that aim to harmonize the world's cultures under the aegis of a single globalization project. In contrast to ideational ideologies, some of which rest on the principle of natural law and rights (Gray 1995, 40–2; Morrow 2005, 201–25; Huntington 1957, 458; B. Williams 2005), conservatism does not have an ideational basis with claims to universal significance. This further underscores the positionist nature of conservatism, for in this case it defends not a particular *value package* but a mere idea of the multiplicity and multivariance of such packages. As I mentioned above, there is no such thing as a 'conservative utopia' in which institutions 'must be reshaped to embody the values of the ideology' (Huntington 1957, 458). Therefore, conservatism of all types inherently denies universalism as fundamentally non-conservative thinking. Huntington (1957, 459, n6), Mannheim (1936, 116–19), Burke (see Cobban 1962, 40, n75), Strauss (1953, 13–14), and Gray (2000) claimed in one way or another that there are no transcendent institutions or universal traditions that could sustain such institutions.

Hence, a conservative ideal includes acceptance of differing paths of arriving at the good life, paths that might be contingent on cultural factors and run through different incommensurable logical deductions. German Romanticism could be seen as a precursor to this ideational complexity. In Herder, this trend of thought expressed the Romantic hope that the world must be built upon a multiplicity of different cultural and historic traditions and that nations could flourish based on their national spirit and idiosyncratic historic roots (Bowle 1954, 33; Berlin 1994; Pinkard 2002). In the mind of Romantics, God has chosen no specific nationality; yet it is through communication and interconnectedness of nations and cultures that humanity can find the cause for common good. 'No nationality [in Europe]' may separate itself sharply and say 'with us *alone*, with us dwells *all* wisdom' (Mazzini, cited by Bowle 1954, 33).

This approach represents the nerve of Russian conservatism. Russia's conservatives insist on the preservation of cultures, nations, civilizations, and religions, and on the maintenance of various local ways of life, ethical norms, and, most importantly, political systems. As Vitally Tretyakov (in Kiselev et al. 2009; see also Akopov 2014) claims, 'I am always repelled by the division of "normal" and "abnormal" countries that our friends or foes in the West are trying to impose. Russia has existed for over one thousand years, and how come it held up together for so long, if it is not normal?' Hence, this thought impugns the universal validity of liberalism and views the universalist drive of the West as a challenge to the extant diversity of political forms world-wide. These thinkers compare contemporary Western universalism, seen in the promotion of democracy programmes, with the pre-existing global aspirations of the two superpowers of the Cold War era, in which political and existential myths of liberalism and Communism alike struggled for the right to be a supreme judge of right and wrong in the torn-apart world.

Natalya Narochnitskaya (2014) argues that 'Europe is ruled by a post-modernist, almost Trotskyist, left-libertarian elite. During Soviet times, the Central Committee Propaganda Department advocated the Marxist-Leninist utopia, which called for everybody to be granted an equal share of bread and expected all nations to merge and fuse on this basis.' 'The Brussels propaganda department,' she continues, 'proposes something similar: it aspires to give everyone similar democracy and human rights and hopes that everybody will think the same about the meaning of life. Both universalist projects completely ignore fundamental differences in religious and philosophical worldviews of peoples and nations.' Hence, this perception of a multiplicity of cultural approaches to the good life forms one important element of Russian conservatism, and this school of thought sees the greatest injustice of the age in the idea of international unipolarity and in the 'end of history' ideology, in which the Western way of life triumphs in every corner of the planet, absorbing authentic cultures into its own image.

This forms the Russian idea of international justice. Russian conservatism becomes an advocate of intercultural and intercivilizational justice, in which cultures are intertwined in a complex web of plurality, rejecting and denouncing the universalization of global life. We will discuss these ideas in detail in Chapter 7 of this volume. It is important to state here, however, that most of Russia's conservatives extend this view to the European continent, which they see as a uniquely complex conglomerate of nations with distinct traditions and cultures. Left-conservative critic Maxim Shevchenko (2014), for example, insists that the spiritual essence of Europe has always been seen in the plurality of different peoples and nationalities. Hence, he warns that the people of Europe will at some point rebel against the universalist ambitions of European Union bureaucracy. This bureaucracy largely pursues a 'neo-Marxist policy' of creating a 'faceless uniformly thinking mass of people, once referred to by Herbert Marcuse (1969) as victims of liberal totalitarianism.' This is seen in the political desire of the elites to 'socially construct a mediocre person with an embedded value matrix that erases the perception of one's own history, the uniqueness of one's own ethnicity, territory and religion.' This mass of mediocre consumers, according to Shevchenko, is 'being dictated to from the cabinets of the international institutions. It is easily managed and controlled by the friendly media through modern discursive technologies and fads.'

It is important that this refusal of globalist universality finds a response among conservatives of all types, in Russia and beyond. The new-right circles in Europe and conservatives in Russia share an admiration of institutions that shape political traditions and practice, as well as the right of people to defend these institutions. Putin's conservative sentiment reflects this position. In his 2013 Valdai speech he spoke against the attempts to 'civilize Russia from outside'. He insisted that Russian society rejected the drive to impose Euro- and America-centric ideas on Russian soil and outlined the desire of Russians to construct institutions that could better reflect their traditional, cultural, and historic realities. He also claimed that 'the attempts to install alien institutional systems on other nations' is a mistaken strategy that would malfunction world-wide.

On a final note, it is important that this thinking relies heavily on the nineteenth-century philosophical debates of both the conservative and liberal factions. Vladimir Solovyov in his 1891 debate with Nikolay Grot writes: 'any insistence on the exclusive rights of one's personality, on one's own personal truth is an imposture. It is the imitation of an alien, strange spirit. All mockery over the truth only because this truth is not *my* truth is an insult to the eternal humanistic truth.' In their dialogue, Both Grot and Solovyov insist that Russia must never indulge in propagating her national exclusivity – a trend that they saw as accepted by the West in its Eurocentric ways of dealing with the rest of the world. The task of Russian philosophy, they argued, is to give way to the propagation of universal kindness, even if it comes in many different shapes and forms (Grot 1891). Furthermore, Rogger (1966, 210) argues that Russian conservatives of the nineteenth century refused the word 'freedom' in its abstract sense. In turn, they had an idea of 'freedoms' which rested not in 'abstract theory but in history and in the groups' institutions that history had created.' These were the rights and freedoms of concrete Englishmen and Germans as opposed to the rights of men and citizens. It is important to bear in mind that those principles were not nationalist principles but rather culturalist and religious arguments that defended the multivariance of European cultures of the age seen in the emergence of distinct European nation-states.

Furthermore, reading various conservative texts of the nineteenth century, in particular those related to the liberal institutional reforms of 1861, one might find many striking similarities with those uttered by conservative ideologues of the twenty-first century with regard to the liberal reforms of the 1990s. The main resentment against both the reforms of 1861 and of the 1990s was their vague nature, which in both cases was detached from the cultural and historic realities of Russia. Reflecting on the liberal reform of 1861, Alexei Pazuchin (1885), Konstantin Pobedonostsev (2011), Rodion Fadeyev (in Thaden 1964, 144 and 154), the minister of the interior, Count Dmitry Tolstoy (see Rogger 1966, 200–1; Baddeley 2011, 184–190) all complained that the changes were conducted in a universalist liberal fashion, thus destroying Russia's civilizational foundations and transplanting alien values and political systems on Russia.

These conservative thinkers were convinced that the liberal reforms denationalized Russia, 'impugned patriotic feelings of gentry and nobility', and built the new institutions upon 'false principles', which resulted in the 'destruction of honour and duty' and the rise of corruption (Pobedonostsev 2011). Equally, they complained that capital had begun to rule a 'faceless, featureless, denationalised mass of people', for which money had become the 'measure of all things' (Rogger 1966, 198–9). Those authors represented the government-led branch of conservatism at the end of the nineteenth century. Their counterparts from the Slavophile camp reinforced such sentiments by claiming that the Western liberal experience and its institutions were not suitable for Russia. Yuri Samarin, Ivan and Konstantin Aksakov, Nikolay Danilevsky, and Fedor Tyutchev believed that Russia represented a specific civilization, whose values and existential self-perceptions were different from those in the West (Tsymbursky 2008; Christoff 1991, 224; Rogger 1966, 322; Kelly 1999, 6; Duncan 2000).

Conservative Modernization

It is also important to discuss the modernizing and future-oriented drive of Russian conservatism. It is mostly applicable to the socio-economic realm, in which it claims that there are no contradictions between conservatism and modernization. Vitally Averyanov (in Ilyashenko et al. 2014), a founding member of the Izborsky Club, claims: 'there are some layman delusions that conservatism equals to reaction. Some often link it to the attempts to find a "golden age", which is left in the past but which needs to be restored without allowing any change. In reality conservatism is a proponent of development; but prudent development, a development that is based on the flourishing of tradition.' Such support of modernization does not seem odd in light of the classical conservatism of Edmund Burke, who chose to stand by the French Revolution and the progressive developments that came with it. His intellectual position also revealed an antinomy, in which conservatism – a guardian standpoint rather than a programmatic ideology – backs revolutionary change. Yet this is perfectly logical from the point of view of a purely conservative thinker. For Burke (as well as for Hobbes), once the change has taken place, new institutions – as long as they serve political stability and development – must be supported and cherished. These institutions, as Huntington (1957, 461) points out, must be accepted as fate.

On a similar note, most Russian conservative thinkers realize that erecting walls to the global world and resisting the process of globalization altogether is futile. Yet, for them, the answer to this fateful challenge lies in a form of acceptable adaptation. Hence, conservatives are at pains to find political and economic responses that could combine new global realities with the range of traditional identities and nationally oriented modernization strategies found in Russia. This adaptation aims to modify the workings of the globalization project in Russia on the economic, ideological-political, and institutional fronts. In the economic sphere, the 'conservative modernization' project has gained popularity within intellectual circles, political elites, and the general public. Such modernization is geared towards the stable development of the country's economy, consolidating her international status, and achieving this through the reliance on the experience of previous generations (Averyanov, in Ilyashenko et al. 2014; Remizov, in Tretyakov 2013a). As Sergey Markov (in Tretyakov 2013b) claims, Russia's conservative modernization assumes 'moderate progress in the framework of order'.

Practically, this conservative modernization is seen in attempts by the Russian government to invest in strategic industries that could consolidate and promote Russia's potential leadership in the international arena and help Russia to become one of the key players in the resolution of global challenges. These include the development of a variety of technologies to assist the ambitious project of Arctic exploration, the restructuring of the army and the relevant modernization of Russia's industry and technology, as well as the launch of important infrastructure projects to develop and logistically link Siberia and the Far East (the east part of Russia) (Rogozin 2014, 2013; Yakunin 2014). It is hoped that these large, almost existential, industrial projects can give impetus to adjacent sectors of the economy and subsequently serve as engines of progress for smaller and medium-sized business.

It is also clear that such projects in effect merge economic and ideological-political factors. This does not differ starkly from the Western situation, in which economic development is based on fundamental ideological principles of personal autonomy, inviolability of private property, growth, and freedom of enterprise. Russian conservative plans do not deny these principles, and in many ways support them. Yet, it is with this in mind that Russian conservatives also focus on the ideas of strategic, large-scale developments that have a nationally oriented character, with overtones tending towards the tradition of large-scale economic, industrial, and technological achievements. As Yakunin (2014) observed, the 'global financial crisis [of 2008] is also a moral crisis. Hence, developing large infrastructural and industrial projects will aid the resolution of this crisis also, and more importantly, from an ethical point of view.' Some of Russia's ideologues referred to these plans as 'dynamic conservatism'. Vitally Averyanov (in Ilyashenko et al. 2014), states that 'dynamic conservatism' reflects 'renewal without the loss of identity'. It is a drive towards change and development 'but without changing our core identity ascribed to us by God and our ancestors. This concerns individuals, as well as communities and cultures as a whole.' Such an approach has a statist flavour, in which the state aids and assists the implementation of these goals (Delyagin et al. 2013; Prokhanov 2012).

This economic thinking is reminiscent of previous periods of Russia's history. Leaving aside the case of Soviet industrialization, the rules of Alexander III and Nicolas II witnessed successful conservative governments that pushed Russia onto the road of rapid industrial development, at the same time making successful compromises with the traditionally autocratic political system and conservative population. Industrial reforms of Sergei Witte, Nikolay Bunge, Ivan Vyshnegradsky, and Dmitry Mendeleev at the end of the nineteenth century represent an example of conservative modernization, or – to use Witte's exact terminology of the day – 'modernized autocracy' (Von Laue 1958, 26–7; Kobyakov, in Ilyashenko et al. 2014; Harcave 2004). The prime minister, Peter Stolypin, was often referred to as 'a conservative politician who wished to preserve the traditional institutions of autocratic Russia, but who recognized that conservatism did not mean a slavish adherence to an unchanging world' (Waldorn 2002, 621).

MAIN ACTORS AND POLITICAL ACTIVITY

Conservative ideology has a sizeable representation in Russian politics. Russia's largest and leading United Russia Party is the main representative of this ideological direction. Its official doctrine states that the party espouses conservative, right-centrist, and liberal-conservative ideology. United Russia is spread across various ideological platforms or discussion clubs, many of which are conservative. Examples include the Centre for Social Conservative Politics, the State-Patriotic Club, the Patriotic Platform, and the Business Platform. There are also a number of smaller parties and movements that espouse ideological conservative trends. The Great Fatherland Party, led by historian and writer Nikolay Starikov, is one such conservative force. Starikov praises the Soviet and particularly Stalin eras, although he does not advocate a return to Soviet socialism. In turn, he proposes to link various periods of Russia's history and move forward with this foundation in mind. The party runs in various regional and local elections and holds seven mandates in the regional legislature of St Petersburg. Conservatism has a sizeable representation within the Russian government, state structures, and business elites. Business leaders Gennady

Timchenko and Arkady Rottenberg, both close associates of Vladimir Putin, stand on such state conservative positions. Vladimir Yakunin, former head of the Russian Railroads and close ally of Putin, openly espouses conservative views. He established the Dialogue of Civilizations think tank, which holds an annual international political-academic forum in Rhode Island.

There are in addition a large number of alternative (Internet) media outlets that pursue a conservative standpoint. Alexander Prokhanov, an eminent writer and editor-in-chief of the *Zavtra* newspaper, espouses left-wing views while supporting a generally conservative stance. Alexander Babakov, a Federation Council member from the Just Russia Party, finances his newspaper. Conservatives have sizeable representation in Russia's intellectual circles and among central public-opinion makers. Nikita Mikhalkov, eminent film producer, Karen Shakhnazarov, director of the *Mosfilm* film studios, Evgeny Satanovsky, the leader of Russia's Jewish Congress, Vitaly Tretyakov, eminent journalist and professor at Moscow State University, and many others form the public intellectual backbone of Russia's conservative discourse. Many of them are members of the Izborsky Club group of intellectuals and public-opinion makers. The club is focused on drafting various conservative strategies and the cardinal ideological direction for Russia.

To conclude, conservatism is an ideology that enjoys sizeable political representation and popularity in Russia. It has both positionist and ideational overtones. In the ideational sphere, this trend of thought ponders some serious issues relating to the effects of globalization and postmodernity on the culture and values of contemporary humans. Within this framework, Russia's conservatism attempts to devise an alternative value package for itself and the rest of the world and makes multiple attempts to narrate a *New Man* of the postmodern era. In doing so, conservatives attempt to recreate the core values of modernity in the newly emerging postmodern world.

In the positionist sphere, Russia's moderate conservatism is similar to its Western counterpart. It strives to sustain a strong Russian statehood that could ensure the country's territorial integrity and political, economic, and cultural security.[2] It also proposes a new model of international relations based on the plurality of world cultures. In many ways, this ideology harks back to history and inherits Russia's conservative political thought of the nineteenth century. In some other ways, this position is still evolving as its proponents weigh various issues of development and modernization and strive to look at the future, which should, for them, be recreated on the basis of the best elements of tradition. The value of this approach lies in the fact that it has the most decisive influence on Russia's contemporary domestic and international policy. Hence, its importance to Russia and the rest of the world cannot be overestimated.

4

Fundamental Conservatism

This chapter examines the main dimensions of fundamental-conservative (or radical-traditionalist-conservative) thought in Russia. The discussion shows that Russia's fundamental conservatism seeks to recast the entrenched interpretations of Western modernity in Russia. Fundamental-conservative thinkers do not reject modernity as a project, but rather propose to develop a culturally specific Russian version of it. In pursuing this task, this intellectual tradition draws inspiration from many diverse branches of Western philosophy, internalizing and interpreting the Western discourse to its own particular needs, and methodologically deploys Russian Eurasianism. This chapter consists of two main parts. The first part will discuss the method and tasks of Russia's fundamental conservatism, while the second will examine the main dimensions of its philosophical arguments.

POINTS OF DEPARTURE:
METHOD AND ARCHAEO-MODERNITY AS A DIAGNOSIS

Before embarking on their philosophical project, fundamental conservatives have provided a 'diagnosis' of Russian society. They claim that Russia has a specific developmental condition termed *archaeo-modernity* (Dugin, 2008), in which the ideological, political, economic, and institutional matrix of modernity is superimposed on a society that still has the outlook and unconscious social interactions characteristic of premodernity (Dugin, 2009e). To explain this situation fully and to flesh out the political objectives of fundamental conservatives on this basis, one must examine their methodology.

As noted at the outset, Russia's fundamental conservatism is firmly embedded in various currents of structuralism, which is in turn intellectually indebted to Eurasianism in its linguistic, geographic, and Russia-specific streams. Hence, the supporting pillars of fundamental conservatism come from the fields of linguistics (de Saussure, Jakobson), psychology (Jung and Freud), sociology, and anthropology (Mauss and Lévi-Strauss).[1] Structuralism views societies through the duality of conscious and unconscious segments. These segments are locked into a permanent struggle and a mutual exchange. The unconscious segment constitutes the structural base of each society. It is composed of language, moral narratives ('myths'), and culture in general. This unconscious structure influences conscious behaviour and rational interpretations of morality in each particular context. It could be argued that structuralism finds its intellectual origins in the Durkheimian-Maussian inquiry into the 'collective consciousness', which sought to explain the roots of social narratives in each society (Harkin 2009, 40). However, structuralism seeks to expand the idea of collective consciousness in order to complement the study of the conscious aspects of thought with factors that go beyond rational experience and influence the formation of opinions beyond logic. Thus, the search of the 'unconscious foundations of human life' became the prime task of structural anthropology (Lévi-Strauss 1963, 18). This subject of inquiry, in turn, had distinct intellectual similarities with the notion of the 'collective unconscious', which originated in structural psychology.

The popularization of the notion of the 'collective unconscious' started with Carl Jung (1991). Jung, a student of Sigmund Freud, believed that, in addition to a conscious that belongs to the area of experience and socialization, each person has an area of the unconscious that has a large influence on the conscious ego. More importantly, the unconscious is not only strictly personal but is divided onto two different parts: individual and collective. The collective unconscious is formed by non-reflexive memories of societal experiences of each individual, and therefore contains a number of archetypes unique to each particular society (Jung 1991, 43). From this point of view, 'myths', assumptions, and socially accepted forms of behaviour imprint the collective unconscious of a human mind and shape activity on a par with the personal unconscious and conscious ego. Levi-Strauss often discussed the societal unconscious in the framework of 'myth' – 'a projection of a culture's values and sense of being on a transcendental plane' (Harkin 2009, 44). He contended that the reliance on 'myth' is a universal condition of humankind that sustains all human societies, be it the modern Western community or others (Giddens 1979, 21; Harkin 2009, 45–6).

The study of the collective unconscious determines intellectual links between Russian fundamental-conservative thought and various schools of structuralism. Aleksandr Dugin, Russia's influential radical-conservative philosopher, ponders the evolution of social systems in the structuralist vein. How at the level of a specific society are historical actions (i.e., praxis) shaped by and in turn shape mythical thought (i.e., ideology)? What makes a change of myth possible? How can a small window of opportunity appear within the entire social paradigm that can effect the change of a myth and its conscious reception and interpretation? How can we explain this process in the framework of Russian realities? To trace this process, Dugin (2010) proposed a trilateral approach to social paradigms, as shown in Figure 4.1.[2]

The lowest level in Figure 4.1 represents the structure. It is the realm of the collective unconscious, which contains language and implicit societal myths. Dugin (2010) brands this level as *mythos*. The second level is the level of collective consciousness, which Dugin sees as articulated practices, institutions, and established and 'rationally' explained traditions of a religious and secular nature. This level is called *logos*. The third and uppermost level of this societal paradigm is formed by the so-called *kerygma* – a term borrowed from theological discourse and translated from the Greek as 'proclamation' or 'announcement'. In Dugin's interpretation, *kerygma* stands for 'sharing the word' – a word that belongs to a radically new interpretation of the myth and its *logos*, or the word that is aimed at deposing the myth altogether. The *kerygmatic* level exists in the minds of philosophers, artists, intellectuals, religious leaders, economists, and young people, who apprehend slight societal changes most perceptively. *Kerygma* therefore opens the way towards unravelling existing unconscious myths. Such demystification represents a very long process that stretches far beyond the span of human life or even over the lifespan of a number of generations. The evolving *kerygma* gradually changes the *logos* and *mythos* to achieve some healthy functional balance, which results in a transition to a new social paradigm.

Two observations spring to mind. First, Dugin does not make a clear distinction between the structure and the system that in further argument seem to unite *kerygma* and the most conscious parts of the *logos*.

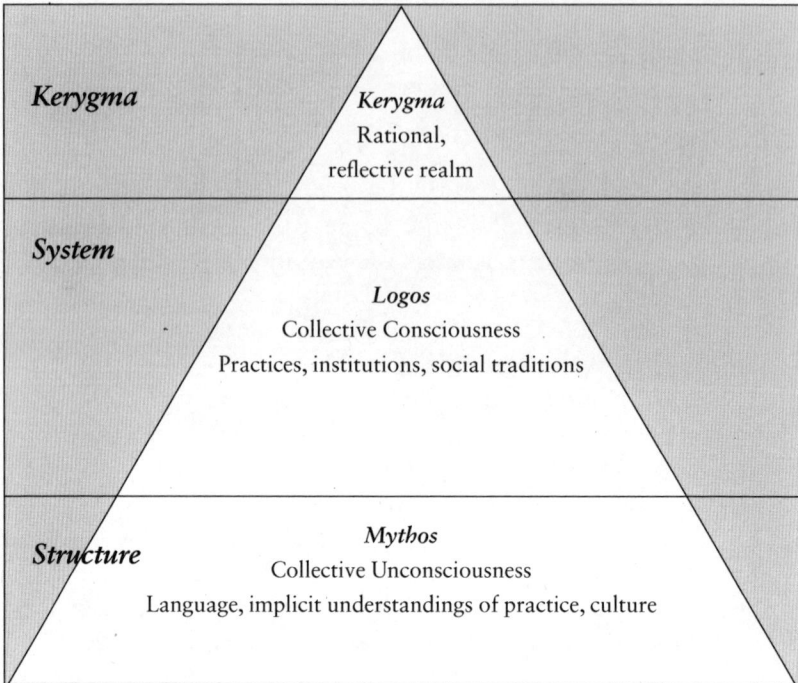

Figure 4.1 The trilateral approach to the social paradigm adopted in Russian conservative thought.

Source: Dugin, 2009a, 2009b.

Many elements of the structure often fall within the system and vice versa. Such confusion often leads to an interchangeable use of these terms. This criticism has been previously made of the entire field of structuralism. Giddens (1979, 23) argues that structuralists provide just the 'physiology' of social life, and not its 'anatomy', and do not systematically distinguish between the structure and the system. Second, Dugin's methodological proposals come close to the ideas of culturalists (such as Stuart Hall and his followers) whose thought is at times considered as a variation on the theme of structuralism. These thinkers select ideology and culture as 'sites of domination, resistance, and change' – an idea that they borrow from Gramsci (McMahon 1999, 207–11). To make this intellectual link clear, Dugin often favourably spoke of the Gramscian concepts of hegemony and civil society and viewed those as important elements involved in changing social order (see Dugin 2012e).

Dugin analyses three main social paradigms: premodernity, modernity, and postmodernity. Following Ferdinand Tönnies, Dugin reminds us that the paradigm of modernity structures social interactions within the framework of society (*Gesellschaft*). *Gesellschaft* is composed of citizens, or individuals, who possess two main qualities: the Cartesian reason and Kantian free will, understood as the 'will to reason' (Fukuyama 2003, 118; Taylor 2011, 55–6). These citizens act as *subject*s of politics, shaping the course of history by the use of their reason and will. Among other factors of an economic nature, the notion of a free and rational individual gave rise to the ideals of equal opportunities and political rights that 'have been formalized as the foundations of the modernity political project' (Habermas, cited in Outhwaite 1996, 338; see also Aronowitz 1988, 46; and Mouffe 1988, 38–9). Premodern life, on the other hand, is based on the traditional commune (*Gemeinschaft*). *Gemeinschaft* features hierarchy, tradition, and mystification, or 'sacralization', of the world, instead of rationality. The absence of the subject of politics is a distinct characteristic of such a paradigm.

Transition from premodernity to modernity in the West took place against the backdrop of a century-long process of subject formation. The emergence of modernity's *Gesellschaft* first occurred at the intellectual (*kerygmatic*) level during the Reformation and Enlightenment and then broadly represented a 'bundle of processes' that have been 'cumulative and mutually reinforcing' (Habermas, cited in Outhwaite 1996, 338). Of particular importance was the process of gradual 'de-sacralization' (Weber 1971, 270) of the premodern world, and the deconstruction of its myths and notions of traditional religiosity. This process resulted in the emergence of rationality and the tradition of Reason, 'in which European modernity understands itself' (Habermas, cited in Outhwaite 1996, 339). Free will came hand in hand with rationality, as the will to reason and a sign of liberation from the constraints of traditional premodern life.

What do Russian fundamental conservatives make of this history? Dugin argues that for historical reasons Russia has not been able to internalize Western modernity in a functional manner. He claims that Russia's history took a particular turn when abrupt, forced, and rapid modernization was conducted by Peter the Great and continued over two centuries later by the Bolsheviks. Thus, the bundle of 'cumulative and mutually reinforcing processes', such as the gradual and consistent de-sacralization of the world, the secularization of values and norms, and the proliferation of political rights – has not taken place as part of an endogenous historical trend. This dynamic precluded the gradual harmonization between the *kerygmatic* interpretation of new realities and the corresponding rationalization of the *logos* and *mythos*. As a result, much of the *logos* and most of the 'collective unconscious' *mythos* retained their premodern outlook (Dugin, 2008). Thus, Dugin argues that an external *kerygma* has been built over the recalcitrant structure in a disorderly and dysfunctional manner. In this light, archaeo-modernity can be viewed as a conflict between starkly different 'operating systems' – one that operates the structure, the premodern collective unconscious, and another that sustains the *kerygma*. The *logos*, which is partly modern and partly premodern, is torn by the conflict between these two operating systems. 'In archaeo-modernity,' Dugin (2008) writes, 'the structure and the *kerygma* take each other hostage; they become like Siamese twins, who are conjoined by their backs so that neither side can look each other in the eye.'

The condition of archaeo-modernity, Dugin follows, could partly explain a peculiar image that Russia presents to itself and to the outside world. The struggle between the *kerygma* and the structure creates many diverse and often ugly social forms of archaeo-modernity. Dugin sees the period of Soviet rule as a heyday of archaeo-modernity. Western Marxist theories have been subverted by the structure and have created ironic patterns of socio-political interaction. Ambitious projects of launching space missions to Mars and Venus coexisted with peculiar forms of sacralization of power, such as placing Lenin and Stalin in mausoleums and creating personality cults (Dugin 2008). The post-Soviet period repeated these forms of archaeo-modernity. The early liberal reforms, which aimed at exorcising the structure of its sacrality by implementing the radical measures of Yegor Gaidar and Anatoly Chubais, faced the quick and equally radical retaliation of the 'unconscious'. The archaeo-modernity was rapidly revisited with the all-too-familiar caricatures of Tsar Boris (Yel'tsin), his court (the family), and a close circle of boyars-oligarchs – all mythical expressions of sacralization of power that came from the deeply entrenched unconscious structure (Dugin 2008). Putin, Dugin continues, represents an archetypal feature of archaeo-modernity, for he genuinely believes in the possibility of coexistence between the Western kerygmatic level of modernity and the archaic structure without being willing to take a step in reforming either side. This has been a source of political stability for his system during the past decade (ibid.).

This diagnosis of Russian society has been internalized and reinterpreted by various conservative commentators. Andrey Konchalovsky, one of Russia's eminent film producers, brands this as modern feudalism (Konchalovsky 2012). He claims that Russian society lives in a different historic era, which is still feudal in its socio-cultural outlook, while the institutional system of politics and economics comes across as modern and European. Konchalovsky writes (2012):

> Feudalism is nesting in every village shed, in every worn *valenki*,[3] under the seats of luxurious Bentleys, and in every Rolex watch on a well-groomed wrist! And every Russian husband in a Rolls-Royce will treat his lady in the good old tradition of the nineteenth century. Thus, *reyderstvo, krysha*s,[4] murders for refusal to pay protection, courts based on customs and not laws, and the all-round readiness to break the law of any legitimate representative of power are familiar patterns of our everyday life.

Journalist Sergey Dorenko agrees with the feudal terminology, claiming that Putin's vertical of power is a mere smokescreen for the feudal distribution of authority, and that in every region of Russia only bribes and subsidies could ensure genuine compliance to the federal centre (Dorenko 2007).

Fundamental conservatives see this situation as a diagnosis for the Russian social and politico-economic matrix. This moves them somewhat closer to the radical liberals discussed in Chapter 2, yet both camps offer radically different remedies to the situation. It is all too familiar to mention the three-hundred-year-old debate between Westernizers and Slavophiles. Nevertheless, I will allocate some space to this problem here in order to provide clarity for the subsequent discussion. Westernizers, the forerunners of Russia's contemporary liberals, advocated a radical recasting of the Russian structure, which could be viewed as a logical, albeit harsh, remedy. Slavophiles, on the other hand, called for the return to the traditional premodern (pre-Petrine) structure and the destruction of the *kerygma* and partly the *logos*, which they viewed as an alien and harmful imposition.

In contrast to the principals engaged in that debate, the project of today's fundamental conservatives is to find a third way. They wish to reinvent the *kerygma* on the basis of a gradual understanding, desacralization, and reinterpretation of the structure. The new Russian *kerygma* must call for a change, but this change should be based on the internalized *mythos* and *logos* of the existing Russian reality. Such gradual internalization and reinterpretation of the Russian structure and its myth might, and should, lead to the formation of the specifically Russian subject of politics with its idiosyncratic interpretations of reason and rationality (Dugin 2008). That, in turn, could open ways towards Russia's endogenous pattern of modernity and bring the three-hundred-year conflict between the *kerygma* and the structure to an end. Therefore, Russian fundamental conservatism represents a search for new forms of rationality and new forms of citizenship rooted in the Russian socio-historic context. From this point of view, fundamental conservatives consider themselves as the only 'true' modernists of the endogenous project of Russian modernity (ibid.). Konchalovsky (2012) writes that creating a citizen from the midst of Russia's feudalism is an uneasy and time-consuming task, but at the same time is an imperative that Russia will have to address. Mikhail Leontyev, Aleksandr Prokhanov, and Patriarch Kirill write and speak incessantly on the same theme (e.g., Leontyev 2004).

Clearly, fundamental conservatism represents an intensely critical project. To achieve their proposed ends, fundamental conservatives must dethrone the main Western narratives that do not sit well with the Russian structure and simultaneously determine their own paths towards deconstructing Russia's premodern myths. This task seems as ambitious as it is perhaps utopian, for many tenets of Western modernity, as well as Russia's own archaeo-modernity, have now become internalized as part of the Russian collective unconscious. Facing the difficulty of this task, most fundamental conservatives are engaged in debates of a distinct metatheoretical character; they work on broad normative and ontological concerns and devote their energies primarily to demolishing the philosophical foundations of the Western modernity project that to their view are incompatible with Russia's structural realities. In this intellectual endeavour, Russian fundamental conservatives deploy the reasoning of Western anti-liberals and postmodernists. Of particular importance are postmodern revisions of the liberal and Marxist traditions, cultural and structural anthropology, comparative history, as well as the revolutionary conservatism of Carl Schmitt. In the following subsections, I will analyse the fundamental-conservative critique of modernity, trace its intellectual origins and analytical apparatus, and link it to potential ideological proposals.

CONFLICT WITH MODERNITY

Reason: Universal or Particular?

Western modernity's tradition of Reason is intimately linked to the idea of universalism. Indeed, the central perception of modernity is that Reason is not only capable of explaining Nature (and thereby 'desacralizing' the world) but also developing an ideal model for social systems that will ensure universal peace and harmony. As John Gray (2000) has argued, modernity, and its Enlightenment project in particular, began not with the recognition of difference but with a demand for uniformity. Generally, this tradition of thought was central to Western modern philosophy. It derives from the ideas of all major Greek thinkers, with the exception of a few groups of Sophists. They depart from the idea of natural law – an eternal set of correct notions established by Nature and instinctively understood by humans. This leads to a particular view on ethics, in which right action cannot contain wrong. The natural-law idea then travelled to Christianity, when Aquinas insisted that the origins of this law derive from God's will. The Enlightenment took the idea of human nature from the Greeks as a given and identified human reason as the source of natural law (see Gray 1995, 40–2; Morrow 2005, 201–25).

The notion of the universality of Reason creates an ethical justification for the export of the Western conception of modernity to various human societies in the hope that, in time, they will catch up with 'progressive' and 'civilized' parts of the world. This logic was indeed deployed in Russia by various generations of modernizers, from Peter to the post-Soviet liberals of today, which, as fundamental conservatives would argue, has resulted in the rise of archaeo-modernity. The fundamental-conservative project works to subvert this notion of universality, as it argues for the development of Russia-specific dynamics of modernity. In pursuit of this task, they side with many Western thinkers who defend the particularity of Reason and reject the idea of universalism.

In the liberal spectrum, the Western notion of value pluralism gains instrumental significance. The twentieth-century idea of value pluralism was initially inaugurated by Isaiah Berlin and further developed by John Gray (2000; 2003) and Bernard Williams (1979; 2005), with some qualifications by Richard Rorty (1983). This idea ran parallel to the comparative-history thinking and propositions of liberal-conservative philosophers, such as Samuel Huntington (1996) and his 'clash of civilizations' thesis. Huntington's own ideas have been tightly interconnected with the comparative-history method largely associated with the name of Arnold J. Toynbee (1946). Toynbee defended the multiplicity of different civilizations, claiming that the history of human development is not based on the rise and fall of nations, but rather on the rise and fall of civilizations as cultural and religious communities. The comparative-history method claimed that the history of such civilizations is not based on the Enlightenment idea of progress, but rather depends on the internal logic of each civilization and on external factors that subject civilizations to change. In the Marxist tradition, the same logic emerged in the shape of the radical-democracy doctrine advocated by Ernesto Laclau and Chantal Mouffe (1985; see also Daly 1999).[5] Intellectuals of both persuasions reject the Enlightenment ideal of the universality of Reason and place it in the cultural, societal, and socio-historic context. They insist that, while it is always possible to distinguish between the just and the unjust, as well as the legitimate and the illegitimate, this can be done only within a particular socio-historic milieu and within a particular cultural tradition.

John Gray (2000), whose thought has had a serious impact on fundamental-conservative writing in Russia (Dmitriyev 2011), argues that, while humanity shares a set of universal values – such as justice, courage, compassion, and prudence – each society would use different reasoning and paths for implementing those values. Following Berlin, he claims that human demands are often conflicting, while meanings that uphold values are incommensurable. Each society would interpret the ideas of what is good in a different manner, and, paradoxically, each would be right in its own way (ibid., 14). Mouffe (1988, 37) agrees that 'there is no point of view external to all tradition from which one can offer a universal judgement.' Bernard Williams (2005, 23) deploys the very same logic and reminds us that the liberal ideology is no better than its non-liberal counterparts in the sense that it still has the problem of 'forcing itself on the recalcitrant world'. He further argues (ibid., 25–6) that 'there is no way in which theory can get all the way ahead of practice and reach the final determination of what can make sense in political thought.'

The work of Western cultural and structural anthropologists further upholds the ethical foundations of difference for Russia's conservatives

(Dugin 2009d). Franz Boas and Bronislaw Malinowski challenged universalism and argued that the world consists of a multiplicity of different cultures. They claimed that each cultural group has its own unique history which depends on its peculiar social development and partly on external influences that are subjecting a culture to reactive change (Firth 1960; Giddens 1979; Baker 2004). A similar line of logic is used in the structural anthropology of Lévi-Strauss (1966),[6] who argues that the primitive, archaic (or premodern) life is as complex as civilized existence in terms of its taxonomy, narratives, and social-relational ties. Such reasoning was partly deployed by Western communitarian multiculturalists, such as Charles Taylor (1994, 42–3), who warned Western societies against Eurocentrism and feeling superior to other forms of cultural expression. Thus, the body of literature working within this trend is based on the principles of human equality and defends the right of various cultures to live and develop within their own historically chosen path.

This laid the foundation for the central claim of Russia's fundamental-conservative discourse, which rejected the inevitability of Western-type civilization and refused to accept a Eurocentric vision of modernity. Interestingly, Western postmodern thinkers of all spectra are aware of being in the intellectual company of fundamental conservatives. Mouffe (1988, 38; see also Williams 1995; Gray 2000; and Gray 2003) observed that:

> [B]ecause of the importance it [radical democracy] accords to the particular, to the existence of different forms of rationality, and to the role of tradition, the path of radical democracy paradoxically runs across some of the main currents of conservative thinking. One of the chief emphases of conservative thought does indeed lie in its critique of the Enlightenment's rationalism and universalism, a critique it shares with post-modernist thought.

At the same time, while accepting particularity as a cornerstone notion, post-Marxists, value pluralists, and fundamental conservatives come to some varying conclusions. Value pluralists remain committed to Isaiah Berlin's idea of freedom as the ability to exercise a 'meaningful choice between incommensurable ideas of the good life'. Post-Marxists, in turn, expose domination within society associated with hegemonic interpretations of identities. They draw inspiration from Michel Foucault, who linked validity and power and suggested that validity is always associated with a certain regime of truth connected to power.

Fundamental conservatives, in turn, deploy the notion of particularity in defence of non-interventionism in global affairs. They argue that Russia must abandon her role of a perpetual student who is unsuccessfully learning how to transplant Western economic and political blueprints; and the West, at the same time, must also abstain from mentoring Russia on how to conduct her affairs in a 'civilized manner'. In this context, Deacon Andrey Kurayev, one of Russia's Orthodox intellectuals, argues: "I do not share the perception that modern language is the language of Western liberalism. There are other value systems, which operate in different languages, and modern society is morally plural rather than ideologically liberal' (Shevchenko and Kurayev 2012).

Following on this, Russia's fundamental conservatives have become critical of the central Western idea of continuing progress, which is uncritically considered as the driving force of human development. They claim that the very idea of progress contains a strong tendency towards universalism and the modelling of all world cultures on a global, neo-liberal, capitalist pattern. Here they side again with the structural anthropology of Lévi-Strauss and Boas, who struggled against the myth of progress as the defining myth of Western society (Giddens 1979, 46; Harkin 2009, 53). Drawing on these various sources, Russia's fundamental conservatives claim that human history is not an incremental progression from lower to higher forms of civilization, in which Western neo-liberal capitalism represents the most 'developed' form. Implementing the 'evolutionist' vision of progress, they argue, would result inevitably in the victory of a Western liberal utopia for Russia, in which the victorious system would destroy and subvert the resisting structure at devastating cost. They further deploy the ideas of Lev Gumilev, Oswald Spengler, Nikolay Danilevskiy, and Alfred J. Toynbee, to claim that various societies have different trajectories of life, and progress is not an ultimate destiny of humanity (Shevchenko and Dugin, 2012). Russia's fundamental conservatism holds both liberalism and Marxism responsible for entrenching 'the dogma of progress' and calls for a redefinition of these notions of modern eschatology. Dugin claims that Soviet society accepted ideas of 'progress' uncritically due to its modernist and progressivist Marxist basis. The notion of 'progress' was particularly well packaged in the Gorbachevian idea of *uskoreniye*, and it still dominates contemporary

Russian political discourse in its liberal and Marxist guises (Dugin, 2009c). Konchalovsky (2012) also claims that we should not pass progressive value judgments on societies that experience traditional feudal (and from a progressivist point of view backward) mentalities. He writes: 'it is difficult to understand that living in varying historic times is not a vice or a shortcoming. Rather, I can't see any qualitative difference between a person going to a university and a person going to a primary school. They are just different, and a primary school student can even be in some ways better!'

Negative Freedom and Deconstruction of the Subject

We now investigate the conservative critique of liberalism as the main component of modernity's hegemonic discourse. Philosophical deconstruction of liberalism's central narratives becomes a matter of paramount importance for fundamental conservatism (see Dugin 2012c). Russian fundamental conservatives follow the most widely adopted method of Western critique (Nietzsche, Freud, Derrida, Heidegger, Schmitt), and point to the nihilistic potential of the modern age. They claim that, during the period of modernity and postmodernism, the Western subject has evolved and experienced the process of rejecting its original conceptions of Reason and rationality. They place the blame for this process on the idea of negative freedom, which, in Dugin's mind, represents the central notion of Western liberalism.[7] Negative freedom – as seen in the absence of external constraints on self-regarding action – should not be accepted uncritically as a given good. Rather, it raises a host of ethical concerns that need careful deliberation. A Western-communitarian (as well as liberal-conservative) critique of negative freedom serves as a point of departure for these efforts.

Charles Taylor (1979, 175) claims that freedom must be regarded through the prism of motivation and purpose that could be fundamental to a human's life. He ponders what one is going to do with his/her freedom in the absence of external constraints. How is freedom going to be implemented? From this point of view, unimpeded fulfilment of all inner desires could not be considered as fundamental to freedom. A purpose, on the other hand, is hardly found in isolation and cannot help but depend on society. Taylor (ibid., 180) argues that 'the subject himself can't be the final authority on the question [of] whether he is free; for he cannot be the final authority on the question of whether his desires are authentic, whether they do or do not frustrate his purposes.' Francis Fukuyama (2002, 92–3) also raises some similar points. Echoing Taylor, he claims that human desires are not formed independently from society (ibid., 94). In turn, they are influenced by social constructs of fads, cultural impositions, and ideologies. Fukuyama (ibid., 100) warns against the common translation of immediate wants and interests into the notion of fundamental human rights – something that could be socially and politically explosive and result in the unleashing of the power of the unconscious. A similar critique of the human-rights notion can be found in Bernard Williams's essays 'In the Beginning Was the Deed' and 'Human Rights and Relativism', in which Williams attempts to detach the idea of fundamental (or the most basic) human rights from the ideological framework of liberal ideology and its 'most disputed theses' (B. Williams 2005, 74) and constructions.

The idea of motivation and the purpose of liberty figure as the central points of fundamental conservative thinking in Russia. Dugin argues that the marriage between negative liberty and technological Reason has led humanity to experience the 'surplus' of the Enlightenment, which induced a crisis of ethics and morality. Echoing Fukuyama and deploying the philosophy of Deleuze and Guattari (2004), he sees the ethical crisis in unleashing the power of non-Reason – something that the Enlightenment sought to revoke in the first place (Dugin and Kapitsa 2006). He claims that, in the postmodern world, the emancipated individual is trying to liberate him/herself from all forms of social constraints, and when nothing is left, he/she begins to target his/her own Reason with the view to liberating unconscious desires. On this path, however, a person is making a gradual transformation from being an individual (understood as an indivisible autonomous entity) into becoming a *dividual* – a being free from the modern understanding of rationality and acting upon his/her inner desires and impulses. Incidentally, Anthony Giddens (1979, 38) refers to this process as 'decentering of the individual'. In an article entitled 'The Dawn of Freedom', Dugin (2012a) attacks the idea of negative freedom as mainly responsible for this gradual deconstruction process. Echoing Taylor, and to a broader extent Nietzsche (May 2011), Dugin embarks on the quest for the substantive purpose of freedom. To what ends is a 'liberated' individual going to apply his freedom?

Dugin takes this problem to its extreme and builds a rather bleak picture. He argues that, without substantive rationality, freedom becomes a goal in itself, and this will trigger an endless reiteration of liberating projects. He claims that, having dispensed with the most-obvious forms of totalitarian state oppression, the logic of negative freedom pushes liberalism to search for those forms of social constraints that do not seem explicitly oppressive but could be branded so for the mere purpose of liberation. Yet many such constraints could arguably be seen as integral to human life, or the 'human nature' that Fukuyama (2003, 97–100) so convincingly defends. One such project is gender. It is one perceived form of collective identity that has traditionally played a part in creating various forms of social domination. The drive to relieve an individual of gender constraints is seen in the decisive ideological divorce between the notions of socially constructed behavioural gender and biological sex. Combined with modern gender/sex-change technologies, this step makes the choice of gender/sex a matter of individual preference. Orthodox Patriarch Kirill (2012), who is one of Russia's most influential conservative intellectuals, warns against this new ideological narrative very much in line with Dugin, viewing it as a threatening imposition of modern techno-liberal morality.

Family is yet another form of collective identity that could be regarded as oppressive. The radical redefinition of the traditional bourgeois family in the postmodern world could be seen through a broad range of policies around artificial procreation, surrogate motherhood and freezing biomaterials, highly intrusive child-abuse prevention policies, as well as the redefinition of the traditional idea of marriage. Physical reality, Dugin argues, becomes another target. The Internet, which liberal economists and ideologues of globalism often hold up as an ultimate symbol of progress, assists in creating a virtual reality. Humans can then choose multiple forms of identity and become free from the constraints of the outside world (Dugin 2012a). In line with that, many fundamental conservatives (Leontyev, Prokhanov, Dugin) claim that the world turns into a perpetual set of simulacra (to use the Baudrillard's [1981] expression) – a chain of reproduced images and ideas that have long since lost touch with the original. Even the very idea of freedom becomes a contemporary simulacrum of the Kantian original concept of personal autonomy. As Fukuyama (2003) argues, the Kantian view of free will was seen as the subjugation of internal inclinations to Reason, while contemporary understanding reverses this and grants prime importance to internal wishes. This process of nihilistic liberation destroys substantive aspects of freedom and yet retains the formal rationality of liberation as a goal in itself. This crisis between 'formal' and 'substantive' liberty raises a multitude of questions. This provides the basis for fundamental conservatives to argue against Russia following such a path and to brand postmodernity as 'the ultimate oblivion of Being,' 'the midnight, when nothingness (nihilism) begins to seep from all the cracks' (Dugin 2012c, 29). In pursuing this logic, Dugin compares this nihilism with the Nietzschean idea of the 'will to nothingness', which throughout the course of its history led to the devaluation of the traditional values of Platonic-Judeo-Christian morality (May 2011, 98–103).

Andrey Fursov, an influential conservative publicist, also points to the ethical dilemmas of Western modernity and postmodernism as its next stage. He echoes Dugin and argues that Western civilization is going through the process of de-individualization and the derationalization of society. He sees this as the deconstruction of Weberian capitalist ethics ('de-Weberization of modern capitalism'), which were broadly based on Christian (and primarily Protestant) reasoning about norms. Fursov, much in the vein of Durkheim (1972, 115), sees capitalist individualism and rationality as a moral condition that demands a person lives and works as a specialist and acts like a responsible citizen. Yet he claims that Western society engages in the deliberate destruction of this original notion of individual responsibility. As an example, people abstain from forming meaningful relationships as a way of getting away from responsibilities. Modern culture evinces a preference for high-tech gadgets over meaningful personal attachments. This dynamic, Fursov argues, shows that postmodern people want to work less, receive more, and feel less responsible for their actions and the actions of others (Fursov, 2010).

This philosophical discourse extends to wider public debates, in which Russia's religious groups become particularly active. Journalist Mikhail Leontyev (2008) laments a situation in which a liberal intellectual of today 'visits the Church with the view to reforming the Church and not with the view to reforming himself'. A public debate held on Russian television between Father Andrey Kurayev and producer Lolita Milyavskaya follows a similar line. Kurayev, echoing the Western liberal-conservative critique (Fukuyama 2002, 106–8), claims that modern society tends to convert people's immediate wants into rights and picks and mixes sacred readings in a way that suits individual impulses. At the same time, people overlook the fact that the Church is not modern. Christ was not modern; he did not always forgive, and God does not correspond to human expectations of a wish-granting Being. From this point of view, Kurayev (Kurayev and

Milyavskaya 2012) argues that 'a person must have the courage to hear a decisive "no" to his/her desires ... Church should not be cozy, comfortable, and lenient.' Kurayev (Kurayev and Milyavskaya 2012) continues: 'We are downgrading traditional values to the supermarket, in which spirituality is bought and sold at affordable prices ... But talking within this fashion, there is also a right "not to be modern".' Geidar Dzhemal (2012b), the leader of Russia's Islamic Committee, laments that the postmodern project 'has eaten up all values, meanings, and signposts. Platonism is dead. Hegelianism, Heideggerianism are just small puddles of thought which have no real influence apart from narrow circles of "intellectuals"' (ibid.).

If the West is progressively decentring its subject and moving consciously from society to some new forms of post-society, why should Russia follow this example in attempting to create her own version of modernity? This is a question that fundamental-conservative philosophers want their readers to ponder. These arguments create ethical foundations for Russia's conservatives to claim that Russia must construct its own logic and ethics of modernity, and qualitatively define her own 'subject', removed from the Western subject that has travelled the road from being endowed with Reason and responsibility towards narcissism and whimsical satisfaction of internal desires.

Post-Secularism

This thinking logically brings us to the discussion of a potential return of religious ethics. In this sphere, Russia's fundamental conservatism paradoxically crosses intellectual paths with the post-secular doctrine of some Western liberals. The post-secular approach admits the continuing global value of religion and presses for dialogue between religious and non-religious segments of society. Jürgen Habermas (2011, 28) agrees with John Rawls in that secularization of the state did not mean secularization of society. In this light, he hopes that 'the public use of reason by religious and non-religious citizens alike may spur deliberative politics in a pluralist civil society and lead to the recovery of semantic potential from religious traditions for the wider political culture.' It is significant that, while the post-secular doctrine presses for a dialogue between secular and religious members of society, it places the responsibility for transcribing religious semantics into a 'universally accessible language' on the latter (Mendietta and Vanantwerpen 2011, 4–5).

These post-secular ideas further fuel Russia's fundamental conservative search for alternative ethical narratives of Russian modernity. In line with this discourse, conservative thinkers argue that these should not be the self-founding narratives of Western liberalism but ethics that draw on the norms and values of Russia's main religions – Islam, Christianity, Judaism, and Buddhism. Interestingly, in an engaging debate with physicist Professor Sergey Kapitsa, Dugin has argued that this type of ethical foundation does not contradict the search for Reason – that is, Reason can have sacred and spiritual qualities (Dugin and Kapitsa 2006). He claims that the pre-modern world had religion and nature at its centre, which was considered rational. The modern world placed science in a similar position. While religion was suppressing science prior to the Enlightenment, science *de facto* began suppressing religion during modernity. Moreover, technology and liberalism – the main engines of modernity – obtained some sacred forms of their own, as John Stuart Mill once noted and as the practice of the Positivists Auguste Comte and Saint-Simone would confirm (Mill 1973; see also Gray 2003, 34). Continuing with this logic, fundamental conservatives view a partial merger between the state and the Church as a rational, conscious, and distinct feature of the Russian tradition. They often recite the Justinian idea of a symphony, in which the Church and the state form a symbiotic symphonic alliance and become jointly responsible for the fate of the country within their own spheres (Meyendorff 1980, 200–2; Kharkhordin 2005, 48–51).

Thus, finding a common ground between Russia's various religious traditions and secular lifestyles becomes an important part of this conservative project. These thinkers look at the Church as an institution of power that could help define the main directions of Russian modernity. Marina Mchedlova (2012), a professor at the Institute of Philosophy (Russian Academy of Sciences), argues that religious values form a large part of the Russian political and social culture. She claims that traditional morals have firmly entered the public space, and an inversion of sorts is occurring between the political and non-political realms. Religion, which formerly belonged to the realm of the non-political, is becoming increasingly political, not only in Russia but in the world as a whole. The secular paradigm, Mchedlova claims, has exhausted itself, and a new civic matrix needs to emerge in its place. Mchedlova (2012) cites a survey by the All-Russian Centre for the Study of Public Opinion (VTSIOM) that shows that 63 per cent of

Russians long for social justice and only 20 per cent value individual freedom. Yet the idea of 'social justice' is not clearly defined. Given that there is a distinct lack of trust in the state, the Church could help develop ideas that might become relevant to the Russian appreciation of social justice.

Thus, the idea of a Church playing a political role has become increasingly important. The Pussy Riot scandal was not accidental, for it exhibited the *de facto* politicization of religion in Russia and the social tensions that this process entails. This case led to the introduction of a bill that considers insulting religious feelings a criminal offence (Zakon, 2012). A large number of fundamental conservative voices spoke in defence of this proposed law. Yegor Kholmogorov, public intellectual and civic activist, insisted that:

> the liberal part of the Russian public defends the right to spit in the face of millions of our ancestors and contemporaries, for whom religion is sacred and Christ the Saviour Cathedral is an embodiment of that sacredness. Instead of merging societal forces in the discussion of how we could repair this moral and ethical damage, we are discussing the wrongs of the Russian Orthodox Church and how we could best befoul it!
> (Otkrytiye 2012)

Fedor Shelov-Kovedyayev, Russia's historian and Deputy Foreign Minister in 1991–92, claims that 'The Church is one of the most important institutions of society. Assaulting it should be made illegal. If society loses moral signposts, it could quickly fall into chaos, revolution, and mass destruction (ibid.). Vladimir Solov'yev (in Shevchenko and Svanidze 2012) concurs, noting:

> Today people are tired of seeing the banality, abomination, and soullessness of the modern world. Seventy years of the Soviet period have been spent creating a quasi-religion, while the subsequent twenty years have been imposing the pseudo-American way of life. In return, we have received smoking and drinking women, an obscene number of abandoned children, impoverished and deserted elders. If there is no God, everything is allowed. Perhaps, it is best to reinstall those barriers that traditional morals place on us and modern ethics dismantle?

RUSSIA AS A COUNTRY OR RUSSIA
AS A CIVILIZATION?

The search for a particular version of modernity leads Russia's fundamental conservatives to ponder the country's image in the international arena. Chapter 7 will discuss the theory of a multipolar world as Russia's philosophical contribution to the contemporary discourse on international relations. It is fruitful, however, to introduce this theme here, in the framework of fundamental conservative thought. To follow this point, fundamental conservatives deploy the logic of large cultural-civilizational spaces (*Grosraum*) developed by Carl Schmitt and the ideas of cultural coalitions proposed by Lévi-Strauss (see Harkin 2009, 54).

Even in the 1960s, Schmitt understood that the bipolar world order was unsustainable. Yet, he thought that the post–Cold War organization of the world would represent a plurality of large spaces with several centres of cultural and political influence, rather than the politico-ideological imposition of a winning side (Schmitt 1963; Mouffe 2007; Zolo 2007). The multiplicity of cultural and political poles could create, in Schmitt's mind, a legal equilibrium of international relations. Schmitt saw these large spaces as pluricultural areas, in which all ethnicities composing the space would find their historic place. The centre of such a cultural space would be called upon to protect the surrounding areas from political, ideological, and economic impositions of similar outer spaces. Schmitt derived this idea from the American Monroe Doctrine that initially regarded the entire American continent (North, Central, and South America) as a single large space and viewed the United States as a core that could protect this cultural-civilizational area from European colonialism (Schmitt 2003; see also the critique by Zolo 2007, 155–6). Lévi-Strauss also speaks of the possibility of cultural 'coalitions', which could operate rather like trading blocs at the cultural level. Individual societies would choose to open themselves up to some of these, while at the same time maintaining adequate barriers (Lévi-Strauss 1966, 257; Harkin 2009, 55).

Following that line, Russia's fundamental conservatives argue that civilizations coincide with cultural, rather than territorial, borders. At the moment, they encompass a constellation of nation-states that share similar moral, ethical, and political values that have been formed on the basis of their socio-historic transmission. Dugin has argued that 'if Russia is a European country, then it cannot talk about its own system of values and it should then unequivocally embrace the global universalism of the West. If Russia feels that her values are different to those of the West, she should define her civilizational identity and self-perceptions' (Dugin, 2012d).

Kirill, the Patriarch of the Russian Orthodox Church, has promoted the idea of Russia's cultural-civilizational distinctness from the larger European space. This theme will also be detailed in Chapter 6, which deals with the state dimensions of Russian nationalism. Kirill argues that Europe has been evolving against the background of Greco-Roman-Semitic cultural influences. Yet, following the Great Schism, Eastern and Western parts of Europe took distinct developmental paths. This resulted in the development of the two separate, but intrinsically interconnected, European civilizations that represent two branches of a common Christian tradition (Gvozdev 2006, 135; see also Suslov 2012, 582–6). Western Europe, now seen as the Euro-Atlantic civilization, is marked by a philosophy of individualism and human rights that were born during the Reformation and continued during the course of the Enlightenment and European revolutions. Russia, as part of Eastern Europe, did not replicate this historic experience and as a 'result based her values on communitarian wisdom, viewing democracy and rights in the framework of mutual self-support' (*Komsomolskaya Pravda*, 20 July 2006; see also Gvozdev 2006, 136). In this light, Patriarch Kirill (2005; see analysis in Gvozdev 2006) argues that Russia represents a European, but not Western, civilization, noting that 'Eastern Europe does not want to blindly follow the rules developed some time ago by someone without its participation and without the consideration of its inhabitants' philosophy of life simply because these rules are applied at present in the materially prospering countries of the West.'

Many fundamental conservatives believe that Russia can exist only as a separate civilization and that joining an external civilization would result in her cultural-civilizational 'self-destruction' (e.g., Starikov 2012). In most cases, the word 'civilization' is used interchangeably with the word 'Empire' or 'pseudo-imperial formation'. Mikhail Leontyev (2012; see also Fursov 2010; Dugin 2012d; and Kushanashvili 2012) insists that the Russian existential essence is seen in an empire-like formation. By empire Leontyev means a civilizational-cultural coalition that is based on a voluntary interaction of people who share a common moral and ethical matrix, as well as a social philosophy. He wishes to avoid the exploitation, injustice, and coercion that spring to mind with the notion of empire, and hopes that the peoples of the former Russian space would be willing to form a new geopolitical, cultural, economic, and socio-historic alliance (not much structurally different to that formed in Europe). This union must be based on the traditionalist communitarian ideas of the Russian cultural space and would eventually become a pole of cultural-political influence on the globe, capable of a meaningful dialogue with similar civilizational poles, such as Western Europe, China, the United States, and Latin America (Krechetnikov 2007; Demidov and Leontyev 2007).

For many conservative thinkers, the ideas of neo-imperial forma-tions obtain a particular significance as an answer to the rapid desov-ereignization of nation-states spawned by globalization. Dugin, Fursov, Leontyev and others view civilizations as the new subject of sovereign agency, while common history, religion, and social ethics become identifiers of civilizations. Thus, instead of the universal ideology of human rights, the fundamental-conservative concept views the group rights of cultures and civilizations (cultural and national spaces) as the new subject/instrument of sovereignty in the global world. They also propose that these large civilizational spaces could become new subjects of global politics, so that we could meaningfully speak of civilizational sovereignty. Dugin (2012c; see also Dzhemal 2012a and 2012b) argues, that

> as soon as we dispense with the global universalism of liberals, a single-scale measure for human societies will also disappear. Each civilization will gain the right to declare its prime values. For some civilizations, it will be human rights (implementing Protagoras's statement that 'Man is the measure of all things'), for others it will be religion; for some others ethics; and yet for some others – matter.

Having said that, these intellectuals do not view civilizations as uni-form, homogenous, and static formations. Their idealized civilizations are involved in a constant dialogue, interpenetration, mutual reinforce-ment, and change. They promote multiple, preferably peaceful, pat-terns of interaction, contrary to Huntington, who insisted on the single idea of a *clash* of civilizations. In various settings, conservative thinkers have insisted that contemporary civilizations are heterogeneous, enclaves of separate civilizations existing within larger civilizations (e.g., Islamic islands are part of the Western scene; similarly, Western communities exist in the Arab world), and these larger civilizations are developing on the basis of the interpenetration of values and ideas existing within them, as well as those brought in from outside (Sleboda and Dugin, 2012; see also Fursov 2012).

CONFLICT AS THE WAY OF POLITICS

The idea of cultural unions and the radical attempt to reject liberal universalism in pursuit of the Russian modernity project invariably pushes fundamental conservatives to embrace the Schmittian notions of conflict and the political. Ironically, the advancement of the Schmittian concept of the political makes Russia's fundamental conservatives once again an intellectual ally of Western post-Marxists. The concept of the political, and its friend-enemy distinction, has influenced many Western postmodern Marxists and radical democrats, who emphasize the significance of conflict as a means of advancing dialogue. John Keane (2003, 179–81) groups various thinkers who embrace the Schmittian understanding of the political into the School of Cantankerousness. These thinkers welcome the idea of conflict in politics as an instrument for giving people a meaningful choice between varying conceptions of the good life (Laclau and Mouffe 1985, 127; Daly 1999, 75). Mouffe, in support of Schmitt, contends that the belief in the possibility of rational consensus on liberal grounds, which we have discussed in previous chapters, has hollowed out the meaning of democracy and precluded the development of a meaningful dialogue between opposing points of view and various hegemonic discourses. Following Schmitt, Mouffe (2005, 3) advocates the creation of 'an agonistic public sphere of contestation' where different hegemonic political projects can be confronted. She further defends the existence of a meaningful choice within the global political discourse as a precursor to all democratic deliberations and dialogue (ibid., 6).

Russian fundamental conservatives also push for the establishment of a radical value pluralism, in which their socio-economic proposals could provide a meaningfully different non-liberal alternative with independent non-liberal purchase power. The Izborsky Club, which unites Russia's foremost fundamental conservative thinkers, sets the idea of drafting a meaningful non-liberal alternative to archaeo-modernity as its prime purpose. Fundamental conservatives claim that the immediate post-Soviet Russian discourse has been substantively liberal, even though it has attempted to dress in traditional garb since the late Yeltsin era. Even the very word 'conservative', they claim, bears liberal connotations and stands on a liberal foundation – as indeed many liberal conservatives would agree, for they see Russia as part of Europe and Europeanization as a trend that needs to be preserved as part of Russia's natural tradition (Polyakov 2004). Thus, fundamental conservatives aspire to create a substantive epistemic choice, in which liberal and non-liberal, even anti-liberal alternatives, will be clearly divorced and meaningfully articulated. Fundamental conservatives see the arrival of their project as livening up Russia's democratic discourse in a manner similar to the postmodern radical democracy proposed by Europe's new left or post-liberal value pluralism (Dugin, 2012b; see also Antivaldayskaya 2012). Indeed, by suggesting a meaningful non-liberal alternative and struggling for this position in the public space, they hope to enrich the discussions on Russia's future and introduce politics of difference.

Like other liberals seeking consensus on humanistic grounds, Russia's liberals have been extremely cautious about the potential for conflict with fundamental conservatives. An exchange between Alexandr Dugin and Yurii Pivovarov, Professor of Modern History at Moscow State University, is indicative. As a liberal, Pivovarov stood staunchly against the idea of agonistic politics, and indeed publicly refuted Schmitt as a dangerous precursor to fascism, whereas Dugin promoted it as a step towards defining the grounds for real alternatives and political positions (Voskresnyy vecher 2012). Yet, the idea of conflict and the Schmittian concept of the political often led to the radicalization of discourse. For example, Maxim Shevchenko (Shevchenko and Svanidze 2012) has argued, 'I am not afraid of divisions. I think that the war has already been declared. This is the war between those who love traditional Russia and fight for her freedom and those who would want to see Russia as a slave to the Western liberal pattern.' By 'traditional Russia' Shevchenko means the multiplicity of Russia's composite cultures, religions, and ethnic groups united by common history. The 'common ground' is found in the language, pluricultural mutual support and co-operation, the tradition of a holistic vision of politics and society, as well as traditional ethics based on Russia's religions. Arkadiy Mamontov agrees that the Russian political landscape reveals the two warring parties as liberal universalists and conservatives: 'this is the war of meanings, the war of symbols, the war of thought, and the war of spirit' (Mamontov 2012). On a more radical note, Aleksandr Prokhanov claims that 'liberalism represents a metaphysical, religious, cultural project that strikes a deadly blow into the heart of the Russian state.' The present victory of the liberal project, according to Prokhanov, 'took place with the active assistance of the liberal state that emerged from the ruins of the Soviet Union' (ibid.). Prokhanov further argues that:

> Liberal culture, liberal ideology, liberal values were propagated, forced, and imposed on the reluctant population that was unsure of its future direction after the fall of the Communist ideology. Now, the time has come for a comprehensive conservative project to get revenge. The goals of that project are propagation of the Rossiyan culture, Christian Orthodox, and other traditional religious values, the ideas of a strong state that are instinctively understood by the majority of the population, and patriotic values based on Russia's multicultural identity.

This critical and radical reinterpretation of post-Soviet liberal realities, as well as the Soviet project of modernity, points to the serious shift that is taking place at the *kerygmatic* level of Russian society. Whether this shift will effect a serious recasting of Russia's structure remains an open but very serious question.

MAIN ACTORS AND POLITICAL ACTIVITY

Fundamental conservatism has lower levels of political representation than pluralist liberalism, conservatism, or even nationalism, in terms of political parties, organizations, and movements. At the same time, this philosophical and ideological position has a substantial following in Russia's influential political and social institutions, as well as in academic circles and among the general public. It has become clear from the discussion above that the Russian Orthodox Church largely shares the position of fundamental conservatism. Hence, religious circles and many influential religious activists, such as Andrey Novikov, Arkadiy Maler, Andrey Kurayev, and on many occasions Patriarch Kirill – all share a highly critical attitude to Western postmodernity. Given that the Church has an historically important function in Russian society, this view could have far-reaching consequences on public opinion and policy in Russia.

Furthermore, various monarchist movements and parties emerged in Russia with the collapse of the Soviet Union and thereafter. These movements are based largely on fundamental-conservative ideological positions. Such activists and organizations often become situational fellow travellers with moderate conservatives at various political junctions. These are backed by a number of influential political and business figures. Natalya Poklonskaya, former Prosecutor of Crimea and currently (2020) State Duma Deputy from the United Russia Party, acts as a media promoter of the pro-monarchical position. There are many popular Internet television resources, such as Tsar-Grad TV, that stand on fundamentally conservative and pro-monarchical positions. Dugin initially organized and led this television station in order to desseminate his philosophical ideas. He subsequently left his editor-in-chief position, yet the media outlet retained his general philosophical and ideological stance. Moreover, the channel is established and financed by Russia's eminent philanthropist Konstantin Malofeyev. Malofeyev also sponsors a number of Orthodox Christian organizations and movements that promote traditional family values and Christian education.

Finally, Alexandr Dugin formed a political movement entitled the Eurasian Youth Union in 2005. This organization participates in various civic actions, joins protest rallies, and holds intellectual public meetings and debates. It co-operates with other youth social movements such as Young Russia, which pursues a pro-government position and organizes rallies aimed at defending Russia's foreign policy and repudiating a liberal point of view. The Eurasian Youth Union also works together with the Trade Union of Russian Citizens – a political movement organized by writer Nikolay Starikov. The movement stands on fundamental conservative positions in the realms of foreign and social policies, and it is often critical of governmental neo-liberal initiatives in the economic sphere. The Movement for People's Liberation, led by the State Duma Deputy Evgeniy Fedorov, is another radically conservative organization and is allied with the Eurasian Youth Union and Starikov's Trade Union. Fedorov's central idea is that Russia is currently under Western economic, political, and ideological occupation and that she should struggle against it by all possible political means.

In conclusion, Russian fundamental conservatism proposes a new and systematic search for radically different dimensions of Russian modernity. Fundamental-conservative thinkers have launched an ambitious attempt to harmonize the conscious and unconscious aspects of Russian society and break away from the debilitating pattern of archaeo-modernity. This involves a radical recasting of the main myths of Russian archaeo-modernity, as well as of Western modernity. While such discourse has significant anti-Western overtones, its essence is rather more non-liberal, anti-liberal, anti-globalist, and anti-interventionist than it is anti-Western *per se*. Russia's fundamental conservatives view the West as a self-sufficient functioning civilization, whose historical development can be seen as a remarkable drama that witnessed a triumph of philosophy, scientific thought, and human spirit. Yet they advocate only a productive dialogue with this civilization and argue against a full transplantation of its values and developmental patterns on Russian soil. They insist on a rational borrowing of various elements of Western civilization that could be useful to Russia, and reject a situation in which Russia would act as a pupil of this civilization (Dugin 2012f).

It is also important to say that fundamental conservatism does not equate its anti-liberal ideas with illiberal politics. In turn, most fundamental conservatives seek to avoid, at least rhetorically, illiberal politics, which they see in totalitarianism, coercion, and elitism. Fundamental conservatives insist that their reformed political project draws on some positive experiences from Russia's past and casts aside anything that can be perceived as totalitarian. At the same time, they focus on social justice (instead of individuality), a strong and effective state, focused on protecting the public good and national interests (instead of a minimal neutral state), tradition and religion (instead of the constructionist approach to values), and the formation of an alternative to the Western pattern of modernity.

5

Socialism and Left-Wing Ideas

POLITICAL ALTERNATIVE OR *TELOS* OF DEVELOPMENT?

Socialism is often viewed as a paradigmatic alternative to capitalism. It was considered as such during the Soviet project of 'alternative modernity', as well as in the political programs of various Western European socialist-democratic parties. At the ideological level, socialism pursues the values of equality, freedom, and social justice. At the economic level, socialism emphasizes state planning as opposed to the free market, an elaborate system of welfare, and redistribution. To achieve those ends, socialism envisages state or collective ownership of the means of production within large industries. Socialism is subjected to a sociological and economic critique which supposedly demonstrates how and why the socialist path is inferior to the capitalist mode of living and how socialist societies failed to deliver on their promises. The situation is exacerbated by the fact that most socialist experiments, starting with the Soviet Union and its client states and ending with Sweden's Social Democratic middle way, Labourite Britain, and Israel's Kibbutzim, 'claimed the title socialist to themselves' (Malia 1994, 23). At the same time, as American historian Martin Malia (ibid.) aptly notes, 'none of these living systems have been truly socialist.'

Against the backdrop of many such criticisms, contemporary Russian socialists insist that socialism must not be viewed as an alternative system to capitalism but as a project of the future and the ultimate purpose of human socio-political development. The Soviet state attempted to achieve this end in the most comprehensive manner to date but failed due to various historical reasons – an underdeveloped working class, an insufficient technological base, international pressures, and an overly powerful bureaucracy that appropriated the gains of the October 1917 revolution (Tretyakov 2017; Kurginyan 2018). From this point of view, Russian revolutionaries launched a project that leapt hundreds of years towards the future, even though attempts to fulfil it at that point were futile. Nevertheless, the metaphysical essence of this project, its ideational, anthropocentric, and cultural foundation, remains a distant ideal for masses of people around the world who are striving for a just society. Therefore, in retrospect, the Soviet state should not be examined as an alternative to contemporary capitalism. Rather it must be viewed as a futuristic experiment which was attempted prematurely at a particularly problematic junction of history.

Some Western scholars concur with this approach. Malia, for example, argues that 'socialism, as the just and humane system, is not an alternative to, but is higher than capitalism. So, socialism also comes to mean the culmination of history, the *telos* of human development; in this guise, it generates a theory of history, or shades off into what has been called meta-history or "historiosophy"' (Malia 1994, 22). From this point of view, socialism as a system and ideology of organizing social life can not be dead or dated as long as humans are striving for a fairer society, justice, equality, and creative freedom. As Jean-Paul Sartre declared, socialism is 'an inescapable horizon of our age' (cited in Malia 2006, 184). More importantly, Malia claims that the modern project of democracy treats the ideas of equality as a target towards which society must evolve. This makes modern democracy an ultimately socialist project that has yet to be fully achieved in contemporary settings.

The socialist paradigm promises equality, justice, harmony, abundance, mutuality and reciprocity, opportunities for personal growth and development, and unlimited knowledge of the outer world as a futuristic mission that might change the very nature of men. A very brief excursion into the history of Western thought reveals a centuries-deep longing for an equal and just society – the type of society which was resistant to being implemented in its entirety at most junctions of human history, and therefore has been postponed to better days. The Platonists, and especially Plotinus, argued that the perfect world exists in connection with the absolute. Man's true being could be achieved by unifying his soul with the absolute through the process of decline and reascent, by casting off the empirical, factual, and material world. Thus, achieving equality, justice, and true knowledge is fully possible only in the next world (Kolakowski 2005, 13–15). Christianity, which absorbed much of Platonism, also promised the return to a lost paradise, to a 'native home' beyond everyday reality, 'a place where man might be what he truly was' (Kolakowski 2005, 15).

Renaissance thinkers continued the search for the equal and just social order by breaking the hitherto-existing link between the noble lineage of a person and his honour and propensity towards noble conduct (Skinner 2002, Vol. 2, 228–9). The philosophical task of divorcing noble lineage and virtue had serious repercussions on the subsequent understanding of the nature of power and governance. Yet again, these thinkers believed that this fully ideal order could be only a utopian one. The quest for equality, justice, and freedom was omnipresent but all these values were to be found in the "objective" outer world, existing beyond human imagination and with all probabilities in the afterlife (Skinner 2002, Vol. 2, 230). Thomas Moore was one of the first systematic Renaissance theoreticians of a socialist society, which he depicted in his book *Utopia*. Moore subverted the understanding of virtue as being based on wealth and splendour by abolishing money and private property in his fictitious society on the island of Utopia. In this case, the ideological task of separating virtue from noble lineage, faced by humanist thinkers of the Renaissance, was resolved automatically, in that all wealth became truly common.

Such theorizations gave impetus to further thought about the ways to achieve justice and equality. Starting from 1517, Reformed religion limited the power of the King by endowing the general public with rights and the responsibility to monitor the way in which the King fulfilled his divine duties of governance. New religious teaching has described the relationship between the King and his subjects as that derived from a particular compact, which mirrored the compact between Man and God and between King and God. Subsequently, the Glorious Revolution of 1688 in England and the 1640 Civil War introduced the idea of a constitutional monarchy (Malia 2006; Kissinger 2014). Succeeding social theorists presented further means towards equality and governance by the people. Jean-Jacques Rousseau argued that evil, and with it inequality, came to the world not through some innate flaw of human nature, but through the defective constitution of society, which was founded on the 'usurped lordship of the strong over the weak' (Malia 1994, 30; Rousseau 2016, 52). The

Scottish Enlightenment proposed an economic solution to the way in which a just society should be organized. Its main thinkers advocated the equality of economic opportunity seen in open participation in the free market.

The French Revolution of 1789 represented an apex of these philosophical ideas in that it clearly formulated the demands for legal equality, universal suffrage, and popular sovereignty. If we suppose that during the French Revolution the bourgeoisie tactically allied with the Third Estate and represented an antagonistic stratum to royal officials and nobility, then this revolution could be considered a precursor to the Great October Socialist Revolution of 1917. For if the bourgeoisie had not taken its class victory in 1789, then 'there would be no development of the proletariat and the emergence of its corresponding class interests, and as a result the social analysis of the evolution of rights' (Malia 2006, 186–7). From this point of view, demands for greater equality and the expansion of rights towards the social dimension were a predetermined outcome of the French Revolution. Malia argues that, if we understand modern democracy in terms of the cardinal values of the French Revolution (equality, justice, and expansion of rights), socialism becomes the inevitable conclusion of democratic development and democracy's highest point. Malia (1994, 33) states:

[S]o long as there are differences of wealth in society, there will be differences of power and status; and so long as there are differences in power and status, there will be exploitation of some men by others, and domination of some human beings by other human beings. But any exploitation and subordination are a denial of human dignity, a profanation of the sacred persona of Man. Inequality, therefore, is dehumanization, and thus a moral scandal that must be ended if the word is to become truly civilized.

This distinctly eschatological approach to socialism creates a unique area of discourse and a disruptive force that inserts thorns into the otherwise smooth story of capitalist narrative. From this point of view, it does not come as a surprise that the re-emergence and consolidation of left-wing discourse in Russia after the collapse of Communism at the close of the twentieth century has the potential to undermine the long-established Russian debate between liberals and traditionalists.

The left-wing strand comes across as the third alternative that disrupts the established paradigmatic alliances within a number of important spheres. Therefore, I will begin the detailed discussion of the Russian left-wing scene by considering the potential of the socialist project to disrupt the existing status quo between the two classical ideological paradigms: liberal and traditionalist. I will then proceed to examine the critique of global capitalism by the contemporary Russian left and their proposed plan of political change.

FRAGMENTATION OF THE HEGEMONIC DISCOURSE

The consolidation of the post-Communist left-wing discourse showed that, in addition to the traditionalist and liberal paradigms of Russian modernity, another serious rupture is slowly coming to the fore. The nature of this rupture is economic, and it is mainly expressed through a conflict of interests. It represents the eternal conflict between 'haves' and 'have-nots' – using the E.H. Carr lexicon – or conflict between those with wealth and power and those without it. The evolution of this conflict reflects the consolidation of newly formed economic classes in Russia. These processes turn the usual paradigmatic split between liberals and traditionalists upside down, almost negating the previous Western-centric socio-cultural debate. Thus, this new socio-economic conflict throws an entirely new light on existing ideological divisions by invoking new political alliances and changing the centuries-old trajectories of the ideological debate. This development is largely a feature of a developed capitalist society and has been observed by a number of Western researchers of mature capitalism. French-Greek Marxist philosopher Nicos Poulantzas (1978, 32) points at the economy-conditioned discourse migration using the example of Western capitalist states. He argues that the 'state does not produce a unified discourse, but several discourses that are adapted to the various classes and differently incarnated in its apparatus' according to their class destination. Or, put another way, it produces a discourse that is broken into fragments according to lines intersecting the strategy of power.

Russian state and political elites exhibit this economy-conditioned discourse fragmentation within the areas that might jeopardize the newly established socio-economic status-quo. While the state usually follows a hegemonic traditionalist line, calling for a continuity of all periods of Russia's history within the spiritual, cultural, and eschatological realms, the issue of the Soviet past remains a touchstone of division. Indeed, an overly positive assessment of the Soviet past and the October Revolution of 1917 will subsequently raise questions that compare the level of social justice within the Soviet Union with inequality and the lack of meritocracy in contemporary Russia; Soviet industrial achievements will be scrutinized, and the way in which the privatization of large enterprises was conducted during the 1990s will be challenged. Such questions are inconvenient and detrimental to the economic interests of contemporary Russian elites. Therefore, the otherwise traditionalist segments of the elites often adopt a sceptical stance towards this cardinal period of Russia's history. From this economically deterministic point of view, the fragmentation of discourse in Russia mainly entails attitudes towards the Great October Socialist Revolution, Soviet industrial, scientific, and international achievements, Stalin's modernization, as well as matters of humanism and historicism. Hence, economic interests often topple cultural and civilizational considerations. In many ways, this strategy of the elite indicates that Russia, having travelled a long road from the dissolution of Communism at the close of the twentieth century, is about to complete the consolidation of her bourgeois state. Let me examine those rupture lines.

Attitudes to the Great October Socialist Revolution

Russia's left-wing theoreticians generally praise the 1917 socialist revolution in the three most important ways. They insist that: (1) the revolution had a social rather than political character; (2) the revolution followed the political and social dynamics of other European revolutions and grand transformations around the world; and (3) October 1917 produced the project of alternative modernity, which enriched the world's civilization from technical, scientific, social, and political points of view.

First, the attitude to the 1917 revolution remains one of the central and highly debated issues in the ideological landscape of contemporary Russia. The narrative of the revolution's causes, dynamics, and outcomes has far-reaching implications for the legitimacy of the contemporary Russian state. Let us assume, for example, that the character of this revolution was political and not social. In this case, the state formed in the wake of this revolution reflected the interests of a narrow group of political-activists-turned-elites. This means that the socialist nature of the revolution was not predetermined, for it did not reflect the general will of the Russian people to create a just social order and to free themselves from the chains of pre-existing exploitation and oppression. In this case, revolution could be reduced to a mere *coup d'état* or power takeover. From this point of view, the outcome of such a revolution was not strictly legitimate, notwithstanding the fact that state power was firmly entrenched in its wake.

Expanding this speculative argument to its extreme, those who fought in the Great Patriotic War, in the interest of the state formed in the wake of this political revolution (or as we may say, *coup d'état*), were mistaken. At the same time, those who took up arms with the German army to 'liberate' Russia from its illegitimate government could be vindicated in the eyes of history. This invalidates the contemporary Russian understanding of the Great Victory, which often serves as a socio-political platform upon which Russian people unite into a single socio-historical whole. Such an interpretation would invoke a serious historical reassessment of the very foundations of contemporary Russia's historical myths, as well as her core positions in the international arena which largely rest on the Yalta-Potsdam understanding of the results of the Second World War. With this in mind, Russian socialists (largely supported by other ideological groups within the traditionalist bracket) defend the idea of the socialist character of the October 1917 Revolution.[1]

Soviet historiography was aware of these potential discursive and political dangers and had a unified view on the revolution, assessing it as a social revolution with political consequences. In this assessment, it relied on the idea that the Russian Empire was a backward state with extreme socio-economic stratification and inequality. Revolution was therefore brewing within Russian society for over a hundred years and had social liberation as its principal purpose. Soviet classical writer Maxim Gorky (1949) sustains this argument in *The Life of Klim Samgin*: in 1877, sixteen years after the abolition of serfdom, Russia's population stood at one hundred million people, of which ninety-one million were peasants, seven million were workers, and just one million were nobility, landowners, clergy, and bourgeoisie. Some one and a half million were soldiers, police, prison guards, and secret police. Seventy-three-million people were illiterate. Russia had the highest levels of birth and child mortality in Europe. Inefficient government, an illiterate population, and immense class differentiation, Gorky argues, generated discontent among the educated intelligentsia and ordinary people. They joined the struggle against the tsarist regime, which culminated in the October 1917 socialist revolution.

Similarly, Alexandr Blok, one of Russia's foremost twentieth-century poets, despite subsequent disillusionment, supported the revolution enthusiastically during the years 1917–18. He paints an artistic and radical picture of the events in his long poem *The Twelve* – written in 1918 and still one of the central texts of the Russian revolution – as well as in historical-philosophical essays such as *Catiline* (1918) and *The Decline of Humanism* (1921). For Blok (1918), the revolution was sanctified as a profound spiritual, social, cultural, religious, and political transformation, reflecting the deeply held desires of the Russian people. Blok argued that the tsarist regime became anti-Christian and lost its legitimacy, as well as its 'holy status', in contrast to the Red revolutionary guards marching towards the new idealistic future. Vladimir Golstein (2018) observes that, despite subsequent reservations, Blok wanted to see October 1917 as 'the revolution that merges Christian values with social goals, and the one that is ready to challenge the corrupt and rotten regime from the perspective of these values and ideals. Such a revolution could truly transform things, as opposed to one that simply reverses the haves with have-nots.' Moreover, Blok compared the tsarist regime with the declining Roman republic, which was saved and transformed from its political and spiritual downfall by the Christian revolution (Kalb, 2000). By the same token, the Russian Empire was a degenerate and ailing organism, whose salvation hinged upon the revolution, which was blessed, in Blok's vision, by Christ. To sum up, the social character of the Russian revolution was evident through literary and cultural expressions of Soviet, as well as Russian, writers and poets, buttressed by the official historiographic position.

With the dissolution of the Soviet Union, opinions began to diverge, gravitating largely towards the argument that the Russian Revolution was a political *coup d'état* which had grave social consequences. These critics argue that the political conditions of the time were propitious for such a *coup*. In particular, they point to the general crisis of Russia's imperial state institutions, the betrayal of monarchy by its closest cognate allies – the nobility, military, and industrial bourgeoisie – and to external factors, such as the entry of the Russian Empire into the Great War. Numerous conspiracy theories brand the October Socialist Revolution as the first 'Western-orchestrated' attempt at a 'Colour Revolution' similar to those that occurred in 2003 in Georgia and

2014 in the Ukraine.[2] These critics argue that revolutionary workers'
rallies in imperial Russia were organized with Western, mainly British
and German, financial help (Starikov 2014). Others (Miler 2004)
emphasize the participation of British intelligence in the Rasputin
murder, which has been acknowledged in Britain with the emergence
of new data. This fact consolidated the opinion that Britain pressed
for Russia's continued participation in the Great War – a policy that
Rasputin attempted to torpedo at all costs. Participation in this war,
meaningless for Russia's geopolitical interests and costly from the
socio-economic point of view, led, in the view of many such observers,
to the Russian revolution of February 1917 and the subsequent illegitimate Bolshevik *coup*. Some other commentators underscore the
role of German industrial capital in the Russian Revolution and
pointed at Lenin's close association with Alexander Parvus – a wealthy
member of the German Social Democratic Party and a German coun-
ter-intelligence agent. Creative and popular arts advance this point
of view. Of particular significance are the hundred centenary
Revolutionary biopics on Lenin (*The Demon of the Revolution*) and
Trotsky (*Trotsky*) both released in October 2017.

Contemporary left-wing theorists vehemently disagree with such
assessments. They argue that this particular view of the revolution
subverts its main ideals, such as people's ownership of the means of
production, equality, classless society, and people's governance.
Admitting that those ideals reflected the genuine wishes of the people
of the Russian Empire would be subversive to Russia's contemporary
bourgeois class interests – hence much of the cinematic production
is financed by this class with the view to discrediting the revolution
at the hegemonic discursive level. Socialists insist that the October
Revolution had a social character and that shortcomings of Russia's
imperial estate system brought the fall of the political regime in 1917.
Moreover, they warn that a similar showdown could occur in contemporary Russia if the issue of economic division is not appropri-
ately addressed. Russia's socialists further argue that, despite the
ensuing oppression that accompanies all great revolutions and
upheavals, masses of people supported the October Revolution and
the Red Army during the Civil War. Without such support the Reds
would not have been able to secure decisive victory and invoke
enthusiasm for the reconstruction of a new country. Socialists also
insist that the Bolsheviks opened immense opportunities for 'growth
and development to all previously dispossessed, gave ordinary folks

a chance to obtain dignity, education, and social mobility and to conduct their lives freely according to their creative plans and wishes' (Shevchenko 2016).

Interestingly, former dissident writers Alexander Zinoviev (2001) and Alexander Solzhenitsyn (1995) (both subsequently disillusioned with the West) saw the roots of the Russian Revolution in reforms of the seventeenth century and argued that the Soviet period of Russian history represented a logical continuation of pre-revolutionary Russia, epitomizing in many ways the best elements of pre-revolutionary times. Zinoviev and Solzhenitsyn (1995) claim that the October 1917 revolution reflected the metaphysical aspirations of the Russian people for justice and God's Kingdom on Earth. It imbibed Russian religious ideas: that the land belongs to God and therefore should belong to people collectively, and that luxury is a sin if it is created for the few by those who live in poverty. Both these authors argue that the events of the October Revolution were predetermined socially and that the Provisional Government and the participants of the February 1917 bourgeois revolution logically gave way to the Bolsheviks.

Russian left-wing thinkers, such as Alexander Pyzhikov (2017), Evgeny Spitsyn, Maxim Shevchenko (2017) (who joined the Communist Party of the Russian Federation [CPRF] during the 2018 presidential electoral campaign), Sergey Kurginyan, and Eduard Limonov, share the view of some Western historians that the October Revolution was a logical continuation of the French Revolution of 1789. They concur with the idea of the historical momentum of the European liberation movement and with Russia being a significant part of this dynamic, culminating in its October 1917 crest. Yet, in contrast to the Marxist supposition of permanent world revolution, the Russian Revolution focused on nation-state building in the wake of Stalin's political victory over Trotsky. This was a nation-state of a new type, however: multinational, multiethnic, and free from imperial and colonial exploitation. Socialists argue that contemporary Russia is still enjoying the fruits of the Russian Revolution via the remains of the welfare state, the federated multiplicity of peoples and ethnic groups, none of which have been fully assimilated, and the achievements in the spheres of science, technology, and creative arts.

Second, Russian left-wing thinkers adopt the argument of many Western philosophers that there is a broad scheme of revolutionary development, which is common to all great revolutions. As Isaac Deutscher argued, any revolution will undergo stages of enthusiasm, public debate, and democracy, and will end up with a growing rift between the revolutionary party and people. In the end, the only way to preserve the gains of the revolution is to silence the voice of the people and impose direct bureaucracy or party rule. Hence, every revolution would produce its own Cromwell, Robespierre, and Napoleon. Every revolution follows this particular logic, be it independent, Jacobin, or Bolshevik, and whether it is 'English, French or Russian' (MacIntyre 1971, 53). Other theorists, such as John Dunn, claim that 'revolutions are facts of nature, analogous to physical process, the release of enormous forces, moving vast masses through space. They are amoral, ineluctable. They crush all in their path ... It is pointless to resist them and absurd ... to put them on trial' (Dunn 1972, 3). Marxists concur with this logic. Engels (1873) stated that any revolution is 'certainly the most authoritarian thing there is: it is the act whereby one part of the population imposes its will upon the other part by means of rifles, bayonets, and cannons, authoritarian means, if such there be at all, and if the victorious party does not want to have fought in vain, it must maintain this rule by the terror which its arms inspire in the reactionaries.'

With this in mind, Russia's left-wing thinkers argue that Russian society must reassess the experience of the October Revolution and its post-Revolutionary terror. Vitaly Tretyakov (2017), for example, insists that the 1789 French Revolution was bloodier than the Russian, and argues that heavy human casualties accompany all great societal transformations. Sergey Kurginyan calls for a comparison of the number of victims of the Russian revolutionary process with the number of victims resulting from revolutions in other European and North American states. More importantly, socialists (Kurginyan 2017a; Zyuganov 2015) repudiate Alexander Solzhenitsyn's claim of sixty-six-million victims of the Soviet experiment between 1917 and 1959 and the forty-million figure for victims of the Great Purge (Medvedev 1988; Antonov-Avseenko 1991; Solzhenitsyn 1973, Vol. 2, 451). They insist that these numbers have been derived from creative literary accounts, which became uncritically accepted as fact in most West European states. Socialists argue that Russian society must conduct a critical reassessment of the real numbers of victims, and serious archival work must be conducted to establish the total of those executed, imprisoned, and arrested during that period.

Viktor Zemskov, professor at Moscow State University, was one of the first historians to work in the OGPU-NKVD-KGB-MVD and State

Archives under the aegis of the 1989 State Commission to establish the extent of the purges. The Zemskov Commission, which did not collude ideologically with either socialists or Stalinists, established that the figures uncritically accepted as facts in the Western academic literature have been seriously inflated. Having investigated declassified State and KGB archives, as well as the correspondence of Soviet leaders, Zemskov (2012) states that, during the period between 1921 and 1953 (thirty-two years post–civil war and Stalin's rule), the total number of citizens convicted in political cases has been 4,051,903. Out of those, 799,257 people have been sentenced to death and executed. It is important to note that this statistic also includes criminals who took part in organized theft from state-owned enterprises (which at the time was considered a political 'counter-revolutionary' crime since state property was a target). In this light, the KGB archives – which aimed to separate criminal and political cases – state that the number of convictions for political cases stood at 3,753,490 and the number of those executed was 815,579. The discrepancy in the number of the executed arises from the fact that the KGB accounted for 23,726 executed for political reasons and espionage in 1941, while the MVD arrived at the figure of 8,011. It is significant that the lion's share of convictions, 35 per cent of the total number (or 1,345,000 people), took place during the Great Purge years in 1937-38. Similarly, the greatest number of executions, 682,000 people, took place during the same period of time (Zemskov 2012).

Comparing these figures to other states, Zemskov (2012) argues that the extent of purges in the USSR was similar to that of Franco's Spain. In the latter case, eighty thousand people were executed for political motives. At face value, this is ten times less than in the USSR, in which around eight hundred thousand were executed for the same reasons. At the same time, the population of Spain in the late 1930s and early 1940s stood at twenty million, while the population of the Soviet Union during the peak of repressions was two hundred million. This signifies that, while the sheer numbers of the dead are ten time greater in the USSR, the population was also ten times larger, meaning that the figures become comparable. Viktor Zemskov further claims that

those who examined the problem of political repression in the Soviet Union become subject to a particular social environment. Researchers could not distance themselves from societal requests within each particular moment ... During the Cold War, Western historiography, tasked with the study of purges within the USSR, developed a range of templates, labels, and stereotypes. It was not socially acceptable to break those barriers. It was customary to assess the total number of victims at forty million and over; the total number of inmates at the end of 1930 was over eight million; the number of victims of the 1937–38 purges was over seven million. Claiming lower figures would be considered socially unacceptable behaviour.

Moreover, Zemskov (2012) points out that, by 2000, of 3,854,000 people convicted for political crimes between 1921 and 1953, 2,438,000 (63 per cent) had been rehabilitated; 1,416,000 (36.7 per cent) had not been rehabilitated, because many of them fell into the category of Nazi collaborators – those who fought with Hitler against the Soviet Union during the Great Patriotic War (1941–45). Despite that, a number of radical liberals, such as Gavriil Popov, Dmitry Bykov, Nikita Sokolov, nationalist, monarchist, and Cossack organizations continually press for the political rehabilitation of the Russian Liberation Army and 15th SS Cossack Corpus leaders such as Generals Andrey Vlasov, Peter Krasnov, Andrey Shkuro, Helmuth von Pannwitz, Timofey Domanov, and Sultan-Girei Klych. The rationale behind the rehabilitation was that those individuals fought for the heritage of historic Russia, represented the ideology of the Civil War, and continued the White cause of anti-Communism. Unsuccessful attempts to overturn the USSR verdicts were made in 1997, 2001, and in 2007. In all cases, Russia's officials confirmed the sentences and charges pressed against those officers (*Newsru* 2001; *Kommersant Daily* 2001; *Tribuna* 2008).

Finally, pondering the nature of revolutions, Martin Malia (2006, 5) observes that 'a European "grand revolution" is a generalised revolt against an old regime. Moreover, such a transformation occurs *only once* in each national history, since it is also the founding event for the nation's future "modernity".' This observation is significant when considering the October Socialist Revolution, for it took place against the distinct order of European industrialization, particularly in England and France. Russia's left-wing critics continue that, despite reflecting on general processes of liberation occurring in European history, Russia took its own revolutionary path by organizing its distinct nation-state and simultaneously launching the project of 'alternative socialist' modernity. They further argue that the existence of the 'alternative modernity' project enabled the world to focus on a range of creative activities (Alferov 2017a). The technical achievements of the twentieth century stemmed mainly from scientific and socio-economic competition between the United States and the Soviet Union. Moreover, the Russian Revolution created a state of workers, which improved the conditions of the working class across the globe by setting higher standards for social justice and equality. Thus the rapid development of the Western welfare state in the twentieth century was largely the by-product of the October Socialist Revolution (Alferov 2017a). The conditions of economic and socio-political competition within the socialist system prompted many capitalist countries to match the Soviet welfare state with their own systems to respond to the demands of their own working classes (see also Piketti 2013).

Attitudes to the Soviet Past: De-Sovietization or Re-Sovietization?

Soviet achievements of the past, such as high educational standards, rapid industrialization and modernization, great power status in the world arena, global leadership in the spheres of space exploration, sport, creative art, and science often generate public nostalgia in contemporary Russia. Soviet societal values and practices, such as comradeship, equality, social justice, a classless society, strict restrictions on embezzlement, and higher levels of meritocracy obtained new significance with the passing of time. Arguments have emerged that working-class people had a high social status and their contribution to the community was genuinely valued, and professionalism was a feature of the age (Zadornov 2017; Zyuganov 2019; Zyuganov 2016). These sentiments indicate that large segments of the Russian population still adhere to Soviet ideals and take pride in the achievements of that period. Indicative of that trend is that Stalin's tomb behind the Lenin Mausoleum is covered with fresh flowers on his birthday each December.

Statistics generated by the Russian Levada Centre in 2016 show that 56 per cent of Russia's population regret the dissolution of the Soviet Union, and 51 per cent think that the USSR's collapse could have been avoided. Only 29 per cent of the respondents suggest that the dissolution of the Soviet Union was unavoidable, and just 28 per cent do not regret this.[3] General interest in and nostalgia for the

Soviet past is well reflected in the sphere of creative arts. Most Russian television dramas and series are focused on the topic of the Soviet past. Russia's contemporary blockbusters – which often outdraw Hollywood movies in the country's cinemas – are mostly devoted to Soviet achievements of the past and the ideology of Soviet patriotism that led people to various victories in sports, art, and politics. Despite the fact that many of these productions often depict negative aspects of the Soviet political climate, such as the pressure of the state apparatus on the public, the interest in those topics is not waning. Similarly, a cursory glance over evening TV entertainment shows demonstrates that people often have eyes clouded with tears when old Soviet films, songs, and programs are being demonstrated and discussed. It is also notable that the participants on many such shows claim that they intend to bring up their children on Soviet popular culture as opposed to contemporary offerings.

More significantly, the legitimation of the extant political regime in Russia rests heavily on the promise to revive various positive achievements of the Soviet past that were demolished during the tumultuous period of the 1990s. Soviet standards in industrial production, achievements in geopolitics, sports, arts, science, and the military often serve as a benchmark in assessing Russia's contemporary initiatives. Hence, Russian political elites often garner public support when they refer to Russia's former Soviet glory in the geopolitical arena and when they pledge to catch up with Soviet standards in the socio-economic sphere. Putin's (2005) sincere acknowledgement in 2005 that the dissolution of the Soviet Union was the biggest geopolitical catastrophe of the twentieth century has drawn a positive response from the Russian public. He reiterated this statement in 2015 at the Valdai forum and made similar claims in his interview with German television, arguing that the demise of the political party dictatorship should not have been accompanied by the total demise of the Soviet state (RBC 2012). More importantly, contemporary Russia considers itself to be the heir of the Soviet Union, which further suggests that it bases its legitimacy on the Soviet past. This pertains particularly in international affairs, as is seen in Russia's seat on the UN Security Council, her possession of nuclear weapons, and her general international stance as a global power.

At the same time, this situation is precarious for contemporary Russian economic and political elites. Basing (however partially) their legitimacy on the Soviet premise will always mean that there is an air of conditionality to the riches, capital, and political power accumulated by such elites during the post-Soviet period. The question of property ownership, particularly within large industrial sectors, will loom over those elites for as long as the spectre of the Soviet Union is alive and viewed favourably by the general public. To this end, the elites need to navigate carefully between the Scylla of pandering to the wishes of the general population that demands vindication of the Soviet Union, and the Charybdis of the elites' personal desires to obtain radically new sources of legitimacy that could once and for all seal their claims on the riches. It becomes evident that, when matters concern wealth and property, these new sources of legitimacy must be clearly divorced from the USSR, its culture and ideology. To resolve this dilemma peacefully, Russia's extant political elites are engaging in the creeping de-Sovietization of the Russian population.

There are two political factions within Russia's elites. The first group considers the demonization of Soviet history detrimental to the future development of Russia. This group is conscious of Russia's reliance on Soviet achievements in its various international claims, such as the permanent seat on the UN Security Council. Representatives of this group are also trying to forge a compromise with a general population that admires the Soviet past. As we discussed in the Introduction, this compromise could be seen in the ideological attempt to link the three different periods of Russia's history: Imperial-Tsarist, Soviet, and post-Soviet. The second group presses for wide-scale de-Sovietization of Russia and the comprehensive abandonment of the Soviet past at the ideological level. This group is not concerned about Russia's extant territorial and historical integrity and has globalist preferences and orientations. This elite group adopts a particularly critical line towards Soviet history. It focuses on the large extent of political repression during the Stalin era, and it supported opening memorials to the victims of purges in Moscow (the Wall of Sorrow) and Magadan (the Mask of Sorrow) and the Yeltsin Centre museum in Yekaterinburg. Vladimir Putin attended the opening of both the Yeltsin Centre and the Wall of Sorrow, thus indicating his mediating role between the two groups and some ideological ambivalence towards the issue of the Soviet past.

In this light, left-wing thinkers (Kurginyan 2017b) insist that Russia's civil society must struggle against the spread of anti-Soviet sentiments and the creeping de-Sovietization conducted by portions of Russia's political elites. More importantly, these thinkers warn that full-scale de-Sovietization could lead to a serious social, economic, and geostrategic devastation of Russia for the reasons that we have partially outlined above with reference to the Russian Revolution. To reiterate, interpretation of the Soviet past is considered central to Russia's contemporary standings in the international arena. As the heir to the Soviet Union, Russia is also the inheritor of the Soviet Union's victory in the Second World War, which was its most significant geostrategic achievement during the twentieth century. The pre-existing Russian Imperial sphere of influence, which was tarnished in the wake of the Great War and the Revolution, was restored and officially enshrined in the agreements of the Yalta and Potsdam conferences. Discrediting the Soviet Union through the process of comprehensive de-Stalinization, de-Sovietization, and repentance could logically lead scrutiny of the very idea of Soviet victory and a questioning of the geostrategic gains that came with it (Kurginyan 2017d).

The demonization and rejection of the Soviet past would invariably lead to equalization of Nazism and Communism and the subsequent revision of the Soviet victory in the Great Patriotic war, as well as its role in the Second World War. This in turn would logically challenge the place of contemporary Russia in the world arena, her seat on the United Nations Security Council, and her signature on a range of foundational international treaties. Some conservative thinkers concur with the thesis that the international legitimacy of the contemporary Russian state draws heavily on the previous achievements of the Soviet Union in the international arena. Natalia Narochnitskaya (2017) argues that the true reason behind the demonization of Stalin stems from the fact that he detached Russia from the European context and did not view Russia's evolution through the European prism. This helped him to strategically outplay his European counterparts and turn Russia into a geopolitical entity that was equivalent to all of Europe.

Attitudes to the Contemporary Class Structure

The class issue is another divisive subject that accompanies the problematic legitimation of the current Russian state and subverts its extant hegemonic discourse. Reflecting on the future of the Soviet state, Leon Trotsky, in *The Revolution Betrayed*, argued that the new communist bureaucracy evolved into a special political 'caste' that usurped power and turned its guns against workers and peasants. He (2004, 214–15) wrote:

[T]he bureaucracy is not only a machine of compulsion but also a constant source of provocation. The very existence of a greedy, lying and cynical caste of rulers invariably creates a hidden indignation ... Will the bureaucracy devour the workers' state, or will the working class clean up the bureaucrats? Thus stands the question upon whose decision hangs the fate of the Soviet Union.

Lenin concurred with this view by arguing that Soviet power might collapse only from its own partisan bureaucracy, and not from external or internal enemies. Albert Einstein, who was sympathetic to the socialist idea, and to the Soviet Union in particular, expressed a similar concern. In his 1949 article 'Why Socialism?' he worried that the class of emergent bureaucracy within the conditions of a planned economy and consolidated state ownership could grow into a specifically privileged caste and reinforce economic and socio-political inequalities within society. Einstein (2009) writes: 'how is it possible, in view of the far-reaching centralization of political and economic power, to prevent bureaucracy from becoming all-powerful and overweening? How can the rights of the individual be protected and therewith a democratic counterweight to the power of bureaucracy be assured?'

With this in mind, a number of left-wing thinkers in Russia argue that the Soviet state fell into the trap anticipated by Lenin and Trotsky. On the one hand, the Soviet Union liquidated the class of exploiters, created state ownership of the means of production, and passed the land to collective farms. In due course, it conducted rapid industrialization and laid the foundations for victory in the Second World War. On the other hand, the Soviet Union created a bureaucratic class (or 'caste' in Trotsky's words), which appropriated significant segments of political and economic power and evolved into a self-sufficient class of exploiters. Such exploiters wished to convert their political power into tangible economic gains and property by demolishing the socio-political foundations of the Soviet Union (Alferov 2017b; Delyagin 2019, 644–8; Prokhanov 2012; Zyuganov 2016; Starikov 2011; Kurginyan 2009; Shevchenko 2017a; Khazin 2014). Therefore, few from the highest echelons of the party apparatus – the very leaders and political elites of the Soviet state – were interested in rescuing the Soviet Union at the time of its death. From this point of view, the Soviet Communist Party elite is directly responsible for the collapse of the Soviet Union and the dissolution of the

Communist Party. This party elite also relied on dissenting intellectuals who helped to frame new ideas of economic and political restructuring, conceptually and theoretically.

In the wake of tumultuous post-Soviet economic reforms, a campaign of privatization created a new class of proprietors that now possess both power and wealth. A number of contemporary left-wing analysts, such as Mikhail Delyagin, Mikhail Khazin, Maxim Shevchenko (2017b), and others argue that, despite the fact that *perestroika* aimed to achieve greater justice, the post-Soviet reality established a new 'estate' system, cruel and unequal in its nature. By doing so, contemporary Russia repeated and reinforced the grave inequalities of both the Tsarist Empire and the late Soviet Union (Khazin 2017). The new stratum of a large industrial and financial bourgeoisie and political elite represents the most privileged class. Russia's new bourgeoisie controls the country's political institutions and enforces inequalities in the application of law, employment opportunities, moral codes, and behavioural limits, as well as educational standards. Maxim Shevchenko (2017b) argues that the new class of Russia's bureaucracy possess wealth at a level unthinkable for ordinary people: properties, palaces, yachts, foreign Riviera villas, penthouses in the most prestigious cities of the world, private jets, top-range automobiles, and expensive jewellery. Conservative Mikhail Remizov (2017) concurs that contemporary Russian society is highly polarized, with 1 per cent of people statistically owning 70 per cent of national wealth. Russia's statistics agency *RosStat* supports such claims by stating that 13.5 per cent of the Russian population (or 19.8 million people) live below the poverty line. In 2016, 10 per cent of the population owned 46 per cent of the country's income. This figure is higher than in China or Europe, where the top 10 per cent own 41 per cent and 37 per cent of the national income respectively. The figure, however, is close to the United States and Canada, where inequality is known to be higher and stands at 10 per cent of the population owning 47 per cent of the national income.[4]

It is often pointed out that, in addition to economic inequality, the new privileged demand preferential treatment in other spheres of socio-political life. That includes a selective application of the law and differential employment opportunities and education standards. With regard to the application of the law, children of influential officials and business executives can often be acquitted in criminal cases. A number of these cases included grave violations of motoring laws

– some involving fatalities. Children of the management of *Lukoil* engaged Moscow's traffic police in car chases across the city. The offenders drove a luxury G-Class Mercedes over lawns and pavements, trying to evade the police, and simultaneously insulted police officers on their smart-phone cameras. YouTube videos of such Herostratic fame later appeared online and served as evidence in court. It did not come as a surprise that none of the 'rally' participants received a custodial sentence, and most have been acquitted with insignificant fines. In the employment sphere, children of high-ranking bureaucrats usually occupy leading executive positions within Russia's largest and most important institutional and industrial structures. They manage to reach staggering career heights at an age that raises questions over their competence and professional suitability. Spouses of bureaucrats often head multi-million-dollar enterprises, generating annual incomes that significantly surpass the national average.

This situation allows left-wing critics to claim the emergence of a special class (or estate) of people who transfer wealth, political positions, and the privileged application of law enforcement on an hereditary basis. This moves the country away from the principles of meritocracy, legal equality, and equality of opportunity. Left-wing critics argue that this situation could have potentially revolutionary consequences unless the government decides to implement measures capable of altering the existing social structure of Russian society. Konstantin Syomin, a radical left-wing investigative journalist, argues that the showdown with the ruling class and its allies will inevitably take place, should the working class press for greater political and socio-economic equality. To this end, he insists that the working class must establish a parliamentary, as well as a non-parliamentary, base. Building grassroots democracy outside the state and its elites, as well as forging alliances with like-minded personnel within the state who are waging the Gramscian 'war of position', becomes the ultimate strategy of the left-wing political struggle.

While striving towards greater equality and the abolition of the extant estate system, it is important to establish how Russia's contemporary left-wing thinkers understand the idea of equality. Different political ideologies provide us with varying interpretations of the concept. Liberals and conservatives view equality either as the equality of opportunity (in the conservative case) or legal and political equality (in the liberal case). Socialists, in contrast, advocate so-called socialist egalitarianism, which is characterized by social equality, or *equality of outcome* (Heywood 2007, 108). However, the equality of outcome is also understood differently. While classical Marxists and Communists desired absolute social equality, social democrats advocate a relative social equality achieved through the redistribution of wealth through the welfare system and progressive taxation (Heywood 2007, 108). Sergey Kurginyan, Russia's most outspoken and prolific socialist critic, advocates the equality of opportunity and relative social equality at the expense of the absolute equality of outcome. Kurginyan (2017c) argues that attempts to achieve a full egalitarian equality of outcome represented one cardinal policy mistake committed by the Soviet Union, one that led to the ethical and ideological failure of the Soviet socialist project.

At the same time, Kurginyan (2017c) argues that the meaningful implementation of equality of opportunity remains a distant goal in contemporary capitalist societies. He argues that such societies do not guarantee equality of opportunity because people have different starting points in life, a situation caused by embedded economic inequality. The situation is exacerbated by the fact that capitalist education promotes the spirit of capitalist economic competition and a 'survival of the fittest' mentality, thereby institutionalizing the class division of society. Syomin (2016a), who focuses on the problems of contemporary education, argues that, within such conditions, people can not challenge inequality and merely navigate this harsh socio-economic environment to the best of their abilities. In this light, Zhores Alferov (2017a; 2017b) cites Albert Einstein (2009; first published in 1948), who argued that the 'crippling of individuals' within the educational systems represents 'the worst evil of capitalism ... An exaggerated competitive attitude is inculcated into the student, who is trained to worship acquisitive success as preparation for his future career.' Einstein further claimed that 'there is only *one* way to eliminate these grave evils, namely through the establishment of a socialist economy, accompanied by an educational system which would be oriented toward social goals.'

Humanism and Historicism

Historicism and humanism are cardinal aspects of the traditional Marxist-Leninist metaphysics that have been incorporated into contemporary socialist thinking, particularly in light of its criticism of capitalist education. Let us briefly consider the theoretical aspects. Anglo-Polish philosopher Leszek Kolakowski (2005) argues that the human search for higher ideals stems from an understanding of the 'contingent state of man'. Summarizing this problem, he argues that 'finite and conditional beings ... are constantly moving from a past that has ceased to be into a future that does not yet exist; they are obliged to see themselves in terms of memory or anticipation; their self-knowledge is not direct, but meditated by the distinction of what was and what will be' (Kolakowski 2005, 13). Resolving the contingency puzzle would enable humans to obtain full knowledge of nature and by doing so devise the most perfect order that could represent the epitome of human social development. German idealism devoted significant effort to examining the idea of man's contingency. The findings, however, have been ultimately pessimistic. Kant argued the sheer impossibility of full knowledge in this world due to the unsurmountable physical constraints of the human body that determine perception and cognition. Hegel ultimately argued for the 'end of history', at which full knowledge is achievable, albeit at the cost of a significant transformation of human anthropology. Despite that, both Kant and Hegel granted humans an immortal rational soul. Hegel argued that this rational soul is the source of self-consciousness and that the soul finds its apex in the spirit, which unfolds over time towards greater self-consciousness and liberty (Pinkard 2002, 282; Bowle 1954, 39; Malia 1995, 29–30).

Marx placed the theoretical paradigm of German idealism on its head, for his teaching represented a radical departure from the theoretical division of life into the world of ideas and the world of action. Marxism challenged the Kantian idea of the sheer impossibility of full knowledge within this world and the Hegelian concept of the 'end of history' moved by the spirit. He brought humans to the centre of the political experience; and from that point of view, human abilities became endless. For Marx, human intellect was beyond bounds and the possibility of learning in the material world was within reach. Hence, the perfect order, the complete freedom of man, equality, and the transcendence of alienation was possible through reason and action. This would bring the final reconciliation of man with himself, with the world, and with others. Malia claims that, while Platonism, Christianity, and German idealism looked to the other world to achieve a fully self-identified and free state of man, Marxism promised to transcend the contingent state of man in this world. Malia (1994, 30) claims: 'German philosophy with its quasi-divinized idea of man could become a major force in the modern world only if it were translated into politics; and this Marx did.' Marx argued that the future is contingent on the creative energy of humans. The future represents the result of human choice and not the end of history as determined by the Hegelian spirit or any other unknown force of history. Viewed from this perspective, the complete liberation of humanity has become a possibility and an ultimate dream. Human abilities can become endless. Humans are able to learn nature, to change it, and to harness it to their needs (Kolakowski 2005).

Soviet Communism imbibed those theorizations in the socio-economic and political construction of life. Humans were considered to be the authors of their own fate. Nothing was out of reach. Conquering space, breaking the bounds of traditional physics, completing significant industrial projects – all became possible within the motivational narrative of the Soviet state. Humanistic ideals of friendship, comradeship, love, sincerity, and honour obtained new meanings and were not to be measured by the metrics of 'sale', useful and useless, as was often the case within the bounds of capitalist rationality (Zadornov 2017). That communist ideals rested on the foundation of social justice as opposed to the goals of financial gains arguably released the creative energies of the Soviet people. As the Russian Nobel Prize laureate in physics Zhores Alferov (2017b) argues, the Soviet public sphere promoted an ideal of knowledge instead of the myth of success. In this light, contemporary socialist thinkers, such as Alferov, Syomin (2015a), Kurginyan (in Vedeneev 2013, 72–3), and others, often claim that the Soviet people lost their sense of identity at a time when financial considerations superseded metaphysical ones (Alferov 2017b; Prokhanov 2019; Tretyakov 2019). The ideology of financial success, they continue, represents the main feature of capitalist societies; it is linked to physical self-indulgence and slowly steers people away from reason and rationality by swapping the order of human priorities (Alferov 2017a; Kurginyan, in Vedeneev 2013, 72). At the same time, socialists claim that metaphysical preferences (or 'mental pleasures' as Bertrand Russell [1946, 135] called them) drive human progress and give humans the chance to master nature and achieve progress in the realms of justice and equality.

The Critique of Post-Capitalism

Let us discuss the ways in which socialists criticize the existing capitalist order. Similar to the fundamental conservatives discussed in Chapter 4, Russian left-wing intellectuals depart from the analysis of contemporary Western society from the meta-theoretical point of view. Their search for the best possible organization of human community begins with the rejection of the Western postmodernist project, including its left-wing dimension, which, to their view, has been turned into a full-scale recasting of traditional humanism. Russian socialists and communists claim that the world is witnessing the emergence of a post-capitalist oligarchic system that threatens the future of humanity. These thinkers argue that the new system of post-capitalism betrays both classical capitalism and socialism. Moreover, Soviet socialism was competing against classical Weberian capitalism throughout the twentieth century, and from that point of view, the latter is considered a more humane opponent. It is often argued (Fursov, 2010) that post-war capitalism has been restrained by the greater need for the redistribution of wealth, an elaborate welfare state, the social solidarity of workers, the efficiency and functionality of trade unions, and the regulation of finance and elements of public ownership. Contemporary global capitalism escaped those bounds and began constructing the world according to its new principles. The new system refutes modern ideas of nation-states, the Protestant ethics of individualism and responsibility, and many important cardinal principles of the modern age that used to rest on the primacy of reason and personal restraint. The new system has become far more hawkish, power hungry, and anti-human. Such a critique is very similar to the ideas of the fundamental-conservative thinkers discussed at length in Chapter 4. However, it is necessary to consider a number of key points from the left-wing perspective.

First, Russian socialists argue that the political system that is now being established in the West and in Russia could logically gravitate towards fascism. These left-wing ideologues echo Karl Polanyi's thesis (1944) that the most probable destination of unrestrained global capitalism lies in fascism and not in communism achieved via a universal workers' revolt, as Karl Marx envisaged (Dale, 2017; Cornell, Moller, Skaaning, 2017). Polanyi claimed that when markets become 'dis-embedded' from their societies and create great social dislocations, people will revolt. Fascism becomes a natural deterrent to such revolts, for it pledges to restrain capital and instil social order. From this point of view, Polanyi reasoned that democracy could not survive an excessively free market, whose containment is the task of politics (Polanyi 1944; Kuttner 2018). Russia's left-wing thinkers, such as Sergei Kurginyan (2019b), Konstantin Syomin (2015b), Mikhail Delyagin (2014a), and others, follow a similar line by arguing that, without substantive changes to the current political course, global capitalism will result in the establishment of a fascist political system, both in the West and in the rest of the world.

This is primarily seen in the creation of a system of extreme inequality, in which economic wealth and political influence is concentrated in the hands of the few. Growing income disparity, politico-economic persuasion to reduce birth rates and postpone families, emerging rifts in the quality of medical services, and declining standards of education create a distinct division between the very narrow level of elites and the relatively deprived masses. Needless to say, this system suffers from a democratic deficit: the army of unelected professional officials, advisors, and experts who are the subjects of capital conduct decision-making behind closed doors. Public politics, on the other hand, is run via the instruments of moral panics, mobilization over trivial issues linked to identity politics or external threats, as well as thorough thought control implemented via the instrument of corporate media. Such a system will eventually be prying into and controlling all aspects of human life, making sure that everyone thinks, feels, and behaves in a uniform way.

Outside the West, such a fascist system will attempt to physically eliminate civilizations that stand in the way of the global control of markets. It will not be long before technical progress will allow the richest part of the globe to produce endlessly without relying much on human resources. This means that a large number of people from poorer states will not be needed for production and will become unnecessary from the point of view of global capitalism. Hence, wars and chaos will simultaneously resolve the task of dispensing with 'unwanted' masses of people (Syomin 2015a; Kurginyan, in Vedeneev 2013; Kurginyan 2018). In this light, Russian socialists call for the counter-mobilization of people around the world with the view to securing counter-hegemony. Representatives of different nationalities, religions, cultures, and beliefs from the West and beyond should come together in defence of their common interests of culture, civilization, economic equality, freedoms, and human dignity. The extent to which Russia's socialists propose to 'turn to the left' varies among differing thinkers. Konstantin Syomin (2015b), who is often considered as Trotskyist by his critics, such as Sergey Kurginyan, advocates a reversal to the Soviet experience at home and unification of all working classes around the world. Kurginyan (2018), on the other hand, speaks more along the Polanyi line, arguing in favour of establishing 'feasible' socialism.

Second, and following from the above, socialists argue that the new global capitalist system aims to recast the idea of the nation-state and state sovereignty. The notion of state sovereignty emerged at the dawn of modernity to buttress bourgeois nation-state capitalism. Russian left-wing critics argue that the new system of global capitalism moves away from this cornerstone concept, not only by creating supra-national bureaucratic organizations with double legitimacy and democratic deficit (an issue that has been well covered in the Western literature on globalization), but also by creating organized chaos in various parts of the world, with the Middle East being a prime example. Kurginyan (2015) argues that the main goal of this policy is to delay the modernization of those regions and instil political chaos there. In order to sustain control over the extant world markets, the global capitalist minority does not want the rest of the world's populations to modernize and so seeks to eliminate the main tool of modernization – the nation-state.

Third, Russia's left-wing critics also discuss the sphere of human anthropology, though their analysis of the matter is almost identical to the ideas of conservatives discussed in Chapter 3. Just like conservatives, socialists argue that the new post-capitalist system seeks to alter the traditional understanding of human nature to fit the needs of the markets, increase profits, and reduce the potential for genuine human solidarity and resistance. From this point of view, socialist thinkers argue that global capitalism has become increasingly incompatible with democracy and the very ideas of humanism. Russia's leading socialists insist that their political project must shake the triviality of identity politics, which is erroneously ascribed to the Western left but is deployed by global capitalism as a tool of public distraction from pressing economic matters of declining welfare, unfair redistribution of wealth, and inadequate social justice. Mikhail Delyagin, Sergei Kurginyan, and Mikhail Khazin (2018) uphold Europe's foundational ideals – the Christian understanding of human nature, the industrial ethics of professionalism, as well as responsibility and individualism in the modern (Weberian) understanding of those terms. Mikhail Delyagin argues that by doing so Russia could show the world that Europe could be different and that Europe still has the chance to retain her critical, rational, and reasonable spirit.

MAIN ACTORS AND POLITICAL ACTIVITY

Despite the initial expectations that the left-wing discourse could avoid the paradigmatic split on state traditionalism and liberal globalism, the left-wing scene has begun to diverge in this standard direction since the end of 2018. Two main factions have surfaced: left conservatives (or traditionalist left) and left globalists (liberal left). Both factions share the basic ideas and attitudes that we have examined above. Their differences lie in their attitude towards the extant Russian state and their choice of political alliances. Left traditionalists, who represent the majority of Russia's left political forces, refuse to depose Russia's extant political system in favour of establishing a new socialist paradigm. They also reject any politically expedient alliance with pro-Western liberals and liberal nationalists, despite being ideological fellow-travellers at some political junctions.

This approach is represented by Russia's main and largest left-wing movements and parties, such as the Communist Party of the Russian Federation (CPRF), the social democratic Just Russia Party, the Communist Party of Communists of Russia, led by Maksim Suraikin, and the left conservative political movement Essence of Time (*Sut Vremeni*), led by Sergey Kurginyan. These political forces are adamant in their general support of Russia's statehood, despite its numerous ills and failings, and this falls in line with their ideological commitment to the idea of state sovereignty. Such thinkers claim that deposing the extant government by revolutionary means would open the way to the global (US-led) takeover of the Russian state (Kurginyan, 2019a; Zyuganov, 2016). In that event, Russia would lose control over her nuclear weapons and subsequently her current statehood, territories, and resources, and would forever fall prey to the forces of external domination. This would invariably signify the end of contemporary Russia and the world as we know it in its current territorial and political form.

Another strand of the left-wing movement gravitates towards radical liberal or pro-Western liberal lines. This ideological dynamic had fully surfaced by the end of 2018 and is represented by the Left Front – an organization uniting left-wing internationalists; the The Other Russia (Drugaya Rossiya) party, led by Russia's eminent writer Eduard Limonov; the Party of Action (*Partiya Dela*); television journalist Konstantin Syomin and his political support groups; and various Internet discussion portals, such as *Vestnik Buri* (Storm Herald), Goblin (Dmitry Puchkov), Tubus Show, and others who have a substantial base of subscribers and followers. These activists argue in favour of a demolition of the extant Russian state and the construction of a new communist government on its ashes. In doing so, they refuse to support Russia's foreign-policy initiatives, such as those related to Crimea and Syria, arguing that aiding Russia's state interests abroad serves the interests of her ruling capitalist class and thereby perpetuates the exploitation of her people. By advancing those arguments, as well as calling for the working-class struggle world-wide, these activists are often considered Trotskyists or the globalist left in the Russian political scene.

The difference in approaches and priorities determines the nature of the political alliances and strategies of these respective currents of the Russian left wing. The globalist left often unites with various nationalist and radical liberal forces. Many of them support Alexey Navalny's liberal initiatives, as well as the work of the Open Russia Foundation, led and financed by Russia's exiled ex-oligarch Mikhail Khodorkovsky. They often adopt the radical-liberal political lexicon discussed in Chapter 2, in that both ideological currents have the goal of deposing the Russian state and radically changing the views of the Russian society. The globalist left organizes rallies in conjunction with radical liberals and nationalists in order to form a united front of radical opposition. The traditionalist-left faction, more-temperate and greater in numbers, refuses to forge an alliance with any pro-Western or globally minded forces. Traditionalist conservatives insist that monarchists, liberals, nationalists, as well as radical leftists have become a project of global capitalism, and co-operation with them would be tantamount to betrayal of Russia's national interests. An example of this strategy was seen during the 2011–12 protests, when left traditionalists openly declared their disagreement with Russia's political elites, but refused to support the pro-Western liberals (and radical leftists) who organized the White Ribbon movement. Traditionalist-left forces then forged a political alliance with conservatives based on their common resistance to the possibility of a pro-Western takeover of power.

Conservative left-wing movements also propose an alliance with the Russian Orthodox Church, despite the fact that the church represents a serious anti-communist force within Russian society. Both Gennady Zyuganov and Maxim Suraikin, leaders of the CPRF and Communists of Russia respectively, openly declared their friendly attitude towards the Church. Other conservative socialists argue that their political movements should work in unity with those who support the traditional religions of Christianity, Judaism, Islam, and Buddhism. The overtly anti-religious nature of global capitalism ensures that religious political groups could become at least situational allies of the traditionalist left.

To conclude, Russia's left-wing discourse is undergoing a period of formation and consolidation. The fact that large segments of Russia's population feel positive about the Soviet past provides left-wing advocates with the opportunity to break the extant paradigmatic rigidity within the ideological scene. If the split within the left does not fully go ahead, the left-wing political movement in general, supported by those who feel positive about the Soviet past, could appear as a third ideological segment, which houses elements of traditionalism but challenges the existing political system over its most important concerns with class, legitimacy of wealth, equality, social justice, and meritocracy.

6

Nationalism

BASIC THEORETICAL POSITIONS

Nationalist ideology has become increasingly important in the contemporary world, despite the efforts of globalism to create cosmopolitan forms of citizenship, reduce the role of the nation-state, and blur national administrative, cultural, and civilizational borders. Nationalism as an ideology continues to matter as the 'fundamental organizing principle of the inter-state order, as the ultimate source of political legitimacy, as a readily available cognitive and discursive frame, as the taken-for-granted context of everyday life' (Ozkirimli 2010, 2). Craig Calhoun has rightly pointed out that 'even if we are deeply critical of the nationalism we see, we should recognise the continued importance of national solidarities. Even if we wish for a more cosmopolitan world order, we should be realistic enough not to act on mere wishes' (Calhoun 2007, 1). Western academic literature on nationalism could be broadly divided into two main groups that view the root-cause of this phenomenon in a different light. The first group could be conditionally labelled as liberal-constructionist (or civic), while the second group is culture-bound, and therefore could be conditionally branded as conservative.

It is commonplace in the constructionist literature on nationalism to argue that nationalism was born with the onset of European modernity, when the nascent European bourgeoisie embarked on the destruction of the erstwhile European solidarities with a view to establishing well-defined borders, restraints, and parameters on the functioning of the emerging capitalist system of production. Nationalists then created their ideology, endowed with myths and histories to 'imagine' tightly knit national communities that could fight for a state that promotes their economic and political rights and freedoms. This line of thought compels leading theoreticians of nationalism, such as Gellner (2006) and Andersen (1989), to claim that the nation is an artificial, ideological, social construct, which appeared as the result of the disintegration of the feudal commune and the rapid modernization and industrialization of society. In this light, nationalists, who draft the main dimensions of state-constructing historical myths, emerge long before the nation.

If national communities are imagined, and only civic and logical considerations are taken into account while constructing the nations, it could be assumed that some patterns of nation-building, or ways of organizing socio-political life, are more efficient than others. This assumption led a number of nineteenth-century thinkers to claim, in various forms, the existence of more advanced groups, which were entitled to lead others into modernization, and therefore formed a national mechanism that could ensure such a development. Hegel, for example, draws a sharp distinction between the idea of a nation and a state. A national group can exist, according to Hegel, without ever succeeding in building a state. For Hegel, such a nation does not fully participate in world history, for a nation can only fulfil its true historical role if it is capable of creating a state and achieving true freedom. Hegel viewed such stateless nations as 'uncivilized people' with no history (*historyless* people), and since these people were not able to establish a state, they would perish in the stream of history (Nimni 1985, 107–9).

Marx and Engels, having moved from the outright internationalism of the *Communist Manifesto*, adopted the controversial Hegelian distinction between historical and non-historical nations. Historical nations are those capable of independent development and industrialization. Non-historical nations, on the other hand, are those that. without external help, would lag behind in the process of industrialization and capitalist development. Hence, they were supportive of Irish and Polish independence, arguing that both Ireland and Poland were nations capable of becoming industrially developed and independent without the assistance of the United Kingdom or Russia respectively. This approach was fully endorsed by the liberal camp. J.S. Mill, for example, divided nations into 'barbaric' or 'civilized' and argued that 'civilized' nations are those who are able to create an efficient institutional order and form a state, which in Mill's mind represented the minimal mechanism needed to ensure enlightenment, rights, and freedoms. Smaller and 'barbaric' nations that have not achieved a peak of civilizational and national maturity should have joined the civilized and progressive ones en route to historical progress and development (Kymlicka 1995; Hobson 2012). This approach *a priori* assumes some unified 'civilizing', an economically based pattern of development that must result in the development of a 'civic' (or liberal-constructionist) approach to nationalism and nation-building.

An alternative point of view claims that 'imagined' communities had their basis in an ethnic, linguistic, cultural, and communal tradition that served as a framework within which nationalism as an ideology could be fed (Smith 1986; 1991). Anthony Smith (1986; 1991) is often considered as the founding father of this methodological approach to the study of nationalism. This thinking largely grows out of the German Romantic school, in which Herder developed the theory of *Volkgeist* that stands by the distinctness of each and every nation and incommensurability of the world's political and social cultures. Such thinkers develop a cultural (conditionally conservative) approach to nations and ethnicity. They claim that the commune, with its traditions, myths, and behavioural patterns, ultimately serves as a matrix for the subsequent civic and nationalist community. In this way of thinking, all national cultures and particularities should be cherished, and no nation has the right to dictate to others which aspects of traditional life should be deconstructed in order for it to join the cohort of modern states. Herder claimed that there are no 'chosen people', no *Favorit-Volk*. He argued that 'no nationality has been solely designated by God as the chosen people on earth; above all we must seek the truth and cultivate the garden of the common good' (cited in Heater 1988, 79). Hence, modernity must have a multicultural character and a wealth of narratives embedded in the variety of ethnic communities and cultures.

This brief excursion into the particularities of nationalist thought allows us to deploy Kohn's (1958) division between 'civic' and 'political' nationalism and 'ethnic' and 'cultural' nationalism. He claimed that the predominance of each form of nationalism was characteristic of geographic areas of Europe. Hence, civic and political nationalism was prevalent in Britain, France, and the United States (the so-called Western world). Ethnic and cultural nationalism was a feature of the Eastern world, in which he grouped Germany, Russia, the countries of Eastern and Central Europe, as well as Asia. Regardless of the supposed geographic redistribution of these various forms of nationalism, we can see these two groups in contemporary Russia. Vladimir Pribylovsky (2015), pondering Russian nationalism, proposes a similar classification. He claims that Russian nationalism is divided into three important strands: (1) political, civic, or national democratic; (2) ethnic; and (3) state imperialist (conservative traditionalist). The first two strands of nationalism stand very close together, with the second group seeking to construct a civic nation-state with the ethnic Russian group at its heart. The third group is fundamentally distinct from the first two, and represents Russia's cultural-imperial nationalism. Therefore, this chapter will focus on a detailed analysis of political democratic nationalism and state imperial (or traditionalist) nationalism.

STATE IMPERIAL NATIONALISM

Valery Fadeyev (2014), an influential conservative Russian intellectual, follows Anthony Smith's line and states that, while some aspects of national consciousness can be constructed, they nevertheless stem from the depth of ethnic consciousness, shared history, language, and long-standing traditions. Fadeyev argues that Russia currently stands at a historic juncture at which she must 'choose' her national identity. Yet, this 'choice' is limited and a nationalist-ideological construction is not a sandcastle built out of the blue on a whim but something that should have a solid historical and social foundation. The 'choice' is seen in a number of historically cemented options that have been shaped and problematized throughout the course of Russia's evolution.

Referring to Andersen's theorizations, Fadeyev (2014) claims: 'it is not possible to "imagine" a national idea or national identity. It is only possible to extract it from the depth of people's collective unconscious – the contradictory, intuitive, and unconstructed.' From this point of view, Russia's state imperial nationalism is buttressed by two main doctrines: (1) the historical myth of Russia's Byzantium connections, and Russia's inheritance of the Byzantine civilization, and therefore of the Eastern Roman helm; (2) Eurasianism as an idea that Russia belongs to neither Europe nor Asia but exists as a separate historical-developmental space called Eurasia.

Eurasianism was developed at the beginning of the twentieth century by Prince N.M. Trubetskoy (1890–1938) and economist and geographer Peter Savitsky (1895–1965), who are often considered as the doctrine's founding fathers. Eminent historian Georgy V. Vernadsky (1877–1973), jurist and philosopher N. Alexeev (1879–1964), historian and theologian V.N. Il'in (1891–1974), theologian George Florovsky (1893–1979), and historian and philologist Vladimir Lamansky (1833–1914) were all key contributors. The doctrine rests on a set of cultural pluralistic and structuralist ideas that we have discussed in Chapter 4. Eurasianism's emphasis on cultural particularity, its rejection of the West and Western democracy as a political system suitable for Russia, enabled this doctrine to buttress the claim of Russia's political and historical distinctness.

The main contribution of Eurasianism to the state imperial nationalism is its legitimation of Russia as a self-sufficient civilization that has interests in both Europe and Asia and acts as a 'balance holder' between the two (Sakwa 2008, 379; Rangsimaporn 2006, 376–7). From this point of view, Eurasianism substantiated the notion of Russia's Great Power status, which was reflected in various official documents. The 1997 National Security Concept, as an example, termed Russia a 'European-Asian power', the foreign policy of which is determined by 'its unique strategic location on the Eurasian continent' (Rangsimaporn 2006, 377; Kontseptsiya Natsionalnoi Bezopasnosti 1998, 4). Subsequently, Eurasianism served as a tool of narrating Russia as a civilization, empire, and country-civilization that could only survive in the cohort of key international players (Kedmi 2019). Remaining within the paradigm of large spaces enabled Eurasianism to normalize the process of Empire-formation from a theoretical point of view in Russia and beyond. Laruelle (2007, 24) observes that Vasilii Barthold (1869–1930), an official historian of the Eurasian persuasion during both the Tsarist and Soviet periods, pressed for a 'cultural rapprochement between people from different origins' and argued that 'worldwide empires' represented an 'historical necessity'.

The place-of-development (*mestorazvitie*) concept introduced by Peter Savitsky (1997, 293) is perhaps one of the most fundamental Eurasian notions in consolidating state patriotic nationalism. The concept denotes the idea that the geographical place, its climate, and the environment is dialectically linked to its socio-cultural and historical evolution. Differing places of development produce correspondent cultural-historical types or civilizations. It is the idea that space conditions culture and politics and vice versa. From this point of view, the *mestorazvitie* of Russia represents a distinct socio-historic Eurasian realm that differs from Europe and Asia and corresponds geographically to the borders of the Russian Empire or the former Soviet Union (Vernadsky 1926, 35).

This spacial realm conditioned its inhabitants to create a special type of civilization with an imperial flavour that was established on the Eurasian landmass throughout centuries (Vernadsky 1926, 13). This concept treats Russia's statehood as a free-standing value, regardless of its existent political colouring. The latter is situational, invariably fleeting, and largely irrelevant for as long as it advances the logic of Eurasian space as a distinct inland Empire. The state could come across in the Tsarist, bourgeois, communist, or post-Soviet form. Regardless of the shape the actual state may take, the space will invariably influence the state's main actors to adopt the specific developmental logic of the place. This concept serves the purpose of linking the three periods of Russia's history: Imperial, Soviet, and post-Soviet, thus legitimizing Russia's extant state and its high geopolitical ambitions.

While Eurasianism is focused on vindicating Russia's overarching state aspirations in foreign policy, the idea of Russia's links to Byzantium is geared more towards narrating the country's position in Europe. I shall focus on this trend thereafter in more nuanced detail, in that this idea is somewhat older than Eurasianism and that relations with Europe reflect the historical and deeply held dilemmas that have had a large part in shaping Russia's discursive narratives and identity. The revival of interest in the Byzantine Empire and its cultural, religious, and historical impact on Russia's development compose the heart of the philosophical and eschatological elaborations made by Russia's state nationalists. These imperial nationalists argue that the Roman Empire did not fall under the attacks of barbarians and internal socio-political and religious turmoil. Instead, it simply moved towards Byzantium in the East, and Byzantium, in contrast to the Latin West, did not experience the Dark Ages (Nikonov, 2017a). During that period, Byzantium was a thriving empire and promoted learning, education and research, culture, art, and science. Russia's historical links to the Byzantine empire have become useful to numerous theorists of contemporary state nationalism that put forward the idea of Russia's political and cultural distinctness and her unique political and ethical model.

These historical theorizations lent philosophical foundations to Russia's perceived entitlement to an independent and usually missionary role in European affairs. The state has actively supported this idea and funded various media campaigns focused on researching the history of Byzantium and its historical links with Russia. A prominent

example is a multi-series televized dramatization of the life of Sophia
Palaeologus – a Byzantine princess who became the wife of Ivan III
and grandmother of Ivan IV, known as Ivan the Terrible in the West.
Similarly, a documentary series produced by Fr Andrey Shevkunov
promoted the idea of the Byzantine Empire as the spiritual and cultural cradle of Russia. An avalanche of print publications and media
discussions emerged to sustain this thesis. Russian historians and
public opinion-makers charge Byzantium with a crucial role in the
evolution of European and world affairs. They also view Russia's
Byzantine links as the cornerstone of both Russia's European-ness
and Russia's otherness.

How does Europe treat Byzantium? Western classicists, medieval
historians, and historians of Byzantium diverge in their assessments.
Many contemporary historians of Byzantium (Mathews 2010; Harris
2015; Herrin 2007; Frankopan 2012) insist that Byzantine art, culture,
and literature became the most significant bridge between ancient and
Renaissance Europe. Moreover, some authors go as far as to claim
that Byzantium contributed to the preservation of certain political
and educational systems that were later utilized in Western Europe.
As Herrin (2007, 322–3) insists, Byzantium was

> active, surprising and creative, as it reworked its prized traditions
> and heritage. It bequeathed the world an imperial system of gov-
> ernment built upon a trained civilian administration and tax
> system; a legal structure based on Roman law; a unique curricu-
> lum of secular education that preserved much of classical, pagan
> learning; orthodox theology, artistic expression and spiritual
> traditions enshrined in the Greek Church; and coronation and
> court rituals that had many imitators ... Without Byzantium,
> there would be no Europe.

These authors also lament that some European scholars have purposely neglected Byzantine history, hidden it from the public eye, and
shown it, particularly since the Enlightenment, as vulgar, unimportant,
despotic, and irrelevant (Harris 2015, 242; Herrin 2007, 321).

Through centuries of cultivation, the sceptical view of Enlightenment
scholars towards Byzantium (Gibbon 1998; Lecky 1868) has seeped
into contemporary studies (Meyendorff 1981; Dawson 1991; Harris
2015). This cohort of historians views Byzantium as an alien, insignificant, and dark period in the history of European affairs. Classicists

consider the 'Rome that did not fall' (Byzantium) as a preposterous replica of the once-great Roman Empire. Gibbon (1998) presents the Byzantium period as a betrayal of Antiquity and an era of historical stagnation and accumulation of political malpractice. Lecky (1868, 13) insists that there has been no 'other enduring civilization so absolutely destitute of all forms and elements of greatness, and none to which the epithet "mean" may be so emphatically applied.' A number of contemporary theologians argue that Byzantium made only cursory and weak contributions to the European Renaissance. They claim that, while Byzantium kept ancient Greek literature and some cultural traditions alive, there was no real ground for a true Renaissance. In turn, Byzantium sustained a 'tradition of peaceful, frequently inconsistent, and sometimes charmingly creative coexistence of cultural features of Greek antiquity with Christian faith and spirituality' (Meyendorff 1981, 121; see also Pelikan 1993, 3–21). Moreover, the culture of antiquity and contacts with ancient Greek works was found only among Byzantine elites.

Returning to our discussion on Russia, it does not come as a surprise that contemporary nationalist authors, such as Egor Kholmogorov, Valery Fadeyev, and others, side with the Western researchers discussed first. They also deploy the views of the second group as evidence of an organized conspiracy of the West against Russia and Russia's particular contributions to European debates and politics. This position becomes a convenient trump card in the nationalist mobilization of Russia; and it is within the context of this debate that such nationalist mobilization obtains a deep-seated metaphysical meaning.

Three main nationalist historical myths can be inferred from this reasoning. First, by transmitting religious and cultural traditions to Russia, Byzantium enabled Russia to make a thousand-year leap into European history and to level her culture with relevant European standards. Byzantium helped Russia to escape the fate of a deep European periphery, whose cultural and political centres are located in Britain, France, and Italy (Kholmogorov 2014b). Being an heir of Byzantium, which represented a distinct cultural-civilizational realm, allowed Russia to challenge Western Europe politically, philosophically, economically, and technologically. Second, Byzantium's particular imperial form of government transmitted itself to Russia and has become deeply entrenched in Russia's evolving political culture. Along with this imperialism came universal aspirations of grandeur and glory. Finally, and more importantly, following the fall of Constantinople and the declaration of Moscow as the Third Rome, Russia obtained an independent standing as a self-sufficient pole of political, religious, and cultural influence in Europe, as well as the centre of a civilizational alternative to the Latin European West.

To sum up, the 'Byzantine idea' legitimizes Russia's search for her special path and unique role in history. It fosters Russia's messianic sentiments centred around the preservation of the Orthodox Christian faith in political, cultural, and theological aspects. From this point of view, Russian state-imperialist nationalism has a particular Christian religious flavour. This factor detaches it from civic and political Western nationalism, which is focused on closed national communities 'imagined' through the onset of modernity and development of capitalism. Let us focus on these foundational myths, moving from religious to political and historical factors.

Theological and Cultural Focus

A religious focus in the historical and philosophical deliberation of state nationalists does not come as a surprise from a theoretical point of view. Societal norms, values, beliefs, along with cultural and behavioural patterns, rules, and perceptions invariably have a religious basis or evolve in a dialogue with pre-existing religious ideas. As Weber notes, 'even though we have dispensed with religious explanations for the rules of the game, the spectrum of religious morals is looming behind them' (Sitton 2003, 9–11). Sergei Bulgakov (1994, 23–4, 44), eminent Russian philosopher and theologian of the early twentieth century, argues that 'the foundations of the national idea are not merely ethnographic and historical, they are primarily religious and cultural; they are based on religio-cultural messianism, into which all conscious national feeling is necessarily cast.' Hence, it is often claimed that the transfer of knowledge from Byzantium to Russia took place mainly through the theological route. Fr John Meyendorff (1981, 122) argues that the 'overwhelming majority of the texts translated into Slavic languages over the centuries that followed baptism of the Rus was religious and ecclesiastic in character.'

Russian monastic libraries contain immense bodies of monastic literature, translations of fourteenth- and fifteenth-century Slavonic versions of works that are considered as the classics of Orthodox Christian spirituality. Russian monks read the same Fathers, the same lives of saints, as their Greek brothers. This placed Russian monasteries on a par with their Greek counterparts and reaffirmed Russia's spiritual connection with Byzantium. Furthermore, in the absence of any unquestioned political centre in medieval Russia, the Church preserved the unity of the nation, thus tying the ideas of national unity with the ideas of Christian universalism. This is partly the reason why many nineteenth-century exponents of Russia's nationalism – Fyodor Dostoyevsky, the Slavophile philosophers – understood the Russian idea in religious and cultural terms, envisaging a mission of universal salvation for the Russian Orthodox Church.

Contemporary Russian theologians and exponents of state nationalism continue this line. Yegor Kholmogorov argues that Russian traditionalist nationalism is driven and determined by Christian ideas and values, and thus it has a universal character. Kholmogorov, however, adopts a highly nuanced justification of this universalism. On the one hand, he argues against contemporary global universalism and claims that every form of nationalism must have a distinct ethnic core. He insists that the differences in cultures, languages, and expressions of ethnicity are natural to human beings. Kholmogorov, like many conservative writers of the nineteenth and early twentieth century before him, points at the tale of the Tower of Babel. It represents a story of human arrogance and ambition, which drove people to embark on a global project that blurred cultural, linguistic, and ethnic distinctions. This particular example crosscuts the Eurasian stream of reasoning, and it was first mentioned by Prince Trubetskoy in his philosophical defence of cultural diversity.

Arguing against the pressures of contemporary globalization, Kholmogorov states that attempts to break down the existing national boundaries by dispensing with the ideas of nationalism could result in a new Babel-like apocalypse. On the other hand, Russian nationalism, in Kholmogorov's mind, should not lead to the isolation of ethnic Russians and the political marginalization of Russia. Apart from the aforementioned ethnic core, Russian nationalism has a religious, and cultural, character. To that end, it becomes inclusive, thus allowing Russia to encompass various peoples and ethnic groups – notwithstanding their ethnic background. Given that the base of Russian state nationalism is contextualized in Orthodox Christianity, Russian-ness becomes an all-inclusive universal meaning that can unite people of different origins on a platform of religious fraternity.

In this light, a number of Russian state nationalists argue that Russia's mission is to preserve Christian values for the rest of the world. Common to this line of thought is the idea of Russia 'saving' Western Europe from decline and degradation. Many state-nationalist philosophers of the nineteenth century and beyond have pondered the question of which moral and ethical foundations could allow Europe to remain 'European'. Incidentally, these thinkers regard Christian values as genuinely European values – a point of view that many public intellectuals of Russia promote in numerous Russian media outlets (Mikhalkov 2015; Konchalovskiy 2019 and 2017; Tretyakov et al. 2009a; Nikonov, 2017a). They also harbour hopes that Russia is endowed with the mission of protecting wider European political and cultural heritage. Among this heritage are the Christian foundations of morality and a pluralistic approach to the organization of human life, as well as the negative foundations of liberty that stand in stark opposition to the positive pressures towards self-actualization pursued by the contemporary politics of identity. Fadeyev (2014), Shchipkov (2017), and other state nationalists argue that Russia is capable of guarding Europe's freedom from the pressures of globalization and of acting as an anchor of traditional (read Christian) European moral-ity. In this light, state nationalists claim that nationalism must be rooted in the idea of community, instead of the individual, as is the case with classical Western nationalism. As Alexander Shchipkov (2017) argues, Russia can only fulfil her historic mission of 'preserving Christian values for the rest of humanity' if Russians understand their nationalism from a communitarian, cultural, and religiously embedded point of view, and abstain from the idea of constructing a civic nation modelled on the theoretical blueprint of individual rights and freedoms envisaged by the European version of political nationalism.[1]

Hence, this political paradigm regards Orthodox Christianity as the basis for the contemporary Russian political nation. As Maxim Shevchenko (who is a frequent contributor to theological and religious debates, despite his socialist convictions) observes, 'Christianity pro-vides a far more serious basis to the formation of Russian democratic politics than does any secular ideology or movement' (Shevchenko 2008).[2] From this Christian point of view, Russian state nationalism has a universalist dimension. It rests on the idea of a spiritual, religious, cultural, and historic unity, and not on the conception of ethnic, blood-based, or even bourgeois civic affinity. From a practical political point of view, such imperial-state nationalists often claim that Russian nation-alism cannot be reduced to the rejection of migration from Central Asia and the extant populist demands of ethnic Russian nationalists to reduce financial resources channelled to the North Caucasus. In turn, Russian state nationalism demands that the state address Russian society as an historically cemented group of people and create a discourse based on those elements of Russia's history that could cater to her ambitions for international influence, domestic prosperity, cultural distinctness, and the uniqueness of her historic mission.

Cultural Distinctness, a Special Path, and an Historic Mission

Let us now discuss the state-nationalist myths relating to Russia's cultural and historic distinctness. As we have already observed, state-nationalist thinkers view Byzantium as the source of Russia's European roots, and to that end they consider Russia as an inheritor of the Hellenistic Greek era. Russia, in their mind, mirrors Western European civilization in the sense that both Russia and Europe share a common heritage in Antiquity. The two civilizational streams (Eastern European–Russian and Western European) parted ways when Constantinople succeeded Rome in 330 and consolidated the split when the Christian Church experienced the Great Schism of 1054. Nonetheless, the Greek-Roman-Celtic West and the Hellenistic-Byzantine-Slavic Russia remain two parallel, and intricately intertwined, civilizational branches of European heritage. Geographically, they share the continent. Intellectually, they sustain two thousand years of common culture and history that evolved via dialogue, conflict, co-operation, and competition (Kholmogorov 2016, 57; Narochnitskaya 2014).

In this light, Russia becomes distinct as a self-nominated leader of the Eastern stream of European Christianity, the alter ego of the West, and its perpetual dialogical partner in moral, ethical, and cultural reflection. State nationalists argue that, following the fall of Constantinople in 1453, Rus remained the only independent Orthodox Christian Empire, which reinforced her position as the possessor of a separate Eastern stream of European civilization and granted her specific 'civilizational' responsibilities (see also Toynbee, Vol. 2, 1946). Fadeyev (2014; see also Medvedev 2016) claims that, 'by declaring itself as the heir of the Byzantine state and the Third Rome, this small and insignificant East European state set itself a monumental mission, a global task of preserving Orthodox Christianity for the entire world.' State-nationalist writers explore a range of specific Eastern Christian traditions that enabled Russia to claim theological and spiritual 'distinctness' from the European West.

The *hesychast* monastic tradition was chosen as one such Orthodox doctrine that distinguished Eastern Christian spirituality from Western Christendom. The *hesychast* tradition signified a particular type of Christian practice that involved contemplative monastic life and specific exercises that involved spiritual prayer' (Fedotov 1950, 6; Ware 1997, 62-70). The practice enabled its followers to spiritually transcend their bodily sensations, approach God as closely as possible, and see the Divine and Uncreated Light, which three disciples saw surrounding Jesus at His Transfiguration. The practice caused a significant rift, known as the *Hesychast* Controversy, between Eastern and Western Christianity. The controversy torpedoed negotiations over the potential unification between Eastern and Western churches during the mid-fourteenth century and ensured that "Byzantium developed a distinctive spirituality which never had any parallel in the West" (Herrin 2007, 200).

The ideological conflict erupted between the Archbishop of Thessalonica, St Gregory Palamas (1296–1359), who was an active exponent of the *hesychast* doctrine, and the Italian monk Barlaam the Calabrian, a contemporary of Palamas, who travelled to Byzantium to explore the possibilities of uniting Eastern and Western churches. Palamas endorsed the use of bodily exercises in prayer by arguing that our body is not an enemy but a partner and collaborator with our soul. He further insisted that knowledge of God is possible through invoking His *energies* (not His *essence*, which still remains unapproachable) through such a prayer, and these energies take the form of Divine light (Ware 1997, 67–8; Herrin 2007, 200–1). In contrast to that, Barlaam insisted on God's otherness and unknowability and argued that God can only be known indirectly (Ware 1997, 66). Philosophically, Barlaam drew on the Aristotelianism of St Thomas Aquinas, or more precisely on nominalism, while the Palamite tradition was closer to Platonism and Neoplatonism (Herrin 2007, 200) – views that contributed to intellectual and political cultural trends within Western and Eastern Europe respectively.

In Russia, *hesychasm* became part and parcel of the country's religious, monastic, socio-cultural, and political life. In the religious sphere, *hesychasm* has made a decisive contribution to a renewal of Russian personal religiosity, individual prayer, and a more conscious understanding of a culture of Christianity. Meyendorff (1981, 142) argues that hypostatic union, Christological doctrine, and the notion of deification – all of which, one way or another, assume that divine life becomes accessible through the human flesh of Christ and of the saints – relies heavily on the theology of Palamite *hesychasm*. In the realm of culture, the incarnational message of Christianity expressed in the Palamite theology promoted the development of Orthodox Christian art and expensive decoration of churches. The Christological doctrine of Christ and the saints offering their human flesh as a path towards obtaining a divine life contributed to the proliferation of icon painting. Theophanes the Greek and his apprentice Andrey Rublev, both the exponents of the *hesychast* theology, left timeless masterpieces of Christian art and church adornments across Russia.

In the sphere of politics, *hesychasm* contributed to landmark historic events. Russia's political and national resurrection from the spiritual inertia inflicted by the Mongol domination began in the fourteenth century. It is important to note that the leaders of this revival were *hesychastic* monks, who 'had taken refuge in the virgin forests of northern Russia, where they lived a life of prayer and contemplation' (Fedotov 1950, 50). Prominent *hesychastic* monk St Sergius, a founder of the famous monastery of Holy Trinity, is often considered one of the most important state 'builders of Russia'. He rendered his services as a counsellor and advisor on spiritual as well as political matters to Russian princes, and was a faithful supporter of Moscow's princely line (Fedotov 1950, 50). St Sergius gave his blessing to Prince Demetrius of Moscow (Donskoi) for the battle of Kulikovo (1380), in which Russians were victorious over the Tatars. This date was officially considered the beginning of the end of Tatar-Mongol domination. St Sergius rose to the eminence of a national hero and a state builder of Muscovy.

Byzantine *hesychasm* also came to comprise the core of Russia's social-conservative values. It has become a consistent world view and a self-perception that came to form the basis of an ethical code seen in much of Russian literature and philosophy. Dostoyevsky's Father Zosima expresses the *hesychastic* world view in the following passage:

> Brothers, have no fear of men's sin. Love a man even in his sin, for that is the semblance of Divine Love and is the highest love on earth. Love all God's creation, the whole and every grain of

sand in it. Love every leaf, every ray of God's light. Love the
animals, love the plants, love everything. If you love everything,
you will perceive the divine mystery in things. Once you perceive
it, you will begin to comprehend it better every day.

Russia's foremost theologians and philosophers of the twentieth
century expressed similar ideas. Sergei Bulgakov, Simeon Frank, Peter
Florensky, and Nikolai Berdyaev all worked within the tradition of
brotherly love and compassion that could change the social fabric of
the world. These thinkers believed that the path towards Russia's
future lay in the spiritual revival of the Russian people and the resurrection of Russia's core traditions of compassionate humanism
(Berdyaev et. al 1994).

This 'unique' moral code becomes a justification for Russia's supposed 'special path' as espoused by theologians, philosophers, state
builders, and imperial state nationalists. Berdyaev underscored the
distinct nature of Russia's human anthropology from that of the West
in those terms. While the West is dominated by a Cartesian logical,
'thinking' Man, Russia expounds a sensitive, sentient Man. *Senito
ergo Sum* (I feel therefore I am), as opposed to the Western *cogito*
(think), is considered to be the motto of Russian ethical life, and once
again echoes the intellectual and philosophical rift between Aristotelian
Aquinas and Platonic Palamas. Sergei Bulgakov (1994, 24) proceeds
to criticize the ethics of rationality of the Western Enlightenment:

> The so-called Enlightenment of the seventeenth, eighteenth, and
> part of the nineteenth centuries is characterized in intellectual
> history as an intensification of the motifs of humanistic individu-
> alism. The Enlightenment drew the most negative conclusions
> from the premises of humanism: in the field of religion, by
> way of deism, it came to scepticism and atheism; in philosophy,
> through rationalism and empiricism, to positivism and material-
> ism; in ethics, through 'natural' morality, to utilitarianism and
> hedonism. Materialist socialism, too, can be viewed as the latest
> and ripest fruit of the Enlightenment.

Contemporary Russian nationalists utilize the historical, philosophical, and theological lessons of their intellectual predecessors. Some
authors claim that the *hesychastic* Christian tradition distinguishes
Russia from the West and grants it a special mission of transmitting

brotherly love and Christian ideals around the world. They argue that the ideational Platonic foundation of *heysychasm* causes Russia to diverge from the rest of Europe (Kholmogorov 2014a). Fadeyev (2014) suggests that Russia's Christian spirituality almost compels her to a constant search for a unique ideational path, higher justice, and absolute truth. Should Russia cease this search for a higher monolithic truth, which would once and for all resolve the problems of moral conduct, she would betray her spiritual roots and inflict imminent destruction upon herself. Fadeyev (2014) argues that Russia 'risks becoming an outcast in human history if she gives up her search for this unique path. Even though Russia is weak at the moment and the *hesychastic* world view is profoundly alien to the ideas of natural rights and political correctness, Russia must persevere in her search for her distinct future' (Fadeyev, 2014). Kholmogorov (2014a; 2016, 57) concurs that the need for a 'distinct future' has been conditioned by the fact that Russia inherited Byzantine religious and political traditions. He (2014) emphatically claims: 'Russia cannot exist as a remote European province, which the cultural and civilizational "radiation" of France and Britain reaches after it had reached Poland.'

Imperialism and Caesaropapism

It could be argued that the imperial inclinations of Russia's state nationalism also owe a great deal to Byzantine metaphysics. As we have already mentioned above, Byzantium bequeathed to the world an imperial form of government, yet this was a particular form of empire. Metaphysically, this form of imperial government is based on the Byzantine notion of *caesaropapism*. This concept regulates the relations between secular and ecclesiastic authorities and represents a significant deviation from the idealistically envisioned Justinian idea of *symphony* between church and state. The notion of *symphony* assumes close co-operation and coexistence between church and state, which represent the two separate but co-ordinate realms, independent within their respective spheres of influence. Under this scheme, the emperor, or *caesar*, and the patriarch are united in promoting Christian policies although they maintain their separate legal systems (Herrin, 2006, 79; Meyendorff 1974, 283). Together spiritual and secular powers work harmoniously, as opposed to existing in conflict and competition (Codevilla 2008, 121; Kharkhordin 2005, 48–51; Petro 1995, 61–70; Schmemann 1979, 41; Ware 1997, 41).

Caesaropapism diverges from the idea of *symphony* by introducing a rather more hierarchical relationship between the two entities and treating the role of the 'caesar' with greater reverence. During the thirteenth and early-fourteenth centuries, the emperor stood above the law and implemented the ideas of generosity (which allowed him to break civil law and adopt arbitrary decisions for the purposes of generosity) and sacral kingship (Angelov, 2006, 150–4).[3] The emperor had a decisive role in the appointment of the patriarch, as he chose among three candidates presented to him by the synod – the governing body of the Church (Meyendorff 1981, 86). Moreover, despite such coordination with the church, the emperor was considered the political head of the Christian world, promoting the imperial ideology in its realm (Meyendorff 1981, 12–13). As Patriarch Anthony of Constantinople claimed: 'It is not possible for Christians to have a church without an Emperor' (Meyendorff 1980, 264). There was an assumption that the end of the world (or the Antichrist) could not arrive as long as an emperor (*katechon*) who held power was at the head of the Christian Empire. Hence, the emperor was granted eschatological functions in order to *hold* the world together and guard it from apocalypse. The removal of an emperor would signify the end of the world and the arrival of the Antichrist.

As a result, there can only be one emperor across the imperial land, while various territorial units could have their separate patriarchs, which opened the way to a particular imperial structure that allowed multiple political institutional forms and religious interpretations. Different lands under the influence of Byzantium had their own patriarchs, while the emperor exerted supreme influence over the Kingdom of Byzantium. The kingdom's constituent units claimed political allegiance to the imperial centre and accepted court titles, but were not required to become exact replicas of the centre at the institutional and religious levels. Direct obedience was not requested for as long as the units endorsed the principle of a unique and universal Christian empire. The structure of the Eastern Orthodox Church in the centuries since Byzantium reminds us of this model: various ethnic Patriarchates, which could have some variation in tradition and practice, belong to a single Orthodox Church, with some such units forming part of a unified cultural and political space with the political centre in Moscow. More importantly, the spirit of imperial Russia's political system has been somewhat similar. Faithful acceptance of the imperial ideology asserting the unity of lands did not translate into the uniformity of religious, institutional, and cultural patterns. It now becomes clear why, in contrast to most Western European empires, the Russian empire fostered multiple political institutional models, as well as multiple religious domains.

Within this framework, the church has endorsed and sustained the state's main actors as long as their activities have been conducive to the task of *holding* the political empire.[4] The church endorsed members of the House of Romanov as holders of the Russian Empire, and then extended its support to the communist government in the form of the Metropolitan Sergey Declaration of 29 July 1927. At this time, it had become clear that the Communists could create a strong state and reassemble the lands of the erstwhile Russian Empire. (Having said that, this move resulted in the split of the Russian Orthodox Church and the formation of the Russian Orthodox Church Abroad.) During the post-Soviet period, the church selected and supported those political forces/factions, whose positions were the strongest and whose programme was geared towards the restoration of Russia's international influence and domestic stability (Petro 1995, 156). During the 1990s, the church forged strong political links with the Communist Party of the Russian Federation, when the latter held a majority in the State Duma (Shevchenko 2008). In the 2000s, the church has formed cordial links with the Putin government, extending its support to the idea of regaining Russia's geopolitical glory and economic development at home (Willems 2006).

It is important that the caesaropapistic idea led to an imperial, messianic, and civilizational perception of political life in Russia. It has also coloured Russian state nationalism. Patriarch Kirill of Russia (2013) endorses this approach by claiming that 'Russia is a synonym of Rus. We have a new geopolitical reality today. New independent states emerged in the vastness of Russia. Many of those states are also heirs to this historic Russia. Therefore, when I speak of Russia, I always mean this great civilizational space.' Kirill (2013) continues that Russia could provide a model of interethnic and interconfessional peace to the rest of the world, since Russian society has always functioned on the basis of a solidarity of people.

At the same time, this solidarity was only possible because of the specific nature of the Russian imperial state. The Russian Empire, Kirill argues, sustained the plurality of political institutional models, ethnic cultures, and religions. The cohesiveness of this political construction rested on the thin notion of adherence to the Russian throne and the idea of Russia as a great geopolitical entity. In contrast to the British Empire, Russia did not expect its dominions to adopt political and institutional systems similar to the metropolis. In turn, since the reign of Ivan the Terrible, Russia encouraged the development of ethnic languages, religions, and specific political institutions within the dominions that comprise its territorial borders (see Berdyaev 2008). Yet, despite those characteristics, Russia was an Empire, with Russians the core people and Orthodox Christianity a backbone of its institutional, cultural, historical, and religious framework (ibid.). Patriarch Kirill (2013) also accentuates the civilizational character of Russian state nationalism. Invoking Russia's cultural, theological, ethical, and ultimately geopolitical confrontation with the West, he argues:

> Very often those who deny our sacred sanctities and our values transpose their feelings on Russian people – the people that have become the main creators of our civilization and the carrier of its ideals. These forces attempt to sustain everything that aims to divide, weaken, and disorient Russian people morally. Above all, those circles fear the true revival of the Russian civilization; a revival that could take place on the basis of faith, life, and social solidarity (ibid.).

NON-SYSTEMIC OR DEMOCRATIC RUSSIAN NATIONALISM

Ideological Junctions with Western Nationalism

Non-systemic Russian nationalism, often referred to as 'political' or 'democratic' nationalism (Solovey 2016), is comprised of differing political trends with wide-ranging ideological positions. In the sphere of philosophical and ethical deliberations, political nationalism is reminiscent of classical Western nationalism. It praises individual responsibility, democracy, and a small and efficient state that defends the rights and freedoms of individuals. This nationalism repels the imperialism and grandeur of statist imperial nationalists and proposes a radically different political agenda. The intellectual apparatus of these thinkers is reliant on Western theorizations of nationalism and liberal democracy – factors that often move them into a close tactical alliance with liberals. Democratic nationalists often stress that nationalism and democracy are inseparable. This idea largely coincides with comparative theorizations on democratization which claim that mono-ethnic nation-states, due to the lack of internal fragmentation, are more successful in establishing democratic systems (Dahl 1998).

Russian nationalist democrats agree with Western interpretations that say the nation is a product of the bourgeois development that emerged at the dawn of the New Age as an antithesis to the Holy Roman Empire. The latter claimed to be 'larger' than any nation and, along with the Catholic Church, united the inhabitants of Europe, dictating to them common rules and norms. The crumbling of European traditional internationalism took place in the sixteenth century at the dawn of the Modern Age. This process took place against the backdrop of the socio-political transition from commune (*Gemeinschaft*) to community (*Gessellschaft*), accompanied by modernization, secularization, popular 'disenchantment' with the world, and the growth of a rational and logical appreciation of socio-political realities. As Carlton Hayes (1931, 4) notes, 'from the ruins of Empire and the wreckage of the church emerged the modern state system of Europe.' The nation-state is thus a cardinal feature of the modern age.

In this context, nationalism is bound to demolish ethnicity, for it creates and establishes *one* dominant language, *one* dominant culture, and dominant norms and customs, which are based on the language and traditions of the dominant group. This group is usually the most advanced economically and acts as a locomotive of industrial development. Hetcher (1975) insists that spatially uneven waves of modernization divide the population into relatively advanced and less advanced groups and compel the relatively advanced communities to set political, cultural, linguistic and other normative standards. Representatives of the 'core' or 'advanced' group seek to 'stabilize and monopolize its advantages through policies aiming at the institutionalization of the existing stratification system' (Hetcher 1975, 9). This invariably results in the destruction of smaller or 'backward' ethnicities and their saturation by the more 'advanced' cohort. These dynamics can be observed in almost all modern European nations: Germany, France, Britain, and the Scandinavian countries. Many of these countries have experienced a loss of their pre-existing ethnic diversity and richness and a merging into one coherent national group.

Furthermore, as a child of the Enlightenment, Western nationalism is tightly connected with the ideas of individual liberty and cosmopolitan rationalism. Nationalism becomes part of a social mechanism that upholds a social contract between state and society. Yet, only free, rational, and logical individuals can enter into such a contract. To that end, nationalism promotes the development of an emancipated bourgeoisie, city dwellers, professionals, small landholders, and other rational individuals that constitute the backbone of a nation-state. Through nationalism, this stratum conceptualizes its collective identity and entrusts the state to defend the rights and freedoms of its members in return for taking on a range of obligations and duties. In many ways, nationalism could also be regarded as a Hobbesian idea, in which the nation-state emerges as a constructed Leviathan that enables peoples of different groups to coexist peacefully within a single socio-political territorial unit. Hence, nationalists endow the state with much more significant socio-political functions than liberals do.[5] The nationalist approach to the state has a distinctly Hegelian flavour. The state is concerned with matters of war and peace, transmission of cultural and moral values, the defence of freedoms and liberties from outside interference, and the ensuring of justice, peace, and the public good at home. It represents the apex of human development, whose mission will never be exhausted, but only refined or redefined. For Western civic nationalists, the state has a modern, democratic, and bourgeois nature.

Returning to Russia, democratic nationalists embrace this Western nationalist theoretical paradigm and deploy it as a starting point for their deliberations on Russia's extant political order. These nationalists lay out their political programme in straightforward terms (Fefelov and Krylov 2012). First, they argue that *political* liberalism and democracy are the best forms of organizing human life. Much in the fashion of their Western counterparts, they regard individual liberty, rights, freedoms, and enlightened rationalism as the core principles worthy of cherishing and protecting. Second, they view the Russian state and its structural and political organization as an impediment in fulfilling those principles. They argue that the extant Russian state represents the source of trouble that has befallen Russia's society throughout the course of its history. Third, they wish to reorganize the Russian state in a national-democratic manner, which would involve territorial and political recasting. Such a recasting would require parting with the imperial ambitions of the Russian state in the domestic and international realms. In this light, anti-imperial struggle becomes the focal point of their political platform. They do, however, support irredentist claims of ethnic Russians in the international arena. Finally, democratic nationalists are sceptical about close collaboration with foreign, and in particular Western, powers that they consider a colonizing and domineering foe. Let us discuss those positions in detail.

Dialogue with Liberalism and Communitarianism

In terms of the liberal agenda, democratic nationalists claim a number of important points. They adhere to the idea of individual rights and freedoms as the most important precondition of a well-functioning political system. The package of essential rights espoused by Russian democratic nationalists converges with the principal rights and freedoms adopted in the West. National democrats select freedom of consciousness, freedom of speech, freedom of association, and freedom to form political organizations as the key concepts that buttress their desired state structure. They agree with liberals that such rights and freedoms must be granted to all citizens in a colour-blind fashion, that is, the rights must be granted to individuals, and not to representatives of ethnic groups. At the same time, there are significant nuances in the ways in which nationalists differ from their liberal colleagues.

Russian democratic nationalists clearly articulate that rules, duties, rights, and freedoms must be drafted and established by the majority. Western liberals usually remain silent on this point, which attracts a lot of criticism from their colleagues in the communitarian camp (Parekh, 2006; Kymlicka, 1995; Taylor, 1994). Communitarians argue that in approaching individual citizens in a colour-blind fashion, liberals inadvertently overlook the specific needs of minorities and groups. We will return to this subject in greater detail in Chapter 9, which deals with the ideology of multiculturalism. While Russian democratic nationalists side with liberals on the colour-blind implementation of rules, they claim that such colour-blindness is not an accidental theoretical omission but a deliberate political step. They hope that the colour-blind policy will be adopted at the state level, which should result in the majority drafting the rules of the game. The right to set the rules must belong to the ethnically based majority (Solovey 2016, Fefelov and Krylov 2012; Sergeyev 2017). Krylov (Fefelov and Krylov 2012) argues that liberties and freedoms, as well as the right to define them, are passed through generations, and the simplest benchmark of entitlement is one's bloodline. National democrats therefore claim that the Russian ethnic majority has the right to interpret history, determine the language of communication, draft administrative and electoral borders, and define the main dimensions of foreign and domestic policies. And while every citizen will be admitted to the system of state governance in a colour-blind fashion, most rights, freedoms, and political institutional constructions would cater to the needs of the Russian ethnic majority by default.

Democratic nationalists lament the current state of affairs in Russia, which in their view caters to the needs of Russia's ethnic minorities. This is seen in the grants made to ethnic republics (such as Chechnya and Bashkortostan), which have privileged access to state funding via specialized developmental programmes and sizeable economic subsidies. Democratic nationalists point out that the preferential treatment of minorities is also manifest in divergent legislation that allows ethnic regions to practise particular Islamic traditions related to polygyny and arranged (at times underage) marriages – traditions to which Russia's central state turns a blind eye.[6] Arguably, allowing greater, or specific, rights to minorities is conducted under the aegis of the metatheoretical idea of the pluricultural Russian Empire, in which all ethnic groups are left to pursue their cultural, religious, and political self-expression, while observing a loose allegiance to the centre. Democratic nationalists reject this paradigm, claiming that it results in *de facto* oppression of the Russian majority and in the cascading demands of various groups to expand their rights at the expense of the Russian ethnic group. Their views are somewhat reminiscent of Nathan Glazer's (1975, 200) theorizations on the United States, in which catering for past grievances of particular ethnic and racial groups could lead to granting them unreasonable preferences, arguably just for the time being, but subsequently enshrined in legislation. Hence, the aim of Russian democratic nationalists is to equalize the rights and freedoms of all Russian citizens through the 'elevation' of ethnic Russian rights to the level of the republics and other ethnic groups. Therefore, the equality of individual citizens is seen through the articulation of the colour-blind approach to rights, freedoms, and policies with the assumption that any such policy's 'colour' would have a default 'colour' of the Russian majority.

It is also crucially important that democratic nationalists want to enshrine the 'default colour' in the constitution by stressing that the Russian state is the state of the Russian people, and specifically omitting the extant affirmation of the multiethnic composition of Russia. Nationalists hope that this move influences various ethnic groups of the Russian Federation to join the Russian ethnic group, which, in their mind, should be open to everyone willing to join it. Nationalists also propose to expand the Russian majority numerically by granting Russian passports to all Russians that reside outside the borders of the Russian Federation and are entitled to Russian citizenship by birth (Fefelov and Krylov 2012). In particular, such citizenship must be granted to those who were born in the Russian Socialist Federated

Republic of the u s s r and moved to another Soviet Union republic prior to the breakup of the u s s r, thereby finding him/herself deprived of Russian citizenship.

Another important aspect of rights concerns immigration and settlement. Full rights, democratic nationalists argue, should be guaranteed to ethnic Russians only. The system of rights should have a hierarchical nature, based on a group's status. Groups should be distinguished between indigenous ethnic minorities and migrant minorities. It must be stressed that democratic nationalists propose to adopt the group hierarchy on the assumption that ethnic Russians comprise the majority of the population that establishes this very hierarchy. They argue that nationalism must serve as a framework, which guarantees and implements the rights of minorities (Fefelov and Krylov 2012). Russian democratic nationalists insist that the rights of minorities must be protected by specialist legislation (Kholmogorov 2014b). Minorities must receive all necessary protection of their local languages and culture. They should be allocated financial and political support in pursuing their ties with the diaspora abroad, as well as specific funds to preserve their culture and traditions. These steps must be assured in full compliance with the Framework Convention for the Protection of National Minorities (f c n m) and the European Charter for Regional or Minority Languages. This reasoning resonates with Western European theorizations on multiculturalism and ethnic justice, which we will fully discuss in Chapter 9. However, while Western liberal theorizing on the hierarchy of rights is aimed at achieving greater equality for all members of society, balancing the views of majorities and minorities, Russian nationalist-democrats speak from the position of a wronged majority seeking justice.

Criticism of the State

National democrats have developed some strong criticisms of the Russian state. They approach this problem from an historical perspective and argue that the contemporary organization of the Russian state, despite the novelty of its democratic structure, has inherited cardinal autocratic features of the past. They argue that, in ideal circumstances, democratic development rests first and foremost on the enlightening role of the state, in line with the Western theorizations discussed earlier. This enlightening role must involve the dissemination of democratic and liberal ideals in various sites of mass indoctrination, such as schools, churches, important social institutions, and the media. Nationalists argue that the Russian state has always propagated ideals hostile to Russia's democratic development (Sergeyev 2017). They blame the Russian state for disseminating false information on the nature of Russia and Russians, which ultimately lured the country into the catastrophes of the twentieth century and threw Russia off its 'normal' developmental track since the period of Ivan IV.

National democrats argue that the Russian state has always claimed that Russian people are 'natural monarchists', and to that end they do not need rights and freedoms on a par with other European nations. Hence, the idea of state rule unrestricted by the people led to the formation of despotic and non-democratic regimes throughout Russia's long history. The Russian state, democratic nationalists further insist, has always argued that Russians do not desire material wealth but are geared towards higher spiritual values and strive to follow their invented mission of 'saving humanity' and finding 'absolute justice' (Prokhanov's work [2016] is often cited as an example). The Russian state, nationalists continue, is persuaded that Russians are not the rightful owners of Russia but of a specific nation that 'glues' the country, along with its multifarious ethnic groups, into one geopolitical unit. Russians, the state has reasoned, are long-suffering and patient people who are called to shoulder the burden of the Empire obediently and are prepared to suffer in the name of their supposed higher mission (Sergeyev 2017; Fefelov and Krylov 2012). In this light, national-democratic critics call for an impending reorganization of the Russian state. The state is to abandon its imperial ambitions and its desires to 'hold' ethnic enclaves within its realm at all costs. This is likely to mean the loss of some North Caucasian and other ethnic territories that may wish to leave the federation. This nationalist-democratic doctrine is close to Yeltsin's early ideas that strove towards political democracy and economic prosperity by parting with constituent republics of the Soviet Union at the expense of the USSR's *de facto* imperial nature.

Democratic nationalists also criticize the Russian state for its supposed ties with Western global capital, which, in the view of many such activists, have colonized Russia. At this point, we must highlight an intellectual dualism of Russian democratic nationalists. On the one hand, some Western researchers of Russian nationalism claim that the main ideological vector of these activists is geared towards the Westernization of Russia. Laruelle (2014; Laruelle 2010) claims that new generations of nationalist activists have emerged: younger, speaking foreign languages, able to travel abroad with connections to their Western European and American counterparts, and wanting to anchor their own narrative within more globalized ideological trends, they increasingly advocate for a Europeanization of Russian nationalist values.

This is largely true, particularly in light of our earlier theorizations on the metaphysics of Western nationalism and its Russian counterpart. On the other hand, nationalists suffer from the painful realization of Russia's perceived backwardness and her ideological, cultural, and economic 'colonization' by the West.

Democratic nationalists are aware that Russia largely borrowed political institutions, ideological constructions, and economic patterns of modernity from Western European states. In this light, they resent the West as a source of intellectual and economic domination. Yet, they also look up to it, seeking the best methods of political institutional organization and political ideas. This dualistic attitude to the West is illuminated through the attitudes of democratic nationalists to specific historic figures. While admiring Western institutional structures, national democrats negatively assess Peter I for his sweeping reforms and overzealous Westernization of Russia. At the same time, they admire Nicholas I and Alexander III – the heroes of Russia's traditionalists – for their conservative policies and promotion of the Russian language and culture (Krylov and Kalashnikov 2013). In Russia, such attitudes to these historic personalities are indicative of a thinker's ideological predisposition and could be considered a benchmark of subconscious and deeply held views towards the West and Westernization. It would be difficult to encounter a pro-Western Russian liberal who would be critical of Peter the Great's policies and assessed the rules of Nicholas I and Alexander III positively. Yet, such positions are widespread among Russian nationalist democrats – a fact that testifies to their deep-seated suspicion of the West and Russia's supposed Westernization.

More importantly, these thinkers criticize the Bolsheviks for their purely European and Germanic origins, for entertaining the global political ambitions of global revolution, and for restructuring the nascent Russian nation-state into an internationalist Empire tightly locked in intellectual and economic dialogue with the West. They often speak regretfully about Soviet social and economic policies that resulted in a profound Westernization of the Russian mind. As Solovey and Solovey (2009) write, the Communists, 'within seventy years of their rule, objectively, and without any subjective intentions, achieved wide-scale Westernization of the Russian mind – something that the Romanovs were unable to achieve during the three hundred years of their governance.' They are fearful of the West taking away Russia's territorial space and resources, and claim that the creation of the Russian nation is necessary to ensure that Russians will succeed in their struggle with the West for such space and resources (Fursov 2014).

Consequently, the most radical representatives of the nationalist-democratic paradigm observe that Russia's ideological discourse is torn between liberal and statist-patriotic paths. These nationalists also blame the Kremlin for indecisiveness in refusing the liberal path. They often invoke the political failures of Viktor Yanukovich, ex-president of Ukraine, who was pursuing a policy of European integration combined with economic and political association with Russia. To them, this inconsistency ultimately led to Yanukovich's demise, just as the Kremlin's inconsistency towards domestic liberals and the West could result in the arrival of radical pro-Western politicians in the Kremlin in a *maidan*-like fashion (Strelkov 2016a; Strelkov 2016b). Many radical representatives of the nationalist-democratic camp claim that the Kremlin must steer in an unequivocally patriotic, even revanchist, direction and abandon its futile attempts of reaching a dialogical balance with the liberals (Limonov 2016; Krylov and Kalashnikov 2013). It is unacceptable, they claim, that the statists' discourse contains substantial chunks of Western ideology and liberalism, and that this ideology is presented in Russia's main media channels and state policies. Russia, in their view, must move steadily towards a national revival and cease 'appeasing' the West by openly declaring it as an existential rival rather than a dialogical partner.

Anti-Imperialism

An anti-imperialist struggle is the cornerstone of the nationalist-democratic doctrine. Nationalists agree with conservatives and liberals that nation-building requires individual and national maturity (Fefelov and Krylov 2012). Imperialism or civilization-building, on the other hand, is buttressed by emotional and intellectual immaturity that rests on pure faith in poorly defined ideals, as well as the partial abandonment of rationality and logic. Indeed, many Russian conservative thinkers also observe that the processes of constructing a nation-state and empire-civilization have radically different eschatologies (Mezhuyev 2016).

Following J.S. Mill, Boris Mezhuyev (2016) reminds us that nations require some form of civic maturity that signifies the 'passing of traditional society', the end of barbarity, and the negation of 'nature' by a 'republican order' in order to deploy Kant's theorizations. Simultaneously, a nation sees its collective goals in the dialogical transfer of culture, knowledge, and ethics, as well as in the preservation of its political integrity, thus rebelling against the idea of universalizing political institutional forms. The apex of this process lies in the creation of an efficient and well-functioning nation-state.

Civilization, on the other hand, is a starkly different category and demands the opposite dynamic. Civilization necessitates a *faith* in the unclear-but-predestined End of History that binds participant peoples in a universal push towards creating their unique order, peace, and happiness. That historic push requires participants to develop a universal logic in the application of political forms and to exercise a common *Kultur*, to use the Fichtean idea, which expresses true common goals of unity. This approach renders a transcendental flavour to the very notion of civilization. In contrast to the rigid rationality of a nation, civilization requires mere *faith* in the natural ability of civilization's participants to accept their chosen universal order based on the goodness of their chosen epistemology. The movement of civilization through time represents the will of history itself, whose true intentions and logic are unknown to the participants (Mezhuyev 2016).

In this light, small and compact European nation-states with a clearly defined future and clearly defined political goals represent an eschatological ideal for Russian democratic nationalists. They argue that Russian nationalism 'could become a vehicle of Russia's return to her European roots ... This could become a means of destruction of the utopian idea of the multi-national Soviet people and endorse a European-style Russian nation-state building' (Milov 2016). This invariably leads to an ideological struggle between Russian nationalists and those who still espouse the Soviet or Russian imperial mentality. Nationalists lament the fact that the Russian Empire was built before the Russian nation-state and that the imperial consciousness was substituted for national consciousness – a line that continued with the USSR.

At the same time, the anti-imperial claims of Russia's nationalist democrats stop short before a number of ideological hurdles. Despite their strong dislike of the empire as a political form of organizing the Russian state, these thinkers agree on the need to support the irredentist claims of ethnic Russians across the former Soviet Union. For example, Russian nationalists invariably refer to Northern Kazakhstan, a sizeable Russian ethnic enclave established in Kazakhstan after the Soviet redrafting of republican borders in 1939 (Solzhenitsyn 1990), as Southern Siberia. Similarly, Russian nationalists ardently supported the 2014 incorporation of Crimea into the Russian Federation and the insurgency in Eastern Ukraine, whose ultimate, albeit unachieved, goal is to join the Russian Federation. Being overtly sceptical and even hostile to the idea of Eurasian integration and the Eurasian Economic Union, Russian democratic nationalists insist that the unity between the Russian Federation, Ukraine, and Belarus is an historic necessity. Some nationalists, such as Alexei Navalny, Egor Prosvirnin, and others, claim that all those nations form essentially one people, or Russian super-ethnos (Laruelle 2012; Prosvirnin 2014).

MAIN ACTORS AND POLITICAL ACTIVITY

The main problem of Russian nationalism in general, and democratic nationalism in particular, is that the state partakes in nationalist movements. By doing so it co-opts cadres from both streams of nationalism and provides them with strong ties to political state structures and legal enforcement agencies (Solovey 2016; Kurginyan 2014 in Tolstoy). This does not come as a surprise, given that most legal enforcement agencies are staffed with patriotically minded people who would gladly lend their support to the nationalist ideology. The co-operation between various state structures and nationalist activists impedes the formation of a force that is self-sufficient and independent from state nationalists, with a clear political platform. Another problem is that, despite being buttressed by the silent support of financial elites and security services, nationalist ideology is gradually losing its grip over Russia's societal and political ground. Researchers of this trend (Solovey 2016) claim that by 2016 nationalists had become so marginalized and fragmented that they could not meaningfully discuss participation in parliamentary or regional elections. This happened for a variety of reasons that could come down to the emerging rift with the Kremlin, a parting of ways with the liberals, and the events in Crimea that altered the entire discursive scene in Russia.

As for the Kremlin, following the initial success of the Russian March in 2005 (an annual Moscow rally of nationalists), it sensed the danger associated with unleashing the nationalist force. The failure of nationalists to protest against the West and their preoccupation with the problems of internal immigration (the Russian Marches were dominated by the Movement Against Illegal Migration [Dvizhenie Protiv Nelegalnoi Immigratsil – DPNI] and not by anti-Western movements) indicated that, instead of protecting Russia's political regime from potential Western interference, this force tended to turn its guns against the Kremlin itself. The first signs of rupture between the Kremlin and nationalists took place in 2007–08, soon after the state adopted a range of punitive measures against ethnic hatred and extremism (Chebankova 2013). The immigration process was systematized; the judicial review for racial crimes was revised and expanded; and the possibilities for the dissemination of xenophobic literature were restricted. Political nationalists then fully emerged as a stronghold of opposition to the Kremlin.

Of particular importance have been the Movement Against Illegal Migration (recognized as extremist and banned in April 2011), the National Bolshevik Party, which was also recognized as extremist and transformed into the Other Russia Party (*Drugaya Rossiya*) in 2010, the Party of Freedom (dissolved in 2009), and many other radical nationalist movements. Some members of less-radical nationalist parties, even state nationalists, have also become renowned critics of the Kremlin. The Russian All-People's Union, a political movement headed by politician Sergey Baburin, hold state-nationalist views and took part in almost all rallies of the radical opposition. The same could be said of the Congress of Russian Communes (*Kongress Russkikh Obshchin*) and the Motherland (*Rodina*) party that emerged from it. These are Russian state-nationalist-conservative organizations, with intimate links to Russian elites. The Motherland Party is unofficially headed by Dmitry Rogozin, one of Russia's top-ranking officials, who openly suggested in 2011 that Putin should join the Congress of Russian Communes movement. Rogozin also took part in the formation of the Great Russia Party (*Velikaya Rossiya*) in 2007, which failed to obtain an official registration, despite promoting state-nationalist views. At the same time, the intellectual public leaders of these three movements – such as Konstantin Krylov, the leader of the Russian

Public Movement (*Rossiiskoe Obshchestvennoe Dvizhenie*), and Andrey Savelyev, the leader the Great Russia (*Velikaya Rossiya*) party – have been the most outspoken proponents of the liberal nationalist-democratic ideology that stands against the Russian state. It is interesting that Savelyev was also working with Rogozin within the *Rodina* party in 2004–05 and was a State Duma Deputy representing *Rodina* between 2003 and 2007.

Following their split with the Kremlin, nationalists had a chance to unite with liberals and form a single front against the statists who controlled the dominant discourse. It is not surprising that, during the December 2011 protests, opposition liberals united with nationalists to form a single anti-Kremlin front (Laruelle 2012). The nationalist cohort as a whole hoped to capitalize on the failures and shortcomings of the Kremlin's policies in the international arena – souring relationships with the West, as well as in the state's failures in the domestic field – by pointing to the problems of corruption and economic crisis. These groups promoted two broad agendas that have been generally approved by the liberals. The first agenda focused on the relationship between the central Russian regions and the North Caucasus and advanced the 'Stop Feeding the Caucasus' campaign, which was supported by some influential liberal figures such as Stanislav Belkovsky, Alexey Navalny, Igor Iurgens, Evgeny Gontmakher, and many others. The second agenda was a general anti-immigration campaign geared towards the introduction of a visa regime with the Central Asian republics.

However, events in Crimea and the subsequent civil war in Donbas turned the tables radically and virtually obliterated this discourse. A large number of nationalists initially supported the 2014 *Maidan* revolution, attracted to the fact that their Ukrainian equals played a decisive role in the radical change of the Ukrainian political regime. Yet they quickly faced disappointment, for it transpired that the Ukrainian revolution had an anti-Russian ideological colouring, which was unacceptable to the nationalists (Limonov 2016). The subsequent outbreak of bloody conflict in Eastern Ukraine led this group to adopt a radically pro-Russian agenda, arguing in favour of Russia's direct military involvement in order to rescue the 'Russian world' in Eastern Ukraine. This policy, however, resulted in further disappointment, for it transpired that the real mobilization potential of Russian nationalists was minimal. Nationalists failed to mobilize the general public domestically and could not attract a substantial number of volunteers who would agree to fight for the 'Russian world' in Donbas (Solovey

2016). This was mainly linked to the fact that Russia's general public was not in favour of the country's direct military involvement in the conflict, but wished to support the Russian population in Eastern Ukraine, both politically and rhetorically.[7] This led to a significant narrowing of the discursive niche in which nationalists could engage.

It is also important that the political field previously occupied by the revanchist ideologists has been gradually taken over by moderate liberals and statists. Following the failure of the December 2011 protests, moderate liberals began rhetorically appealing to socially significant values by praising patriotism, 'love of the motherland', and the development of the welfare state. This trend deepened in the wake of events in Crimea. Then, the overwhelming majority of Russians backed the Kremlin's move to incorporate the region into the bounds of the Russian Federation, and by doing so squeezed the liberal support base. The statists also accelerated their patriotic rhetoric, seeing it as a useful tactical instrument in the struggle for a dominant position in the discourse. Sergey Karaganov (2016), professor of International Relations in the Moscow Higher School of Economics, argued in March 2016 that contemporary Russia still remains a non-ideological state, thus adhering to our initial proposition of paradigmatic pluralism. Yet, Karaganov (2016) argued, Russia possessed two consolidating concepts: sovereignty and defence. Those two ideas have been united under the overarching notion of 'patriotism'. This change within the main discursive stream has deprived nationalists of their usual rhetoric.

An important indication of the fragmentation and weakness of this nationalist force was its attempt to unite into a single group, setting aside profound ideological differences. The 25 January Committee, established in January 2016, represents a union of extremely diverse and largely incompatible forces. It includes nationalist monarchists, led by Igor Strelkov, radical national-democrats, represented by Konstantin Krylov, national-Bolsheviks, led by Eduard Limonov, ultra-nationalist-fascists such as Egor Prosvirnin, and oppositionist former security-service officers, such as Anatoly Nesmiyan. Diverse ideologically, this group supports the irredentist claims of ethnic Russians in the post-Soviet space and the idea of establishing an ethnic Russian state based on the principles of justice, legality, and equality.

The committee is driven by a mutual suspicion of the West and the search for internal enemies within Russia's state apparatus. Assessing the ideology of its participants and the goals of the movement, prominent Russian journalist Konstantin Syomin (2016b) claimed it has similarities to the initial aspirations of the ideologues of the Third Reich and the Russian Liberation Army, pointing at their messianic stance, habitual advocacy of erstwhile German fascism, and unification around the 'heroic' figure of Igor Strelkov. The slide of Russia's nationalist discourse, from a formerly viable political force to a marginalized group of intellectuals driven by dubious aspirations, is perhaps unfortunate for those who wished to create a sustainable political paradigm based on Russian democratic nationalism. Yet, their current discursive and political weakness suggests that the arrival of representatives of this paradigm in the highest echelons of Russia's power structure is highly unlikely, even at a time of economic and political crisis.

To conclude, Russian nationalism is deeply divided into two competing groups, which contradict each other on many important positions. The first group espouses imperial, cultural, and civilizational ideas and looks back at Russia's historical links with Byzantium. This group of thinkers researches cardinal elements of Russia's Christian religiosity and defends the ideas of Russian imperialism, its special path and strong authoritarian state. The second group belongs to the Western nationalist-democratic cohort. It argues against the ideas of imperialism, the multiethnic and multinational composition of the state, and the civilizational course of Russia's development. Instead, ity offers to create a compact nation-state in place of the contemporary Russian Federation, at the expense of territorial integrity, if necessary. Both strands of thought generate some serious concerns over their proposed policies. If any of these intellectual lines are taken to their logical and extreme conclusion, the political consequences could be devastating, not only for Russia but also for Europe.

7

Multipolar World Order Ideas

MAIN POSITIONS AND ACTORS

Deliberations on the nature of the extant world order are becoming increasingly important in the global political discourse. Two competing interpretations dominate this debate. The first is seen in the idea of unipolarity, buttressed by the global advance of liberal democracy and capitalism. The second interpretation lies in the idea of multipolarity, which advocates multiple centres of political and economic influence. The existence of these multiple centres of influence is sustained by normative pluralism in cultural and ideological spheres and a multiplicity of political forms in the institutional area. The arrival of the multipolar discourse in in the international arena is defined by the fact that the American-led Western hegemony is being challenged in the discursive, economic, and military spheres. The world is being increasingly divided into subjective spheres of influence, and the erstwhile hegemony of the Western realm is in need of redefinition. The prospect of having to share global power could lead to a confrontation and invokes a range of contradictions. These are the contradictions between hegemony and multipolarity; between globalization and identity politics; as well as between social justice and globalization of the economy. More importantly, some forms of civilizational confrontation, invoked by substantive differences in the discursive-cultural realms, require the development of meaningful forms of civilizational realism.

This confrontation will require political management, because new conditions are difficult to comprehend using existent theories of international relations. Despite being engaged in the polarity discourse for some decades (Waltz 1979; Deutsch and Singer 1964; Krauthammer

1991), the literature on international relations is generally confused over developments taking place in this sphere. The relations between major powers have a significant impact in shaping the nature of the global order, and therefore the number and nature of major centres of power are likely to be important structural factors in world politics. Thus, the development of an ideology that could legitimize the practice of managing the newly emerging civilizational realism has become a necessity. Russia's official line (National Security Concept 2000), as well as her major ideological paradigm of traditionalism, considers the multipolar world order an ideal model of international relations, grounded in the normative principles of equality, fairness, plurality of cultures, and the 'great variety of interests' of the modern world. The idea of constructing a multipolar world order took on key metaphysical and political significance in the Russian public discourse during the period of Yevgeny Primakov's diplomacy (1996–98). It has subsequently turned into an official foreign-policy doctrine with Vladimir Putin's accession to power. The fact that these ideas often coincide with the official position of the Russian state makes the discussion of the ideological foundations of this doctrine ever more important. It is a doctrine that informs Russia's international conduct, as well as a theory/discursive practice that Russia wants to offer to the world as a means of fulfilling new alternative hegemonic ambitions. From this point of view, the newly emerging theories about world polarity in Russia represent an important strand of thought that needs to be examined within the framework of Russia's intellectual ideological landscape and political theoretical landscape.

We could argue that this theme sits between the rubrics of ideology and political theory. At the same time, it could still be contextualized within the discussion of Russia's ideologies, because its normative and theoretical foundations rest on metaphysical approaches to the organization of human life. Its principles look to the future, legitimizing existent political actions that challenge normative conventions of the age, and developing a theory of political change (all of which falls into the toolkit of ideology, according to Martin Seliger's classical propositions made in 1976). At the political level, these ideas are enshrined in *Russia's Foreign Policy Doctrines*, issued in 2008, 2013, and 2016 (The Foreign Policy Concept of the Russian Federation 2016). At the theoretical level, such ideas are attempting to recast classical approaches to the study of international relations, even though they combine the elements of the realist school on the structure of power as well as the English and constructivist schools on perceptions of power, agency, and performativity.

This chapter examines the main dimensions of the ideological conventions that uphold the emergence of the multipolar world order. It departs from the discussion of the chasm between the universal and particular as discussed by Western philosophers, emphasizing those authors that advocate the particular. The focus then shifts towards historical Russian debates of a similar nature and deliberations over the significance of cultures and civilizations in human evolution. The final section examines Russia's contemporary reflections on the multipolar world order and its main practical dimensions. Given that multipolarity is called on to address the limitations of the unipolar world order, the chapter concludes with a metatheoretical analysis of problems posed by both architectures of international affairs.

DEBATES WITHIN WESTERN LITERATURE: IN DEFENCE OF PARTICULARITY

The moral and philosophical core of the multipolar world order evolves from the Western philosophical debate over the universal and the particular.[1] This chasm stems from modernity's efforts to devise a universal political arrangement for human collectives via logical deduction. Most recently this belief was demonstrated in Francis Fukuyama's famous text *The End of History*, written after the end of Cold War in 1992. This work stated that history had come to its logical conclusion, because humanity was finally able to deduce the most harmonious world order, based on the ideals of liberal democracy and progress. When the subsequent reality showed that the universal spread of these ideals had stagnated, some policy-makers attempted to encourage it politically and militarily. This led to turmoil in various areas, clearly demonstrating that the end of history remained a distant goal and that alternative metaphysical deliberations were necessary.

A plethora of Western writers and intellectuals called for reconsideration of the use of political theory and the philosophy of ethics in the practice of international relations. The argument was that a sense of egoism began to reign in contemporary inter-state interaction at the expense of considerations of justice, ethics, and morality (Lebow 2003, 16; M. Williams 2005, 4–6). Such justice and ethics demand the recognition of various regional and state interests, as well as the recognition of difference in the world's political cultures (Kissinger 2014;

Lieven and Hulsman 2007; Kaplan 2002; Kagan 2003). Broadly speaking, we began witnessing a deepening of the intellectual chasm between the ideologies of universalism and particularity. Universalism looks at the possibility of summing up the experience of human beings and binding it into a totality of universally applicable laws. In contrast, the ideas of particularity see the development of a tightly knit political community that can only be judged by the standards of its internal culture and history. This chasm transfers the discussion of international *relations* theory to the discussion on international *political* theory (Shilliam 2009; Brown et al. 2002; Beitz 1979; Linklater 1982; Williams 2007). International-relations theorists opened broad dialogues with writers on political philosophy, invoking the logic of Aristotle, Machiavelli, Burke, Weber, Kant, Hegel, Foucault, Strauss, Schmitt, Oakeshott, and others. This debate builds upon a never-ending series of 'hidden dialogues'.concerning fundamental meanings of truth and knowledge, freedom and responsibility, ethics and justice.

With the emergence of the Cambridge School of Historiography (led by Quentin Skinner, John Dunn, and J.G.A. Pocock), a philosophical approach to knowledge has become increasingly contextual, thus somewhat exonerating the ideas of particularity. As we have already mentioned in the introduction, Skinner contends that knowledge is not produced in the framework of a search for a universal philosophical position, but as an exercise conducted within a specific context (Skinner 2002, Vol. 2, 104–5; Shilliam 2009, 10; Tully 1988, 5–8; Ward 2007). The contemporary postmodern and poststructuralist socio-intellectual environment further reinforces the dependence of an observer on the context (Lyotard 1979). Foucault (1977, 38) goes further than anyone by 'depriving authors of significant agency and claiming that the "author" *qua* subject disappears and that "the subject (and its substitutes) must be stripped of its creative role and analysed as a complex and variable function of discourse."' (Ward 2007, 242; Shilliam 2009, 11; Foucault 2002, 112–16; Foucault 1991, 144–6 and 148–9).

The Cambridge School and its related ideas unleash debates with liberal universalists (such as Leo Strauss), who often claim to uphold some ubiquitous principles of transcendent 'morality'. The realist opponents of this liberal position claim that the idea of different moral foundations within different cultures, as well as an awareness of context dependence, represents a moral position in *itself*. It is a position of mutual recognition and respect, which prevents a full-scale conflict. In this light, Isaiah Berlin's observation that Machiavellian values are moral but not Christian raises the possibility of several just-but-incompatible value systems existing side by side (Kaplan 2002, 62; see also Gray 1995). Weber, the 'first modern thinker to systematically develop a realist approach to international relations' (Smith 1990, 15–16), proposed the study of the international environment with the assumption that one could not mount value comparisons across different cultural systems and that each system had to be critically appreciated by its own standards (Barkawi 1998, 163; Shilliam 207, 128).

Morgenthau, on whom Weber had formative intellectual reach (Barkawi 1998; Pichler 1998; Turner and Mazur 2009), sustains this position. He (1948a, 267–9) argues that, despite the hopes of the liberals, there is no agreement on ethics, but only ethical frameworks that arise from specific contexts defined by nationalist experiences. His criticism of the universalist claims of the most prominent political players in the world throughout the twentieth century indicates his pessimism at the very possibility of drafting a single international order based on uniform morality. It is also important that many Western writers consider the universalist approach immoral, arguing that its purpose is to deceive the world by using its favoured ethical project as a cover to pursue hidden interests. E.H. Carr (2001), for example, criticized 'utopian moralising as a strategy employed by the 'haves' against the 'have-nots'." Just like Morgenthau, Carr connects this with the introduction of politics, in which the two poles with competing universalist claims advanced their positions in the Third World, meanwhile expanding their political, economic, and trading interests in those areas.

As a final point, intellectual efforts to use this approach to devise a more stable world order rest on the idea that societies should develop freely according to their own histories and distinct moral and political paths. Some societies may be liberal-democratic, some monarchic, some republican, some autocratic. In some ways, the defence of the particular gives rise to the idea of large civilizational coalitions that would unite states with similar cultural, historical, and political patterns, as Schmitt and Huntington each envisaged independently. At the same time, this is not the idea of cultural relativism, in that relativism draws a mistaken conclusion over the nature of the relationship between differing societies by expecting members of other societies to accept practices that seem vulgar or unacceptable to them (Williams 1972). Two major differences from relativism can therefore be inferred. First, disagreement with the moral principles of other societies is the right of any society. Second, there is a fundamental layer of the rules of morality that, however thin and generic it may be, is applicable to the human community as a whole. From this point of view, accepting violent atrocities, gross violations of human body integrity, and other fundamental forms of security, could be considered as a vulgar deprivation of other societies' very idea of being human.

These Western debates have had a critical influence on the development of the Russian contemporary school of international relations that took a decisive turn towards the particular and the contextual in the vein of the classical realism of E.H. Carr, Kissinger, Morgenthau, and others (Bordachev et al. 2015; Tsygankov 2016). Yet, prior to dealing with Russia's contemporary ideas, let me discuss Russian historical philosophy, which made its own significant contribution to the defence of cultural-political particularity.

RUSSIAN HISTORICAL PARALLELS

Traditionally Russian philosophy leaned towards particularity, which resulted in the idea of cultural alliances and civilizations as the main units of international political conduct. It was originally envisaged that societies could organize into distinct civilizational cultural coalitions, and such civilizational coalitions could be engaged in a constructive intercivilizational dialogue and exchange. Apart from Western deliberations on this subject, nineteenth-century Russian theorizations could be viewed giving birth to those ideas. As we previously observed, Russia's intellectual life in that age had been split into two competing groups: Westerners (P. Chaadaev, T.N. Granovsky, V.G. Belinsky, A.I. Hertzen, N.P. Ogarev, K.D. Kavelin) and Slavophiles (I. Kirievsky, A. Khomiakov, the Aksakov brothers, Iu. Samarin, N. Danilevsky, K. Leontyev). Westerners admired and supported the European developmental path. Slavophiles revered a distinctly Russian way of life and developed a thesis on Russia as an independent civilization distinct from Europe in the religious, cultural, and socio-political sense (Walicki 1979, 93–9).[2] At the same time, lenience towards cultural particularity at the expense of universalism was a distinct tradition of nineteenth-century Russian philosophy across both spectra.

While the Slavophile stance on the multiplicity of politico-cultural forms is self-evident, some Westerners also criticized universality. Many such thinkers, including Peter Chaadaev (Maslin 2008, 129–30; see his letters to A.I. Turgenev, written in the mid-1930s in Chaadaev

1991) and revolutionary socialists such as Chernyshevsky, did entertain, at some points in their lives, the idea of Russia's civilizational
distinctness – something that divorces them from Russia's contemporary radical liberals and proponents of global universalism whose
ideas we discussed in Chapter 2.[3] Decembrists, ideological precursors
of the Westerners, believed, in a similar vein to the German idealistic
approach, that while there can be a universal standard of freedom
developed by external civilizations, it is up to the national spirit, love
of the fatherland, and patriotism, to set Russia on the path of
Enlightenment. As Christoff (1970, 118) writes, 'beneath the richness
and complexity of ideas and ideological currents and crosscurrents
in Russia during the first three decades of the nineteenth century,
there throbbed a third and most vital heart. It was the focus on the
Russian individual and national self-consciousness, and in it and
through it the Decembrists sought a solution to Russia's major problem, that of freedom.'

These thinkers searched the Russian spirit in the process of enlightenment, reproducing the Hegelian idea of *Volksgeist* (Copleston 1986,
23–4; Walicki 1979, 93; Miscevic 2008). Venevitinov (cited in Christoff
1970, 99) writes: 'among all independent nations, enlightenment
developed from, so to say, a patriotic principle. Once their products
had achieved even a certain degree of perfection and as a consequence
had entered into the composition of the universal achievements of
the mind, they did not lose their distinctive character.' Rajevskii,
Kjuxel'beker, and Odoevskji all advocated the development of Russian
culture and philosophy that would not be a blind copy of French,
German, or English counterparts but would 'inscribe the Russian spirit
in the history of the human mind' (Christoff 1970, 108).

Yet, in their advocacy of cultural particularity, neither Slavophiles
nor Westerners deployed the terms of political geography. They pondered the epistemology of the Russian space, focusing solely on the
specificity of its religious, cultural, and socio-political forms. They
did not pay attention to the spatial dimension of world cultures and
their implications for political relationships between states. Russian
pochvenniki, who are considered more recent and more mature
Slavophiles, worked with these ideas via a civilizational analysis
of the world's geographic areas – ideas that sustain Russia's subsequent theorizations on the multipolar world. Nikolay Strakhov and
Nikolay Danilevsky were pioneers in this field (Kline 1968; Kelly
1999).[4] Strakhov and Danilevsky examined civilizational geography

through the idea of cultural-historical forms. Danilvesky believed that civilizations, like humans, undergo various stages of evolution, seen in inception, development, maturing, and decay. He distinguished ten existing cultural-historical forms or civilizations: Egyptian, Chinese, Assyrian-Babylonian, Indian, Iranian, Jewish, Greek, Roman, neo-Semitic or Arabian, and Germanic-Roman or European. The eleventh type was Russian-Slavic, which Danilevsky believed, was in the process of inception during the nineteenth century (Christoff 1991, 406–18; Kline 1985, 194). This theory is similar to Huntington's 'clash of civilisations' thesis. Yet, it allows some additional conclusions that are consequential to the development of the multipolar world order and to contemporary ideas of multiculturalism.

First, Danilevsky stresses the importance of examining the distinctness and originality of existing world cultures. It is important that the comparison of cultures is conducted on the basis of a culture's structures and developmental laws, and not on 'external' achievements. This idea is close to the contemporary 'politics of recognition' advanced in the twentieth century by the multicultural theories of Charles Taylor (see the following chapter) and to the Cambridge School spectrum of ideas discussed earlier. Second, Danilevsky insists that people's traditions and customs buttress the uniqueness of all cultures and must be cherished. Third, he warned against the danger of mimicking and imitating other cultures. This again reminds us of the Taylorian (1994, 31) 'politics of recognition', in which 'a *volk* should be true to itself, that is to its own culture. Germans should not try to be derivative and (inevitably) second-rate Frenchmen ... The Slavic peoples had to find their own path. And European colonialism ought to be rolled back to give the peoples of what we now call the Third World their chance to be themselves unimpeded.' Finally, Danilevsky refuted a claim that one culture (in particular the European one) has an absolute universal value (Belov 2010, 12–13) – a thesis endorsed by many contemporary critics of Eurocentrism (Hobson, Eisenstadt, Gray, Williams, Parekh) and the realist international-relations thinkers discussed earlier. In this light, many Russian intellectuals (Mezhuyev 2016; Tretyakov 2016; Bordachev et al. 2015) claim that Danilvesky's ideas could be invoked in the defence of the equality of the world's political cultures and defence of their peaceful coexistence, mutual questioning, and recognition.

It is important that some Western historians of ideas (Walicki 1979, 114; Christoff 1991, 406–18; Ryazanovsky 2005; Kelly 1999,

154–5; Coplestone 1986; Kline 1985; Duncan 2000, 30–47) charge Danilevsky and Strakhov with pan-Slavism and nationalism. We may, however, argue that Danilevsky did not believe that the eschatological task of the Slavs was in finding the right solution for all of humankind. In turn, many Western positivist philosophers and policymakers of the nineteenth century shared this ambition in the framework of European colonialism (Kymlicka 1995, 52–3). Danilevsky, on the other hand, believed that the Slavs must organize their own civilization in such a manner that it would be capable of developing alongside other historical-cultural forms. While Russians were indeed to be the leaders of their civilization (a thesis that allowed his critics to accuse him of nationalism), this idea still laid a foundation for a multipolar vision of the world, in which various countries of a similar cultural and historical path could merge into larger civilizations and develop these civilizations into the main subjects of history. Danilevsky was the first to touch upon geographic issues and the legitimacy of the use of power outside civilizational borders. Departing from Danilevsky's theorizations, Strakhov considered the Polish revolt of 1863 as entirely legitimate. Poland, in Strakhov's view, belonged to the West European civilization, and it was unjust to hold it within the bounds of the Russian civilization (Belov 2010). Hence, he did not believe in the moral virtue of crushing the uprising. This raises a more significant question of the proportionality of state power and its moral significance – an issue discussed by Morgenthau, Weber, and Schmitt that remains topical in many modern conflicts in which success in military warfare is rarely matched by political, moral, and discursive achievements.

This thought gave rise to early Eurasianism, which advocates cultural particularity from a territorial and geographical point of view. As a distinct method of thought, Eurasianism also had a general philosophical application, for it exerted intellectual influence on structuralism through the work of Roman Jakobson (1896–1982), as well as on various strands of conservatism and nationalism that we discussed earlier. Prince Trubetskoy, one of the founding fathers of Eurasianism, granted to cultural diversity an almost divine nature. He deployed the Tower of Babel tale to argue that the Bible preferred a variety of languages to just one – an argument deployed by state nationalists examined in Chapter 6. Trubetskoi viewed cultural and linguistic homogeneity as a sin that led to spiritual emptiness and the arrogant project of erecting the Tower. The ensuing 'confounding of languages', which was essentially an imposition of cultural diversity, was not a curse but a benign solution given to humanity in order to prevent it from the sin of cultural homogeneity (Ryasanovksy 1993; Miscevic 2008, 94; see also Chapter 6).

Eurasianism concurs with the claims of the Cambridge School that knowledge, beauty, and ideas are contingent on the socio-historical and cultural context. Based on this, Eurasianism concludes that the world must be viewed as a multiplicity of civilizations, each of which exists within its own time, deploying its own taxonomy of goods and traditions and relying on its own incommensurable value systems. Those civilizations survive synchronically, being scattered throughout space and undergoing differing stages of inception, growth, and decline. From this follows Eurasianism's criticism of the modernist idea of progress, in which each stage of human development is superior to its predecessor. They claim that such an understanding represents a socially constructed myth that judges a culture's achievements by an external measure. This myth states that the social being is a function of time and that each stage of human development internalizes the best from its predecessor and creates new and superior forms of being.

CONTEMPORARY RUSSIAN DEBATES ON THE MULTIPOLAR WORLD

Let us now examine the conclusions drawn from the lessons of Western and Russian thought by those contemporary Russian intellectuals who advocate a multipolar world order. The definition of a *pole* of influence is perhaps the cardinal point. Upon it would depend the future construction of the multipolar world order. There are a number of potential forms that could be considered as a way of constructing a multipolar world architechture. Multiregionalism, polycentrism, great power management, balance of power, and multilateralism are the leading models pondered by scholars of international relations and governments, both in Russia and the West (Morozov and Makarychev, 2011, 357). Great power management, or a 'concert of power' (advocated by a number of Russian realists [see Nikonov, 2017b; Dugin 2013]) departs from the idea that poles of influence are constructed on the basis of leading great-power countries that will agree to manage the world collectively. In this situation, leading centres of power are bound to resolve a range of global problems in union, often bypassing the opinion of smaller secondary states. In the case of the balance-of-power model, the system is also run by a handful of leader states, albeit geared towards avoidance of conflict. The overall construction therefore generally lacks a meaningful dialogue and co-operation (Haas, 2008, 45).

Multilateralism is focused on the functioning of international institutions dominated by a number of strong countries who draft the rules of global development, trade, and inter-state relationships (Makarychev and Morozov, 2011, 353). Polycentrism, in a similar fashion to multilateralism, assumes that states are no longer central actors of international order. In this situation, however, states take much less responsibility, moving the centre of international influence to a territorially dispersed multi-layered and globalized power in the shape of non-state actors, international organizations, outlets of civil society, and – where necessary – leading states (Scholte, 2004; Gul, 2009). Such centres, lodged in different geographical realms, would co-operate and manage the system of international relations, deploying the means of intellectual and cultural soft power, as well as coercive methods of sustaining discipline – such as pre-emptive strikes conducted by common military networks and rigorously enforced WTO trade regulations (Haas 1958, 213–14; Haas, 2008, 44). Russian observers view this model as a logical continuation of the unipolar world order and an argument for a new, only subtler, *type* of unipolarity. They argue that this model departs from the assumption that peace in such a model could be achieved only if most countries have adopted a liberal-democratic (or invariably Western) path of development (Dugin 2013; Bogaturov 1999, 28; Kedmi and Satanovsky 2017). Hence, the idea of polycentrism is almost absent from the Russian understanding of the multipolar world order.

Finally, multiregionalism, or *dialogue of civilizations*, represents a multipolar-world-order option favoured by the official Russian state and its leading intellectuals (Primakov, 2003; Kazarinova 2017; Yakunin 2017; see also Tsymbursky 2007 and Mezhuyev 2016 on civilizational realism). The global community, these intellectuals insist, developed the need to adopt checks and balances in the international arena and to establish a set of international laws applicable for all. Every country must take part in establishing those rules. Cultures must be respected, and no one country, or group of countries, can claim superiority in the spheres of politics and culture. All countries must be able to decide which cultural, trading, and political union or alliance they would like to join and they must be able to choose their institutional frameworks on the basis of their history and culture (Russian Foreign Policy Concept 2016). Yakunin (2017) argues that the dialogue of civilizations advances the idea of 'unity in diversity', interdependence, and 'infrastructuralism'. He insists on communication between civil societies within different countries that do not necessarily share similar cultures and values but are prepared to listen to and interrogate each other's positions and engage in a constructive dialogue in order to build dialogical bridges between countries and peoples.

The emphasis on cultural distinctness and civilizational dialogue among world communities leads to further development of the notion of *civilization* as the subject of international politics. This is perhaps the cardinal difference between multipolar-world-order theory and its rational, critical, and postmodern counterparts. Contemporary Western theories of international relations propose the state (realism and liberalism) or international discourse (postmodernism and critical theory) or social class (Marxism) as the main subject of international relations. Multipolar world ideologists such as Bordachev, Dugin, Fursov, Leontyev, Kholmogorov, Tsymbursky, and others shift away from this understanding and consider civilizations as a new subject of international politics.

At this point it is important to discriminate between theoretical and practical dimensions of multipolarity. The difference stems from the impact that the idea of civilization as a subject of international politics has on the idea of state sovereignty. At the theoretical level, the multipolar approach to the world tends towards a diminished state sovereignty within the framework of cultural-civilizational alliances. Sovereignty, as it presently stands, is a category that must be transcended in the future in favour of sovereignty of the alliance or *civilizational sovereignty*. However, at a practical level, recasting the idea of state sovereignty seems premature. Taken from this point of view, multipolarity could be considered an argument for a strengthened role of the state. This latter practical position falls in line with the position of Russian officials and intellectuals who ardently defend nation-state sovereignty. From this point of view, practical multipolarity considers state sovereignty as a transitory ally and an expedient instrument for preserving cultural distinctness and self-standing in the rapidly globalizing world. Let us examine the reasoning of both sides of the multipolar world theory spectra more closely.

Sovereignty and Civilization: Theoretical Dimensions

At the theoretical level, taking civilizations as the main actors of international relations would necessitate a precise definition of 'civilization' in terms of size, borders, and structures of internal governance. To define a civilization in the most flexible terms, Dugin proposes to deploy the Platonian notion of *politeia* – which represents a political unit of unidentified size (a city, a country, or a union of countries). A civilization can then be viewed as an imprecise form that unites a number of countries on the basis of their culture, history, philosophy, traditions, and religious consciousness. From this it follows that a civilization, as a cultural political union, would require the process of regional integration and redefinition of sovereignty as a result.

From a philosophical point of view, moving away from the idea of state sovereignty to the notion of *civilizational sovereignty* partly rests on English School theorizations. This is because the English School questions the nature of state sovereignty in the contemporary world and implies that the division of states into varying categories is based on their ability to influence the discourse of international relations. At the international level, the English School views sovereignty as the ability to pursue an independent course of action within the given social environment of a state's interaction (Manning 1975; James 1986). English School advocates claim that order between sovereign states is sustained via international institutions that involve established social practices of interaction and a variety of non-state and non-territorial actors (Manning 1975, 177 and 201; Bull 2000, 252; James 1986). Ikenberry and Kupchan (1990, 292) stress the role of international organizations erected by hegemonic states that lead the alliance: 'through frequent participation in the institutions ... elites in secondary states are exposed to and may eventually embrace the norms and value orientations that those institutions embody.'

Indeed, much of Western literature on international relations (of various persuasions) argues that the socialization of secondary states by hegemonic nations within a given sphere of influence plays a serious role in altering the political atmosphere at home, influencing norms, value orientations, and policy preferences (Waltz, 1979, 127–8; Rowe and Torjesen 2009, 2; Ikenberry and Kupchan, 1990). Deutsch and Singer (1964, 392) insist that: 'as a nation enters into the standard coalition it is much less of a free agent than it was while non-aligned. That is, its alliance partners now exercise an inhibiting effect – or perhaps even a veto – upon its freedom to interact with non-alliance nations.' Hence, the multipolar world arrangement could expect some form of diminished sovereignty from member states of other civilizational alliances, but endorse full sovereignty of an alliance as a cultural and political union and a member of the world political process. This process is closely intertwined with the proliferation of international rules in the economic sphere. It is also accompanied by the *de facto* division of countries into rich industrialized states that determine the parameters of interactive practice and peripheral poorer areas that have to follow the established rules (Suganami 2010).

This dynamic concurs with the suspicions of E.H. Carr, Morgenthau, and other writers, such as Desch, Owen, Oren, and Williams, who posit that, since the world order is buttressed by the system of sociopolitical interaction among states, this order must benefit the powerful within the system. Here, Russian intellectuals follow the ideas of Western thinkers in believing that the social narrative is intimately linked to power. Hence, those countries that are able to influence the interactive discourse within the society of supposedly sovereign states would have a privileged position in drafting the rules of conduct for the others (Ivashov 2015, 775–7; Russian Foreign Policy Concept, 2016; Dugin, 2013). Russian intellectuals, much in the vein of their Western colleagues, lament the fact that this path would compel states to comply with global, and thereby America-centred, standards of political behaviour, on both the domestic and international scenes. Moving towards such a system, they argue, would invariably lead to a homogenization of political norms and forms across the globe – a process they could not agree with when armed with the Western and Russian historical theorizations examined above. This essentially violates the principles of the Westphalian system, in which all sovereign states are considered equal (Bogaturov 1999, 40; Lavrov, 2015). This arrangement also compels weaker states to function within a system run by rules in which they had no active hand in drafting.

Multipolar world theorizations deploy these ideas advocating civilizational integration of states based on a state's cultural and political similarities. Such integration, this theory claims, would help weaker states to obtain more of a voice in the process of drafting a world-order discourse. It could also explain the weakening of state sovereignty and its replacement with *civilizational (or alliance) sovereignty*. In this light, 'pluralism of civilizations' becomes a cardinal value in the Russian interpretation of the multipolar world model. Each civilization, it is argued, must have the right to its own value system and its particular path of development (Yakunin 2017). International anarchy can therefore be considered as the anarchy of civilizations as opposed to the anarchy of states, which, according to the English School of international relations, is becoming increasingly obsolete. Once we accept the civilizational interpretation of international reality, the Euro-Atlantic civilization loses its claim to universality and obtains a local character. Other civilizations may adopt what they see fit from the Euro-Atlantic experience and cast aside what they deem harmful to their existence.

This thought echoes the arguments of many of the Slavophiles and *pochvenniki*. In particular, it continues Danilevsky's theorizations on selective transfer of knowledge in the course of inter-civilizational evolution. These theorizations claim that civilizations could selectively borrow those elements from other civilizations which they deem useful and discard those they consider inapplicable. Such ideas would ensure that civilizations will remain in a dialogue, but a critical and mutually interrogating dialogue. The relationship between civilizations would therefore rest on the concept of normative pluralism and the multiplicity of cultural and political forms (Sakwa 2015, 557–8).

Sovereignty and Civilization: Practical Dimensions

From a practical point of view, the redrafting of the idea of sovereignty would invariably entail a significant recasting of the extant world order. Russian officials view a strong state as a vehicle for stability and continuous economic development. Hence, at the practical level, they would be reluctant to curb the state, even within the framework of multipolarity. Russia's Minister of Foreign Affairs Lavrov (2015) argues that state sovereignty, and the ability to sustain the multiplicity of cultural and political forms based on sovereignty, remains the cornerstone of international security and lasting peace. A substantial section of Western literature concurs with this Russian understanding and insists that, under multipolarity, quite different domestic systems are considered legitimate. This exonerates states' flexibility of action and is in contrast to unipolar or bipolar arrangements that require a strict ideological adherence of states to a chosen political system (Vayrynen 1995).

Indeed, in a multipolar world environment, smaller states obtain a more significant status derived from their greater room for manoeuvring between the existing poles of influence (Deutsch and Singer 1964,

394). Given that no hegemonic state exerts a commanding influence on the general international climate, the socializing effect under multipolar systems is markedly weaker than under unipolar or bipolar ones. This could partly explain the fact that there is more tolerance towards 'deviant' behaviour within domestic political systems (Vayrynen 1995, 362–3). Under multipolarity, hegemons would rather seek compliance via non-coercive means of persuasion, using soft power, media, and non-state actors. Hence, under the multipolar arrangement, ideological and political pressures exerted on secondary states by a hegemon become less significant.

This means that, at the practical level, multipolarity attempts to sustain the extant world order based on the Westphalian systems, with some minor-yet-consequential modifications. It adopts a somewhat conservative outlook, seeing this arrangement as a transitory alliance *en route* to the full-fledged practice of civilizational multipolarity consisting of the strong regional alliances advocated at the theoretical-ideological level. Let me reiterate that the extant order is based on five main principles: (1) the Westphalian notion of state sovereignty; (2) the formal assumption that the United Nations is the most important international institution; (3) the fact that composition of the United Nations Security Council consists of the victors of World War Two; (4) the existence of a strategic nuclear parity between the United States and Russia; and (5) the presence of the Bretton Woods financial system. The fall of the USSR and the dismantling of the 'socialist bloc' added another layer to this system, creating a supposition on the part of the world community that Russia's international standings have been significantly weakened compared to what they were in the 1970s.

At the same time, this additional post-1991 layer can be considered as cursory, since the essence of the five-tier construction remained unchanged. Russia's geopolitical retreat of 1991 has not been institutionalized. No comprehensive document was signed to state that Russia was a losing party in the Cold War and must, due to this situation, take upon itself certain obligations that could restrict her sovereignty or freedom of action in the international arena. Russia retained her seat on the UN Security Council. She preserved her nuclear potential and inherited the remaining arsenals from the former Soviet Union's republics. Despite the visible economic slowdown that took place during the 1990s, Russia remained the only country that enjoys scientific-technological and research potential that competes with the United States in the spheres of the military and the exploration of space (Leontyev, 2015). Therefore, with the exception of the fifth principle and the minor modification of others, practical multipolarity hopes to see this order stable and gradually evolving towards a more inclusive multipolar arrangement. Let me discuss these points in detail.

Russian intellectuals uphold the classical idea of state sovereignty as a means of preserving the cultural and political distinctness of various states in the world and combating the uniformity of the global culture narrated in the West, without the full participation of the 'rest' of the world. Sovereignties must be sustained as an expedient instrument that could allow the idea of normative pluralism to capture the dominant discourse. Simultaneously, countries should unite into cultural, political, and civilizational unions to advance the idea of civilizational diversity. These two processes – sustaining sovereignty and forming cultural unions – could move in parallel, mutually reinforcing each other. Such an approach is seen in the ideology of the Eurasian Union that proposes integration of the post-Soviet space based on the idea of a plurality of cultural and political forms within the union, thus accepting the idea of domestic sovereignty of each state. This offers integration on the basis of a common history and common understanding of political processes taking place in the contemporary world.

Lavrov (2015), in his address to the Russian State Duma, insisted on creating a more just, polycentric, and stable world order. He claimed that imposing a particular political and developmental recipe on various countries would lead to increased chaos and anarchy, and would be met with resistance from many states. He pointed out that Russia does not expect other states to sacrifice their prosperity for the sake of particular ideas or political doctrines and that no country must try to fit any particular developmental model which is considered optimal by other states. These claims may seem odd, particularly to Western observers, in light of events in Crimea, Donbass, South Ossetia, and Abkhazia, in which Russia influenced political events. Yet, as Sakwa (2016) notes, most official statements by Russia on such occasions deal very little with normative and ethical notions, but do reveal Russia's disdain and ideological resistance to 'Western mentorship' in all spheres of socio-economic and political life. Maria Zakharova, the spokesperson of Russia's Ministry of Foreign Affairs, often adhered to this line of reasoning when faced with criticism of Russia's international behaviour.[5]

Following this logic, the role of the UN also seems central for Russia in the framework of the multipolar world order. Putin (2015) in his speech to the seventieth UN General Assembly claimed Russia understands that 'the world is changing and that the United Nations must be consistent with this natural transformation.' At the same time, Russia considers all

> attempts to undermine the authority and legitimacy of the UN as extremely dangerous. This can lead to a collapse of the entire architecture of international relations. Then indeed we would be left with no other rules than the rule of force. We would get to a world dominated by selfishness rather than collective work. A world increasingly characterised by dictate rather than equality, genuine democracy and freedom. A world where truly independent states would be replaced by an ever growing number of de facto protectorates and externally controlled territories.

Being adamant about sustaining the idea of sovereignty, the particularity of political-cultural development, and the central role of the UN as a guarantor of international legal framework, Russia is aiming to change the fifth principle concerning the Bretton Woods financial system. This could be done through trading with regional currencies and the introduction of regional financial institutions as alternatives to the World Bank, the IMF, and US credit-rating agencies. This change would challenge the dominance of the US dollar as the world's reserve currency, and as a result would challenge the political power of the United States in the world arena. It could also ensure a redistribution of control over financial resources across the globe, thereby giving more tangible sovereignty to other states and centres of influence.

The Significance of the Multipolar World Approach

The multipolar world propositions remain significant in that they have come into being as a response to a number of processes taking place in the contemporary world. Three main factors invoked the development of the multipolar world theory. First, the unipolar order began to experience significant difficulties in the course of its entrenchment. Turmoil in the Middle East, the refugee crisis, and political challenges in other parts of the globe have demonstrated that a single force cannot run world affairs successfully and that the participation of other players is necessary to ensure lasting peace and stability.

Second, the unipolar world order has not been framed institution-ally, which results in further predicaments in terms of legitimacy. Indeed, during the past quarter of a century the United States created a series of precedents – such as 'humanitarian intervention', 'regime change', and 'disarmament' – that could consolidate its global leader-ship and draft the main dimensions of the unipolar world. The doctrine of Responsibility to Protect (R2P), a political commitment endorsed by all UN members states at the 2005 World Summit, has been dis-cussed by many Russian scholars of international relations. These scholars (*Kruglyi Stol* 2012) argue that the emergence of R2P is a response to the unclear nature of 'humanitarian interventions' and welcome the doctrine as a step towards clarification of the circum-stances under which interventions can take place and towards the enforcement of the role of the United Nations Security Council in the process. Yet, as Maria Zakharova (2015) insists, all such steps repre-sent a series of practices in differing political conflicts that have yet to be converted into positive and comprehensive international law, con-solidating unipolarity.

Moreover, the adherents of both uni- and multipolar world orders avoided the enactment of Brazil's 2011 Responsibility while Protecting (RWP) initiative (Tourinho, Stuenkel, Brockmeier, 2016). Both Russian and Western policy-makers left the doctrine to academic debate, eschewing intense public discussions. The RWP doctrine calls for improvements to the use of force in acts of protection to guard against causing more damage to the country where the intervention takes place. It also calls for the establishment of a set of *extremely* specific criteria for the authorization of military intervention, thereby prevent-ing the R2P doctrine from being used with ulterior motives. Finally, the initiative wished to expand the role of the UN Security Council once the use of force has been delegated to other parties. The aim of the initiative was to grant the R2P doctrine a new ethical dimension and redefine the *way* in which actors operate the intervention.

This RWP doctrine relies on Weber's ideological chasm between the ethics of ultimate ends and the ethics of responsibility. The first relates to an uncompromising just action. From this point of view, the moral quality of an act correlates with actions that are undertaken with good intentions. The second perspective, however, treats acts on the basis of their consequences (Weber 2004, 119–22; Sitton 2003, 12). The main idea here is that political actions should be determined by ratio-nal considerations dictated by the state's survival pertaining to power politics and not by ethical or 'ideal' considerations (Smith 1990, 15–16; Barkawi 1998, 163; Hennis 1988, 79–84; Mommsen 1984). Hence, ethics of responsibility contrasts with the universalist ethics of 'absolute conviction in which only actions ethical from the point of view of one's ultimate values are undertaken' (Barkawi 1998, 163). This position also invokes the Machiavellian logic that assumes the virtuousness of a policy is defined by its outcome: if it is not effective, it cannot be virtuous (Kaplan 2002, 53). Therefore, within this logic, the morality of results is more important than the morality of intentions.

Criticism of 'absolute conviction' and 'just war' doctrines also comes from Morgenthau. An intellectual student of Weber, he (1948a and 1948b) ponders the link between moral intentions and outcomes, arguing that human beings are limited in their ability to predict the results of their moral actions. Because of this 'natural ability of human intellect' (Morgenthau 1945, 11), good intentions will inevitably go awry. For Morgenthau (1945, 18; see also Lang 2007, 28–9), morally informed political action is possible only if one acts within the bounds of the Aristotelian virtue of prudence, exercising restraint, political wisdom, moral courage, tempered judgment, and consideration of others' interests.

It now becomes clear why neither the West, which stands as the main proponent of the unipolar world, nor Russia or China that advance the multipolar world structure, promoted the RWP doctrine. All sides quietly reserved the right to advance their geostrategic interests (civilizational or unipolar) at the time of conflict and intervention, thus taking us back to positions of classical realism. It is indicative that both Russia and the West accused each other of egoistic behaviour in almost all cases that invoked R2P. Russia pointed at the Western ulterior motives during the Libya, Iraq, Syria, Yemen, Afghanistan, and Serbia campaigns. The West lamented Russia's initiatives in South Ossetia and Abkhazia, Donbass and Crimea. In Syria, where both Russia and the United States have tangible stakes, the countries' respective officials deploy the higher language of 'protection' and 'fighting terrorism'. At the same time, they often avoid the problem of balancing outcomes and intentions, as the RWP logic would prescribe.

The third challenge stems from regional alliances that emerge in various parts of the globe. The formation of BRICS, the integration processes in Latin America, the post-Soviet space, and Asia and Africa could all challenge the global domination of the West. On the other hand, multipolarity has not become a permanent structure of international relations either. The world is now locked in a stalemate, a rather unstable balance, between multipolarity and unipolarity. As to Russia, advancing the ideas of multipolarity has become expedient in pursuing her aim to remain a significant voice in the international arena. Dugin (2012) argues that contemporary Russia is incapable of defending her national interests alone. Apart from the ideas of multi-polarity, Russia does not have a coherent ideology that could be exported as, for example, Marxism and Communism had been during the Soviet period. Neither does she have adequate military means to sustain such an ideological export. Hence, the return to a bipolar world, in which Russia is able to act as a counterweight to the West, is no longer a possibility. That defenders of the unipolar world have a coherent ideology, a military complex, and the economic means to advance their political project makes Russia's position more tenuous. Indeed, human rights, globalism, consumerism, cosmopolitanism, and capitalism sustained by the neo-liberal project are easily exportable and appealing to many of its supporters across the world.

In this light, forming alliances with those who are critical of the unipolar world order is a powerful instrument left for Russia in her claims to assert global influence. Hence, Russia's elite considers this civilizational ideology a distinct intellectual product that it can offer to the world (Tsygankov 2016). Proponents of this ideology claim that the multipolar world architecture can only have a dialogical character as opposed to the unipolar world, which is mostly based on the normative monologue of liberal-democratic states. The task of the multipolar world ideology, they argue, is to reconstruct the extant discourse on international affairs in a way that could incorporate the ideas of particularity, cultural-historical context, multiplicity of political forms, and unimpeded independent development.

These ideas have become a leitmotif of Russian intellectuals and foreign-policy ideologues of the late-Putin period. Russia's insistence on multipolarity is often framed as a proposal to create a new 'world order' that could be fairer to all and devoid of various forms of 'crusading universalisms' (Williams 2001). In the wake of the Iraq war, this debate took on an increasingly metaphysical character. Russian intellectuals often deploy Western philosophical deliberations to argue in favour of particularity of knowledge, the link between knowledge and power, and the critique of proportionality of results and intentions. Critical of the very possibility of universalism, a number of Russian intellectuals began to argue that, if the framework of unipolarity is to be built, the United States and its allies must show the world a new metaphysical project that could ultimately serve a universal public good. This project, in their view, should be mindful of the Weberian (and Morgenthau's) dilemma of balancing the ethics of ultimate ends and the ethics of responsibility that we discussed earlier.

Maria Zakharova (2015) claimed in September 2015 that

> we criticize Western ideology not because we disagree with it. Moreover, we would have accepted it, if we saw any tangible results of Western actions in the Middle East during the past ten years. What we see now is that no modern prosperous state has emerged in the region so far. The most recent refugee crisis in Europe demonstrated the ultimate failure and immoral nature of such political practices in the area.

Sergey Kurginyan (2015) laments that the United States, through its foreign-policy actions, dismantles the paradigm of modernity in those areas that need modernity most. He questions, much in the Machiavellian fashion, the balance between results and intentions of such policy-making. Kurginyan (2015) argues that the process of de-sovereignization of formerly secular sovereign states of the Middle East during the Western-backed Arab Spring was meant to trigger the de-sovereignization dynamic world-wide and could ultimately create a new 'global disorder'. He insists that, if the unipolar world model were to have a chance of success, its proponents should demonstrate the tangible socio-political benefits of such an arrangement.

Russian intellectuals also shift away from the 'just war' ideology, claiming that, while liberal democracy might be an effective form of governance, it should not delegitimize alternative forms of political structure.[6] Their ideas often echo the laments of Western philosophers that we have examined above. Evgeniy Tarlo (2015), professor at the Moscow Institute of Foreign Relations, insists that Russia is not against the idea that the vast majority of nations across the globe embrace democracy as a form of government. Yet, he claims that 'Russia is against the imposition of "democracy" via military methods or change of political regimes by sponsoring "colour" revolutions, organizing Western-backed political movements, and manipulating those countries into the Western geopolitical orbit through uprooting economic and politico-cultural systems of those areas.' Sergey Karaganov (2015) supports this point by insisting that the direct imposition of democracy in the past two decades discredited the very idea of democracy. He claims that this is similar to the situation when the idea of Communism was discredited by the Soviet Union's actions in the international arena. 'Democracy is a wonderful idea and a political system,' Karaganov (2015) claims, 'but it was made a caricature by Western attempts to spread it forcefully across the globe, using it as a dogmatic rhetorical token in political argument, and imposing it where it was not appropriate or necessary.'

MULTIPOLAR WORLD ARCHITECTURE: PROBLEMS AND CAVEATS

While the multipolar approach to the architecture of international relations has serious claims to justice, normative pluralism, and peace, it contains a number of limitations that need to be examined. This could provide us with the sober realization that the establishment of the most just world order is still a distant goal. I have selected four main points.

First, the multipolar-world-order theory does not provide adequate answers to the problem of conflict. While the multipolar architecture strives to assure lasting peace within civilizations, it does not rule out conflicts between civilizations. More importantly, such a conflict has the same chance of evolving in the 'just war' fashion as do contemporary wars that stem from the extant order of international conduct. Hence, we can meaningfully construct a *co-operative* security system (as defined by Wendt) only within civilizations and examine the conflictual security system when we refer to inter-civilizational dialogue. Cross-civilizational interaction does not guarantee peaceful coexistence, even though proponents of this theory claim that dialogue and co-operation must be a feature of the inter-civilizational dynamics of recognition.

Second, a multipolar model of world development does not solve the problem of rising managerialism, a lack of transparency, and the growing power of large corporations. The unipolar world structure invariably leads to a disproportionate increase in the power and political significance of global transnational corporations and bureaucratic networks, which could adversely impact not only the population of the periphery but also the inhabitants of the centre. Vladimir Putin (2016), in his 2016 Valdai speech, pointed to the breakdown of the previous politics of consensus that until recently marked the political systems of most Western states. He argued that populations of many of those states often withdraw their consent from supranational economic elites, global oligarchies, and international bureaucracies, which have not been elected but have gained power to influence the dominant discourse. In other words, he claims that Western politics is experiencing a political-historical conjuncture (to deploy the Gramsci terminology) at which radically different choices for the political future begin to struggle for hegemonic discourse.

Having said that, the multipolar world order is not immune to such problems either. Civilizational unions and centres of influence would invariably have clusters of supranational bureaucracy, with strong political-economic ambitions and a lack of democratic legitimacy. Corporations could influence such a bureaucracy and seek its political assistance in the international arena for the advancement of their interests. A number of multipolarity proponents in Russia, while advocating large civilizational regions, often observe that those regions will have their financial instruments and economic elites with private stakes in those territories. Andrey Fursov (2012), an outspoken critic of unipolarity, also remains pessimistic about the multipolar construction. He is convinced that, in the near future, the world will be composed of empire-like formations highly influenced by supranational bureaucracy, economic elites, and legal enforcement services. Mikhail Delyagin (2016; 2019, 293–314) concurs with this idea and laments the natural growth of supranational economic elites.

Third, multipolarity theorizations come across as contradictory in the discussion of civilizational borders. On the one hand, proponents of multipolarity argue that cultural-political unions could become subjects of international politics and define the future of the globe. This adheres to the essentialist approach to culture which claims that, as part of a culture, people feel strongly attached to its features and to sharing a particular way of life (Keesing 1994, 303). On the other hand, multipolarity thinkers endorse the liberal argument that cultures are not clearly demarcated and that membership in one culture does not exclude membership in the other. More importantly, multipolarity thinkers often agree with liberals that cultures are not homogenous internally and that a person's cultural identity could be plural rather than singular (for a liberal argument see Tully 1995, 10; Mason 2007, 223–5; for a multipolarity argument see Dugin and Sleboda 2012; Shevchenko et al. 2012; Dugin 2012). They argue further that parts of one civilization could be lodged within the other, that borders of such civilizations are fluid due to migration, communication, and development (Sleboda and Dugin 2012; Fursov 2012). This theoretical inconsistency raises some questions. If cultures are viewed from the essentialist point of view as subjects of international politics, it is difficult to account for their blurry borders and the proclaimed lenience towards eliminating clear cultural demarcations.

Fourth, multipolar world construction could not adequately deal with the problem of the aggressive propagation of civilizational interests (which in the case of unipolarity takes the shape of advancing the centre's interests into the periphery), adverse image construction of enemies, and hybrid war scenarios. To achieve fairness, multipolarity theorists argue that all members of civilizations, when disagreeing with the common civilizational 'we', must be granted the right of exit from their civilizations and the opportunity to join other civilizations (Sleboda and Dugin 2012; Fursov 2012; see also Chapter 4). This position aligns them with moderate liberal theorists who endorse a 'political' conception of liberalism rooted in the value of tolerance, rather than a comprehensive conception of liberalism rooted in the value of autonomy (Galston 1995; Okin 2002; Kymicka 2007; Hirschman 1970).

At the same time, while it fends for the rights of individuals, this concept is problematic to implement in practice. From the essentialist point of view, Kymlicka (2007) argues that cultures have strong influences on people's subconscious and collective way of life. Threats of exit, if plausibly seen through, can ignite serious internal dissent and jeopardize the culture's survival (Hirschman 1970; Okin 2002, 214). If a culture were to survive, the destabilizing impact of internal dissent should not be too threatening. Yet, the means, or to use Kymlicka's (2007, 31) term, 'internal restrictions' with which civilizations (or cultures) could keep the dissenters in, may vary, from persuasion and popularization of the culture's way of life to forcefully restricting the real opportunities of exit (Kymlicka 2007, 32; Kymlicka 1995, 152–8) or waging hybrid wars with the dissenters.

Indeed, if we were to adopt this concern about internal dissent as serious, it would be logical to consider that, within the conditions of anarchy and a conflictual inter-civilizational security system, civilizations would probably develop financial and geostrategic interests and feel strongly about guarding their perceived civilizational borders, along with their right of exit from the civilization's spheres of cultural and political influence. The means and methods of 'internal restrictions' may be various, starting from hybrid wars, the igniting of internal political turmoil, the exertion of financial pressures, persuasion and propaganda, and the like. The conflict over Ukraine perfectly illustrates this point. Set on the border between the West European and Russian civilizations, Ukraine became torn by these warring parties. This cross-civilizational border conflict demonstrates the potential for war and breakdown of the security system if we were to adopt a civilizational approach to world politics.

To sum up the main positions of this chapter, the emerging multipolar world ideology stems from Western philosophical deliberations in defence of the particularity of knowledge, interpretation, and culture. Russian philosophy of the nineteenth century has also played a decisive part in the evolution of multipolar world ideas. The discussion showed that Russian thought leaned towards the ideas of particularity since its inception in both liberal and traditionalist strands. This subsequently led to Russia's civilizational approach to world politics and the gradual formation of its geographical dimension. The main feature of this approach to international relations is that it has become adopted as Russia's official foreign-policy line. Therefore, Russian officials at the highest level, her main political parties, and political actors who adhere to the state conservative line become the main exponents of this ideational approach.

The chapter demonstrated that the main intellectual contribution of all those actors to the debate on international relations remains their proposal to shift away from the Western rationalist and postmodernist understandings of the subject of international politics and propose civilizations as the main subject of international conduct. Hence, large cultural and political spaces would form the core of international dialogue, promote regional integration, and fight for the particularity of world cultures and political forms. Moreover, I argued that this civilizational ideology has both practical and theoretical dimensions with practical considerations, defending traditional ideas of state sovereignty as a contemporary guarantee of lasting peace and stability.

Besides metaphysical explanations, Russia's advocacy of multipolarity also has practical considerations. The multipolar world arrangement has become one of the most important aspects of Russia's soft power in the global arena and one important instrument for retaining her international influence since the collapse of the Soviet Union. Russia deploys the ideas of civilizational particularity in defence of her territorial and political integrity and in attempts to curb the advance of global democratization and the economic interests of third parties that come with it. She calls for the establishment of strong regional alliances that could help a supposedly fairer redistribution of power and resources across the globe – a process in which Russia could play a decisive role. The theory of the multipolar world arrangement could be developed into a stronger and more coherent political ideology, given its substantial metaphysical and political basis. Whether this arrangement could contribute to longer-lasting peace and stability remains an open question, as the comparative discussion of both political orders above demonstrates. Yet the study of its main tenets and evolution represent a matter of paramount importance for both academics and practical policy-makers.

8

Multiculturalism

Modern Russia faces a plethora of challenges in the area of inter-ethnic and national relations, as well as several struggles to accommodate varying types of subcultural diversity. Intermittent waves of extremism and xenophobia necessitated the development of appropriate models to forge societal harmony. In this light, multiculturalism has become an important theme within Russian political discourse. It is even more significant that Russian public figures and philosophers examine the idea of multiculturalism with constant reference to similar practices and debates taking place in the West. Therefore, the extent to which the Russian idea and practice of multiculturalism correlates to the ideological commitments of the Western practice becomes a matter of interest. This chapter will show that the Russian idea of multicultural-ism shows procedural similarities to Western liberalism but exhibits an ideologically different substance. The discussion is presented in four parts. The first two sections set out a theoretical framework and outline the main dimensions of the Western liberal and communitarian understanding of multiculturalism. The following two sections exam-ine procedural and substantive aspects of Russian multiculturalism. The notions of toleration, as well as aspects of subcultural diversity, will be discussed separately in some detail.

WESTERN DEBATES ON MULTICULTURALISM

The Liberal Approach

Two broad trends can be distinguished in the sphere of multicultural-ism: the neo-liberal tradition, which builds solely on the ideas of classical liberals such as John Locke, and the reformed liberal doctrine, which attempts to marry classical liberalism with changing social realities, often taking into account select tenets of communitarian reasoning (Kymlicka 2005; Parekh 2006).

The neo-liberal tradition focuses on the universal application of human rights. The universality of human rights for these thinkers essentially means that the rights and freedoms of ethnic minorities can be guaranteed by default (Walzer 1994, 100–1). The push towards universality is seen in a strategy of 'benign neglect' (Glazer 1975, 25), 'non-discrimination', and 'colour-blind' politics that ultimately seek equality among all members of society. These ideas have fundamental historical origins and go back to the initial objectives of classical liberals to create a nation-state. The task of creating a nation-state necessitated the formation of a civic nation. The core of the civic nation was composed of the culturally and politically dominant majority ethnic group, while the stabilization of the nation-state institutions often took place at the cost 'of obliterating minority cultures and imposing enforced homogeneity upon people' (Kymlicka 1995, 57; Parekh 2006, 9; see also Keane 2003; Deutsch 1953; see also Chapter 6). A strict division between public and private realms was an expedient practice intended to achieve universality – as expressed in the original ideas of the French Republic. This implied that religious, cultural, and ethnic preferences were to remain in the private sphere, while civic matters were taken to the public domain (Walzer 1994, 100–1; Kymlicka 1995).[1] Finally, the neo-liberal doctrine, despite its claims of cultural neutrality, was prepared to tolerate only liberal expressions of cultural autonomy and unwilling to endorse practices that might impede individual freedom (Heywood 2007, 323; Parekh 2006, 9; Fitzpatrick 2011, 77). Apart from overtly violent and extremist trends, the outcast practices inadvertently included a broad range of attitudes, customs, and beliefs that belonged to a non-Western cultural tradition, but were acceptable in non-European ethno-national contexts.

It soon became clear that such a model could not answer the challenges spawned by globalization, migration, and the revival of ethnic nationalism. While the universality-of-rights concept claims to achieve equality among different peoples, it overlooks some important aspects of particularity. Which ethnic language should we use while exercising the freedom of speech in a multi-ethnic state (Kymlicka 1997, 23)? How do we draw the constituency boundaries to exercise the civil right to vote? How do we interpret historic events in educational processes (Kymlicka 1995)? These and many similar issues were the challenges of multiculturalism that fell beyond the reach of the liberal universality. Liberalism strove to adapt to the growing social complexities by giving answers to some of these questions in the reformed liberal doctrine.

Will Kymlicka, one of its main proponents, mapped out a new liberal strategy to meet the challenges of diversity. True to classical liberal thinking, he takes the principle of individual rights and autonomy as a basis and extends it to the idea of granting particular collective rights to various ethnic and cultural minority groups. Kymlicka claims that, in a multinational state, membership in a subnational community is the essential basis for autonomy and a fundamental human right. This somewhat links him to the communitarian idea of expressive freedom initially proposed by Rousseau and Herder. I will elaborate on the communitarian approach later. Here it is essential to mention that the freedom to express oneself depends on a society within which an act of expression takes place. In multi-ethnic and multicultural societies, this becomes particularly important. This is because an individual cannot choose his/her national/subcultural community of origin, and parting with one's roots is a most difficult, and in many cases impossible, task. Thus, the freedom to express one's familial and cultural background becomes an important part of a liberal-democratic society. In this context, the state is expected to protect not only individual autonomy but also the autonomy of its composite subnational, and subcultural, cultures.

In Kymlicka's mind, ethnic majorities and ethnic minorities have equal rights to cultural self-preservation and cultural autonomy. The breadth of such rights, however, varies between cultures and types of minorities based on their histories of settlement (Kymlicka 2002, 349; see also Weinstock 2007, 246–7). Migrants are granted polyethnic rights sufficient to maintain a meaningful way of life in terms of preserving some fundamental elements of their ethnic cultures (see also Walzer 1994, 103; Glazer 1983, 149). Indigenous peoples and substate nations could be entitled to rights of political self-determination, which include the erection of structural or ideological institutions of federalism. John Rawls is another seminal thinker who attempted to adapt traditional liberal ideas to new challenges. He revised his original idea of comprehensive liberalism, proposed in the *Theory of Justice* (1971), towards an idea of political liberalism and offered it in the 1993 revision, entitled *Political Liberalism*. The former doctrine was supposedly hostile to non-liberal ideas and lifestyles, while the latter pledged to encompass differing ideas of the good life into one societal framework. Thus the political concept of liberalism aims to provide a 'workable and shared' basis of co-operation between citizens who hold differing comprehensive doctrines of the good life based on their cultural particularities (Rawls 1993, 12).

At the same time, both Kymlicka (1997) and Rawls (1993) invariably follow the early tradition of locking these processes into a single, ideologically liberal framework. These thinkers (like many other liberals, such as Dworkin 1978 and Ackerman 1980) hope that liberalism will entrench itself in society and make a transition from being part of political culture to becoming an essential component of 'social culture'. Kymlicka (1997, 24), in particular, suggests that his differing rights should be granted in the framework of a base 'societal culture' which provides people with meaningful tools for self-realization, common linguistic ground, and the educational standards needed to achieve adequate employment and productivity (Kymlicka 1997, 31). More importantly, Kymlicka insists that this culture should have liberalism as its base. All potential lifestyles and traditions will be considered only on the condition of their compliance with liberal practices or on the condition of granting their participant the 'right of exit' from the wider liberal culture. Kymlicka (1995, 168 and 171) suggests that the wider liberal society has the 'right and responsibility to speak against illiberal opinion, and in general, to put pressure on [those holding such opinions] to mend their ways.'

Rawls's idea of political liberalism also faces the challenge of *creating* a consensus framework, within which composite ideas and values can be housed (Parekh 2006, 84). Rawls (1971; 1993, 13) claims that this framework would resemble 'one rather precisely articulated system' which will encompass all recognized values and virtues. This framework is invariably liberal and seeks to extend its liberal nature to all its composite elements. Rawls (1993, 13) insists that one important feature of his consensus framework is that it is 'expressed in terms of certain fundamental ideas seen as implicit in the public political culture'. The spread of these ideas takes place through various 'societal institutions that must have "*accepted* forms of *interpretation*" that are seen as a fund of implicitly shared ideas and principles' (Rawls 1993, 14). These interpretations, as they are for Kymlicka, are distributed through the 'culture of daily life, of its many associations:

churches and universities, learned and scientific societies, and clubs and teams, to mention a few' (Rawls 1993, 14).

Parekh (2006, 110) in criticism brands this intellectual trend as the 'absolutization' of liberalism. The absolutization of the liberal doctrine often travels to the political discourse. The way in which such thinking feeds itself into the public discourse is seen in various political speeches. Former British Prime Minister David Cameron's statements made at the February 2011 Munich Security Conference (Cameron, 2011) are indicative:

> We need a lot less of the passive tolerance of recent years and a much more active, muscular liberalism. A passively tolerant society says to its citizens, as long as you obey the law we will just leave you alone. It stands neutral between different values. But I believe a genuinely liberal country does much more; it believes in certain values and actively promotes them. Freedom of speech, freedom of worship, democracy, the rule of law, equal rights regardless of race, sex or sexuality. It says to its citizens, this is what defines us as a society: to belong here is to believe in these things. Now each of us in our own countries, I believe, must be unambiguous and hardnosed about this defence of our liberty.

Another former British prime minister, Tony Blair, suggested shaping the ideology of British Muslims in a more liberal direction and changing the attitudes of this group to the nature of American and British foreign policy. A range of similar statements was made by various politicians from left and right (Pugh 2009, 173).

It is now clear that the liberal model, in its reformed and original sense, expects the expressions of cultural particularities to develop within a framework of a common 'societal culture' or base 'societal consensus', whose borders remain ideologically liberal. The framework includes 'reasonable' ideas of the good life and excludes, even 'contains', 'unreasonable' and 'unacceptable' doctrines (Rawls 1993, 64). Those ideas that 'support a free-standing political realm', liberty, and individual autonomy are considered reasonable and receive access to the framework consensus, and those that do not are kept outside. This point reveals important procedural aspects of liberal multiculturalism, which will form a central point of reference in our subsequent discussion of the procedure of Russian multiculturalism.

The Pluralist-communitarian Approach
and Critique of Liberalism

The pluralist-communitarian treatment of multiculturalism differs from its liberal counterpart in a number of important ways. First, the two different models of society, liberal and communitarian, presuppose a different idea of moral commitments. The first model claims value neutrality and suggests that state and society should not have a substantive idea of common good. Rather, a liberal society should have a moral commitment to granting its members personal autonomy to pursue their favoured ideas of a good life without forging a consensus on its substance (Taylor 1994, 56; Rawls 1985; Dworkin 1978; Ackerman 1980; Ingram 2003, 21–4).[2] Communitarians, on the other hand, posit that the state and society can and should have an idea of common good. They often see this in the sustaining of particular cultural, religious, and socio-political traditions of a given society (Fitzpatrick 2011, 77). This means that, in practice, society is often bound by some substantive ideals.

Second, while liberals emphasize individual rights, communitarians speak of 'collective rights granted to minority groups as exceptions with the view to guarantee the sense of cultural belonging and self-expression of these groups' members' (Taylor 1995, 31). Third, communitarians criticize the liberal idea of individual choice and the proposition that an individual can choose cultures autonomously. They argue that the choice can not be meaningful without the *ability* to exercise it in a mature form. Such ability, on the other hand, depends on the process of maturation, which is inexorably linked to society, and thus has a dialogical character (Smith 2002, 145; Taylor 1994, 33). Parekh (2006, 110 and 304–13) speaks of reasoning, values, choices, options, and even the very capacity for autonomy as being structured in a particular culture-dependent way. He writes (2006, 110):

[A]lthough human beings are not determined by their culture in the sense of being unable to take a critical view of it and appreciate and learn from others, they are not transcendental beings contingently and externally related to it either. Their culture shapes them in countless ways, forms them into certain kinds of persons, and cultivates certain attachments, affections, moral and psychological dispositions, taboos, and modes of reasoning.

Fourth, and following on from above, communitarians introduce a concept of equal respect and equal recognition of cultures, and thus stretch the liberal notion of equal individuals to groups. The concept of equal recognition is rooted in the idea of authenticity and expressive freedom (Smith 2002, 154; Taylor 1994, 70–3; Fraser and Honneth 2003).[3] At the community level, the notion of authenticity is closely tied up with cultural expressions. In this context, Charles Taylor (1994, 73) insists that 'we should express our commitment to examine critically other cultures by departing from the principle of their equal worth. By admitting equal worth of other cultures, regardless of our like or disliking them, we are invariably granting all cultures equal *recognition* and the right of their place in our community.' This logic is linked to Isaiah Berlin's (1969) idea of 'value pluralism', which suggests that the world is composed of the multiplicity of cultures, and therefore no culture or moral tradition has moral authority or primacy over any other (see also Gray 1995).

Finally, the notion of recognition is somewhat logically linked to the criticism of the idea of toleration. The liberal notion of toleration is based on a reciprocal recognition of negative freedom (Berlin 1969; Heywood 2004, 267–9) and intimately linked to the ideas of personal autonomy, non-interference in the private sphere, and universality of human rights. Many critics of this notion argue, however, that the concept of toleration cannot be considered as a free-standing humanistic value and that it should not be based on the premise of personal autonomy. Bernard Williams (2005, 128) claims that toleration 'requires us to accept people and permit their practices even when we strongly disapprove of them.' (We must limit Williams's phrase, however, to those practices which, according to the classical liberal doctrine, cause no physical harm to other individuals or their property.) If we link the idea of toleration to the liberal concept of personal autonomy, we could face difficulties in drawing clear boundaries at which we can express our disapproval/dislike of a tolerated practice effectively. Neither can we give a clear answer as to which areas of life should be hiding behind doors of personal autonomy.

Bernard Williams (2005, 132) claims that providing such answers is 'manifestly ... not available under the present construction of the tolerant attitude, since it is precisely the value of the other's autonomy which is supposed to be drawing the limits to what the tolerant but disapproving agent is permitted to do.' For these reasons Williams (2005, 134) claims that the 'idea to ground the practice of toleration in a moral attitude directed to the value of autonomy is bound to fail.' Indeed, a range of questions arises. Could we effectively engage, critically evaluate, and call into a dialogue various moral, ethical, and aesthetic choices of individuals? To what extent are we restrained by the framework of political correctness that rests on the liberal idea of respecting individual autonomy? Could a critical and disapproving group invite a different group into an open dialogue without being considered prejudiced and intolerant? In order to resolve these difficulties, contemporary forms of toleration remove the aspect of disapproval from the idea of toleration. This, in return, hollows out its true meaning, for toleration is impossible without the initial disapproval. Bernard Williams (2005, 128–9) claims that toleration in its current form has become a mere political practice, rather than an entrenched attitude. He insists that, instead of the notions of personal rights and autonomy, the attitudes that underlie the idea of toleration should include virtues such as the 'desire to co-operate and to get on peaceably with one's fellow citizens and a capacity for seeing how things look to them.' This tension between recognition and toleration will occupy a large share of the debate on multiculturalism in Russia.

RUSSIAN MULTICULTURALISM

Three important observations must be made with regard to the Russian idea of multiculturalism. First, if we examine Russian multiculturalism through the Western theoretical prism, it could come across as communitarian in substance but liberal in procedure. The communitarian substance of Russian multiculturalism is seen in its connection to the idea of public good, its lenience towards select group rights, its discourse on the importance of cultural authenticity, and its struggles to replace the notion of toleration with philosophical doctrines of acceptance and recognition. The liberal theme appears when Russian philosophers and public figures begin the discussion of the practical steps that must be taken in order to achieve these desired objectives. In this case, they talk of creating a civic nation based on the common 'base consensus' or a 'societal framework' whose main contours must be developed carefully. In this light, the form and substance of Russian multiculturalism should be examined separately. Second, despite some apparent similarities with the Western discourse, we should analyse the varying dimensions of Russian multiculturalism through the prism of Russia-specific conditions, her distinct history and politics. From this point of view, neither the communitarian substance nor the liberal procedure of Russian multiculturalism converges completely with Western ideas. This particularly concerns liberalism, which has a fragmented and limited character in the Russian case.

Finally, and most importantly, the Russian idea of multiculturalism, just like its Western counterpart, is not uniform. Moreover, Russians have not yet arrived at any coherent articulation of a systematic multicultural policy, even though the ongoing debates allow the determination of some dominant approaches. In line with our initial thesis on paradigmatic pluralism as a political system in Russia, we can select three main strands from the public discourse. The first set of ideas belongs to the Russian liberal project that pursues the construction of a liberal nation-state by the formation a civic nation. These thinkers also strive to achieve 'normality' for Russia, which is seen as compliance with Western institutional standards and practices of multicultural accommodation. The second strand of thought is nationalist. It advocates the creation of unequal identities through policies that would implicitly, and explicitly, favour the ethnic Russian nation. I will eschew the discussion of this thought here for we have already dealt with it in Chapter 6 while discussing Russia's ethnic and democratic nationalism. The third approach, which we may call traditionalist, focuses on Russia's historical multi-ethnic complexity, her inherent cultural multi-vectorness, and religious pluralism. Vera Tolz (2001, 1) writes that thinkers of this type define Russia and the Russians as 'creators and preservers of a unique multi-ethnic community.' They usually maintain a position of tension with Russian and Western liberal political thinkers. It does not come as a surprise that the main chorus of voices belongs to the traditionalist approach, which forms the ideological and instrumental basis of Russia's multiculturalism. This approach also has an ideological leverage over politics, in that many proposals put forth by Vladimir Putin have significant vestiges of traditionalist thought. Given this ideational complexity, the following discussion will have four main vectors. It will refer to the Western liberal and communitarian ideas embedded in the Russian discourse, and also examine the ongoing tensions between the Russian liberal and traditional debates on multiculturalism.

Procedural Aspects

Let me begin with the procedural outlook. Most Russian thinkers, just like their Western liberal counterparts, advocate the creation of a societal-consensus framework, within which various ideas and cultural practices can be accommodated. However, Russian thinkers and politicians propose to find this societal consensus amidst historical interpretations, language, religious traditions, and culture, instead of grounding it on the Western liberal notions of personal autonomy and individual rights. Thus, while Russian thinkers insist on the need to *create* this framework, they avoid – consciously or subliminally – making its contours ideologically liberal. In this procedural aspect, both Russian liberal and traditionalist thinkers are united. At the same time, the two strands of thought emphasize differing themes of importance. Liberals carry much less substantial ideological baggage than the traditionalists. Liberals are content to select cultural and linguistic similarities among Russia's peoples, and by doing so to approximate the procedure of Western liberal universalism as closely as possible. This thinking brings them close to the reformed liberal thought articulated by Kymlicka (1997, 31), who also signified common language, as opposed to ethnic customs, religious beliefs, and family traditions, as one important tool of forming his proposed version of 'societal culture'. Traditionalists, on the other hand, take a step further and focus on the existential aspects of the common future, history, and culture of Russia's composite substate nationalities. More importantly, while the liberals remain deliberately silent on the ideological contours of the 'base consensus', most traditionalists are vocal in rejecting the plan for painting it with liberal colours.

Vladimir Putin (2012a) stands between the two approaches and translates them into some vague political language that draws on ideas from both spectrums. In an article published in the *Nezavisimaia Gazeta* daily in 2012 he insists that Russia needs to recreate its original *cultural code* in order to create a framework for base consensus. In the traditional fashion, Putin (2012a) sees this 'cultural code' as creating common ground on interpreting Russia's culture and history. He claims that Russia should reach some basic civic consensus in which 'every Russian citizen be he/she a descendant of the White or the Red Army members [the two opposing parties of the 1918–1921 Civil War] feels part of our painful, difficult, contradictory, but at the same time great history.' From the ethno-cultural point of view, he thinks (2012a) that the idea of moral, cultural, and historical co-operation among the peoples of Russia should form the contours of societal consensus. Despite the pressures from Russian nationalists to recognize the leading role of ethnic Russians in the course of the country's history, he claims that the Russian cultural code 'belongs to peoples of all religions and ethnicities who share our unique inter-civilizational identity and not only to ethnic Russians.'

As is the case with Western liberal proposals, Putin (2012a) grants various institutions of social life – universities, churches, entertainment industries – the leading role in promoting and maintaining the 'cultural code'. He refers to the example of the United States, in which the code of multicultural unity was disseminated through such institutions. Following the cultural-code idea, Putin (2012a) proposes civic patriotism for Russia, which at this stage begins to obtain more liberal connotations. Putin writes: 'every person living in our country should not forget about his/her faith and ethnicity. But above all he/she should be a citizen of Russia and be proud of it. Nobody has the right to place their ethnic and religious particularities above the state law. At the same time, these very laws must take into account such ethnic and religious features.'

This partial accommodation of liberal and traditional aspirations allows representatives of both strands of thought to emphasize differing aspects of importance in Putin's ideas and claim affiliation with the official policy line. Valery Tishkov (2008, 172) of the Russian Academy of Sciences, a liberal writer who has promoted the idea of civic nationalism enthusiastically, acknowledges how close the official approach is to the Western procedure. He writes that 'the Russian authorities, including the current and former presidents, Dmitry Medvedev and Vladimir Putin, have embraced this final characterization, which advances the notion of the Rossiyan people as a historical entity or civic nation.' Tishkov (2008, 173) is delighted that '[this] formula is in line with the state (civic) national identity that has been adopted and proven successful in other major multi-ethnic countries around the world.'

Alexey Venediktov, the chief editor of the Echo of Moscow liberal radio station, welcomes the idea of developing an implicit public cultural consensus and disseminating it in schools, universities, and other important places of state influence. He also views this as an important step towards forging procedural similarities with the Western liberal practice of multicultural accommodation. However, he qualifies Putin's proposals by arguing that, in order to develop the common 'cultural code', these institutions should assume responsibility for translating the cultures of *all* peoples of the Russian Federation to younger generations. Instead of giving students a choice of culture-related subjects (which could most often result in students choosing to study their own culture), the state should adopt a uniform policy of explaining the particularities of all Russia's cultures to young people. By doing so, Venediktov argues, 'we can gradually create a common cultural denominator that could be implicitly understandable and acceptable to future generations.' Thus, in a classically liberal fashion, personal cultural preferences would remain in the private realm of home and family, while multicultural civic teaching would be kept in the public domain of civic education (Shevchenko et al. 2012). Nikolay Svanidze (Shevchenko and Svanidze 2012), an eminent liberal journalist and historian, emphasizes the importance of public media, which should actively promote the values of Russia's differing cultures and thus disseminate the idea of a cultural consensus and a basic code of recognition.

Peter Shchedrovitskiy (2000a), of the Institute of Philosophy, also speaks on the need to develop a distinct cultural framework that could reflect Russia's growing societal complexity. He claims that the development of cosmopolitan multiculturalism – a version of liberal multiculturalism in which people have multiple 'hyphenated' identities – is the main trend of the global Western dynamic. Yet again, he does not view the proposed societal consensus in terms of ideological value. Rather, he focuses on the communicative sphere that could create particular 'perceptive configurations' and construct new implicit forms of understanding reality. He advocates the formation of 'a communicative space for possible and *acceptable* actions within this newly created *framework*.' For Shchedrovitskiy (2006a), language plays a decisive role in influencing the formation of behavioural patterns. Thus he believes that those who think and speak Russian can feel affiliated with the Russian state and Russianness.

Traditionalists, on the other hand, consider the liberal understanding of the 'cultural code' as too thin. Maxim Shevchenko, a left-wing conservative journalist and politician, criticizes Shchedrovitskiy's solely communicative idea. Instead, he calls for finding a 'common interpretative ground' for the Russian 'culture code'. This 'common interpretative ground' should be based primarily on 'the interest of participant peoples to pursue common fate and history'. Shevchenko (2004) argues that 'without this implicit understanding of the common fate, the creation of Russia's civic nation will remain a field for manipulative games amongst financial elites who might have linguistic unity but lack ontological loyalty to the Russian world.' Thus, successful integration in Russia should take place through the creation of a 'political nation that unites various people regardless of their nationality, race, and religion by some common political principle' (Shevchenko 2004). Despite these somewhat procedurally liberal connotations, the 'common political principle' for Shevchenko (Shevchenko, in Prokhanov et al. 2012) is seen in the articulation of the idea of 'inter-civilizational plurality' based on a societal pact between various cultures, traditions, and 'civilizations' forming the Russian state.

Dugin (2009f), the leader of Russia's radical-conservative thought, has become an avid supporter of the 'cultural code' or the 'base consensus' idea. He claims that without the base societal consensus 'there will be no history, no coherent state policies, and no sense of nationhood.' In line with traditionalist thinking, he embarked on the search for a common 'interpretative ground' for the 'culture code' notion. In this light, Dugin sees the main value of Putin's proposals in the emphasis on historical interpretations. Dugin lends to this a theoretical backing. Armed with the logic of Foucault and Wittgenstein, he claims that 'there is no historical or philosophical fact as such. Rather there is an interpretation of events, and as a result, a conflict of existing interpretations.'

Dugin (2009f) outspokenly advocates the creation of a new 'Russian myth', which could help establish the idea of Russian national identity. The word 'myth' is not used in a negative sense, implying that the events it describes are not true. Rather it has an interpretative meanings. As Vera Tolz (2001, 7) explains, 'often scholarly assumptions constitute substantial parts of such myths.' This reasoning links him closely with many modernist and postmodernist theoreticians of nationalism, who claim that national identities are constructed by cultural and political elites (Tolz 2001, 7; see also Hroch 1985; Breuilly 1985). This 'myth' should be grounded on a few significant 'historical facts' that can be implicitly accepted by all peoples in Russia. Multiculturalism must become one of the most important features of this myth. Dugin (2009f) insists on an official recognition of the 'equal contribution of all peoples of Russia to the process of Russian state building', and proposes to 'outlaw claims that state otherwise'. Dugin (2012g) also thinks that Russia has some previous experience at creating her 'culture code'. He points to the relative success of the Imperial and Soviet eras, when the presumed culture code was based on Orthodox Imperial and Soviet ideas respectively. At the same time, he (2012g) argues that modern Russia finds herself in differing circumstances and faces the challenge of inventing a 'new framework of acceptable interpretations'. This is a complex task, for it would first require developing the new 'culture code' on the basis of historical interpretations and customs and then forging an adherence among all ethnicities to the new 'base consensus'.

It has now become clear that, at the procedural level, the Russian idea of multiculturalism, in both liberal and traditional versions, proposes a type of hierarchical identity structure. The base identity layer – which could be called the framework identity – is forged on the foundation of a common societal consensus. The upper identity layers belong to cultural, linguistic, religious, and other particularities. It also remains implicit that the base identity layer is more significant than the other layers built on its foundation – as seen in Putin's proposals above. Divergence between the Western-liberal and Russian interpretations of the base layer's nature is also clear: the first instance assumes ideological adherence to liberal practices, the second focuses on the yet-to-be-established cultural, historical, or communicative commonality.

Substantive Aspects

The difference between Western-liberal and Russian multicultural ideas deepens when we move from procedural to substantive issues. Which ideas, debates, practices, and cultures do we allow in the base framework, and which do we leave out? Answers to these questions reveal that, while both strands of Russian multiculturalism could be viewed as somewhat liberal in form and procedure, they are predominantly communitarian in content. It is important that liberal overtones are minimal and only appear when these thinkers express a desire to create the framework, societal, or 'base' consensus. Pursuit of the common good, on the other hand, is one central feature that links Russian traditionalists and liberals to the communitarian domain. While their ideal of the public good differs substantially, both charge the state with the responsibility to sustain their favoured interpretations of the good life. It is important that neither traditional nor liberal thinkers emphasize the ideals of personal autonomy and individual rights as a criterion necessary for entry into the 'base consensus'.[4]

Liberals often view multiculturalism in economic utilitarian terms. Development, economic growth, and progress are their main priorities that create the ultimate public good. To some extent, this hollows out ideological debates on the importance of inter-ethnic dialogue and reduces it to the discussion of expedience in pursuit of economic growth. Leokadiya Drobizheva, for example, argues for the removal of cultural stereotypes, because they could be detrimental to economic development, the job market, and investment. Drobizheva (2003, 9–11) criticizes Max Weber's idea of drawing the link between religion and political-economic culture, arguing that the latter is context-dependent and changes continually. She (2003, 6–8) also claims that various ethno-cultural hostilities must be viewed through the lens of a competition for economic benefits and employment. This brings her close to the Western liberal idea of conceptually divorcing but politically linking the notions of recognition and redistribution (Tully and Owen 2007). Shchedrovitskiy (2006a) also thinks that multiculturalism is a necessary precondition for creating a successful economy based on intellectual resources and educational services. Pointing at the experience of the United States, he claims that various cultural groups within this country contributed to the emergence of innovative technologies and varying types of businesses and allowed the country to secure leadership in the post-industrial world. He points to America's large corporations and research institutions, which include a large number of European scientists and intellectuals. Thus, he argues in favour of promoting cosmopolitan multiculturalism as a necessary step towards a post-industrial society. The latter could help Russia to be more Western, and hence achieve her political-cultural 'normalization' (Shchedrovitskiy 2000a and 200b).

Vladimir Malakhov's analysis of Western multicultural practices is also based on explanations of economic expediency. Malakhov (2012) argues that many European countries allowed labour immigration with the view of restoring their postwar economies. However, they did not expect those migrants to remain in their countries once their labour was no longer needed, and the multicultural mosaic policy was a mere tool to prevent the migrants from full integration. At the same time, after the 1973 economic crisis, it became clear that migrants had settled in their host countries and were not willing to leave. The launch of generous welfare-state packages, in Malakhov's mind, was to prevent the emergence of a social underclass, in which people would suffer from multiple forms of deprivation – ethnic as well as economic. Yulia Latynina (2011), Russia's eminent liberal commentator, supports this conspiracy theory by claiming that the European multiculturalism of the 1960s onwards was nothing but an 'export of a welfare-state-dependent voter who would be a client of the state and not a citizen.'

The link to economic expediency leads to another common line of liberal reasoning that refuses to treat the problems of multiculturalism as independent issues and views them as consequences of the socio-economic and political difficulties troubling Russia. Many such liberals deploy the 'ethnic conflict/multicultural' card in their political struggle. They often claim that, if the existing government is removed, the problem of ethnic conflict will be resolved automatically. Alex Alexiev (2010), Visiting Fellow at the Hudson Institute in Washington, provides a rather extreme example of this point of view. Alexiev writes that the cause of ethnic extremism in Russia 'is to be found in the undemocratic and politically oppressive regime, the predatory nexus between the interests of business oligarchs and the Kremlin and the corrupt law enforcement apparatus that is more adept at being a political police than in dealing with terrorists. A root cause many call Vladimir Putin.' Many liberal public figures in Russia agree with this. They raise important problems that are challenging Russian society: pending judicial reform, corruption, growing tariffs for communal services, and the absence of civic spirit within the population. Leonid Gozman (Zhirinovsky and Gozman 2011), an eminent radical liberal activist, claims: 'Tadjiks, Afghans, Vietnamese, and other ethnic minorities do not commit crimes against our country. The crimes against our country are committed by those officials who created the corrupt system, who trade our rights for cash, and who could sell these rights to those who would pay more.'

Clearly, beyond the economic and socio-economic debate, liberals can not offer any further substance to the multiculturalism discourse. Traditionalists, on the other hand, propose a more elaborate ideological pattern. As opposed to the thin economic-utilitarian view of the liberals, traditionalists list the items that they wish to include in the common 'culture code', and the items that they want to keep at bay. This list is based on the traditionalists' understanding of the public good. In their view, public good is seen in their two most important values: (1) preservation of Russia's territorial integrity and (2) preservation of Russia's distinct polyethnic character, which has been formed throughout the past centuries. The two objectives are somewhat contradictory on the surface. At the same time, they correspond in many ways to the Western communitarian arguments on similar issues. First, traditionalists are concerned about the possibility of Russia's territorial disintegration. Stanislav Govorukhin (in Shevchenko et al. 2012), the former State Duma spokesman for cultural policy, worries about the

challenge of the political nationalism of ethnic minorities. This challenge stems from the fact that Russia 'has emerged as a union of nations
or peoples who developed as independent subjects in the course of
their history.' He thinks that most such minority nations have erected
their own cultural institutions within the Russian Federation, created
national elites, and established their own historical myths, which are
being rapidly entrenched within local societies. He thinks that such
enclaves exist within Russia as autonomous cultural-political, and
even institutional, units. This genuine mosaic structure, Govorukhin
worries, could result in Russia following the fate of the USSR. From
this point of view, multicultural integration should avoid forging the
mosaic pattern and curb the dangerous trends towards disintegration.

Second, the objective of preserving Russia's polyethnic nature
stems from the traditionalists' understanding of the country's history.
Traditionalists usually view Russia as a historical inter-civilizational
polyethnic polycultural entity. Articulation, promotion, and maintenance of this concept form the basis of their proposed multicultural
policy and one of the most important normative common goals of
Russian society. In this context, they present Russianness as a cultural, political, and civilizational concept, and not an ethnic one.
Most traditionalist intellectuals claim that Russian history was one
of coexistence between various ethnic groups, who through cultural,
economic, and political interchange, as well as war and conquest,
came to form one Russian nation. Alexandr Tsipko (2010), professor of philosophy at the Moscow State University, compares the idea
of Russianness with the notion of Polish Catholicism, which has
'transcended religious interpretations and obtained cultural, political, and social connotations.' From this point of view, traditionalists'
Russia is a complex political-cultural and polyethnic constellation,
which includes 'Russians, Ukrainians, Byelorussians, Tatars, and North
Caucasus people, who culturally feel Russian (Rossiyan), who were
part of Russian history, and who are prepared to support the Russian
state and sovereignty in the international arena' (Shevchenko 1997).

These normative goals compel traditionalists to form a clear
content for a multicultural-consensus framework. First, Dugin, in
agreement with Shevchenko and Govorukhin, argues that the new
multicultural policy should avoid all forms of chauvinism and radical
nationalism. It should primarily exclude the ethnic-minority political
nationalism described above. Secondly, it should avoid Russian ethnic nationalism as a dangerous precondition of potential territorial

disintegration. Third, traditionalists hope to promote the idea that all peoples of the Russian Federation have equally contributed to the building of the Russian state (Shevchenko et al. 2012; Dugin 2012g). Shevchenko (1997) claims, for example, that Russia is located at the crossroads of three 'civilizations': the Judea-Christian, Islamic, and Buddhist. Each of these 'civilizations' is responsible for Russia's inherent multi-vector and multicultural outlooks. Judo-Christian origins determine Russia's European features. Islamic components shape her Central-Asian outlook. The Buddhist-Confucian foundations are responsible for Russia's Far Eastern cultural components. These cultures, the late Geidar Dzhemal continues, have been complementary in the construction of the Russian state and identity. Traditionalists further insist that denial of this 'myth' and the promotion of mono-ethnic, monotheistic, and monocultural interpretations of Russia's history must be cast aside as unacceptable.

Fourth, they claim that the state should make all the effort in cultivating cultures, histories, religions, languages, and other particularities of peoples populating the Russian Federation. Maxim Shevchenko (Dzhemal and Shevchenko 2012) proposes some steps towards achieving such goals, using the example of the North Caucasus. Concerned with keeping the area an integral part of the Russian Federation, Shevchenko (2010) claims that the primary policy objectives in the region are not economic, but cultural, historical, and political. He observes that the extant interpretations of the Caucasian war gloss over some bitter historical truths and evoke hostility from local people. 'The myth of the Caucasian war,' he argues, 'is dominant in the process of mobilization of the anti-Russian sentiment in the region.' The only way forward is to adopt policies that could cherish the memory of extinct regional cultures and promote the 'varying cultures of the remaining people, carefully avoiding trends towards assimilation' (ibid.). In support of this, Dugin and Govorukhin point at Russia's history of cultivating varying ethnic cultures. They quote Lev Gumilev, who insisted that, in the Middle Ages, France was composed of over one hundred ethnic groups – Gascons, Basques, Occitans, Bretons, and others. However, the policies of ethnic assimilation resulted in the formation of a largely uniform French civic nation, in which only Basques and Bretons sustained their distinct identities. A similar situation took place in Germany, Spain, Italy, Sweden, and, to some extent, Britain. Russia, in Govorukhin's mind, has followed a different path of cultivating ethnic particularities. Therefore, despite the odds and dangers, she should continue this policy in the future as one means of preserving her multi-ethnic identity (Shevchenko et al. 2012). This logic links Russia's traditionalist multiculturalists with their Western communitarian counterparts who argue the significance of culture in a person's life and the importance of sustaining one's cultural authenticity.

Taking this a step further, Russian traditionalist multiculturalists advocate legal recognition of group rights – which is also a step in the Western communitarian direction. Shevchenko (Shevchenko and Nemtsov 2012) suggests that the peoples of the North Caucasus should receive legally enshrined permissions to practice various Islamic traditions. He suggests that these traditions may include polygyny, special religious dresses at schools and other public places, the slaughtering of animals during religious holidays, and so on. Interestingly, polygyny is already *de facto* tolerated in Russia's Islamic regions. Chechen President Ramzan Kadyrov (2006) spoke in favour of legalizing the practice – a policy proposal that got support from the Council of the Grand Muftis in Russia. It is important to mention that many traditionalists, while speaking in favour of group rights, refuse to view such rights as an extension of individual autonomy. Dugin (2012g), for example, argues that Russia has never built her cultural and ideological traditions on the concept of individual rights. Russia, in Dugin's mind, has always had holistic approaches to social problems, in which the whole was more important than the part. Other participant cultures of the Russian space were also rejecting individualism. Georgians, Armenians, Central Asian, and North Caucasian cultures were based on communitarian values and holistic attitudes. The conglomerate of these holistic cultures defines Russia's cultural distinctiveness, and group rights must be granted under this understanding.

Finally, the vast majority of traditionalist multiculturalists think that Russia should avoid following Western blueprints in dealing with migrants. Mikhail Leontyev, an eminent conservative commentator, argues that migrants in Russia, who mainly come from the former Soviet Union republics, represent 'our former countrymen and from that point of view they do not differ from internal North Caucasian migrants who come to settle in the European parts of Russia' (Leontyev and Gusman, 2010). He claims that migrants are foreigners in the legal domain only, but an integral part of Russian society in the cultural sphere. Claiming that these people are culturally alien to Russia would be morally wrong and could threaten Russia's historical multicultural essence. In this context, voices are heard in advocacy of the cultural and political recognition of migrants as 'our own citizens' – recognition that they lack at the moment (Leontyev and Gusman 2010).

Toleration vs Acceptance and the Conflict Model of Toleration

This discussion brings us closer to the issue of toleration. In this area, views expressed by the liberal and traditional sides of the spectrum are very similar. Therefore, I will refer to the Russian understanding of the idea of toleration as an umbrella term for various liberal and traditionalist interpretations that have some common ground. Given that toleration is an important moral doctrine and political practice of the West, it has both legally and morally binding overtones for many radical liberals. Russian traditionalist philosophers reject this understanding of the concept as hypocritical, arguing instead in favour of genuine *recognition* and *acceptance*. Logically, we can distinguish two main points of disagreement between the Russian and Western ideas of toleration. First, following some Western critics (B. Williams 1993; 2005), Russian philosophers insist that linking toleration to the liberal notion of personal autonomy is inadequate. They are concerned with the fact that such an approach hollows out the meaning of the concept of toleration and oppresses political dialogue. Second, Russian philosophers develop the conflict-antagonistic model of toleration. They insist that the idea of conflict and disagreement should be treated as an integral and unalienable aspect of toleration. This could help to maintain the genuine nature of this moral attitude and political practice.

Alexandr Pertsev (2005, 32), Professor of Philosophy at the Ural State University, insists that the failure of the politics of toleration in both Russia and the West stems from its tendentious interpretation. He writes that toleration, 'both moral and political does not automatically guarantee true understanding between representatives of different cultures. Many proponents of toleration view it as a panacea from all social ills, while toleration is just an intermediate stage on the road from conflict to true understanding and co-operation.' Thus, omitting the conflict component from this chain of events could break its internal logic and subsequently deny the possibility of a genuine dialogue and interpenetration of cultures. It will create a mosaic society whose basis for peace is temporary and tenuous. Thus, the idea of toleration as an intermediate stage between conflict and harmony leads Russian philosophers to argue that we should cease treating toleration as an end goal. Rather, we should view it as a policy that leads to new forms of dialogue (Pertsev 2005, 33).

Furthermore, Maxim Khomiakov (2003, 27–8), the head of the Ural Institute of Philosophy, claims that it is almost impossible to combine moral integrity of principled individuals with the need to tolerate something that they find unacceptable and wrong. When we adopt the practice of toleration, we do not change our attitude as such but merely hold back disapproval or replace it with scepticism and indifference. This is procedural but not substantive toleration. In this light, Russian philosophers argue that disagreement, which is best channelled to the realm of critical discussion, represents an unalienable component of toleration. This leads them to propose the conflict model of toleration. Many Russian analysts examine the idea of toleration within the framework of its intrinsic relationship to political violence. Svetlana Ilyinskaya (2004, 122–6) of the Moscow Institute of Philosophy (RAN) argues that tolerance is almost always associated with violence – be it in the shape of value offensive doctrines or physical acts of a political struggle. A minority group becomes an object of toleration only when it is capable of challenging society politically and only when it relocates its ideas of the good life from the private to public domain, i.e. when it becomes the subject of politics. The subsequent toleration rhetoric emerges in the course of political struggle. It is driven by the inability of majorities to ignore the growing political significance of 'tolerated' minorities. Following Marcuse (1969), Ilyinskaya (2004) claims that in modern societies political technologies replace substantive means of political struggle. Thus, the idea of toleration emerges as one such technology aimed to impose a temporary status quo.

Thus, removing conflict from the political scene entirely is not always beneficial. Ilyinskaya (2004) writes that in the course of a conflict various cultures begin to learn each other's ways of life and this may lead to the formation of genuine foundations for recognition that could ensure peaceful coexistence in the future. In this argument she echoes Boris Kapustin (2003), who thinks that recognition of the initial antagonism always assumes distinguishing a common ground between differing parties and thus provides a starting point for reconciliation. Monistic avoidance of conflict, on the other hand, promotes suppressed discontent and a subsequent backlash. In this context, open recognition of the conflict component could help society to relieve itself from the chains of self-censorship and moral oppression. This in turn could ignite a move towards genuine inter-penetration of cultures, their mutual interrogation, criticism, and eventual enrichment. On a final note, Pertsev (2005, 37) argues that true inter-penetration of cultures requires spiritual efforts. Superficial partnership and stereo-typic forms of co-operation do not invoke such feelings. As he (2005, 37) notes, such forms of partnership lead to the 'Kingdom of the Heideggerian das Man – a non-personality which is now endowed with the burden of responsibility and decision-making.'

Philosophical struggle to provide the concept of toleration with genuine substance feeds back to Russia's civic-political discourse. This is manifest in two main developments. First, Russian public figures speak in favour of genuine recognition, as opposed to toleration. Second, in such debates they refuse the means of political correctness as an instrument capable of instilling the practice of toleration. Nikita Mikhalkov (2011), Russia's eminent film director, emphasises the importance of implicit cultural recognition and acceptance. Toleration, to Mikhalkov, is a dialogue between 'falsely polite guests and equally false hosts' who have little genuine interest in each other. He insists that, instead of toleration, 'we should feel internal (spiritual) necessity of a dialogue between nations' because the 'Russian landscape is as dear to a Muslim as it is to an Orthodox Christian living in our country.' Mikhail Veller (in Shvydkoy et al. 2011), an Estonian-born Russian writer, insists that 'toleration proclaims the primacy of morals over the truth. If these two values converge, then this is fine. If they do not, a tolerant person has to make a deal with his conscience.' Vladimir Solovyev (2011b), Russia's influential political commentator, also speaks of toleration as a political imposition intended to contain a conflict but often producing a backlash as a result. He points to the examples of the Thilo Sarazin book (*Germany Does Away with Herself*), the English Defence League, and the British National Party, as well as their West European counterparts that emerged across Europe as a result of the 'suffocating climate of political correctness, which often acts as a pressure cooker mechanism.' Valery Solovey, formerly Professor at the Moscow Institute of International Relations, also claims that, because of the 'oppressive mechanisms of political correctness and toleration, the level of domestic xenophobia in Europe is much higher than that in Russia' (Dzhemal and Solovey 2011).

Dugin claims that 'love instead of toleration' should become the primary goal of multicultural politics (Shevchenko et al. 2012). By this

Dugin does not imply a literal but rather a spiritual, Abrahamic understanding of this word seen as either brotherly love of one's neighbour
or assumed collective responsibility for the fate of one's compatriots
and people. Vladimir Gurkin (in Shvydkoy et al. 2011), Russia's film
and art director, claims that 'institutionalised toleration, as well as
intolerance, are both the results of manipulation of the human mind.
Genuine toleration, on the other hand, shows inner moral integrity of
a person, her strength and devotion to the values of the good life. It
relates to compassion, sensibility, and is a feature of kindness that is
available to all human beings without institutional imposition and
ideological cliché.' The search for the genuine within aspects of toleration brings Russia's debates close to Western communitarianism, which
also advocates the ideas of 'recognition.' Oksana Gaman-Golutvina
(in Shvydkoy et al. 2001), Professor at the Moscow State Institute of
Foreign Relations and the Chair of the Russian Academy of Political
Science, comes very close to this line of reasoning. She argues that
'toleration is often linked to some form of arrogance. It *a priori* considers the dominant culture's superiority and falsely demands it to be
"tolerant" or indifferent to minorities.' This echoes Bhikkhu Parekh's
(2006, 110) passionate criticism of the liberal practice of toleration,
which has a '... persistent tendency to ... divide all ways of life into
liberal and non-liberal, equate the latter with illiberal, and to talk of
tolerating and rarely of respecting or cherishing them.'

Finally, the absence of any meaningful tools of political correctness
in Russia's public discourse is the reflection of the proposed conflict
model of toleration. Vladimir Solovyov (2011a) is particularly critical
of the idea of political correctness. He (2011a, 78-9) insists that 'the
failure of multicultural policies in Europe also testifies to the official
line towards political correctness that harbours domestic expressions
of mistrust, fear, and suspicion.' The speeches and public relations acts
of the State Duma deputy speaker and the leader of the Russian Liberal
Democratic Party Vladimir Zhirinovsky, as another example, often
evoke fear and misunderstanding among Western observers, but
mainly amusement or disgust among his Russian listeners. Yet,
Zhirinovsky acts within the 'no political correction' framework and
often diagnoses some painful areas of Russia's political life that could
not be otherwise articulated in such a direct style. It is also important
that his speeches usually invoke public rejection of Russian ethno-
centrism, showing the dangers of ethnic hostilities, as well as practical
intolerance, and lead to further critical discussion of these issues.

Struggles with Sub-Cultural Diversity

The theorizations above function until we meet the bounds of sub-cultural diversity. Representatives of subcultural diversity, while sharing a broadly common Russian culture, entertain various lifestyles and practices that challenge the ideals of traditional/mainstream customs. This concerns unconventional family structures, gender and sexuality choices, and the like. The problem is best discussed in the framework of Russian conservatism, which we dealt with in Chapter 3. Yet I find it important to devote a few words to this subject, for it is relevant to the debate on multiculturalism. While the liberals remain largely indifferent, and often abstain from the debate, the fear of subcultural diversity leads many Russian conservatives to denounce the very meaning of multiculturalism, if such 'multiculturalism' is understood in terms of promoting subcultural diversities. Moreover, Russian conservative thinkers claim that the acceptance of subcultural diversity has led to the crisis of values in Europe and to the 'dusk of European civilization'.

Natalya Narochnitskaya (2012; 2010) argues that the liberal endorsement of the moral diversity of the West constructs the 'prison of values, within which traditional morals have no place'. She writes that the 'freedom of morals, personal autonomy, and diversity took their toll too quickly, and humanity is rushing down this path, ignoring all road signs.' Veller (in Shvydkoy et al. 2011) also claims that the detraditionalizing aspects of multiculturalism have reached their peak in Europe. As a result, we 'lose the meaning of words such as moral, sin, the good, promiscuity, perversion, consciousness, egoism, and betrayal. Instead, we are driven by the moral of self-expression, the desire to have things here and now, and as a result, by the pressure to be tolerant to the same wishes of others. We are observing the destruction of a Great Civilization (Europe) that is eating itself from within.' Thus, it is often claimed that the West is overly welcoming of unconventional forms of self-expression, such as radical-looking tattoos, hairstyles, outfits, and lifestyles, but is sceptical of traditional religious dresses, symbols, and customs. The goal of this criticism in Russia is not to suppress subcultural diversities as such, but to keep them outside the bounds of political visibility. Pursuit of unconventional practice is permitted if it stays within the private sphere or the domain of entertainment and does not publicly threaten the traditionalist moral values of the mainstream.

As this logic unfolds, religious thinking often merges with the secular traditional mentality and forms a unified front of mainstream morality that is hostile to subcultural trends. Shevchenko (2011) reasons that the multicultural conflict in the West is not a conflict between cultures and religions but an 'ideological struggle between secularism and tradition'. Liberal secularism, in his mind, bears the most blame. He argues that, because Western liberal politics divorced religious and civic domains in the age of Enlightenment, liberal ideology now 'wages war against all traditional way of thinking, be they Catholic, Orthodox, Muslim, Jewish, or anything whatsoever.' He continues that 'liberalism broke the back of the Catholic Church in Europe, and now it aims to clash with Christian, Islamic, and Jewish civilizations that promote tradition and faith. Liberalism is antagonistic to traditions, and multicultural conflict is a falsely imposed conflict of faiths and cultures that is meant to disguise the true conflict between liberalism and tradition.' Traditional cultures, according to Shevchenko, are capable of carrying on a dialogue aimed at mutual enrichment, interrogation, and criticism. Representatives of different cultures could question each other's interpretations of the good life and disagree on some issues 'as long as they are not degraded to the status of mere consumers, autonomous individuals who are denying moral codes of traditional religiosity. Therefore, we see a conflict between the world geared towards secularism and the world based on traditional morals, cultures, and spirituality. There is a kingdom of matter, the "here and now" ideology, the "bodily needs", and a realm of spirituality, high culture and tradition.' In this context, Shevchenko (2011) claims that multiculturalism in its Western-liberal interpretation is a 'trap intended to divide religions and peoples. Europe is not going through a crisis of multiculturalism but through a crisis of religious, cultural, and moral consciousness.'

This approach to the Western idea of subcultural diversity, as well as the fear of detraditionalization of society, causes concern among Russian thinkers and public figures. Nikita Mikhalkov (2011) claims that Russians 'should fear secular propagandists and their destructive potential more than they should fear unification of all religious denominations.' Boris Mezhuyev (2012) explains the unexpected success of Rick Santorum, a staunchly conservative Catholic, during the 2012 Republican primaries, in terms of the public fear of the ongoing redefinition of traditional religious morals and self-perceptions of humans that, to his mind, represent the result of scientific progress breaking the conventional bounds of Nature. This relates to gender and genetic engineering, new methods of human procreation, stem-cell research and other technologies that shatter the traditional reach of human abilities and redefine the pre-existing relationship between Man and Nature that was based on the norms of religiosity.

MAIN ACTORS AND POLITICAL ACTIVITY

The Russian idea of multiculturalism reveals a complex mix of philosophical approaches. It is evolving against the backdrop of Russia's distinct culture and history, although it has not yet developed as a fully formed doctrine or political practice. From this point of view, there are no coherent or clear political parties and movements that can defend the specific ideas of multiculturalism. Having said that, all Russia's political organizations, in one way or another, take a stand on the subject. Russia's highest echelons of power, represented by Vladimir Putin, often adopt a traditionalist approach to multicultural practice in Russia. As we have discussed in this chapter, Putin's speeches, articles, and policies are geared towards sustaining Russia's substantively pluri-cultural, multi-religious, and pluri-ethnic historical tradition. This attitude has had an impact on Russia's foreign policy and her moral standing in the international arena. Russia's foreign minister, Sergey Lavrov (2018), often insists on granting the ability to all people around the world to pursue their cultural and religious roots and to resist the norms of 'pseudo-liberal morality' that lead many countries, and Europe in particular, to the 'rejection of its traditional cultural roots'.

Lavrov (2018) also claimed that more and more people around the world are looking to Russia as a 'defender of traditional values'. Russia's main political parties – such as United Russia, the Communist Party of the Russian Federation, and Just Russia – tread the traditionalist multicultural line in their policies and speeches. It is also significant that various nationalist organizations of the state-conservative lenience, which we have discussed in Chapter 6, also adopt a traditionalist approach in the multicultural debate. The vast majority of left conservative movements – with Essence of Time being at the forefront, as well as fundamental conservative associations such as the Union of Eurasian Youth and the Great Fatherland party, also consider Russia as a multi-cultural, multi-religious, multi-ethnic union of peoples united by common history and traditional values of patriotism, family, and humanistic compassion. Russia's liberal parties of both radical and pluralistic lenience adopt a less-substantive attitude to multicultural policies and depart from the positions of liberal multiculturalism that we have discussed in this chapter.

Nonetheless, the main tenets of Russia's multiculturalism are constantly in the making and being shaped by political debates between liberals and traditionalists, with permanent reference to similar practices and ideologies in the West. However, despite the ongoing Western reference, we can regard Russian liberals as 'liberals' only conditionally. The only liberal element in the Russian debate on multiculturalism is the procedure of forging a base 'societal consensus'. The contours of this base consensus are sought in cultural, historical, and linguistic factors, as opposed to liberal practices and values, as it is understood in the West. Fundamental tenets of classical liberalism, such as the autonomy of the individual, freedom of association, strict division between the public and private spheres, and limited government, face either criticism or avoidance in the Russian discourse on multiculturalism. With regard to the content of proposed multicultural models, the Russian idea of multiculturalism has some communitarian overtones. Yet again, these are understood in Russia-specific terms. The emphasis is on the political consensus of big government and the primacy of a state-centred political community. In the area of subcultural diversity, Russia differs ever more radically from the West. The fear of subculturalism leads Russian thinkers in a staunchly conservative direction entering the realm of religious conservatism. These trends are instrumental in understanding the subsequent institutional choices and policy directions that might be adopted by the Russian government in the sphere of multicultural and multi-ethnic accommodation.

9

Feminism

Feminism has become an essential part of the ideological landscape of any modern state. This chapter examines the main theoretical trends within this ideology in contemporary Russia. The analysis adopts a theoretical framework established in the West some decades ago, at the time active debates on the subject began. It splits the idea of struggle for women's rights into two broad categories. One claims total equality between men and women. Another strives to accommodate differences between the two sexes and account for the ways in which women may be disadvantaged in contemporary society due to their differences from men. Even though the Western critique has developed significantly to include new broad variations of feminist trends, many Russian conservative observers (Tretyakov, Babayan, Solovyov, Kurginyan, Dugin, Goricheva), who look at the development of the problem in contemporary Russia from outside the gender-studies cohort, hold to this pre-existing Western methodology. This approach is therefore important, in that it represents an examination of Russian feminism from the point of view of Russia's conservative centre. It also helps to sustain the existing paradigmatic division between traditionalism and liberalism that has run as a major thread through this book. This chapter is in three parts. The first part introduces a brief history of feminist ideology and its ensuing conceptual split. The second part examines the idiosyncrasies of Soviet feminism and its impact on the emergence of equality feminism in post-Soviet Russia. The third section considers themes and problems raised by both types of feminism in reference to the Russian case.

THEORETICAL REMARKS:
TWO CONCEPTS OF WESTERN FEMINISM

Feminism is concerned with the issue of male domination of aspects of socio-political and economic life. This mode of social relationship that is often referred to as patriarchal has been formed throughout many centuries of human development. A short tour of history would start with Ancient Greece. The emergence of private property and the household, along with the division of *oikos* (domestic) and *polis* (the state and the public) that took place at that time largely benefited men. Gradually, *oikos*, in which women were naturally more active by virtue of their role in rearing children, began to lose its socio-political importance. This resulted in the rise of various myths that glorified male activities, such as war, travel, and exploration, and explicitly excluded women (Coole 1993, 6–7; Squires 1999; Pateman 1998). By that time, Aristotle and Plato had a large body of preconceptions to rely on.

To Aristotle, the division between *oikos* and *polis* was natural. *Oikos* was a lower institution, a sphere of production and reproduction that existed on behalf of the higher institution – *polis* – that represented the good life. The good life meant a condition in which a man could implement his finest qualities and self-determination. However, the achievement of the good life is only available to those who are free from financial constraints and chores. This meant liberation from the daily rounds of productive and reproductive life. Within this paradigm, women, slaves, and children existed for the sake of rational male citizens, who could enjoy the good life in the realm of *polis* (Coole 1993, 30). Hence, the household served the purpose of providing the good life for the few.

Western feminists argue that this logic was later consolidated in the Bible, which claimed that Adam had natural superiority to Eve by virtue of his sex (Pateman 1988, 86–7). Subsequent Christian theology sustained this line in the writings of Thomas Aquinas and the Church Fathers – St Augustine, St Jeremy, St Gregory, St Ambrose who wrote between the fourth and sixth centuries. In a way similar to the tradition of the Greeks, St Jeremy and St Augustine divided body and soul into two distinct categories. They claimed the supremacy of the soul over the body, attributing the former to men and the latter to women. The body was associated with lust, uncleanliness, pleasure, and childbirth. St Jeremy insisted that, if a woman chose to serve Christ and focus on her soul, she would have to cease to be a woman and would have to become a man (Coole 1993). This was perhaps the first intuitive introduction of the idea of gender in the history of political thought.

Following the Renaissance, when the female role in society was briefly exonerated, modernity invented new ideological justifications for patriarchy. During the Reformation, the state struggled to maintain absolutism, which faced challenges from rising Protestant movements. This invoked an intense philosophical debate between defendants of patriarchy and proponents of the new contract theory. Patriarchalists, led by Robert Filmer, drew parallels between the positions of the head of state, the head of the Church, and a male head of a family (Pateman 1988, 77–115). The role of the father then became instrumental in the defence of state authority and in the stabilization of social relationships (Coole 1993, 53). In contrast to this, contract theorists, such as John Locke and Thomas Hobbes, argued that all people are born free and that there is no law of nature that could subordinate women to men. At the same time, both Locke and Hobbes drew similar parallels between the family and society. They claimed that authority within families belonged to men, albeit on a contractual, as opposed to a natural or divine, basis. Hence, the emergence of the social-contract idea represented the reorganization, but not the abolition, of patriarchy (Pateman 1988, 90; Coole 1993, 64–7).

Furthermore, modernity, through philosophy, art, and literature, established a new image of secular masculinity as a social norm and a cardinal behavioural pattern. Affirmation of the male sex helped to advance the idea of liberating humans from God. Lucifer was the only angel who defied God. It was perhaps not accidental that he was also the only angel who had sex and genitals. In contrast to other, sexless, angels, he was a male, often depicted with biphallic features. Subsequent political and philosophical secularizations of life, which culminated with the Nietzschean 'death of God' thesis, led to a situation in which a secular Man emerged as the main subject of politics. Man, as opposed to God, King, or Nature, assumed responsibility for the course of history, the fate of humanity, and the environment. Rational, aggressive, egoistic, economically active, and – above all – secular, this Man became the hero of the age.

His mastership accumulated gradually in the fields of art, politics, and philosophy. It began with the Cartesian reverence of reason. It continued with what Francis Bacon called to 'conquer the nature', through logic, exploration, and science. It asserted itself in Goethe's idea of the God-defiant male, who discovered the moment of ultimate happiness in the realm of the social. It was consolidated in Marxian proposals to 'change the world'. Hence, modernity built economic, political, and social relationships on masculine terms. It exalted aggression, egoism, and a competitive ethos, defined by the newly established and rapidly developing capitalism. Ownership of private property, acquisitions, hostile takeovers, nationalism, economic and political expansion, stock-market speculation – all represented masculine characteristics. Politicians and philosophers of that period had men in mind as beneficiaries of the new world structure and the parameters of the new social contact (Elshtain 1986, 7; Foucault 1990).

With consolidation of patriarchy, women had no choice but to struggle for their rights. Yet initially this struggle took two essentially different paths. The first option assumed fighting for equal rights with men in a world designed by men. These groups of feminist theorists, whom the literature occasionally refers to as liberals, 'integrationists', 'assimilationists', and 'feminists of equality' (Elshtain 1986, 2; Freedman 2001, 9–10), are 'concerned with the ways in which politics has structured gender relations' (Squires 1999, 17). They search for ways to include women within the extant structure of power relations. Such theorists propose to adopt a gender-blind androgynous society, in which biological differences have no relevance in the course of social, political, and economic affairs. They represent a liberal trend of thought, considering people primarily as individuals and only then as representatives of particular gender, ethnic, or religious groups. From this it follows that they are generally tolerant of the public-private divide, in which the matters of sex and gender remain in the private sphere.

Complementary to them are feminists of difference (Freedman 2001, 9; Kymlicka 2002, 378–9; Frazer and Lacey 1993, 214) or 'transformation theorists' (Squires 1999, 17), often referred to as 'rejectionists' (Elshtain 1986, 3). They claim that there are cases in which differential treatment of the sexes is legitimate and even desirable. They begin with sports, job placements, and separate washrooms, and end up with proposals to redefine the entire spectrum of social relationships to include and integrate women's perspectives and problems. Their project requires reconstructing the entire ontology of social science to include gender as one of its concepts and to conduct an epistemic shift in the study of power relations. Such thinkers claim that gender had already been taken into account while designing social institutions.

They insist that justice and equality can not be achieved if men are allowed to build social institutions in accordance with their standards and expect women to compete in an environment which they have not originally created (Mackinnon 1987, 36; Kymlicka 2002, 379). In this sense, these feminists argue that equality 'does not mean to be like men, as they are today, or have equality with one's oppressors' (Kymlicka 2002, 384; Frazer and Lacey 1993, 214).

Hence, the debate between the feminism of difference and the feminism of equality became central in the political literature of the early stages of the development of feminist thought. Subsequently, different and more-nuanced trends of feminism appeared. These included postcolonial, Marxist, queer, poststructuralist, and other trends. For the purpose of this volume, however, I will focus on the two oldest and more prominent debates between the feminism of equality and the feminism of difference, as those are the most pertinent to Russia. There are many areas in which the feminism of equality and feminism of difference seriously diverge. Let me consider those areas of debate relevant to the subsequent discussion on Russia. These are: (1) the division between public and private, (2) labour relations, (3) conceptions of power, and (4) models of citizenship.

First, the separation between the public and private spheres is a central element of the liberal ideology. Following the Greek tradition, the idea re-emerged in late-medieval Europe, signifying the end of the religious wars. The goal was to separate religion and politics and drive matters of religious consciousness into the private sphere (Habermas 1987). Many other aspects of an individual's life soon followed: family matters, personal views on culture and ethics, ethnicity, sexuality, and gender. Despite the fact that the separation between public and private realms formed the cornerstone of liberal thought, the two branches of feminism do not find consensus on this issue.

Feminists of difference claim that the division between public and private must be broken. The 'personal is political' slogan represents the locus of their critique. They reject the traditional idea that the political is located strictly within the sphere of institutions and government. Rather they claim that politics are ubiquitous and all-encompassing (Squires 1999, 23; Di Stefano 1996, 95–116). Politics is power, and power exists in all spheres of human life, including the private. They argue that exploitation, abuse, and neglect of women have taken place in the private sphere since antiquity. Domestic work is unpaid and not recognized as a socially and politically significant occupation. This leads to the disproportionate concentration of women in low-income part-time positions or in positions that do not require serious responsibilities and overtime work commitments. As a result, women begin to depend on men financially and politically (Kymlicka 2002, 381).

Liberal feminists, in contrast, are reluctant to part with the public-private distinction. This type of feminism merely seeks to open the public sphere to equal participation for men and women (Friedan 1960). These theorists suggest that if women stay in the sphere of domestic life, it is their personal choice and even their predisposition. This thought appeals to women who have a higher educational and social status and who could presumably take part in the political sphere on equal terms with men. As Heywood (2007, 245) notes, 'liberal feminism reflects the interests of white, middle-class women in developed societies, but fails to address the problems of working class women, black women and women in the developing world.'

Second, labour policy is an area in which the two strands of feminism also part ways. Feminists of difference argue that many job descriptions have been drafted to fit a male image. Gender inequalities, they argue, are built into the very definition of various positions in the spheres of blue-collar work, the military, education, public politics, and academic work. There may be gender-neutral pledges to employ men and women equally, but job descriptions favour men indirectly. For example, employers prefer hiring persons who are free from child-care responsibilities or those who have the height, weight, and strength to operate the equipment that is invariably designed for men (MacKinnon 1987, 37; Radcliffe-Richards 1980, 112–14; Kymlicka 2002, 379). Liberal feminists are reluctant to accept the argument that job descriptions must be composed in a fashion that could take the difference between men and women into account and create conditions that could adapt to women's specific needs. Instead, they take pride in women's capabilities to occasionally take part in male-dominated jobs and prefer to ignore any existing physical differences.

The definition of power is the third area in which the two strands of feminism find differences. Liberal feminists tend to support the so-called male definition of power, and argue that women are good at deploying this model in business and politics. This definition, initially proposed by Stephen Lukes, is based on the idea of conflict. In this model, A, using various methods, 'can get B do something that B would not otherwise do' (Lukes 1978, 11–12). Methods, in which A makes B do something A wants, diverge from a direct imposition of rules to agenda setting and mobilization of bias, and ends with the tools of hegemonic control of mind. This model of power assumes that there is a conflict of interests between *A* and *B* and that *A* wants to dominate *B* and have power 'over' *B*.

The feminist conception of power is rather different. It assumes that *A* and *B* seek consensus and want to co-operate. It departs from the idea that power is not possessional but relational and takes multiple directions. Hannah Arendt (1969) gives the best description of this power model. She (1969, 44) writes that power

> corresponds to the human ability not just to act but to act in concert. Power is never the property of an individual; it belongs to a group and remains in existence only so long as the group keeps together. When we say of somebody that he is 'in power' we actually refer to his being empowered by a certain number of people to act in their name. The moment the group, from which the power originated to begin with, disappears 'his power' also vanishes.

This model of power mainly refers to informal methods of influence and excludes zero-sum games. This is an important step forward in the definition of power, in that it has a gender-based foundation. Indeed, male forms of 'power over' represent the formal aspect of power, while female versions of 'power to' stands for the type of informal empowerment that has always characterized female influence (Squires 1999, 40). Elshtain (1986, 116) claims that 'one thread that seems to run through the tangle of historical and ethnographic evidence is a picture of *formal* male power being balanced or even underlined by *informal* female power.' Feminists of difference argue that women usually apply this model of power in politics and international relations (Grant and Newland 1991, 5; Harding 1986; Zalewski 1995; Foucault 1977, 168–9; Elshtain 1986, 106).

Finally, in the sphere of theories of citizenship, two clearly defined categories can be distinguished – one promoting the gender-neutral approach and the other advocating gender-differentiated thinking. In the first case, citizenship assumes a gender-blind attitude to all members of society and advocates the idea that both men and women should have equal access to and take equal part in the public sphere. This is reminiscent of the liberal model of citizenship (Heater 1990), in which rights are considered universal and primary to duties. The second approach claims that the contribution of women and their difference from men must be taken into account. These authors argue that women have 'specific capacities, talents, needs and concerns, so that the expression of their citizenship will be differentiated from that of men' (Pateman 1989, 196–7). Moreover, such theorists claim that the ideal of gender-neutral citizenship is unattainable and that women, in order to receive full citizenship, will have to adapt to the citizenship template fashioned and defined in a male image (Vogel 1991; Lister 2003, 94–6). This idea of citizenship emphasizes the concept of the public good, in which the duties of each citizen are viewed as sustaining good public life and order (Etzioni 1993; Heater 1990).

The two models of citizenship seem incompatible, and they have radically different side effects. The second model runs the risk of indulging in essentialism, in which the role of women as mothers and carers is overly exaggerated and they become unnecessarily confined to the private sphere. The first model, on the other hand, strictly demands that, in the patriarchal welfare state, women should either conform to the male-defined model of citizenship or continue their role as carers whose contributions and unpaid domestic labour are not valued by society as public or political deeds (Pateman 1989, 196–7). Similar theoretical and practical debates have evolved in the field of Russian, and even Soviet, feminism. The rest of this chapter will discuss the division of Russian feminism into two similar branches and apply those conceptual issues within both theoretical camps.

RUSSIAN FEMINISM

Soviet Patterns of Gender Socialization: Feminism of Equality

Researching the landscape of contemporary Russian feminism, one can arrive at an interesting conclusion. Thinkers and activists of the Soviet generation usually espouse feminism of equality and stand on the liberal positions, both theoretically and practically. Younger generations of women who were brought up under the post-Soviet system usually espouse feminism of difference. This interesting observation could be explained by the particular system of gender relations that was formed under the Soviet and partially Russian Imperial systems (Akulova 2013; Arbatova 2013; Gessen 1998; Goricheva et. al, 1980).

Liberal feminism, as we have discussed above, concerns itself with the issues of general equality and fends for women whose socio-economic interests have been already observed. Patterns of gender relations of both the Imperial and Soviet periods were generally geared towards gender equality and therefore conducive to the emergence of the liberal version of feminism at the post-Soviet stage. It is consequential that Russia, in its Imperial and Communist interpretations, was the first country in the world that granted women the widest political and economic rights (Seltser 2003; Khasbulatova 2004; Zdravomyslova 2001; Chirikova and Lapina 2011; Akhmedina, Shnyrova, Shkolnikov 2007). Women's rights organisations initially emerged between 1861 and 1917. This period gave rise to women's political solidarity and helped formulate demands towards state and society. Women became active in business, delivering impressive results in various industries and trade. A number of feminist literature journals emerged. Among those were the *Zhenskii Vestnik* (Women's Times), *Zhenskoe Delo* (Women Affairs), and *Drug Zhenshchin* (Women's Friend) (Chirikova 1998, 7). The February 1917 Revolution granted women the right to vote and run for office. Russia's Interim Government gave women the right to occupy any state power positions, including ministerial ones, in 1917 (Khasbulatova 2004, 343; Chirikova and Lapina 2011, 8).

The subsequent Bolshevik ideology, which won the dominant discourse after the October 1917 Revolution, also sided with the cause of female liberation. At its incipient stages, it held radical aspirations to fully recast the extant model of the bourgeois family. This trend chimed well with the general purpose of creating a radically new human anthropology based on the ideas of total equality and communal lifestyle. One of the first bills that the Bolsheviks passed upon their arrival in power was the abolition of church marriage and simplification of the divorce procedure. They also legalised civil partnerships, same-sex marriages, as well as marriages between three or more people, and were the first government in Europe to allow abortion. The initial radicalism of the Great October Socialist Revolution rhetoric gave way to the conservative restoration during the 1930s onwards. Traditional family, i.e. that which comprised one man, one woman, and a number of children, had become an essential "unit of society" without which building a meaningful Socialist system seemed impossible. At the same time, the idea of gender equality had not left the ideological scene. Men and women were expected to take equal paths in life. They received equal education, applied for jobs equally, with both expected to work and equally contribute their respective financial shares to the family budget. The state also inadvertently favoured women in the ideological, educational, and social spheres. In many ways, the post-Stalinist Soviet state purposefully neglected matters of masculinity and explicitly emphasised women's problems (Ashwin 2000; Kukhterin 2000). In line with the new family-friendly policy, the Soviet system sided with "mother and child" to socially protect them from potential life adversities. This strategy ideologically killed two birds with one stone. On the one hand, it maintained the initial Marxian-Bolshevik line of liberating women from the shackles of a patriarchal family and gave them some start in the socio-economic hierarchy. On the other hand, the policy sustained the new conservative idea of protecting families by encouraging birth and motherhood.

State alignment with women was clearly visible in the sphere of education, where girls were taught an active and self-sufficient approach to life. Most educational, nursing, and caring personnel were female, who gave girls initial ideas on how to be a professional self-sufficient woman. Boys, on the other hand, found themselves in a different situation. Boys were often told off for playing active and aggressive games. At the same time, they were expected to be different from girls: they could not cry, they could not behave in a girlish manner, and they could not play with dolls (Aleshina and Volovich 1991, 75). In this light, girls grew in a more relaxed emotional environment with clearly defined socialisation patterns, while boys had a serious challenge to recast their behaviour later in life to the yet-to-be-defined principles of masculinity. Moreover, in contrast to capitalism, the Communist economic and ideological system was based on the principles of mutuality, common property, sharing, and integration. Returning to our previous discussion on the nature of capitalism and its explicitly masculine qualities, Communism, in its idealistic ideological form, represented the reverse, feminine, paradigm.

Aleshina and Volovich (1991, 77; see also Brofenbrenner 1962) argue that patterns of Soviet education were mostly feminine, much in line with the feminine nature of Communism as a political system. Soviet school discipline relied on methods of public encouragement and deterrence. It assessed pupils' behaviour on the basis of their contributions to the common good. It awarded co-operation and help to other members of the collective and punished excessive individualism and selfishness. Hence, feminine qualities, such as bonding with others, consensual behavioural strategies, and expressive attitudes, have been encouraged. This was a stark difference to the American or

West European patterns of education that were based on masculine forms of socialisation. While Western settings encouraged children to be independent and self-sufficient, the Soviet pedagogical milieu motivated a child to be a good member of community and society.

This environment resulted in a situation, in which the Soviet generation of women developed overtly active, almost masculine, qualities. Women often engaged in quintessentially male jobs – from the mid-twentieth century Western perspective such as hammering bolts to railroad lines, driving trams and trolley buses, completing various physical tasks in factories, reconstructing street buildings and indoor premises. Hence, for most women family was not the main but a complementary form of self-realization. Women often had equal, even leading, family roles. Employment was a must, and equal sharing of a family budget was a norm, which again contrasted the position of women in the mid-twentieth century West. To buttress these suggestions, 44 per cent of the 2006 FOM (Foundation for Public Opinion) poll respondents, of the Soviet generation, claimed that they grew up in a family headed by women and only 31 per cent answered that their family was headed by a man (Vovk 2006). Fascinatingly, this state of affairs has been well reflected in Soviet cinema, literature, and art. One of the landmarks of the Soviet monumental art – the Worker and Collective Farm Woman (*Rabochii i Kolkhoznitsa*) statue located at the *VDNKh* exhibition centre – is a vocal statement of the Soviet idea of gender equality. The Moscow Metro boasts mosaics and sculptures that express the idea of a physical and social equality between men and women – an idea which at the time was not immediately evident in other parts of the world. This attitude to women invoked criticism from a small group of religious conservative feminists within the Soviet Union, such as Julia Voznesenskaya, Tatiana Goricheva, Nataliya Malakhovskaya (1980), who could be conditionally classed as USSR's first feminists of difference. They published their feminist critique in the *Woman and Russia* collection, which gained popularity in West and forced its authors to be expunged from the country as dissidents.

At the same time, a serious antinomy was lodged into this pattern of Soviet gender socialisation. Despite these advances towards the gender-equal environment, the Soviet Union remained a patriarchal society at a deep-seated psychological level (Sperling 2006, 170). Soviet employment patterns reflected that patriarchal psychological attitude. Boys were favoured at university placements in scientific and technical fields.[1] In the higher echelons of power, the *nomenklatura* rules demanded that candidates had specific qualifications and experience, which, though equally applied to both men and women, still unofficially required that women were hired to departments concerned with the social, cultural, and educational spheres (Chirikova and Lapina 2011; Aleshina and Volovich 1991, 80). Therefore, during the collapse of the Soviet Union, the share of men employed at the highest positions of power at the federal level has been 94 per cent. Eighty-five per cent of men occupied executive positions within the same bodies of power, and 68 per cent of men were employed at positions that assumed important decision-making responsibilities (Chirikova and Lapina 2011). By the same token, lower positions of power, such as support staff, consultants, and heads of departments, have been comprised of 50 per cent women.

At the ideological-theoretical level, the state ignored the problem of women's personal development (Voronina 2004, 132–3). The idea of women as self-sufficient subjects was lost in the ideological confusion. At the same time, notions of a collective struggle of women for the cause of the liberation of the proletariat class have been predominant. Liberated women were supposed to work for the benefit of the Soviet people's economy on an equal footing with men (Aivazova 1998; Voronina 2004, 132–3). In this light, Khasbulatova (2004, 398 and 401) writes: 'resolution of the "women's question" in the Soviet Union has always had two levels: declared goals, i.e. ideological aspirations, and realisation practice. This is because aspirations to create the conditions for female self-realisation have always been accompanied by pragmatic applications of this challenge to the current tasks of the party and the state.'

FEMINISM IN RUSSIA: EQUALITY AND DIFFERENCE

The fall of the Soviet Union, along with the ensuing liberalization of the ideological environment and labour market, created more opportunities, as well as personal and professional aspirations for women. Hence, pressures towards changing the extant pattern of gender relations in favour of greater recognition gradually surfaced. Due to the reasons outlined above, women of Soviet generations were more open to the ideas of feminism of equality than they were to the ideas of feminism of difference. Writers working within the feminism-of-equality strand are inclined to think that, in Russian society, typically male or typically female behavioural models are very rare, and mixed androgynous behaviour is more common (Kon and Temkina 2009). Therefore, they propose to study masculine and feminine behaviour as complementary (Temkina, Zdravomyslova, and Rotkirkh 2009; Chirikova and Lapina 2011; Iusupova and Kon 2009; Pozniakov 2006; Aleshina and Volovich 1991; Nikulina and Kharlamenkova 1998; Kagan 1989). These writers mainly focus on successful women who achieved high social status and impressive careers within commercial and political spheres (Chirikova 2001; Chirikova and Lapina 2011).

Feminism of difference emerged with the evolution of the capitalist economic model in Russia. Gradual withdrawal of the state from the sphere of social welfare left women face to face with an economic and political system that had been drafted to benefit men economically and politically. The 2000–01 administrative reform liquidated departments for the Affairs of Children, Women, and Families. The Commission for Women's Affairs, which was usually managed by the deputy Prime Minister for Social Development, has also been abolished. Family was gradually becoming the sphere of exploitation for women in lower-income and less-educated groups. Feminists of difference struggle against political and economic domination and its social consequences. Their main goal is a profound change of the social consciousness that sustains a world constructed on the principles of patriarchy (Temkina and Zdravomyslova 2009a). These feminists research the problems faced by younger, lower-income, less-educated, and socially excluded women. In many ways, feminists of difference purposely eschew case studies of Russia's successful women. They claim that such women embraced capitalist rules of the game constructed by men and that they represent men from the gendered point of view.

Let me examine the attitudes that both of these strands of Russian feminism hold towards conceptual issues of labour relations, power models, and the public and private divide.

Public and Private

In the spheres of the public and private, feminism of difference advocates that the borders between the private and political be blurred and that private matters be made the focus of political attention. They tackle the problems of domestic violence, lifestyles, family duties, and abortions. Feminism of equality, on the other hand, supports the principle of non-intervention in the private sphere. These researchers often discuss the lifestyle of Russia's emerging middle class, thus observing the convergence of their perceptions with those practised in the West during the late-modern era. Temkina and Zdravomyslova (2009a, 10–12) claim that with the fall of the Soviet Union the family became a realm of private life. Middle-class members ardently guard this sphere from external interference; they chose their circle of friends and individuals that they admit to this sphere very carefully. They are also careful not to let the state (and the public) intrude into their private sphere. For many middle-class women, the private sphere has become an arena of self-realization. In some respects, guarding the private realm and viewing it as an area in which each member has a particular private function represents a compensatory dynamic adopted by Russia's emerging middle class with the fall of the Soviet Union.

Liberal feminists also criticize any intrusions into private life, primarily on theoretical grounds. I have already observed that, on a theoretical note, authors working within the feminism-of-equality tradition advocate a type of equality between men and women that could transcend the biological distinctions that exists between the sexes. Some authors, such as Aivazova (1998) and Temkina and Zdravomyslova (2009b), side with the advances in medical technology that allow women to postpone motherhood or allow men to give birth. These medical advances, they argue, allow us to destroy the usual perceptions of gender duality. Therefore, intruding into family matters by overly protecting women would invariably result in recognizing differences between men and women and buttressing the binary vision of the sexes. Liberal feminists claim that this position leads to a theoretical fallacy, for it undermines the very idea of equality between men and women – a departing point for the entire theory of feminism and its main political objective (Voronina 2004, 125–9; Shisheliakina 2015).

This leads to further criticism of contemporary Russian state policies towards increasing birth rates, the promotion of motherhood, and the institutional defence of the 'working mother'. These authors (Chirikova and Lapina 2011, 10; Temkina and Zdravomyslova 2009a, 9; Iusupova and Kon 2009, 115; Borisova and Gorshkov 2008; Lapina 2007; Aivazova 1998; Shisheliakina 2015) censure the state for its newly embraced political conservatism, excessive advocacy of the 'mother and child' idea, and patriarchal and state-patriotic rhetoric. Shisheliakina (2015), analysing the political discourse since 2000, regrets that the state began to marginalize women as child-rearers for the state. By doing so, she argues, officials actively intruded into the private realm, criticizing women for their decisions to have abortions or to choose a child-free lifestyle. Aivazova (1998) further insists that giving birth has long become a right and not a duty of women. Both authors lament the return to the old Soviet patterns of intervention into private family matters.[2]

These thinkers also insist on gender-blind equality within contemporary families (Mezentseva 2003; Maltseva and Roshchin 2006, 11; Kon and Temkina 2009). They claim that each spouse must assume the particular sphere of responsibility in which his/her output is the highest. These responsibilities must be located either in the public or private realms. A person's gender plays no role in the overall campaign to achieve equality within a family. Family members must calculate the costs of living and the household work and determine the best professional arrangement for both parties and the family as a whole. This would mean that, if earning power of women in the public labour market is lower than that of men, and women's productivity is higher in the household, then it makes more sense for men to work in the public sphere and for women to focus on the private domain.

Finally, liberal activists accuse those who promote a feminism of difference of being in collaboration with radical movements that use eccentric political expressions and challenges to the Russian tradition.[3] Feminists of equality feel that such behaviour breaks down the border between public and private and hollows out political debates. They call for a focus on 'serious' issues of public significance. Maria Arbatova (2013), one of the most long-standing representatives of the egalitarian feminist movement in Russia, claims that Russian feminism 'needs to be rid of clownish manifestations of feminity and masculinity, artist groups that campaign with the use of outrage and profanity, actionist collectives, such as *Voina*, which, though raising some important socio-political issues, remove the debate from the actual problems of Russian women.' Arbatova (2013) further argues that 'when Russian feminism obtains political seriousness, one can talk meaningfully about the problems and challenges that Russian women face in real life.'

From a sociological point of view, Arbatova's opinion has some truth to it. The perceived lack of 'seriousness' of the radical feminism of difference has a negative impact on Russian public opinion. Various polls showed that the Russian public has been extremely cautious of the ideas of radical feminism and has often confused the very notion of feminism with its radical branch. Opinion polls conducted by the

Integration Agency in 2012 among 8,400 respondents support such attitudes. Thirty-six per cent of female respondents did not support feminist ideas, while 12 per cent spoke categorically against them. Only 7 per cent of female respondents considered themselves as feminist, and forty-five spoke for *some* equal rights with men but did not consider themselves feminists (*Integratsiya* 2012). Male respondents returned similar results: only 3 per cent felt that they supported feminist women; 45 per cent have had very negative feelings about feminists; 14 per cent were generally positive about the ideas of feminism; and 38 per cent were neutral about it.

In contrast to liberal feminists, Russia's feminists of difference are advocates of the 'private is political' idea. These feminists argue that, when the public and private becomes strictly separated, as is the case in Western-liberal and early-capitalist societies, women are forced to face a bitter choice between family and career. These activists back up the argument of their Western counterparts, agreeing that in such social settings the family turns into an arena of women's exploitation. Vera Akulova (2013), a leader of the Moscow Feminist Group, claims that, within a patriarchal family, women become dependent on men financially, which opens opportunities for physical and psychological abuse. Hence, domestic violence becomes the prime object of study for Russia's feminists of difference. Researchers claim that data from the country's telephone hotlines shows that between forty thousand and fifty thousand women are raped, and between twelve thousand and fifteen thousand women die as a result of domestic violence each year. This figure amounts to approximately forty deaths per day (Slobodchikova 2014; Akulova 2013). Data collected from Russia's Ministry of the Interior confirms these figures (Akulova 2013). More importantly, older, less-educated, and lower-income women are among the vast majority of victims. This is significant, because these categories of women require state social protection most.

It is indicative that, until September 2017, Russia had no law to prevent domestic violence. The meant that no criminal investigation against a violent party could proceed without a victim's official statement. Such a situation basically kept perpetrators' hands free. However, given that most victims of domestic violence were older, less-educated women with lower incomes, they were reluctant to call the police or file a statement (Bitten 2013). Hence, over 60 per cent of domestic-violence incidents went unreported. It is also important that a lot of the female prison population in Russia has been composed of women who murdered or physically harmed their violent partners in self-defence.[4] The draft law on the prevention of domestic violence was considered by the State Duma in the autumn 2015 session and finalized in September 2017. It was hoped that its introduction could deter domestic violence and its adverse social consequences, as well as provide care to victims (*Rossiiskaya Gazeta* 2014; RIA *Novost* 2014). Yet, in January 2017, the State Duma decriminalized some aspects of domestic violence, putting domestic physical aggression on the same level as general physical aggression by strangers.

Feminists of difference argue that the delay in the adoption of this law stems from the state's ideological refusal to interfere in the traditional realm of the family. Vladimir Putin (RIA *Novosti* 2014), in particular, pointed out, in a conversation with Russia's Human Rights Representative Mikhail Fedotov, that family legislation must be drafted in a such a manner that the state would not have the right to interfere in the private realm of the family. At the same time, the notion of non-interference in the private family sphere has a peculiar double meaning. The state treats families as a single, indivisible unit, in an effort to ensure higher birth rates. The state and Church in Russia united in this approach to the family, advocating traditionalist values and a traditionalist understanding of family structure. Both institutions emphasize that it is necessary for women to give birth. To reflect this institutionally, the state restricted women's right to abortion in 2012.

Prior to 2012, women could get national-health abortion funding for so-called 'social reasons'. These included lower incomes, unemployment, and difficult personal circumstances. The 2012 amendments to law No. 5487, 'On the Health of Citizens of the Russian Federation' (*Ob Okhrane Zdorovya Grazhdan Rossiiskoi Federatsii*) restricted the range of such reasons to cases in which pregnancy originated as the result of criminal activity, that is, rape (*Demoskop* 2012). The law particularly affected women from lower-income groups who are often more in need of assistance with abortions. Indeed, women of higher- and average-income groups could afford an abortion in a private clinic, while their lower-income counterparts find themselves in a different situation. The outcome was further instances of domestic violence and an increased mortality rate for lower-income women due to unprofessional abortions and self-harm.

In the family realm, feminists of difference argue that children should not be treated as the property of families, but as self-sufficient individuals. The shift in attitude, they claim, has already taken place. People have fewer children and parents attempt to give each child a better education and quality of life. Postmodern and post-capitalist living conditions played a key role in these developments. Due to technological evolution, fewer people are needed for manual work and labour. Labour is becoming more creative, less mechanical, and less structured. Produce is now manufactured outside the family realm. This means there is less need to have more than two children per family, and creates pressure to give those children an education that can prepare them for creative, intellectual, socio-political, commercial, or managerial activity (Akulova 2013).

Finally, in contrast to the feminism of equality, feminists of difference are overtly nostalgic about Soviet gender policies. They claim that Soviet consistency in pursuing the 'mother and child' line created a more comfortable environment for women. They also support early-Communist undertakings aimed at sharing domestic duties equally between spouses and rewarding domestic work. It is important that this early radical ideological outlook irretrievably breaks the separation between the public and private. Some early-Soviet ideologues advocated communal living, in which child-rearing and domestic work would be the task of various social institutions, instead of a private family matter. This was reflected in early-Soviet architecture journals that drafted designs for Communal Living Houses (Kuzmin 1928; Kollontai 1923, 23; Temkina, Zdravomyslova, and Rotkrikh 2009, 7), as well as in the general Soviet house designs that had very small kitchens.

Leo Trotsky, in *The Revolution Betrayed* (2004, first published in 1937), was the most ardent advocate of these ideas. He (ibid., 109–10) argued that

> the place of the family as a shut-in petty enterprise was to be occupied, according to the plans, by a finished system of social care and accommodation: maternity houses, crèches, kindergartens, schools, social dining rooms, social laundries, first-aid stations, hospitals, sanatoria, athletic organizations, moving-picture theatres, etc. The complete absorption of the housekeeping functions of the family by institutions of the socialist society, uniting all generations in solidarity and mutual aid, was to bring to woman, and thereby to a loving couple, a real liberation from the thousand-year-old fetters.

Russian feminists of difference explicitly support those ideas, which starkly separates them from their liberal counterparts. Bitten argues:

> [W]e must recast social mentality and provide women with workplaces in social outlets such as nursery schools, restaurants, fast-food-preparation services, launderettes, and other outlets, which could relieve them from domestic work and bring them out into the public realm. This could make women more independent and help constructing a symmetrical equal family" (*Radio Liberty* 2015).

Labour Relations

In the sphere of labour relations, both strands of feminist thought deal with similar issues. However, they come to different conclusions and thereby raise different points of importance. First, feminists of equality usually focus on women's participation in business and power institutions (Pozniakov 2006; Chirikova 2001; Chirikova and Lapina 2011, Maltseva and Roshchin 2006; Zaslavskaia 2006a; Zaslavskaia 2006b; Ogloblin 1999; Mezentseva 2003). They optimistically claim that women are gradually occupying important positions of power within Russia's financial, political, and business spheres. Feminists from the 'difference camp', in contrast, usually focus on women of lower-income groups. They tackle the issues of professional, social, and economic discrimination that face women and the problems associated with pay gaps for both male and female labour. Second, both strands of feminism examine issues of professional gender segregation. In the feminism-of-equality case, thinkers claim that such segregation does not always represent the result of deliberate discrimination against women. Feminism of difference, on the other hand, claims that professional gender segregation takes place as a result of the masculine domination of the entire structure of social relationships. Let me discuss these matters in detail.

First, feminists of equality usually point out that, due to a multitude of historical and ideological reasons (Ogloblin 1999), Russia is among the leading countries of the world in the sphere of women's employment. In the Soviet Union, the share of women in the labour market equalled 77.4 per cent and 88.2 per cent in 1960 and 1980 respectively. These figures looked considerably higher than during the same years in the United States, with 37.8 and 51.3 respectively, France, with 44.5

and 57.0 per cent respectively, Germany, with 46.5 and 56.2 per cent respectively, and Britain with 43.4 and 62.3 per cent respectively (Gunderson 1989, 47). In 1985 the share of employed women in the USSR stood at 96.8 per cent, compared to 71.1 per cent in Northern Europe, 55.6 in Western Europe, and 37.1 in Southern Europe (Barr 1997, 174; Maltseva and Roshchin 2006, 16). It is interesting that, even in the 1890s, women composed nearly one-quarter of all those employed in Russia's industrial production. By 1914, this figure had come close to 40 per cent, and it stood at nearly 70 per cent in the textile industry (Chirikova 1998, 5). Liberal feminists therefore are proud that contemporary Russia also sustains a high level of women's employment. Maltseva and Roshchin (2006, 15) show that, in 2006, 60.8 per cent of economically active women (those aged between 15 and 72) participated in the country's labour market, while this figure stood at 70.4 per cent among men. More importantly, within the 25-to-54 age group, this figure was at 85.82 per cent, comparing favourably again to OECD countries, in which employment for the same category of women stood at 69 per cent for the same year.

With regard to women employed in political institutions, these researchers (Seltser 2003; Pozniakov 2006; Chirikova 2011; Chirikova and Lapina 2011, 10–12; Aivazova 2008, 86; Khakamada 2002) also praise recent developments, in which women have begun to occupy important positions within Russia's political structures. Among the women most often mentioned are the head of the Central Bank, Elvira Nabiullina, and her deputy, Ksenia Iudaeva; the head of the Federation Council and former governor of St Petersburg, Valentina Matvienko; Russia's minister of health, Veronika Skvortsova; the minister of social development, Olga Golodets; the presidential advisor and the head of the Accounts Chamber, Tatiana Golikova, and her deputy, Vera Chistova; former minister of agriculture, Elena Skrynnik; the head of the State Duma anti-corruption committee, Irina Iarovaia; the press secretary of the Ministry of Foreign Affairs, Maria Zakharova; the press secretary of Russia's Prime Minister Dmitry Medvedev, Natalia Timakova; the former head of the Union of Right Forces Party, Irina Khakamada; and many others. Aivazova (2008, 86–9) argues that, during the post-Soviet decades, the proportion of women in federal legislative institutions has grown considerably. The 2007 parliamentary elections ensured sixty-three mandates for women, which comprised 14 per cent of all parliamentary seats. This compares favourably to the previous rounds of general elections, in which only thirty-four and forty-four women entered the 2000 and 2003 convocations of the federal parliament respectively. Researchers of the egalitarian trend also observe that women penetrate municipal and regional administrations, city councils, city mayoral and vice-mayoral positions, as well as village and small-town councils. Chirikova and Lapina (2011) argue that, in regional executive positions, the share of women is one and a half to two times higher than that at the federal level. Researchers explain the active arrival of women in municipal and at village levels of power by the relatively unattractive and underfinanced position of these institutions. In addition, they claim that at such levels people have the chance of a genuine/personal choice between candidates, and women often demonstrate productiveness and a positive attitude.

Feminists of difference for the most part point at the problem of a wage gap between men and women. In particular, they claim that, according to the Russian Statistics Service, Russian women earn 30 to 35 per cent less than men (Khasbulatova 2001, 191). The situation seems much worse than in most Western European countries, where women earn on average of 10 to 15 per cent less than men for performing similar jobs. Studying higher-paid segments of the population, feminists of difference claim that Russian women tend to play down their abilities at the recruitment stage. This results in women achieving 20 to 30 per cent less pay than their male counterparts earn for performing identical jobs (*Radio Liberty* 2015). Recruitment agencies point at the problem of 'internalized misogyny'. This means that women voluntarily embrace their socially constructed inferiority in the male-dominated professional fields and act in accordance with those labels. Women habitually refuse to demand wages suggested to them by HR specialists, feeling that they could not earn 'that much'. This is particularly true in the Russian IT industry, which is dominated by men at both the educational and professional stages. Some HR specialists claim that this state of affairs occurs because women are being educated in a patriarchal framework, and are told at an early stage that they are *a priori* inferior to men in the fields of mathematics, logic, IT, and natural sciences.[5] The capitalist market, on the other hand, demands that employers minimize expenses. Hence, employers benefit from women's inferiority complex by willingly employing a cheaper workforce of equal or superior quality.

This situation is exacerbated by the fact that in nearly 30 per cent of Russian families women assume leading positions, acting as the main breadwinner. Marina Karavaeva, a member of the gender-relations faction of the liberal *Yabloko* party, insists that there are six million Russian families in which women raise children alone, compared to only 635,000 families in which men act as single fathers (*Radio Liberty* 2015). In 80 per cent of cases, fathers avoid paying child maintenance, while state support agencies that are tasked with child-maintenance enforcement duties do not perform their job properly. More importantly, official statistics with which to analyse this problem are unavailable. The aforementioned figures are sourced from independent activist groups, which deal with the issue directly. In this light, Russian feminists of difference propose to establish a state child-maintenance fund, which could assist women whose ex-partners avoid contributions. The state, in their mind, should open a specific debt account against such fathers, and consider unpaid maintenance fees as state debts owed by these men.

Second, let me discuss the attitudes of the two strands of feminism to the professional gender-segregation problem. Such segregation takes place when we see a disproportionately high concentration of one or another gender in a particular professional group or in particular hierarchical positions within one professional group. Researchers distinguish between 'vertical' and 'horizontal' types of this phenomenon. 'Vertical segregation' assumes unequal redistribution of men and women in hierarchical positions within one firm. 'Horizontal segregation', on the other hand, assumes industry segregation between men and women in various professional areas. Both types of segregation are interconnected. Horizontal segregation also has a vertical dimension, due to the perceived status difference between various professions (Maltseva and Roshchin 2006, 11).

Liberal feminists usually argue that equating professional gender segregation with purposeful discrimination of women is inadequate. They claim that professional gender segregation is a result of a multitude of factors of social, economic, political, professional, aspirational, and vocational natures, as well as mere individual preferences (Maltseva and Roshchin 2006, 10). They argue that gender discrimination represents the result of a general lack of social mobility existing within Russian society and the idiosyncratic political system that has been established in Russia during the post-Soviet period. Resolving these problems through consistent policy-making in a gender-blind fashion would help to alleviate the problem of gender imbalance in the workplace (Mezentseva 2000). This approach is reminiscent of the Engelsian (1884) idea of mending the capitalist society in general in order to resolve the 'women's question' in particular.

Focusing on vocational explanations, these feminists argue that the concentration of men in various professional positions to some extent represents a choice by women, who prefer to assume domestic responsibilities for historical – as well as contemporary economic – reasons. Roshchin (1996), following an analysis of Russian women's preferences during the 1990s, observes that almost 20 per cent of respondents would have been willing to leave the labour market in order to focus on household duties, if they had had an alternative source of income, including that provided by their husbands. Hence, these researchers claim that the high proportion of women's employment in Russia represents, partly, the inability of men to support their families. Further criticism comes from the Moscow Higher School of Economics (MHSE). Researchers claim that many women in Russia prefer to benefit from the achievements of feminism, as well as from the elements of a patriarchal society. A large number of poll respondents insist that they would like to treat their partner's (husband's) wages as 'household income', while viewing their own wages as personal income. Many women also admitted that they are inclined to play the role of a 'weaker gender' in the workplace in order to pursue career progression.

Speaking of the professional segregation of women in politics, feminists of equality complain about the general lack of transparency within Russia's political institutions. They do not focus on patriarchy, unlike their counterparts from the feminism-of-difference camp. These liberal authors (Kryshtanovskaya 2005; Maltseva and Roshchin 2006, 95; Chirikova and Lapina 2011, 12–13; Khakamada 2002, 122) claim that the construction of a 'power vertical' narrowed the space for public politics in Russia in general and affected the cause of women's liberation in particular. The process of women's recruitment to power remains informal and lacks any meaningful structure. Arrival of women (and, as a matter of fact, men) in politics mostly depends on the arbitrary choice of the most senior persons in executive positions or the financial status of candidates (Chirikova and Lapina 2011, 13). Hence, the existing 'caste structure', in which most decisions are taken arbitrarily, serves as a barrier for talented and educated women on their path to power (Kanakianova 2006; Chirikova and Lapina 2011, 12).

Chirikova and Lapina (2011, 13) further claim that the newly emerged conservative trend in Russia, in which state-patriotic ideas have gained significance, further impeded women's chances to enter political institutions. This is because the *style* and the language of politics have become masculine, inadvertently gearing towards the selection of male candidates for important political positions. Opinion polls show that both men and women have internalized this position. In an Institute of Sociology survey/poll, 60 per cent of respondents claimed that a woman president would have a negative impact on Russia's socio-political evolution (Chirikova and Lapina 2011, 13; ISPI RAN 2002, 14). In 2017, VTSIOM (*VTSIOM* 2017) polls showed that, while 54 per cent of the respondents claimed that they did not care about the gender of a potential presidential candidate, only 5 per cent would vote for a woman (which was reflected in the 2004 and 2018 presidential votes for Irina Khakamada and Ksenia Sobchak respectively) and 38 per cent would consciously vote for a man. Feminists of equality arrive at the conclusion that the general liberalization of Russia's society and a change of a dominant ideological paradigm could result in the achievement of a fairer gender balance in politics. It now becomes apparent that such an egalitarian approach attempts to resolve women's problems by enhancing general institutional transparency and struggling for human rights in the 'colour-blind' fashion reminiscent of liberal feminism in the West (Kymlicka 2002).

In contrast to their liberal counterparts, feminists of difference are inclined to think that the 'vertical' and 'horizontal' professional segregations occur because Russia's contemporary society is constructed on the basis of a male image as a social norm. Natalia Bitten, a member of the *Za Feminizm* social movement, argues that women are punished for the fact that they perform child-bearing functions. Bitten claims that

> women are less likely to be promoted because of their perceived hormonal 'instability', because they could consider leaving their career to focus solely on child-rearing engagements, because they might already be splitting their attention between their job and child care, because, in case of a child's illness, women, and not men, would have to take sick leave. Men, on the other hand, are considered more stable, more mature, and better job applicants if they have family and children (*Radio Liberty* 2015).

Marina Baskakova (1995), researching a number of Russia's regions, further observess that motherhood in contemporary Russia often involves the loss of a woman's professional status and an impact on her career progression. Women with children could search for jobs for years, while employers habitually violate the Constitution by refusing them placements. The state is being deliberately silent on these matters, usually based on ideological grounds of non-interference in traditional family matters. This pushes women further into a socially excluded group and results in the loss of self-confidence. In this light, Vera Akulova (2013) claims that 70 per cent of all Russia's destitute are women, and 60 per cent of all Russia's illiterate population are also women. The elite echelon segment is only 14 per cent women. This situation, she argues, is a little better than in the United States and North America, but much worse than in most European and, in particular, Scandinavian countries.

From this point of view, many feminists of difference (Bitten 2013; Neifeld 1998) suggest that the state must introduce equal statutory benefits for child-care sick leaves and equal terms for maternity and paternity leaves. This would create a situation in which employers would experience no difference with male and female employees, as both parties could be engaged equally in the child-rearing process. This could give women more chances for fairer treatment in the job market and break away from social exclusion and poverty. Akulova further points out that Russian women work in the lowest-paid jobs involved with pre-school education, lower skilled health-care provision, nursing, and cleaning. Russia's increased military spending and ensuing government cuts within the social-care segments exacerbate this situation. This has led to a significant reduction in statutory pay and benefits within professions mostly populated by women – a situation that will plunge women further into poverty and dependence on their male partners (*Radio Liberty* 2015).

Conceptions of Power and Citizenship

Weighing different models of power practised by Russian women within political and business institutions, proponents of equality feminism adopt a rather nuanced approach. In the sphere of politics and business administration, researchers of egalitarian trends often claim that the style of management in powerful Russian institutions, as well as in medium-sized and small businesses, is androgynous. They argue that there is no fundamental difference between male and female forms of management. At the same time, they note that, despite no significant gender difference in the style of management, women can be more flexible and inventive by deploying both female and male styles of directorship. In sensitive situations, women could be more compassionate and ready to seek consensus. Yet, if the situation demands, they can be firm, aggressive, and uncompromising to match all the socially perceived masculine traits (Chirikova 2011, 146–7). Hence, the description of Russia's women in power is sophisticated. On the one hand, liberal authors tend to notice that women adopt the Arendtian consensual model of power, in which a leader relies on the group as a source of his/her influence. On the other hand, these writers claim that such a behavioural model does not represent a hard and fast rule. Hence, despite admitting *some* behavioural differences between men and women in business and power, researchers refrain from drawing fixed dividing lines (Chirikova 2011; Pozniakov 2006; Pozniakov and Titova 2005; Pozniakov and Titova 2002; Pozniakov 2001).

In the first case, Irina Khakamada (2002, 138 and 154), describing women's behaviour in politics, claims that their role is to mitigate conflicts, placate opponents, and seek consensus. Khakamada further argues that women can tame their ambitions and adopt a consensual style of governance. Chirikova (2011), following her rigorous research of day-to-day situations, insists that most women prefer to rely on the so-called 'expert' or 'charismatic' models of power, which is reminiscent of the Arendtian idea of consensual power. At the same time, Chirikova's (2011) focus-group respondents claim that they combine consensual power practices with conflictual methods of influence when necessary. In consensual situations, such women deployed their expert knowledge to motivate subordinates into submission through respect and recognition. At the same time, when the situation called for it, these same women deployed the conflictual style, acting in an uncompromising fashion, drafting company rules, and compelling employees to submit (Chirikova 2011; Chirikova 1998).

Pozniakov and Titova (2005; 2002; see also Pozniakov 2006), from the Russian Institute of Sociology, go a step further. They claim that women in top positions of power adopt masculine models of behaviour and achieve similar results as men who rely on the conflictual model of power alone. In general, these authors claim marginal behavioural gender differences in important positions of power. Statistical analysis within chosen focus groups demonstrates that the number of women and men choosing competition, co-operation, compromise, and avoidance as means of resolving conflicts does not differ significantly (Pozniakov 2006; Chirikova 1998). The authors further assessed business focus groups for various models of power behaviour from the point of view of risk-taking strategies, an attitude to competition, and self-confidence. Drawing on statistical analysis, Pozniakov and Titova (2005 and 2002; see also Pozniakov 2006) claim that perceived behavioural stereotypes, in which women are less prone to risk-taking or seek to avoid conflict and competition, do exist, but do not lead to any satisfying conclusion. For example, only 13.6 per cent of women respondents did not like competition against 10.7 per cent of male respondents. Yet, 15.7 per cent of men strongly prefer a competitive style of management against just 9 per cent of women exhibiting a similar preference. Nevertheless, women respondents assessed their success in business to 5.14 points out of ten on average, while men had a 4.68-point result. Both groups assessed the results of their activity at 4.5 and 4.24 points and their abilities at 5.32 and 5.0 points respectively. These findings testify to a relatively similar level of self-confidence among men and women (Pozniakov 2006). These researchers do not lament the situation that women 'voluntarily accepted' male forms of behaviour, as would their counterparts from the feminism-of-difference camp. Rather, they conclude that contemporary Russia formed a relatively homogenous group of business entrepreneurs and industrial leaders that has similar psychological features and only marginal gender differences.

Feminism of difference remains silent on the issue of power models. It does however ponder the ideas of citizenship in Russia. These feminists usually consider both liberal or rights-based and republican paradigms, making their approach to the problem nuanced and multi-faceted. Let me consider their view on both models of citizenship. In the liberal sphere, feminists of difference claim that their movement contributes to the expansion of political and social rights in Russia. Elena Petrovskaya, a senior research associate at the Institute of Philosophy RAN, claims that, apart from the rights of women, feminist movements in Russia also fight for a more active implementation of the liberal rights-based idea of citizenship. Women's movements, she argues, could help expand the social rights of pensioners or contribute to the drafting of clearer legal codes for the humane treatment of animals. 'Feminism,' Petrovskaya claims, 'becomes a synonym for tolerance and a particular ethical standpoint. It stands against general

patterns of repression, social exclusion, and inequality. It is an eman-
cipatory position that manifests itself at different levels of socio-
political life' (*Radio Free Europe* 2011). In this light, Russian feminists
of difference advocate greater rights for various segments of society.
Women's rights are as important as any other aspect of human rights,
and they must be included as a separate item in the entire range of
rights that the state and society consider in their policy-making (Gessen
1998; *Radio Liberty* 2015).

Within the republican model of citizenship, feminists of difference
claim that the public good is best served by protecting the rights of
women. They insist that women must obtain greater social rights. Such
rights must consider women's problems relating to childbirth and
motherhood. Only through creating an environment in which women
feel greater protection for themselves and their children, can the state
have fully participating and committed citizens (Bitten 2015). It could
then succeed in securing a harmonious and just society – an achievement that represents the most important aspect of the public good
(Akulova 2013).

Regardless of the emphases that such feminists make in their theorizations on citizenship, they all agree that the model citizen in Russia
is built around the norm, ideal, and lifestyle of men (Akulova 2013;
Bitten 2015). In this light, these feminists argue that the Russian government must introduce the position of a human-rights ombudsman,
who would specifically defend the rights of women. As Bitten argues,
any gender-blind ombudsman position in Russia would mean a systematic defence of the rights of men (*Radio Liberty* 2015). Hence,
women's rights must be defended separately, as women are permanently
discriminated against by the very fact of a male-dominated society.

MAIN ACTORS AND POLITICAL ACTIVITY

Having reviewed the academic, theoretical, and intellectual debates
on the condition of women within Russian society, it is important to
state that contemporary Russia has not produced strong political
movements that reflect those ideas in practice. The heyday of Russia's
feminist movement was in the early- and mid-1990s and since then
this group's activity has steadily declined. It is common for feminist
activists to communicate on a one-to-one basis rather than forming
sectoral political networks. Some of those individuals are united with

liberal parties, such as *Yabloko* or the Party of People's Freedom, and they often let those organizations air feminist claims that have been developed during their political and theoretical debates.

There are number of feminist groups operating in Moscow and St Petersburg. Of particular importance is the Moscow Feminist Group – an organization of radical feminists that was formed in 2008. This group focuses on holding political debates, taking part in various political rallies in conjunction with other movements and networks, and translating Western literature on the subject into Russian. At the same time, the group, due to its very small membership, cannot conduct wide-scale political activity and send activists to participate in the wider political process.

There are a number of adjacent feminist networks operating in both Moscow and St Petersburg: the Moscow Radical Feminists (*Moskovskie Radikalnye Feministki*); the Tea Group (*Chainaia Gruppa*); the Feminist Initiative (*Feministskaya Initsiativa*); the Youth Movement 'Stop Violence' (*Molodezhnaya Gruppa 'Ostanovim Nasilie'*); the Campaign Against Discrimination and Exploitation of Women – the Committee for a Workers" International (*Kampaniya protiv ekspluatatsii i diskriminatsii zhenshchin – Komitet za Rabochii Interantsional*); and For Feminism (*Za Feminizm*). The participants in these movements are mostly in their twenties and thirties; only a few active network members are over forty or in their fifties. Those younger activists stand by a radical feminist programme and are often critical of the misogynistic attitudes of current left-wing movements in Russia that, as discussed in the previous chapters, stand on a conservative platform. More importantly, mainstream debates on the condition of women in Russian society reflect those conservative positions and, for this reason, have been given serious consideration in this chapter.

To sum up, the conceptual split between the feminism of equality and the feminism of difference occurs mainly within the academic and intellectual sphere, and is very similar to the Western feminist critique that occurred at the inception of these debates. The ways in which such theorizations have been applied to the Russian case are interesting and relevant. The discussion reiterated the argument of many Russian feminists that the immediate post-Soviet generation of women often espouses the feminism of equality due to the pre-established patterns of gender socialization that existed in the Soviet Union. At the same time, the development of a capitalist mode of politics and economics also led to the emergence of a feminism of difference that raises qualitatively different themes and problems. Both strands of feminism are relevant to Russia's pressing economic and political challenges and represent an important part of the country's ideological landscape. Feminism of difference is concerned with issues and problems experienced by lower-income women that face socio-economic exclusion at various levels. These thinkers call for a recasting of the entire spectrum of social relationships in order to deal with women's unique problems and perceptions. They fight against domination and patriarchy. They focus on issues of socio-economic exclusion, domestic violence, and exploitation. Feminists of equality, on the other hand, focus largely on economic and labour relations. They concentrate on the rights and problems of successful women. They press for an equal number of women within Russia's institutions of power, viewing power in mostly masculine terms. They do not press for the destruction of the public-private divide, treating family as an area of private relationships. Regardless of the debates and differences that exist among Russian feminists, however, it is significant that such ideas and movements emerge and function in contemporary Russia. Being among the first countries in the world to consider the rights of women, Russia continues to work on the improvement of the extant state of gender relations.

10

Conclusion

This book has examined the evolution of ideologies, as well as political thought at large, in Russia during the beginning of the twenty-first century, and has made ample reference to Western social and political philosophy, discussing critical junctures at which a dialogue between Western and Russian narratives takes place. The discussion has referred to nineteenth- and twentieth-century Russian politics and philosophy and attempted to draw links between pre-existing and contemporary ideas. The account also reflected on the political situation in Russia during Vladimir Putin's leadership, which corresponds to the period of ideological study covered in the book. The discussion elucidated the links between the political motivations and goals of Russia's extant elites, its domestic and international socio-political climate, and the political ideologies, rhetoric, and public debates found in contemporary Russian society. It is hoped that the discussion in this book illuminated the connection between the political motivations of Russia's extant actors and the new ideological and philosophical arguments which they advance in the public sphere.

As explained earlier, twenty-first century Russia is driven by a plethora of complex problems and challenges inherited from the country's momentous past. Russia is torn by the painful memories of the two state collapses in the twentieth century. Her national self-consciousness is indelibly marked by the heroic and horrific experience of the Second World War, which claimed, even by the most modest estimates, over twenty million Soviet lives. Russia is also beset by the increasingly challenging international climate that is considered adverse to the country's vital economic and security interests. In addition, the country is faced with the broken narrative of her history and the need to create a logical continuum between the tales of her inception, her transformation into a modern European Empire, that empire's collapse and reincarnation as a Soviet state pursuing a path of alternative modernization, and the contemporary post-Soviet country that now follows its socio-cultural particularities. Such a coherent narrative is needed to fuel the country's future evolution. A contemporary intellectual conundrum exists in Russia. How does she reconcile the idea of positioning herself as a modern 'corporation', capable of fitting into global economic and political realities, and the idea that she is a state-civilization, seen as a norm-giving and norm-altering pole of international influence.

Finally, the post-Soviet redistribution of power and property exerted considerable influence over the evolution of Russia's post-Soviet ideology and public political debates. The need to legitimize the new state of affairs in politics and economics, as well as to vindicate the newly emerged class of proprietors, had a serious impact on Russia's new philosophical, ethical, and ideological doctrines. A good deal of debate emerged between those who wished to reassess the Soviet experience and apply its most positive aspects to Russia's post-Soviet development, those who were repelled by the Soviet past as criminal and unacceptable, and those who vigorously exposed the privileges of the newly emerged elites as opposed to the relative equality of the pre-existing Soviet state and comparative modesty of its erstwhile political elite.

From these diverse positions two large ideological groups (or paradigms) have surfaced. In this account I have referred to them as 'traditionalist' and 'liberal'. The 'traditionalist' branch envisages a separate developmental path for Russia, insisting on her ideological, civilizational, and cultural freedom from external pressures. The 'liberal' paradigm promotes Russia's convergence with the Western cultural and political orbit and is apprehensive about insisting upon Russia's civilizational distinctness. Thus, both paradigms pursue divergent political goals and envisage a different political trajectory for Russia's future development. Their political premise is predetermined by their respective answers to the complex web of problems outlined above. Each paradigm includes a spectrum of political ideologies, all of which have a similar paradigmatic axis, but exhibit differences in details and tactics. This book has examined each conventionally recognizable ideology – liberalism, conservatism, socialism, nationalism, feminism, and multiculturalism – from the point of view of their split into the two given paradigms. It was also shown that the Putin style of political management endorsed and sustained this paradigmatic division. I have referred to this system as 'paradigmatic pluralism' throughout this book and claimed in the introduction that such a system could also be branded as 'Putinism'. The discussion has demonstrated that representatives of each paradigm operate within Russia's main political parties, at the high echelons of power, in large and medium-sized business structures, and in the main social movements. Putin prefers to balance these socio-political forces without taking sides, and he navigates between traditionalists and liberals situationally.

As an example, Putin took part in the opening ceremonies of the Boris Yeltsin Presidential Centre museum and the Wall of Sorrow, in Yekaterinburg and Moscow respectively. Both are revered by liberals and are of cardinal importance to their political narrative. At the same time, he adopted a firm military and political stance in a dialogue with Russia's international rivals and partners – a move that placates the wishes of traditionalists. Putin also leads Russia's Immortal Regiment, an annual 9th May Victory Day march to commemorate ancestors who fought in the Great Patriotic War of 1941–45 – an event that liberals view with some scepticism and traditionalists acclaim. Such a duality is also seen in Putin's foreign-policy speeches. As we have discussed, Putin presents Russia as a 'European' country or a 'Eurasian' one, or a country with significant civilizational and cultural distinction, depending on his audience and circumstances. Hence, the Putin era in politics, and consequently in ideology and philosophy, has been indelibly marked by this dualistic paradigmatic division.

The question remains as to when and how this dilemma can be resolved. As post-Soviet Russian history has evolved, an acute struggle between these two paradigms has been going on, in which both sides stopped short of a complete victory. The fall of the Soviet Union ushered in an era of liberal triumph, during which the liberal paradigm captured the dominant discourse and liberal policies have been implemented in the spheres of economy, politics, and international relations. Liberal politicians have also become the foremost political figures. Russian and Soviet history has been interpreted from an exclusively liberal angle, thus setting the tone for Russia's future strategic development. That situation led irrefutably to a territorial and political disintegration of Russia and her profound recasting as an international political entity. By the end of the 1990s, however, the pendulum had swung in the conservative direction. This took place with the appointment of Yevgeny Primakov to the positions of Foreign Minister and then Prime Minister. The arrival of Primakov in Russia's mainstream politics signalled the rolling back of the liberal triumph, although it did not herald an unequivocal victory for traditionalists.

Putin continued the Primakov line by curbing the dominance of the liberal perspective, yet, as we have already noted, he abstained from siding firmly with the traditionalists. During the past twenty years of his leadership, both factions have anticipated that he would finally make a choice and side with one or another group. His politics, however, made it clear that the evolutionary strategy of the 1990s (which many traditionalists brand as an era of disintegration, chaos, and disaster) has been held back for the period of Putin's leadership. It was also clear that no steps will be taken towards declaring Russia a fully-fledged civilization-state that steers a firm course towards its traditionalist values. This balancing formula of *paradigmatic pluralism* has been the hallmark of Putin's leadership throughout his entire time in power, and is likely to last for as long as he remains in politics. The paradigmatic balance between traditionalism and liberalism, however, will no doubt be disrupted when Putin leaves the political arena.

It is worth noting that paradigmatic duality has been a feature of Russian political, intellectual, and ethical life in various shapes and forms for many centuries, yet the state has always indicated its preference for one side or the other. This differs from the current formula in which the state is deliberately ambivalent. Various historical periods granted a clear victory to one of the two sides. Those victories were usually short-lived, and newly established realities failed fully to eradicate the opposing paradigm. Exponents of the supposedly defeated paradigms continued to harbour hopes of subsequent revival and restoration.

Broadly speaking, these two separate paths emerged with the Great East-West Christian Schism of 1054, when medieval Rus stood with Eastern Byzantine Christianity, while Western Europe embraced Christianity's Roman branch. Since that period, the question over the strategic direction of Russia (Eastern Byzantine or Western Roman) has been ever present, and has been expressed in different political and rhetorical guises. As discussed in the chapter on nationalism, an adherence to Byzantine faith and tradition has always been associated with traditionalism, and it ultimately enabled Russia to become a large continental empire. Ideals of Europeanization, of individual prayer and individual responsibility, and of the language of economic and political rights have been attributed to the liberals, and they often pushed Russia towards the road of modernity and industrialization. The existential split was exacerbated by the accession of Peter I to the Russian throne. Peter ushered in an era of intense Europeanization in the religious, cultural, social, political, economic, industrial, and military spheres, although he also provoked an intense reaction to these developments from traditionalist politicians and intellectuals.

The dialogue between the traditionalists and liberals (or between Westerners and Slavophiles, as they were branded in the nineteenth century) has never ceased. The nineteenth century saw a flood of books, pamphlets, and articles devoted exclusively to this theme. Likewise, this period led to the significant intellectual split between the two camps. As Isaiah Berlin (2004, 131) notes, the debaters were mostly concerned to prove 'either that Russia is destined to obey unique laws of its own – so that the experience of other countries has little or nothing to teach it – or, on the contrary, that its failures are entirely due to an unhappy dissimilarity to the life of other nations, a blindness to this or that universal law which governs all societies, and which Russians ignore at their peril.' The Soviet era, which to some extent overturned the entire chessboard and swept away all the pre-existing figures, still exhibited the remnants of this centuries-long dialogue.

In many ways, the ideological differences between Stalin and Trotsky bore a significant resemblance to the debate on whether Russia, as a unique society, should choose the path of independent self-development and carry the burden of her alternative norm-giving existence (the Stalin strategy of building a 'communism in one country') or should integrate into the global outward-looking movement of people in search of a better future for the world, which included the universal values of justice, progress, and development (the Trotsky vision of the global revolution). Furthermore, Westernism never disappeared from Russia's academic and intellectual life during the Soviet period. The West has been an example to follow, a rival to 'overtake', and an object of contempt on which perceived Soviet and Russian spiritual and ethical superiority could be exercised. More importantly, the official Soviet preoccupation with the West in all the ways outlined above achieved a profound westernization of the minds of ordinary Russians during the Soviet era.

Contemporary Russia finds herself at a historical junction that ultimately demands a new answer to the question of her preferred strategic trajectory. The international climate, in which Russia attempts to position herself as a country-civilization (a point discussed in

Chapter 7, on the multipolar world order), demands that she articulate the potential alternative ideological direction that she will offer the world. The answer to this trying question should define the future fate of Russia, and largely help determine the political configuration of the future world order. Yet, a choice of this magnitude can not be implemented on the whim of a single person, such as Vladimir Putin. It must be made in conjunction with the reflections and expectations of the people. History shows that, even in the most seemingly brutal impositions of fateful choices, new ideas have resonated with people's innermost hidden feelings and pre-existing subconscious patterns of religious or historical practice. Ideas and practices that did not fit the conventional norms but have been successfully imposed have been, one way or another, pondered, understood, and even practised prior to their official inauguration.

An English parallel is of interest here. The Elizabethan push for the supremacy of the Church of England, despite its harsh measures mixed with brutality and financial persecution, did not stir up angry resistance from the people. They revered the Queen for being 'one of us', due to her English birth, for fighting for the interests of the country against external enemies, and for placing England on the map as a major European country. Similarly, Peter the Great's ruthless policies of Europeanization resonated with the elites' deeply held belief that Russia's technological backwardness must be overcome and the country's industrial development should be accelerated. Peter also garnered the support of ordinary Russians because of his passion for the country's fate, his building of cities, his development of Russia's navy, and his securing of her international military status. Needless to say, the Bolsheviks also spoke to the Russian people by re-interpreting and reinventing the very tenets of Orthodox Christianity, inspiring millions of ordinary Russians to strive for personal and communal growth, and reconstructing the erstwhile Russian Empire in the new modernist Soviet guise. Similarly, the Bolsheviks' eventual demise was in the depth of a faltering Soviet system that experienced a serious crisis of values and legitimacy.

Whoever comes after Vladimir Putin to lead Russia on its new path will inherit many Putinite policies that resonated with the perceptions and conventions of the Russian public. In contrast to many other periods of Russia's history, I anticipate that, by the end of the Putin era, Russians will have the opportunity to select their path within the conditions of free choice. Their choice will grow organically from the depths of Russian society on the basis of thorough deliberations and debates between traditionalists and liberals. Russia was not able to make such a choice freely during the 1990s because of the overwhelming predominance of the liberals. Neither could she choose freely during the Soviet era, for this period was for most part dominated by the traditionalists (Dugin 2018). The conditions of paradigmatic pluralism have enabled Russia to exist in an environment of paradigmatic duality, uncertainty, and a fragile balance, in which both epistemic options are laid freely on the table. Such an environment affords the Russian people some time for reflection on the potential direction they would like to take their country in the future.

Putin's version of the formula of paradigmatic duality is perhaps new and unique in Russian politics, for, as we mentioned above, each period of Russia's development witnessed the relative victory of one or another paradigm and the relative peril of another. Vladimir Putin seems to be the key element buttressing this unusual balance. He ensures Russia's sovereignty from international interference and deliberately abstains from favouring one or another direction, thus endorsing both options for the public.

Will Russia be ready to resist the globalist West and adopt a path of full-scale alternative development, simultaneously showing distinct ethical and norm-giving options to the world? Will Russia choose to integrate into the unipolar world order pursued by the US-centred West and fix herself into the complex web of Western-led institutional structures driven by postmodern morality? The answer to these questions is far from clear. It is evident that Putin will not offer this choice to the people. His function has been to create a system of epistemic (or paradigmatic) pluralism that offers both those options for Russians and to ensure that Russians will have time to reflect and make this choice free from external and domestic pressure. A new volume on Russian ideologies should be written during the post-Putin period, and it will most likely discuss the parameters of the new base consensus rather than approaching each ideology from the point of view of the two potential paradigmatic choices.

Notes

CHAPTER ONE

1 Some critics might suggest that this book could benefit from a discussion on Putinism as a separate branch of ideology. This volume takes the view that Putinism itself does not represent a particular ideology for it lacks a substantive as well as a positionist component. Yet, the political system of ideological balancing could be branded as 'Putinism'.

2 Some authors, such as Andreas Umland and Anton Shekhovtsov, often implicate Alexander Dugin in espousing fascist ideas. Largely in response to these critics, Dugin distanced himself from fascism openly and consistently on various theoretical and practical grounds. He argued that he is a convinced anti-nationalist and anti-racist and does not accept the idea of superiority of one nation (or culture) over another. More importantly, he claims that his thought is essentially anti-modernist, and thus does not fall within the main ideological co-ordinates of modernity, which encompass liberalism, communism, fascism, and nationalism as the principle directions of political thought and activity (Dugin 2012c). From this point of view, he does not consider fascism as an ideological and political alternative to either liberalism or socialism. In addition, Dugin favours the federalist principle of organization of larger states (empires in his view) and is against the centralized method of government. Moreover, he is an advocate of Orthodox Christianity and is sympathetic to all other religions of the world.

3 I thank the anonymous reviewer of the earlier version of this manuscript for insightful thoughts on the matter.

CHAPTER TWO

1 Despite giving rise to competing policies and interpretations, both negative and positive aspects of freedom could be combined and represent mutually reinforcing and interdependent interpretations. Gerald MacCallum (1967, 319) in particular argues for the combination of the two aspects of freedom: 'in recognizing that freedom is always both freedom from something and freedom to do or to become something, one is provided with a means of making sense out of interminable and poorly defined controversies.' Nevertheless, the division serves as a useful analytical tool on many occasions. (More recently, a similar argument has been put forward by Adam Swift [2001].)

2 He granted Catholicism a special role in achieving this goal, due to the distinctly political nature of the Catholic Church. Indeed, Russian thinkers of that period saw the political nature of Catholicism in the perceived movement of the Catholic Church towards the state, with the view to assuming state functions. This project of Catholicism spawned debates within Russian society and gave rise to the conservative 'Dostoyevsky project'. The latter proposed to achieve God's Kingdom on earth through the opposite dynamic. This was seen in the movement of state and society towards the Church, reification of Man, and construction of all terrains of human life on the basis of the New Testament. Thus, while the Catholic Church moves *towards* the state and becomes distinctly political, the Orthodox Church invites the state and society to move towards it, and thus become distinctly religious. The correspondent perceptions of law, freedom, and authority, therefore, become distinctly different in both cases. These issues represented a matter of debate between Westerners and Slavophiles of that period (Kharkhordin 2005, 48–51; Meyendorff 1975, 21; Shmeman 1971, 58–64; Pelikan 1974, 10–11).

3 This could explain the uneasy-but-functioning alliances between various strands of Russian liberalism and the inclusion of radically different representatives of liberal thought into unified political organizations.

4 The extent to which *zemstvo* influenced Russia's political life represents a matter of academic debate. Suffice it to say that the authors cited here hold a somewhat different view on the relative importance of *zemstvo* in the Russian political scene, with some arguing that *zemstvo* faced significant restrictions, and some citing the increase in the *zemstvo*'s budgets towards the end of the Imperial era. Despite the

disagreements, however, it is clear that the *zemstvo* system represented an important political development and fuelled the evolution of liberal thought and practice in Russia.

5 Deploying Kant and Locke moves these thinkers somewhat in the direction of monistic liberalism, for the work of both Kant and Locke, as mentioned above, gave rise to the universalist drive of liberalism and modernity. Nevertheless, intellectual encounters of various strands do not take away from the general pluralistic flavour of this thought. Moreover, the division of liberal thought could be considered for schematic illustrative purposes only and is not always rigidly strict.

6 Vadim Mezhuyev (in Tretyakov 2009b) later somewhat changed his approach to post-modernity, beginning to view it as a positive development and a logical continuation of the modernity project. He then claimed that Russia must first achieve modernity at home – through building institutions of law, order, and equality of opportunity for all – and then proceed to the progressively superior postmodern stage. 'Since I live in Russia,' claimed Mezhuyev in later debates, 'I am a devout modernist, but if I were to live in the United States, I would have stood on the post-modernist positions.'

7 Emile Durkheim (1972, 115) draws a fine distinction between individualism and individuation. Individualism is a moral condition that demands a person lives and works as a specialist and feels like a responsible citizen. Individuation, on the other hand, urges people to 'fend for themselves' and entails the atomization of society.

8 The full implications of such a revision will be discussed in Chapter 5.

CHAPTER THREE

1 Ideological foundation is meant in a traditionalist conservative paradigm, because libertarian, neo-liberal, and technocratic foundations, though proclaiming a limited value package, are still highly ideological.

2 It may seem to some readers that this aspect of Russian conservatism is reminiscent of nationalism. At the same time, we must bear in mind that nationalism does not always entail the support of a strong state or support of existing state institutions, as does conservatism, and in particular Russian conservatism. Nationalism could support the state if the latter pursues an ideological package corresponding to the gist of nationalist policies. Equally, it could be against the state that does not stand by nationalist values. There are multiple examples across

the world, in which nationalism is geared towards the destruction of existing state structures. The 2014 Scottish referendum on independence, the struggle of Basque nationalists against Spain's state structures, Russian ethnic nationalism (to be discussed in Chapter 6) that considers itself part of the non-systemic anti-state opposition are just a few examples in which the goals of nationalism and statism diverge significantly.

CHAPTER FOUR

1 All these fields share a common assumption that an unconsciously accepted structure influences different variations of human socio-political behaviour. They draw this idea from structural linguistics, which makes a distinction between the notions of *langue* and *parole*. *Langue* defines the structure of a language, its grammar and syntax. It is an unconscious and potential side of the language, but not the language itself. *Parole*, on the other hand, belongs to the verbal behaviour, the words we use, and the way we speak. It is the actual, conscious side of the language, its visible interpretation. In this illustration, the structure remains stable, whereas its interpretations in the form of words and their usage could change (Lévi-Strauss 1963, 279–80; Giddens 1979, 10; Rosman and Rubel 2009, 61).

2 In constructing this diagram, Dugin relies partly on Freud and Jung's methods of structural psychology. The *mythos* level could be considered the Id, and the *logos* and *kerygma* could stand for the Ego and Superego, respectively (see Dugin 2009a, 2009b).

3 Traditional rural knee-high felt boots.

4 The terms were introduced during the 1990s and mean an illegal hostile takeover of firms and non-state (usually criminal) protection from takeovers and racketeering.

5 Selection of these two trends is an oversimplification, but nonetheless makes the point that a number of authors have served as an inspiration for Russia's conservatism. At the same time, the universalism of the Enlightenment project has been subjected to revision by many other trends of postmodern thought, such as psychoanalysis, Wittgenstein's philosophy of language, post-Heideggerian hermeneutics, etc.

6 As noted above, the influence of Lévi-Strauss's ideas played a large role in the formation and development of conservative thought in Russia. It is important that Lévi-Strauss himself was seriously influenced by Trubetskoy and Jacobson, Russia's early Eurasian thinkers

(Giddens 1979, 18–19, 20), who worked on the structure of the collective unconscious as a defining feature of social systems. Eurasianism, at the same time, represents the cornerstone of Russia's fundamental conservatism.

7 Dugin's perception of negative liberty as the cornerstone of liberalism, while largely true, must be qualified. For example, Hobbes and Bentham – who were not liberals – deployed the negative interpretation of liberty as freedom from interference in one's plans to implement a chosen course of action according to one's free will. On the other hand, the notions of personal autonomy advanced by liberals such as J.S. Mill and Immanuel Kant could be interpreted in both a negative and a positive sense (Gray 1995, 20; Heywood 2007, 55).

CHAPTER FIVE

1 This is very similar to French public opinion and scholarship of the twentieth century, which has been divided on the issue of the 1789 French Revolution. Public opinion in France underwent various stages of development and approached the French Revolution from a social or political perspective, attributing it to either bourgeois or ultimately Marxist aspirations (Malia 2006). When judged from a class perspective, the French Revolution is seen as the herald of modern democracy and a precursor to the 1917 revolution – a point discussed above. A number of French historians, however, held a different view and judged the revolution as an excessively costly form of modernization with a series of accompanying events that inaugurated France's slow decline as a great power (Chaunu 1989). Some others (Doyle 1999, 17; Taylor 1967, 491) pointed out that the French Revolution did not have a class character, and that its slogans of equality, justice, and liberty were circumstantial rather than historically predetermined. They claim that the French bourgeoisie and nobility belonged to the same economic class, and the wealth of both was landed property and not modern capital. They also argue that the ideology of the Enlightenment was espoused by most social strata of the time, including noble and non-noble notables, as well as royal officials – a circumstance that deprives the bourgeoisie of the right to appropriate the liberating impetus of rising enlightenment (Malia 2006, 186–7). From this point of view, the revolution followed the political logic of a reorganization of society to better fit the social and ideological climate of the time.

2 It is indicative that the Russian state did not recognize the 2014 revolution in Ukraine as a social revolution, but branded it as an externally orchestrated political *coup d'etat* and deployed this fact during its 2014 incorporation of Crimea, in breach of the 5 December 1994 Budapest Memorandum on Security. Hence, the parallel speculative logic that I used above for the October 1917 Revolution does not seem entirely outlandish when looked at from this comparative perspective.

3 See 'Bolee poloviny rossiyan sozhaleyut o raspade SSSR.' *gazeta.ru*, 5 December 2016. https://www.gazeta.ru/politics/news/2016/12/05/n_9412985.shtml.

4 'Zhizn v Rossii: Bednye Stali Nishchimi.' *gazeta.ru*, 15 December 2017. https://www.gazeta.ru/business/2017/12/14/11466530.shtml.

CHAPTER SIX

1 As we have already observed, Western nationalism departs from the ideas of liberal individualism. First, society should make a transition from commune to community. Then it should adopt an urban bourgeois way of life, in which individualism, responsibility, and rights represent core values. Only then, this society could begin fending for itself at a national level, thereby determining the limits and boundaries of its capitalist development.

2 Interestingly, a number of Russian nationalists in the fourth State Duma – including Nikolay Kurianovich, Ivan Demidov, and Yury Shuvalov – formed an Orthodox Christian wing, despite other political differences. Nationalist Sergey Baburin, the founder of the People's Union Party, also positioned his organization as a Christian movement.

3 Late Byzantium under the rule of the Palaiologoi adopted a humbler image of the emperor and introduced an ideology of greater reciprocity between the emperor and his subjects (Angelov 2019).

4 The Western system (with the exception of Britain), on the other hand, relies upon a papacaesaric model that grants this part of the Christian world a different political dynamic. Empire lacks a sacred meaning; hence it is not the sole political condition in which the Western world can exist. In this model, the Pope becomes the superior of many kings. There can be a number of kings that are somewhat subordinate to one religious authority.

5 Liberal thinkers, such as Locke, Kant, and Mill, believe that the state has a limited capacity to educate, enlighten, and civilize individuals

into the core aspects of their duties and liberties (Mill 1974, 187). The state could peter out once it had completed its educational mission, only to be replaced by a civil society of enlightened individuals. Charles Taylor (1995, 215) branded this approach as an L-stream of the civil-society idea. This economically based liberal approach accentuates the importance of society and its management in the modern spheres of production, consumption, exchange, development, and other areas called on to sustain the internal logic of those processes. It views society as a collective of free and rational individuals that precede the state, control it, and might eventually dismantle it, once the state has accomplished its tasks. In this paradigm, the function of the state is to ensure the liberty of such individuals and their peaceful cooperation in the sphere of economic exchange. As John Stuart Mill (1974, 187) observes: 'the worth of a State, in the long run, is the worth of the individuals composing it ... a State which dwarfs its men, in order that they be more docile instruments in its hands even for beneficial purposes – will find that with small men no great thing can really be accomplished'.

6 An oft-cited case is when Chechen wedding participants who indulged in celebratory shooting from their wedding-car windows in the centre of Moscow did not receive appropriate criminal and administrative sanctions.

7 'Tret Rossiyan Vyskazalas za Neitralitet v Konflikte na Ukraine.' *gazeta.ru*, 20 February 2017. https://www.gazeta.ru/social/news/2017/02/20/n_9708653.shtml.

CHAPTER SEVEN

1 Some thinkers might insist that the rift between multipolar and mono-polar world architectures boils down to economic factors. Kenneth Waltz argues that the idea of polarity stems from applying neoclassical economics to the realm of international relations. At the same time, there is a plethora of authors who could, without denying the importance of economic factors, claim the utmost significance of ideological variables. It could be argued that the debate over the primacy of either economic or ideological factors in the discussion on international-relations polarity is reminiscent of the discussion between rationalists and empiricists. This book focuses on the ideological and philosophical line of reasoning and eschews the extensive examination of economic factors.

2 The philosophy of history of Alexei Khomiakov, the idea of organic
    cultures of Apollon Grigoriev, the historiosophy of Nikolay
    Danilevsky, and the anthropology of Nikolay Strakhov have been
    of particular importance.
3 Peter Chaadaev, while setting the division line in Russian political
    thought by arguing that Russia has no future without joining the real
    of European civilization, still argued at some periods of his life that
    Russia's distinctness could advance its development. In a later letter to
    Turgenev, Chaadaev (1991, 98) wrote that Russia has a different civili-
    zational origin from Europe. 'We do not need to chase someone else.
    We need to determine who we really are. We need to leave the lies
    behind and reassert ourselves in truth. Then we can move forward,
    and move faster than others because we arrived here later than them
    but we have all their knowledge and experience reflected in centuries
    of labour that preceded us.' Chernyshevsky and other revolutionaries
    exploited those thoughts of Chaadaev to argue that Russia's civiliza-
    tional distinctness could help it to organize a socialist revolution and
    set Russia on a non-capitalist way of development (Maslin 2008, 130).
4 It is interesting that Strakhov adopted the civilizational approach to
    world politics before Danilevsky and independently from him. An edi-
    tor of the journal *Zarya*, he published Danilevsky's main work, *Russia
    and Europe*, in 1869 and publicly defended it from the liberal critics,
    in particular Vladimir Solovyov.
5 Zakharova argues that, in the case of Ukraine, Western powers have
    been consistently influencing domestic politics since the first Orange
    revolution of 2004, which is indeed well documented by a large num-
    ber of Western scholars from various perspectives (see Aslund and
    MacFaul 2006; Lane 2008). Zakharova also lamented the situation in
    which high-ranking Western leaders frequented the 2014 *maidan* ral-
    lies and publicly supported the demise of the Victor Yanukovich's gov-
    ernment. Furthermore, Western powers did not object to the ousting
    of President Yanukovich the day after the German and Polish foreign
    ministers, as well as a high-ranking French foreign ministry official,
    mediated and witnessed the signing of the roadmap towards settling
    the political crisis. Russian officials argued that, against the backdrop
    of open Western support of political forces that are beneficial to
    Western interests, Russia would support its own interests and enable
    the Russian population of Ukraine to pursue its civilizational choice.
    Hence, we are witnessing a clash of geopolitical interests between

Russia and the West that are linked to the struggle over civilizational
spheres of influence.

6 The medieval doctrine of a 'just war' is often invoked in casual and
   even academic conversations. Yet, its potential dangers are casually
   ignored. The doctrine splits warring parties on 'just' and 'unjust' lines,
   thus allowing the 'just' side to dehumanize and annihilate its adversary
   (Brown 2007, 45–50). Hence, stronger states idealize their moral
   positions and strive to impose them on the 'morally inferior' enemy,
   covering, at the same time, the advance of their power interests
   (Scheuerman 2007, 66). Carl Schmitt, in particular, worried that this
   paradigm demolished state sovereignties, in that those parties that do
   not comply with the overarching 'correct' universalist project. Those
   parties are treated as 'unjust' enemies and become subject to annihilation in the course of creating an international law of a universal
   nature.

CHAPTER EIGHT

1 The idea is also a direct replica of the early liberal principle of separating religion and the state (Walzer 1994, 100–1; Kymlicka 1995). The
   right of religious self-expression belongs to the civil group of rights and
   is articulated in the idea of freedom of consciousness. Thus, religious
   beliefs, and their diversity, are locked within the public realm; civic
   matters not related to religious issues belong to the public domain.
2 Many critics of liberalism viewed this substantive minimalism as a
   form of 'political neutralization'. Carl Schmitt claims that this idea has
   long historical roots and represents the broader process of political
   neutralization. He claims that, following a series of religious wars of
   the sixteenth century, Europe was seeking political neutralization, in
   which an agreement could be reached and conflict diminished. This
   search culminated in the modernity and value-neutral capitalism of the
   twentieth century (McCormick 1997, 44; Meier 1995, 92). Schmitt (in
   Meier 1995, 92) writes: 'the present situation is characterized by the
   fact that a process of three hundred years old has reached its end. The
   age at the end of which we find ourselves is the age of neutralization
   and depoliticization. Depoliticization not only is the accidental or even
   necessary result of the modern development but is its original and
   authentic goal; the movement in which the modern spirit has gained
   its greatest efficacy, liberalism, is characterized precisely by the

negation of the political.' At the same time, Schmitt's criticism of 'political neutralization' is debatable. Arguably, the very idea of substantive minimalism, coupled with the principle of personal autonomy, becomes a highly political doctrine in its own right. Liberalism defends its main tenets rather effectively in both intellectual and political arenas – something that I showed above.

3 The issue of recognition is a complex one. It can be understood in a restricted and comprehensive sense. In the restricted sense, which I use here, recognition refers to the issues related to cultural status. A comprehensive version of recognition advocated by Axel Honneth (Fraser and Honneth 2003) refers to the acknowledgement of the values of others as objects of love, respect, and esteem (see Owen and Tully 2007, 268). In the subsequent discussion on Russia, recognition will be discussed in mostly comprehensive terms.

4 Exception must be made for a small number of liberal thinkers, such as Vladislav Inozemtsev (2012) from the Moscow Institute of International Relations, who place the idea of individual rights at the heart of politics, reject the idea of multiculturalism and group rights as detrimental to individual rights, and advocate the creation of a political-nation-state. Such thinking is reminiscent of a number of his American counterparts – Michael Walzer and Nathan Glazer – who argued in favour of the cultural assimilation of migrants.

CHAPTER NINE

1 This was partly the reason why women performed a lot of physical and unintellectual tasks. The Soviet educational system was heavily focused on the fields of science and technology in order to match the West in the arms race. The humanities were much less prominent and even suppressed. Less choice and fewer university placements in the humanities were available, and the field was largely populated by women. Those who could not get those humanities placements ended up in manual jobs.

2 In reality, however, the state policy towards the family is marked by significant dualism. Apart from the task of increasing birth rates, the state often insisted that it should not interfere in family matters. Russia's President Vladimir Putin supported such rhetoric on many occasions, which had an impact on policy-making. His attitude to the draft law on domestic violence was ambiguous, in that he claimed that the state must not intrude in family matters and must 'act carefully'.

On many other occasions Putin forwarded congratulatory notes to various public conferences (the Congress of Russia's Parents is one such example) that denounced the practice of juvenile justice in West European countries. This practice, in the view of such conference participants, is aimed at the destruction of the traditional family and allows the state to interfere too deeply in the child-rearing process ('Bolshevistskii Opyt Yuvenalnoi Yustitsii', *russia.ru*, 26 February 2013).

3 Pro-Kremlin organizations often deploy similar tactics. Of particular importance were the Rip for Putin (Porvu za Putina) campaign or the pro-Putin calendar photo session (see Sperling's fascinating 2012 account). The Kremlin's promotion of the image of Vladimir Putin also shocks the audience (see Faxall 2012, discussion on the political nature of masculinity in Russia).

4 'Litsa Zony: V Zhenskoi Kolonii Mechtayut o More, Semye, i Fiskashkakh', *gazeta.ru*, 24 March 2015. Accessed 15 December 2019. http://www.gazeta.ru/social/2015/03/23/6611845.shtml.

5 'Pochemy Zhenshchiny Dolzhny Zarabatyvat Bolshe, Chem Muzhchiny: Kak Prevratit Nizkuyu Samootsenku v Vysokuyu Zarplatu'. *gazeta.ru*, 6 March 2015. Accessed 15 March 2015. http://www.gazeta.ru/lifestyle/style/2014/10/a_6250505.shtml.

References

Ackerman, Bruce. 1980. *Social Justice in the Liberal State*. New Haven: Yale University Press.

Ackerman, Bruce. 1998. *We the People. Transformations. Vol. 2*. Cambridge, Mass., Harvard University Press.

Adorno, Theodor, and Max Horkheimer. 1999. *Dialectic of Enlightenment*. London: Verso.

Aivazova, Svetlana. 1998. *Russkie Zhenshchiny v Labirinte Ravnopraviya*. Moscow: RIK Rusanova.

– 2008. *Rossiiskie Vybory: Gendernoe Prochtenie*. Moscow: Moskovskie Uchebniki i Kartolitographiia.

Akhmedshina, Fania, Olga Shnyrova, and Igor Shkolnikov. 2007. 'Opyt Resheniya "Zhenskogo Voprosa" v Sovetskoe Vremia'. In *Vvedenie v Teoriiu i Praktiku Gendernykh Otnoshenii*, edited by Elena Mezentseva, Irina Iukina, Larisa Boichenko, and Irina Tartakovskaia, 71–81. Tashkent: Komitet Zhenshchin Respubliki Uzbekistan.

Akopov, Petr. 2014. 'Globalizatsiya Otmeniaetsia'. *Vzgliad*, 14 March.

Aksyutich, Viktor. 2014. 'Rossiya – eto Sila'. *Politika*, 11 March.

Akulova, Vera. 2013. 'Feminizm v Rossii'. *Zhivoi Razgovor*, 30 March 2013.

Aleshina, Yulia, and Alexandra Sergeevna Volovich. 1991. 'Problemy Usvoeniya Rolei Muzhchiny i Zhenshiny'. *Voprosy Psikhologii'*, no. 4: 74–82.

Alexandrov, Sergey. 2013. 'Izborsky Klub Predlozhil Strategiyu Bolshogo Ryvka Rossii'. *Vzgliad*, 29 January.

Alexiev, Alex, 'The Kremlin and the Root Causes of Terror'. *National Review*, 5 April 2010.

Alferov, Zhores. 2017a. 'Sotsializm Vernetsia'. *Svobodnaya Pressa*, 10 November.

– 2017b. 'Esli By Ne Devyanostye Gody, Iphony be Seichas Vypuskali u Nas'. *Argumenty i Fakty*, 16 November.

Ambrosio, Thomas. 2009. *Authoritarian Backlash: Russian Resistance to Democratization in the Former Soviet Union*. London: Routledge.

Amnuel, Grigory, and Sergey Kurginyan. 2017. 'Chto Takoe Demokratiya? [What Is Democracy?]'. *Poyedinok*, 26 January. Accessed 12 December 2019. https://www.youtube.com/watch?v=20iA-eHZIL4.

Anderson, Benedict. 1989. *Imagined Communities: Reflections on the Origins and Spread of Nationalism*. Cambridge: Polity.

Angelov, Dimiter. 2006. *Imperial Ideology and Political Thought in Byzantium, 1204–1330*. Cambridge: Cambridge University Press.

'Antivaldayskaya vozvyshennost [The Anti-Valday Summit]'. 2012. *Kommersant*, 10 September.

Antonov-Avseenko, Anton. 1991. 'Protivostoyanie'. *Literaturnaya Gazeta*, 3 April.

Appiah, Kwame Anthony. 2005. *The Ethics of Identity*. Princeton: Princeton University Press.

Arbatova, Maria. 2013. 'Maria Arbatova o Feminizme'. *Sobchak Zhiv'yem*, 7 March 2013.

Arendt, Hannah. 1969. *On Violence*. New York: Harcourt, Brace and World.

Aronowitz, Stanley. 1988. 'Post-modernism and Politics'. In *Universal Abandon? The Politics of Post-Modernism*, edited by Andrew Ross, 46–62. Minneapolis: University of Minnesota Press.

Ascher, Abraham. 2001. *P.A. Stolypin: The Search for Stability in Late Imperial Russia*. Stanford: Stanford University Press.

Ashwin, Sarah. 2000. 'Gender, State, and Society in Soviet and Post-Soviet Russia'. In *Gender, State, and Society in Soviet and Post-Soviet Russia*, edited by Sarah Ashwin, 71–89. London: Routledge.

Aslund, Anders, and Michael MacFaul. 2006. *Revolution in Orange: The Origins of Ukraine's Democratic Breakthrough*. Washington, DC: Brookings Institution Press.

Baddeley, John. 2012. *Russia in the Eighties: Sport and Politics*. London: Forgotten Books.

Baker, Lee D. 2004. 'Franz Boas: Out of the Ivory Tower'. *Anthropological Theory* 4 (1): 29–51.

Balzer, Harley. 1991. 'The Problem of Profession in Imperial Russia'. In *Between Tsar and People: Educated Society and the Quest for Public*

Identity in Late Imperial Russia, edited by Edith Clowes, Samuel Kassow, and James West, 183–99. Princeton: Princeton University Press.

Barghoorn, Frederick. 1976. *Soviet Russian Nationalism*. Westport, CT: OUP.

Barkawi, Tarak. 1998. 'Strategy as a Vocation: Weber, Morgenthau, and Modern Strategic Studies'. *Review of International Studies* 24, no. 2 (Apr): 159–84.

Barr, Nicolas. 1997. *Rynok Truda i Sotsialnaia Politika v Tsentralnoi i Vostochnoi Evrope. Perekhodnyi Period i Dalneishee Razvitie*. Moscow: IKTS DIS.

Baskakova, Marina. 1995. 'Zamuzhniaia Zhenshchina: Semia ili Rabota?' *Sem'ia v Rossii* 3, no. 4: 101–8.

Baudrillard, Jean. 1981. *Simulacra and Simulation*. Ann Arbor: University of Michigan Press.

Bauman, Zigmund. 2007. *Liquid Time: Living in the Age of Uncertainty*. Cambridge, UK: Polity.

Beitz, Charles. 1979. *Political Theory in International Relations*. Princeton, NJ: Princeton University Press.

Belov, A.V. 2010. 'Foreword'. In *Bor'ba s Zapadom* [Struggle with the West], edited by Nikolay Strakhov, 5–36. Moscow: Institut Russkoi Tsivilizatsii.

Berdyaev, Nicolas, Sergey Bulgakov, Mikhail Gershenzon, A.S. Izgoev, Bogdan Kistyakovsky, Peter Struve, Semen Frank. 1994. *Vekhi. [Landmarks]*. London: Sharpe.

Berdyaev, Nicolas. 2008. *Russkaya Idea* [The Russian Idea]. St Petersburg: Azbuka Klassika.

Berdyaevskie Chteniya. Samopoznanie. 2015. *Filosof Svobody i Sily*, no. 2. Accessed 12 November 2019. https://politconservatism.ru/upload/iblock/caf/cafa9a7698ba4dd4018a39b41b283801.pdf.

Berlin, Isaiah. 1969. *Four Essays on Liberty*. Oxford: Oxford University Press.

– 1994. *Russian Thinkers*. London: Penguin Books.

– 2004. *The Soviet Mind: Russian Culture under Communism*. Washington, DC: Brookings Institution Press.

– 2006. *Political Ideas in the Romantic Age*. Oxford: Oxford University Press.

Bitten, Natalya. 2013. 'Biet Znachit Lyubit. O domashnem Nasilii i Seksizme v Rossii'. In *Setevizor. Est Takaia Tema s Nikolaem Pivnenko*, 30 May. Accessed 1 May 2015. https://www.youtube.com/watch?v=5YjJRMHltLE&spfreload=1.

Blok, Alexandr. 1999. 'Katilina' (originally published in April 1918) in *Complete Works. Vol. 9*. Moscow: Nauka.

– 1999. 'Dvenadtsat' (originally published in March 1918) in *Complete Works. Vol. 5*. Moscow: Nauka.

– 1999. 'Zakat Gumanima [The Decline of Humanism]', (originally published in 1919) in *Complete Works. Vol. 9*. Moscow: Nauka.

Bogaturov, Alexey. 1999. 'Sindrom Pogloshcheniya v Mirovoi Politike'. *Pro et Contra*, 17, no. 4: 28–48.

Bogdanov, Yuriy, Sergey Riabukhin, Sergey Shugayev, and Yuliya Krokhina. 2014. 'Deofshorizatsiya Rossiyskoy ekonomiki [The De-offshorization of the Russian Economy]'. *Senat, russia24*, 12 March.

Bordachev, Timofey, Elena Zinovieva, Anastasiya Likhacheva. 2015. *Teoriya Mezhdunarodnykh Otnoshenii v XXI Veke*. Moscow: Mezhdunarodnye Otnosheniya.

Borisova, Natalia, and Alexandr Gorshkov. 2008. 'Politicheskii Potentsial Muzhskikh i Zhenskikh Soobshchestv v Sovremennoi Rossii'. *Vestnik Permskogo Universiteta*, no. 1, 34–47.

Botz, Gerhard. 1987. 'Austria'. In *The Social Basis for European Fascist Movements*, edited by Detlef Muhlberger, 242–81. London: Croom Helm.

Bowle, John. 1954. *Politics and Opinion in the Nineteenth Century: An Historical Introduction*. Oxford: Alden Press.

Boyle, Nicholas, Liz Disley, Nicholas Adams. 2013. *The Impact of Idealism: The Legacy of Post-Kantian German Thought*. Cambridge: Cambridge University Press.

Breslauer, George. 2017. 'Reforming Sacred Institutions: The Soviet Communist Party and the Roman Catholic Church Compared'. *Post-Soviet Affairs*, 33, no. 3: 177–99.

Breuilly, John. 1985. *Nationalism and the State*. Manchester: MUP.

Bromley, Simon. 1999. 'Marxism and Globalisation'. In *Marxism and Social Science*, edited by Andrew Gamble, David Marsh, and Tony Tant, 280–301. London: Macmillian.

Bronfenbrenner, Urie. 1962. 'Soviet Methods of Character Education: Some Implications for Research'. *American Psychologist*, 17, no. 8 (8): 550–64.

Brown, Chris, Terry Nardin, Nicholas Rengger, eds. 2002. *International Relations in Political Thought*. Cambridge: Cambridge University Press.

Brown, Chris. 2007. 'The Twilight of International Morality? Hans J. Morgenthau and Carl Schmitt on the End of the *Jus Publicum Eurpaeum*'. In *Realism Reconsidered: The Legacy of Hans J.*

Morgenthau in International Relations, edited by Michael Williams, 42–61. Oxford: Oxford University Press.

Bulgakov, Sergey. 1994. 'Heroism and Asceticism: Reflections on the Religious Nature of Russia's Intelligentsia'. In *Vekhi*, edited by Nicolas Berdyaev, Sergey Bulgakov, Mikhail Gershenzon, A.S. Izgoev, Bogdan Kistyakovsky, Peter Struve, Semen Frank, 17–51. London: Sharpe.

Bull, Hedley. 2000. 'Justice in International Relations'. In *Hedley Bull on International Society*, edited by Kai Alderson and Andrew Hurrell, 206–45. London: Macmillan.

Bunin, Igor. 2008. 'Liberalizm kak politika v Rossii [Liberalism as Policy in Russia]', in Vitaly Tretyakov, Alexey Kara-Murza, Boris Titov, and Igor Bunin, 'Liberalizm kak politika v Rossii [Liberalism as Policy in Russia]'. *Chto Delat*, no. 224 (14 December). Accessed 11 December 2019. http://www.youtube.com/watch?v=eKOfpWPZicw.

Byzov, Leontiy. 2006. 'Konservativnaya Volna v Rossii'. *Zametki Sotsiologa*, no. 9: 152–70.

Calhoun, Craig. 2007. *Nations Matter: Culture, History, and Cosmopolitan Dream*. London: Routledge.

Carr, Edward. 2001. *The Twenty Years' Crisis*. London: Palgrave.

Cassirer, Ernst. 1946. *The Myth of the State*. New Haven: Yale University Press.

Cavallar, Georg. 2001. 'Kantian Perspectives on Democratic Peace: Alternatives to Doyle'. *Review of International Studies* 27, no. 2: 229–48.

Chaadaev, Peter. 1991. *Polnoe Sobranie Sochinenii I Izbrannye Pisma*. Moscow: Nauka.

Chaudet, Didier. 2009. *When Empire Meets Nationalism: Power Politics in the US and Russia*. Aldershot: Ashgate.

Chaunu, Pierre. 1989. *Le Grand Declassement: A propos d'une commemoration*. Paris: Laffont.

Chebankova, Elena. 2012. 'State-sponsored Civic Associations in Russia: Systemic Integration of the War of Position?" *East European Politics* 28, no. 4: 390–408.

– 2013. *Civil Society in Putin's Russia*. London: Routledge.

Chirikova, Alla, and Natalya Lapina. 2011. 'Zhenshchina na Vysshikh Etazhakh Rossiiskoi Regionalnoi Vlasti: Bazovye Tendentsii'. *Politeks* 7, no. 4: 4–72.

Chirikova, Alla. 1998. *Zhenshchina vo Glave Firmy*. Moscow: Institut Sotsiologii RAN.

– 2011. 'Zhenshina-rukovoditel vo vlasti i biznese: sotsialno-psikhologicheskyi portret'. *Politex* 7, no. 1: 142–62.

Chomsky, Noam. 1998. *Profit over People: Neoloberalism and Global Order*. New York: Seven Stories Press.

Christoff, Peter. 1970. *The Third Heart: Some Intellectual-Ideological Currents and Cross-Currents in Russia, 1800–1830*. Paris: Mouton.

– 1991. *An Introduction to Nineteenth Century Russian Slavophilism*. Vol. 4, *Iu. F. Samarin*. Oxford: Westview Press.

Clark, R.T. 1969. *Herder: His Life and Thought*. Berkley: University of California Press.

Clinton, Hillary. 2011. 'US Is Losing the Global Information War'. *RT*, 3 March 2011. https://www.youtube.com/watch?v=NBsALgjLKoU.

Cobban, Alfred. 1962. *Edmund Burke and Revolt Against the Eighteenth Century*. London: Allen and Unwin.

Codevilla, Giovanni. 2008. 'Relations between Church and State in Russia Today'. *Religion, State, and Society* 36, no. 2: 113–38.

Cohen, Jean. 1983. *Class and Civil Society: The Limits of Marxian Critical Theory*. Oxford: Martin Robinson.

Cohen, Jean, and Andrew Arato. 1992. *Civil Society and Political Theory*. Cambridge: MIT Press.

Cohn, Carol, and Sarah Ruddick. 2003. 'A Feminist Ethical Perspective on Weapons of Mass Destruction'. *Boston Consortium on Gender, Security and Human Rights*. Working Paper No. 104, 3–33. http://www.gender andsecurity.umb.edu/cohnruddick.pdf.

Coole, Diana. 1993. *Women in Political Theory: From Ancient Misogyny to Contemporary Feminism*. London: Harvester Wheatsheaf.

Copleston, Frederick. 1986. *Philosophy in Russia: From Herzen to Lenin and Berdyaev*. Notre Dame, IN: University of Notre Dame Press.

Cornell, Agnes, Jorgen Møller, and Svend-Eirk Skaaning. 2017. 'The Real Lessons of the Interwar Years'. *Journal of Democracy* 28, no. 3: 14–28.

Crossley, Nick, and Michael Roberts. 2004. *After Habermas: New Perspectives on the Public Sphere*. Oxford: Blackwell Publishing.

Dahl, Robert. 1956. *A Preface to Democratic Theory*. Chicago: University of Chicago Press.

– 1998. *On Democracy*. New Haven: Yale University Press.

Dahlmann, Dittmar. 1998. 'Liberals in the Provinces: The Kadets and the Duma Elections in Saratov, 1906–1912'. In *Emerging Democracy in Imperial Russia*, edited by Mary Conroy, 88–112. Colorado: University of Colorado Press.

Dale, Gareth. 2017. *Karl Polanyi: A Life on the Left*. New York: Columbia University Press.

Dallin, Alexander. 1972. *The Kaminsky Brigade: A Case-Study of German Military Exploitation of Soviet Disaffection*. Bloomington, IN: Indiana University Press.

Daly, Glyn. 1999. 'Marxism and Post-modernity'. In *Marxism and Social Science*, edited by Andrew Gamble, David March, and Tony Tant, 61–84. London: Palgrave Macmillan.

Dawson, Christopher. 1991. *Religion and the Rise of Western Culture: The Classic Study of Medieval Civilization*. New York: Image Books.

Deleuze, Gilles, and Felix Guattari. 2004. *Anti-Oedipus: Capitalism and Schizophrenia*. London: Continuum International Publishers.

Delyagin, Mikhail, Sergey Glazyev, and Andrey Fursov. 2013. *Strategiya Bolshogo Ryvka*. Moscow: Algoritm.

– 2013. 'Krov v Venakh Ekonomiki'. *russia.ru*, 23 January.

– 2014a. 'Kapitalizm Zakonchilsia. Chto Teper?' *Nevskiy Express*, 8 March.

– 2014b. 'Mavzolei dlia Dzhona Kerry'. 7 March. Accessed 22 December 2019. https://www.youtube.com/watch?v=ja3kn_MjGPg.

– 2016. 'Globalizatsia i Predatelstvo Elit. Oni Zhivut Pod Soboyu Ne Chuia Strany'. *Zavtra*, 14 January.

– 2019. *Obshchaya Teoriya Globalizatsii. Ostorozhno, Dveri Otkryvayutsia. Vol. 1*. Moscow: Institut Problem Globalizatsii.

Demidov, Ivan, and Mikhail Leontyev. 2007. 'Ya ne prinadlezhu k kategorii lyudey kotoryye schitayut, chto vazhen rezultat [I do not belong to the category of people who consider that the result is important]'. *kreml.org*, 19 March.

Demoskop. 2012. 'Novye Ogranicheniya Prava na Abort v Rossii'. 20 February – 4 March. Accessed 15 December 2019. http://demoscope.ru/weekly/2012/0499/reprodo2.php.

Desch, Michael. (2007/08) 'America's Liberal Illiberalism'. *International Security* 32, no. 3: 7–43.

Deutsch, Karl. W. 1961. 'Social Mobilization and Political Development'. *American Political Science Review*, 55, no. 3: 493–515.

Deutsch, Karl W., and J. David Singer. 1964. 'Multipolar Power Systems and International Stability'. *World Politics*, 16, no.3: 390–406.

Di Stefano, Christine. 1996. 'Autonomy in the Light of Difference'. In *Rethinking Obligation*, edited by Nancy Hirshchman and Christine Di Stefano, 95–116. Ithaca, NY: Cornell University Press.

Diamond, Larry, and Gary Marks, eds. 1992. *Re-examining Democracy: Essays in Honour of Seymour Martin Lipset*. London: Sage.

Diamond, Larry. 1996. 'Toward Democratic Consolidation'. In *The Global Resurgence of Democracy*, edited by Larry Diamond and Marc Plattner, 227–40. Baltimore and London: Johns Hopkins University Press.

Dmitriyev, Ilya. 2011. 'Post-liberalizm: Mnogopolyarnaya perspektiva [Post-liberalism. A Multipolar Perspective]'. *Yevrazia Informatsionno Analyticheskiy Portal*, 5 September.

Dodd, Nigel. 2005. *Social Theory and Modernity*. Cambridge: Polity.

Dorenko, Sergey. 2007. 'My velikiy syr'yevoy pridatok Kitaya [We Are the Great Raw Material Appendage of China]'. *Ekho Moskvy*, August.

Doyle, Michael. 1983. 'Kant, Liberal Legacies, and Foreign Affairs, Part 2'. *Philosophy and Public Affairs* 12, no. 2: 323–53.

– 2009. 'A Few Words on Mill, Walzer, and Nonintervention'. *Ethics and International Affairs* 23, no. 4: 349–69.

Doyle, William. 1999. *The Origins of the French Revolution*. New York: Oxford University Press.

Drobizheva, Leokadiia. 2003. *Sotsiologiia Mezhetnicheskoi Tolerantnosti*. Moscow: Institute of Sociology RAN.

Dubin, Boris. 2004. *Intellektualnye Gruppy i Simvolicheskie Formy: Ocherki Sotsiologii Sovremennoi Kultury*. Moscow: Novoe Izdatelstvo.

Dugin, Alexandr. 2001. *Osnovy Geopolitiki*. Moscow: Arktogeia.

– 2008. 'Arkehomodern. V poiskakh tochki, gde i arkhaika, i modern yasny kak paradigmy [Archeo-modernity. In Search of Points Where Both the Archaic and Modern Are Clear as a Paradigm]'. Center for Conservative Research, 10 April. http://www.arcto.ru/modules.php?name=News&file=article&sid=1474.

– 2009. 'Logika Russkoi Istorii i Put Medvedeva-Putina'. *Sovremennaya Identichnost Rossii*, Lecture 3, Centre for Conservative Studies. http://konservatizm.org/konservatizm/ident/240409031315.xhtml.

– 2009a. 'Strukturalistskaya topika sotsiologii [The Structuralist Topic of Sociology]'. Lecture no. 1, Moscow State University, 25 February. http://konservatizm.org/speech/dugin/080309205432.xhtml.

– 2009b. 'Sotsial'naya antropologiya [Social Anthropology]'. Lecture no. 5 in the course 'Strukturnaya Sotsiologiya'. Moscow State University, 25 March. http://konservatizm.org/konservatizm/sociology/270309011304.xhtml#l5_3.

– 2009c. 'Yad Modernizatsii: Monotonnyy protsess progressa kak fatal'naya opasnost' dlya chelovechestva [The Poison of Modernization: A Monotonous Process of Progress as a Fatal Danger for Mankind]'. Center for Conservative Research, 29 March. http://konservatizm.org/konservatizm/theory/290310021447.xhtml.

– 2009d. 'Etnosotsiologiya (lektsiya 1) [Ethnosociology (lecture 1)]'.
Lecture at Moscow State University, 12 September. http://www.evrazia.
tv/content/etnosotsiologhiia-liektsiia-1.

– 2009e. 'Strukturnaya sotsiologiya: Post-obshchestvo [Structural sociology: Post-society]'. Lecture at Moscow State University Sociology
Faculty, 16 November. http://konservatizm.org/161109164821.xhtml.

– 2009f. 'Rossiya Sozdayot Mif (Russia Creates a Myth)'. *Diskurs*, 3 July,
2009.

– 2010. *Logos i Mifos: Sotsiologiya Glubin [Logos and Mythos: A
Sociology of the Depths]*. Moscow: Akademicheskiy Prospekt.

– 2012a. 'Sumerki svobody: Liberal'nyy nigilizm kak poslednyaya stadiya
globalizatsii [The Dawn of Freedom: Liberal Nihilism as the Latest
Stage of Globalization]'. *Odnako*, no. 26, 22 September.

– 2012b. 'Otvetnyy udar konservatorov [The Return Blow of the
Conservatives]'. *russia.ru*, 9 October. www.tv.russia.ru/video/diskurs_
13541.

– 2012c. *The Fourth Political Theory*. London: Arktos.

– 2012d. 'Yevropa v nyneshney polozhenii obrechena [Europe in the
Present Situation Is Doomed]'. *Vis-à-vis s Mirom, Armen Oganesyan*,
15 August. http://www.youtube.com/watch?v=SIC4QUslxC8.

– 2012e. 'Gegemoniya v kulture [Hegemony in Culture]'. *russia.ru*,
13 November.

– 2012f. 'Obshchestvo pobedivshego khama [Society of the Victorious
Boor]'. *russia.ru*, 10 December. http://tv.russia.ru/video/online_199/.

– 2012g. 'Rossiya v Poiskakh Novogo Tsivilizatsionnogo Koda (Russia in
Search of a New Civilizational Code)'. *Yevraziyskiy Soyuz Molodyozhi*
(Eurasian Union of Youth), 27 February. http://rossia3.ru/ news/2012/
02/27/16:04:57.

– 2013. *Teoriya Mnogopolyarnogo Mira*. Moscow: Evraziiskoe Dvizhenie.

– 2018. 'Chto Budet Posle Putina [What Will Happen after Putin]'. *Dentv*,
17 December.

Dugin, Alexander and Sergey Kapitsa. 2006. 'Aleksandr Dugin i Sergey
Kapitsa govoryat o postmoderne [Aleksandr Dugin and Sergey Kapitsa
Talk about Post-modernity]'. *Ochevidnoye Neveroyatnoye*, Center
for Conservative Research. http://www.evrazia.tv/content/aleksandr-
dugin-i-sergey-kapica-govoryat-o-postmoderne.

Dugin, Alexandr, and Avanes Oganesyan. 2012. 'Yevropa v nyneshney
polozhenii obrechena [Europe in the Present Situation Is Doomed]'.
Vis-à-vis s Mirom, 15 August. http://www.youtube.com/watch?v=
SIC4QUslxC8.

Duncan, Peter. 2000. *Russian Messianism: Third Rome, Revolution, Communism, and After*. New York and London: Routledge.

Dunlop, John. 1983. *The Faces of Contemporary Russian Nationalism*. Princeton: Princeton University Press.

– 2010. 'Neoevraziiskii Uchebnik Alexandra Dugina i Protevorechivyi Otklik Dmitriia Trenina'. *Forum Noveiishei Vostochno-Evropeiskoi Istorii i Kultury*, no. 1: 79–113. (English translation by Anton Shekhovtsev).

Dunn, John. 1969. *The Political Thought of John Locke: An Historical Account of the Argument of the 'Two Treatises of Government'*. Cambridge: Cambridge University Press.

– 1972. *Modern Revolutions: An Introduction to the Analysis of a Political Phenomenon*. Cambridge: Cambridge University Press.

Durkheim, Emile. 1972. *Selected Writings*. Cambridge: Cambridge University Press.

Dutkiewicz, Piotr, and Vladislav Inozemtsev. 2013. *Democracy versus Modernization: A Dilemma for Russia and the World*. London: Routledge.

Dworkin, Ronald. 1978. 'Taking Rights Seriously'. In *Public and Private Morality*, edited by Stuart Hampshire, 113–43. Cambridge: Cambridge University Press.

Dzhemal, Geidar. 2012a. 'Vragi mirovogo pravitel'stva [Enemies of World Government]'. *russia.ru*, 27 August.

– 2012b. 'Global'nyy anti-islamskiy zagovor [Global Anti-Islamic conspiracy]'. Conversation with Elizaveta Muratova, *russia.ru*, September. http://tv.russia.ru/video/online_75/.

Dzhemal, Geidar, and Valery Solovey. 2011. 'O Sobytiiakh na Manezhnoi Ploshchadi'. *Dialog RBK*, 20 January, *russia.ru*, 29 February 2012.

Dzhemal, Geidar, and Maxim Shevchenko. 2012. 'Ostraia Diskussiia o Tekushchei Politicheskoi Situatsii', March 1, 2012, available at https://www.youtube.com/watch?v=0PzToE804ww, last accessed 16 July 2020.

Ehrenberg, John. 1999. *Civil Society: The Critical History of an Idea*. New York: New York University Press.

Einstein, Albert. 2009. 'Why Socialism?' *Monthly Review* 69, no. 1 (May).

Eisenstadt, Samuel. 2002. *Multiple Modernities*. Livingston, NJ: Transaction Publishers.

Elshtain, Jean. 1986. *Meditations in Modern Political Thought: Masculine/Feminine Themes from Luther to Arendt*. University Park, PA: Pennsylvania State University Press.

Engels, Friedrich. 1873. 'On Authority'. *Workers Vanguard*, no. 898. Accessed 22 December 2019. https://www.icl-fi.org/english/wv/898/engelsonauthority.html.

- 1884/1972. *The Origins of the Family, Private Property, and the State.* London: Penguin Classics.

English, Robert. 2000. *Russia and the Idea of the West: Gorbachev, Intellectuals, and the End of the Cold War.* New York: Columbia University Press.

Etzioni, Amitai. 1993. *The Spirit of Community: Rights, Responsibilities, and the Communitarian Agenda.* London: Fontana.

Expert. 2013. 'Liberalnaya Platforma. Otkrytoe Zasedanie Liberalnoi Platformy Partii ER po teme Voprosy Deyatelnosti Platformy i Aktualnaya Povestka Dnia'. 20 June.

Fadeyev, Rostislav. 1874. *Russkoe Obshchestvo v Nastojashchem i Budushchem.* St Petersburg: Russkii Mir.

Fadeyev, Valery. 2013. 'Te, kto segodnia nazyvayut sebia liberalami, yavlayutsia protivnikami razvitiya strany'. *Expert*, 30 January.

- 2014. 'Na Tverdoi Pochve'. *Ekspert*, no. 3. http://expert.ru/expert/2014/03/na-tverdoj-pochve/.

Fedorov, Valery. 2010. 'Politicheskaia Sistema Rossii Sozdana'. VTSIOM Publications, 19 January. Accessed 28 May 2015. http://wciom.ru/arkhiv/tematicheskiiarkhiv/item/single/13069.html?no_cache=1&cHash=c41acb2f2d.

Fedotov, GeorgiiPetrovich. 1950. *A Treasury of Russian Spirituality.* London: Sheed and Ward.

Fefelov, Andrey, and Konstantin Krylov. 2012. 'Natsionalnaya Imperiya ili Natsionalnaya Demokratiya'. *Den.TV*, 12 September. Accessed 25 May 2019. https://www.youtube.com/watch?v=O2rrHmCDuNw.

Fichte, Johann Gottlieb. 2000. *Foundations of Natural Right: According to the Principles of the Wissenschaftslehre.* Cambridge: Cambridge University Press.

Filatov, V.P. 2006. 'Osobennosti liberalizatsii i modernizatsii Rossii vo vtoroi polovine XIX-nachale XX vekov v kontekste evropeiskogo razvitiya'. *Rossiya: Varianty Institutsionalnogo Razvitiya*, Conference at Higher School of Economics. http://ecsocman.hse.ru/text/16207777/.

Filippini, Michele. 2017. 'Ideology'. In *Using Gramsci: A New Approach*, edited by Michele Fillipini, 4–23. London: Pluto Press.

Finch, Jeffrey. 2007. 'Neo-Palamite Logic of Essence-Energies Distinction'. In *Partakes of the Divine Nature: The History and Development of Deification*, edited by Michael Christensen and Jeffrey Wittung, 234–49. Madison, Teaneck, NJ: Fairleigh Dickinson University Press.

Firth, Raymond. 1960. *Man and Culture: An Evaluation of the Work of Bronislaw Malinowski.* London: Routledge.

Fish, Stanley. 1980. *Is There a Text in This Class?* Cambridge, MA: Harvard University Press.

Fitzpatrick, Tony. 2011. *Welfare Theory. Introduction to Theoretical Debates in Social Policy.* London: Palgrave Macmillan.

Foreign Policy Concept of the Russian Federation. 2016. Mid.ru (*Ministry of Foreign Affairs*), 1 December. https://www.mid.ru/en/foreign_policy/official_documents/-/asset_publisher/CptICkB6BZ29/content/id/2542248.

Foucault, Michel. 1977. *Discipline and Punish: The Birth of the Prison.* New York, Random House.

– 1990. *The Will to Knowledge: The History of Sexuality.* Vol. 1. London: Penguin Books.

– 1991. 'Oders of Discourse'. In *Post-Structuralist and Post-Modernist Sociology*, edited by Scott Lasch, 134–58. London: Brookfield.

– 2002. *Archaeology of Knowledge.* London: Routledge.

Foxall, Andrew. 2012. 'Photographing Vladimir Putin: Masculinity, Nationalism and Visuality in Russian Political Cutlre'. *Geopolitics* 18, no. 1: 132–56.

Frankopan, Peter. 2012. *The First Crusade: The Call from the East.* London: Vintage Books.

Fraser, Nancy, and Axel Honneth. 2003. *Redistribution or Recognition: A Political-Philosophical Exchange.* London, UK: Verso.

Frazer, Elizabeth, and Nicola Lacey, 1993. *The Politics of Community: A Feminist Critique of the Liberal-Communitarian Debate.* New York: Harvester Wheatsheaf.

Freedman, Jane. 2001. *Feminism.* Buckingham: Open University Press.

Friedan, Betty. 1963. *The Feminine Mystique.* New York: W.W. Norton and Co.

Friedman, Elisabeth. 1995. 'Women's Human Rights: The Emergence of a Movement'. In *Women's Rights/Human Rights: International Feminist Perspectives,* edited by Julie Peters and Andrea Wolper, 18–35. New York: Routledge.

Fukuyama, Francis. 1992. *The End of History and the Last Man.* London: Penguin Books.

– 2003. *Our Post-Human Future: Consequences of the Biotechnology Revolution.* London: Profile Books.

– 2004. *State Building: Governance and World Order in the Twenty-first Century.* London: Profile Books.

Fursov, Andrey. 2010. 'Marks protiv Vebera [Marx versus Weber]'. *Diskurs at russia.ru,* 2 December. http://www.russia.ru/video/diskurs_11281/.

– 2011. 'SShA Ostavliayut za Soboi Khaos'. *russia.ru*, 29 March.

– 2012. 'Konets neoliberal'noy epokhi [The End of the Neoliberal Epoch]'. Interview with *km.ru*, 4 April.

– 'Kholodnyi Vostochnyi Veter'. *Odnako*, 20 March.

Galbraith, John Kenneth. 1992. *The Culture of Commitment*. London: Sinclair Stevenson.

Galston, William. 1995. 'Two Concepts of Liberalism'. *Ethics* 105, no. 3: 516–34.

Gamble, Andrew, David Marsh, and Tony Tant. 1999. *Marxism and Social Science*. London: Palgrave MacMillan.

Garadzha, Nikita. 2006. *Liberaly o Narode*. Moscow: Evropa.

Geanakoplos, Deno John. 1991. *Constantinople and the West: Essays on the Late Byzantine (Palaeologan) and Italian Renaissances and the Byzantine and Roman Churches*. Madison, WI: University of Wisconsin Press.

Gellner, Ernst. 2006. *Nations and Nationalism*. Oxford: Blackwell Publishing.

Gessen, Masha. 1998. 'Litsa Feministskoi Natsionalnosti'. *Itogi*, 8, no. 93. Accessed 25 March 2018. http://www.a-z.ru/women/texts/gessr.htm.

Gibbon, Edward. 1998. *The Decline and Fall of the Roman Empire*. Hertfordshire: Wordsworth.

Giddens, Anthony. 1973. *Capitalism and Modern Social Theory: An Analysis of Writings of Marx, Durkheim, and Max Weber*. Cambridge: Cambridge University Press.

– 1979. *Central Problems in Social Theory: Action, Structure, and Contradiction in Social Analysis*. Berkley: University of California Press.

– 1990. *The Consequences of Modernity*. Cambridge: Polity Press.

Glaser, Daryl. 1999. 'Marxism and Democracy'. In *Marxism and Social Science*, edited by Andrew Gamble, David Marsh, and Tony Tant, 239–59. London: Macmillan.

Glazer, Nathan. 1975. *Affirmative Discrimination: Ethnic Inequality and Public Policy*. New York: Basic Books.

– 1983. *Ethnic Dilemmas, 1964–1982*. Cambridge, MA: Harvard.

Glazyev, Sergey. 2013. 'Net Teorii – net Ekonomiki'. *Izborskiy Kub*, 24 December.

Goffman, Erving. 1959. *The Presentation of the Self in Everyday Life*. New York: Anchor Books.

Goldberg, Jonah. 2007. *Liberal Fascism*. London: Penguin Book.

Golstein, Vladimir. 2018. 'Sacred Violence in Blok's "The Twelve"'. *GreanVille Post*, 23 January. https://www.greanvillepost.com/2018/01/

23/vladimir-golstein-sacred-violence-in-bloks-the-twelve/?fbclid=
IwAR3G-DptFx6uVipjLWalKMHqk2mEKnbYA-5FATWvGwPly5
Ff9cFt_M3HUQk.

Gontmakher, Evgeny. 2010. 'Modernizatsiya: Promezhutochnye otvety'.
Vedomosti, 17 February.

Gorer, Geoffrey, and John Rickman. 1950. *The People of Great Russia:
A Psychological Study*. New York: Chanticleer.

Goricheva, Tatyana, Tatyana Mamonova, Yuliya Voznesenskaya, and
Natalya Malakhovskaya. 1980. *Woman and Russia: First Feminist
Samizdat*. London: Sheba Feminist Publishers.

Gorky, Maxim. 1949. *Zhizn Klima Samgina* [*The Life of Klim Samgin*].
In Complete Works, Vols. 19–22. Moscow: Goslitizdat.

Gorshkov, Mikhail. 2007. 'Rossiya kak ona est'. *Rossiiskaya Gazeta*,
22 December.

– 2009. 'Rossiya kak Realnost. Rossiiskoe Obshchestvo v Sotsiologiches-
kom Izmerenii'. *Mir Rossii*, no. 2: 3–21.

Grant, Rebecca, and Kathleen Newland, eds. 1991. *Gender and
International Relations*. London: Open University Press.

Gray, J. Glenn. 1970. *The Warriors: Reflections on Men in Battle*.
New York: Harper Colophon.

Gray, John. 1995. *Berlin*. London: Fontana Press.

– 1996. *Mill on Liberty: A Defence*. London: Routledge.

– 2000. *Two Faces of Liberalism*. New York: The New Press.

– 2003. *Al Qaeda and What It Means To Be Modern*. London: Faber
and Faber.

Gregor, Anthony James. 1969. *The Ideology of Fascism: The Rationale
of Totalitarianism*. New York: Free Press.

Griffin, Roger. 2006. 'Ideology and Culture'. *Journal of Political Ideologies* 11, no. 1 (Feb.): 77–99.

Grot, Nikolay Iakovlevich. 1891. 'Eshche o Zadachakh Zhurnala'.
Voprosy Filisofii i Psikhologii, no. 6: 1–6.

Gul, Murat. 2009. 'The Concept of Change and James N. Rosenau: Still
International Relations?' *African Journal of Political Science and
International Relations*, no. 3: 199–207. Accessed 5 November 2019.
www.academic journals. org/ajpsir/contents/2009cont/May.

Gunderson, Morley. 1989. 'Male-Female Wage Differentials and Policy
Responses'. *Journal of Economic Literature* 27, no.1: 46–72.

Guttman, Amy, and Dennis Thomspon. 2004. *Why Deliberative
Democracy?* Princeton: Princeton University Press.

Gvozdev, Nicholas. 2006. 'Russia: European but Not Western'. *Orbis* 51, no. 1: 129–40.

Haas, Ernst. 1958. *The Uniting of Europe: Political, Social, and Economic Forces, 1950–1957*. Stanford: Stanford University Press, 1958.

Haas, Richard. 2008. 'The Age of Nonpolarity: What Will Follow US Dominance'. *Foreign Affairs* 87, no. 3: 44–56.

Habermas, Jurgen. 1987. *The Theory of Communicative Action*. Vol. 2: *Lifeworld and the System*. Translated by T. McCarthy. Cambridge: Polity.

– 1988. *Legitimation Crisis*. Cambridge: Polity Press.

– 1989. *The Structural Transformation of the Public Sphere*. Cambridge: Polity Press.

– 2011. 'The Political: The Rational Meaning of a Questionable Inheritance of Political Theology'. In *The Power of Religion in the Public Sphere*, edited by E. Medieta and J. Vanantwerpen, 15–34. New York: Columbia University Press.

Hahn, Jeffrey. 1991. 'Continuity and Change in Russian Political Culture'. *British Journal of Political Science* 21, no. 4: 393–421.

Hamburg, Gary. 2016. *Russia's Path Toward Enlightenment: Faith, Politics, and Reason, 1500–1801*. Yale: Yale University Press.

Hamilton, Malcom. 1987. 'The Elements of the Concept of Ideology'. *Political Studies* 35, no. 1: 18–38.

Hanson, Victor Davies. 2010. 'Obama: Fighting the Yuppie Factor'. *National Review*, August.

Harcave, Sidney. 2004. *Count Sergei Witte and the Twilight of the Imperial Russia*. London: Routledge.

Harding, Sandra. 1986. *The Science Question in Feminism*. Ithaca, NY: Cornell University Press.

Harkin, Michael. 2009. 'Lévi-Strauss and History'. In *The Cambridge Companion to Lévi-Strauss*, edited by Boris Wiseman, 39–59. Cambridge: Cambridge University Press.

Harris, John. 2015. *The Lost World of Byzantium*. Yale: Yale University Press.

Hartley, Janet. 1992. 'Is Russia Part of Europe? Russian Perceptions of Europe in the Reign of Alexander I'. *Cahiers du monde russe et sovietique* 33, no. 4: 369–85.

Hartsock, Nancy. 1996. 'Community, Sexuality, Gender: Rethinking Power'. In *Rethinking Obligation*, edited by Nancy Hirshchman and Christine Di Stefano, 27–50. Ithaca, NY: Cornell University Press.

Harvey, David. 2007. *A Brief History of Neoliberalism*. Oxford: Oxford University Press.

Havel, Vaclav. 1989. 'Anti-Political Politics'. In *Civil Society and the State*, edited by John Keane, 381–99. London: Verso.

Hayes, Carlton. 1931. *The Historical Evolution of Modern Nationalism*. New York: Macmillan.

Heater, Derek. 1988. *The Theory of Nationhood: A Platonic Symposium*. Basingstoke, UK: Macmillan.

– 1990. *Citizenship: The Civic Ideal in World History, Politics, and Education*. London: Longman.

Hegel, Georg. 1946. *The Philosophy of Right*. Translated by T.M. Knox. Oxford: Clarendon Press.

Held, David. 1988. *Models of Democracy*. Cambridge: Polity Press.

Hennis, Wilhelm. 1988. *Max Weber: Essays in Reconstruction*. London: Allen and Unwin.

Herrin, Judith. 2007. *Byzantium: The Surprising Life of a Medieval Empire*. London: Penguin Books.

Hetcher, Michael. 1975. *Internal Colonialism: The Celtic Fringe in British National Development*. London: Routledge.

Heywood, Andrew. 2004. *Political Theory: An Introduction*. London: Palgrave Macmillan.

– 2007. *Political Ideologies: An Introduction*. Basingstoke: Palgrave Macmillan.

Hirschman, Albert. 1970. *Exit, Voice, and Loyalty: Responses to Declines in Firms, Organizations, and States*. Cambridge, MA: Harvard University Press.

Hitchens, Peter. 2014. 'Further Thoughts on Russia'. *Mail on Sunday*, 3 March. http://hitchensblog.mailonsunday.co.uk/2014/03/further-thoughts-on-russia-html.

Hobson, John. 2012. *The Eurocentric Conception of World Politics: Western International Theory, 1760–2010*. Cambridge: Cambridge University Press.

Honig, Bonnie. 1993. *Political Theory and the Displacement of Politics*. Ithaca, NY: Cornell University Press.

Hroch, Miroslav. 1985. *Social Preconditions of National Revival in Europe: A Comparative Analysis of the Social Composition of Patriotic Groups among the Smaller European Nations*. Cambridge: Cambridge University Press.

Hunt, Alan. 1980. 'Taking Democracy Seriously'. In *Marxism and Democracy*, edited by Alan Hunt, 3–15. London: Lawrence and Wisehart.

Huntington, Samuel. 1957. 'Conservatism as an Ideology'. *American Political Science Review* 52, no. 2: 454–73.

– 1996. *The Clash of Civilisations and the Remaking of World Order.* New York and London: Simon and Schuster.

– 2006. *Political Order in Changing Societies.* New Haven, CT: Yale University Press.

Hutchings, Kimberly. 1992. 'The Possibility of Judgement: Moralizing and Theorizing in International Relations'. *Review of International Studies*, no. 18: 51–62.

Iampolsky, Mikhail. 2015. 'Putin's Russia Is in the Grip of Fascism'. *Newsweek*, 9 March. Accessed 14 November 2019. https://www.newsweek.com/putins-russia-grip-fascism-312513.

Ikenberry, G. John, and Charles A. Kupchan. 1990. 'Socialization and Hegemonic Power'. *International Organization* 44, no. 3: 283–315.

Ilyashenko, Andrey, Andrey Kobyakov, and Vitaly Averyanov. 2014. 'Konservatizm – eto Borba s Krainostyami. [Conservatism Is a Struggle with Extremes]'. *Golos Rossii*, 2 February.

Ilyinskaya, Svetlana. 2004. 'Terpimost' i Politicheskoe Nasilie'. *Polis*, no. 6: 122–6.

Ingram, Attracta. 2003. 'Citizenship and Diversity'. In *Mosaic or Melting Pot? Proceedings of a Conference on Cultural Diversity, Dublin 2003*, 14–31. Dublin: Royal Irish Academy.

Inoguchi, Toshio. 2002. 'Broadening the Basis of Social Capital in Japan'. In *Democracies in Flux: The Evolution of Social Capital in Contemporary Society*, edited by Robert Putnam, 359–93. Oxford: Oxford University Press.

Inozemtsev, Vladislav. 2012. 'Rossii Nuzhna Edinaya Grazhdanskaya Natsiya'. *Aktualnye Kommentarii*, 23 January 2012.

– 2013. 'Universal Value at Its Natural Limit?' In *Democracy versus Modernization: A Dilemma for Russia and the World*, edited by Piotr Dutkiewicz and Vladislav Inozemtsev, 29–40. London: Routledge.

Integratsiya. 2012. 'Otnoshenie k Femeniszmu Zhitelei Rossii, Ukrainy i Belarusi'. 17 August. Accessed 15 December 2019. http://gtmarket.ru/news/2012/08/17/4898.

ISPI RAN. 2002. *Zhenshchina Novoi Rossii: Kakaia Ona? Kak Zhivet? K Chemu Stremitsia?* Moscow: ISPI RAN Publications.

Ivashov, Leonid. 2015. *Geopolitika Russkoi Tsivilizatsii.* Moscow: Institut Russkoi Tsivilzatsii.

Jahn, Beate. 2005. 'Kant, Mill, and Illiberal Legacies in International Affairs'. *International Organization* 59, no.1 (Winter): 177–207.

James, Alan. 1986. *Sovereign Statehood: The Basis of International Society*. London: Allen and Unwin.

Janaway, Christopher. 2011. 'Autonomy, Affect, and the Self in Nietzsche's Project of Genealogy'. In *Nietzsche on Freedom and Autonomy*, edited by Simon May and Ken Gemes, 51–69. Oxford: Oxford University Press.

Jung, Carl. 1991. *The Archetypes and the Collective Unconscious*. London: Routledge.

Kadyrov, Ramzan. 2006. 'Polygamy Could Supply More Russians'. *Inter Press*, 7 February.

Kagan, Robert. 2003. *Of Paradise and Power*. London: Atlantic Books.

Kagan, V.E. 1989. 'Stereotipy Muzhestvennosti i Zhenstvennosti I Obraz "Ya" u Podrostkov'. *Voprosy Psikhologii*, no. 3: 53–62.

Kalb, Judith. 2000. 'A "Roman Bolshevik": Alexander Blok's "Cataline" and the Russian Revolution'. *Slavic and East European Journal* 44, no. 3 (Autumn): 413–28.

Kanakianova, Raisa. 2006. 'Sovremennye Tendentsii Preodoleniia Gendernoi Asimmetrii v Gosudarstvennom Upravlenii'. *Vlast*, no. 12.

Kaplan, Robert. 2002. *Warrior Politics: Why Leadership Demands a Pagan Ethos*. New York: Vintage Books.

Kapustin, Boris. 1994. *Ot Absoluta Svobody k Romantike Ravenstva. Iz Istorii Politicheskoi Filosofii*. Moscow: Institute of Philosophy RAN.

– 2003. 'K Poniatiu Politicheskogo Nasiliia'. *Polis* 6, no.1: 6–26.

– 2004a. 'Thomas Hobbes'. In *Ocherki Zapadno-Evropeiskogo Liberalizma XII-IX vekov*, edited by Alexey Kara-Murza, 4–17. Moscow, Institute of Philosophy RAN.

– 2004b. 'John Locke'. In *Ocherki Zapadno-Evropeiskogo Liberalizma XII-IX vekov*, edited by Alexey Kara-Murza, 18–32.Moscow, Institute of Philosophy RAN.

Kara-Murza, Alexey. 1994. 'Liberalizm protiv khaosa: Osnovnyye tendentsiy liberal'noy ideologii na zapade i Rossii [*Liberalism Versus Chaos: Basic Trends in Liberal Ideology in the West and Russia*]'. *Polis*, no. 3.

– 1995. 'Obshchestvennyy poryadok i politicheskaya ideologiya liberalizma [Social Order and the Political Ideology of Liberalism'. In *Kuda idet Rossiya: Alternativy obshchestvennogo razvitiya [Where Russia Is Going: Alternatives for Social Development]*, 413–16. Moscow, Aspect Press.

– 1998. 'Dualizm Rossiyskoy identichnosti: Tsivilizovannoye Zapadnichestvo versus geopoliticheskoye Yevraziystvo [*The Dualism of Russian Identity: Civilizational Westernism Versus Geopolitical Eurasianism*]'. *Russkiy Zhurnal*, 27 October 27.

– 2009. 'Problemy grazhdanstva i identichnosti v Russkom liberal'nom diskurse XI–XX vekov [Problems of Citizenship and Identity in Russian Liberal Discourse of the Nineteenth to Twentieth Centuries]'. Paper presented at the *Grazhdanstvo v Usloviyakh Globalizatsii* [Citizenship in Conditions of Globalization] conference. Moscow, Institute of Philosophy, Russian Academy of Sciences.

– ed. 2007. *Rossiyskiy Liberalizm: Idey i lyudi* [Russian Liberalism. Ideas and People]. Moscow: Fond Liberal'naya Missiya.

Karaganov, Sergey. 2015. 'Reshenie o Vozdushnoi Operatsii v Sirii'. *Pravo Znat*, 3 October. http://www.tvc.ru/channel/brand/id/1756/show/episodes/episode_id/41411.

– 2016. 'Mir Nakhoditsya v Predvoennom Sostoyanii'. *Rossiya v Globalnoi Politike*, 17 February.

Kasparov, Gary. 2013. 'Fascism in Our Backyard'. *kasparov.com*, 6 February. Accessed 14 November 2019. http://www.kasparov.com/fascism-in-our-own-backyard/.

Kautsky, Karl. 1902. *The Social Revolution*. Chicago: Kerr.

Kazarinova, Daria. 2017. 'Dialogue for a New Architecture of Macro-regional Security: From the Clash of Narratives to a Secure Greater Eurasia'. In *Making Multilateralism Work: Enhancing Dialogue on Peace, Security, and Development*, edited by Alexey Malashenko, Vladimir Popov, Peter Schultz, 179–91. Berlin: Dialogue of Civilizations Research Institute.

Keane, John. 1988. 'Despotism and Democracy: The Origins and Development of the Distinction between Civil Society and the State, 1750–1850'. In *Civil Society and the State: New European Perspective*, edited by John Keane, 35–71. London: Verso.

– 2003. *Global Civil Society? Contemporary Political Theory*. Cambridge: Cambridge University Press.

Kedmi, Yakov. 2019. 'Pravo Znat'. 16 November. Accessed 28 November 2019. https://www.youtube.com/watch?v=Kqiv-aHxlhU.

Kedmi, Yakov, and Yevgeniy Satanovsky. 2017. 'Balans Sil v Mire'. *Dialogi in Rossiya* 24, 1 September 2017. Accessed 5 November 2019. http://www.youtube.com/watch?v=OkGeZKbN95k.

Keesing, Roger. 1994. 'Theories of Culture Revisited'. In *Assessing Cultural Anthropology*, edited by Robert Borofsky, 301–12. New York: McGraw Hill.

Kelly, Aileen. 1999. *Views from the Other Shore: Essays on Herzen, Chekhov, and Bakhtin*. New Haven and London: Yale University Press.

Khakamada, Irina. 2002. *Osobennosti Natsionalnogo Politika*. Moscow: Olma Press.

– 2008. 'Liberaly Pbedyat, Kogda Vozmut v Soyuzniki Narod'.
Conference Presentation. http://hakamada.ru/News/1629/1227.html.

Kharkhordin, Oleg. 2005. *Main Concepts of Russian Politics*. New York:
University Press of America.

Khasbulatova, Olga. 2001. 'Rossiiskaia Gosudarstvennaia Politika v
Otnoshenii Zhenshchin (1990–2000)'. In *Teoriia i Metodologiia
Gendernykh Issledovanii*, edited by Olga Voronina, 185–98. Moscow:
MTSGI-MVShSEN.

– 2004. 'Obzor Sovetskoi Gosudarstvennoi Politiki v Otnoshenii
Zhenshchin'. In *Gendernaya Rekonstruktsiia Politicheskikh System*,
edited by Natalya Stepanova and Elena Kochkina, 397–407. St.
Petersburg, Russia: Alteia.

Khazin, Mikhail. 2013. 'Mirovoi Krizis Postavil Rossiiskuyu Elitu na Gran
Raskola'. *Politikus*, 30 September. http://politikus.ru/articles/6963-m-
hazin-mirovoy-krizis-postavil-rossiyskuyu-elitu-na-gran-raskola.html.

– 2014. 'Politicheskaya Logika Disintegratsii: Sem Urokov Raspada
SSSR'. *khazin.ru*, 15 February. https://khazin.ru/articles/10-vlast-i-
obshhestvo/6045-politicheskaja-logika-dezintegratsii-sem-urokov-
raspada-sssr.

– 2017. 'Grazhdane Protestuyut Protiv Soslovnosti. [Citizens Protest
against the Estate System]'. *Khazin.ru*, 13 December. Accessed
20 November 2018. https://khazin.ru/articles/10-vlast-i-obshhestvo/
56267-grazhdane-protestujut-protiv-soslovnosti.

– 2018. 'V Mire Proizoshel Radikalnyi Slom Ideinoi Bazovoi Modeli'.
Radonezh, 2 January. Accessed 16 August 2018. http://radonezh.ru/
recommend/mikhail-khazin-v-mire-proizosh-l-radikalny-slom-ideynoy-
bazovoy-modeli-177885.html.

Kholmogorov, Egor. 2014a. 'Viznatiiskii Vybor'. *Vzgliad*, 27 January.
http://vz.ru/columns/2014/1/27/669716.html.

– 2014b. 'Fenomen Russkogo Natzionalizma'. *Katekhon-TV*, 31 January.
https://www.youtube.com/watch?v=muPERkmgOgU.

– 2016. 'Russkaia Tsivilizatsiia: Kategorii Ponimaniia'. *Tetradi Po
Konservatizmu*, 3, no.1: 39–63.

Kholmogorova, Natalya. 2012. 'Voprosy Beshenoi Sobaki k Ateistam.
[Mad Dog's Questions to Atheists]'. *Russkiy Obozrevatel*,
10 November. http://www.rus-obr.ru/blog/20550.

Khomiakov, Maksim. 2005. 'Tolerantnost i Eyo Granitsy: Razmyshleniia
po Povodu Sovremennoi Anglo-Amerikanskoi Teorii'. In *Filisofskie I
Lingvokulturnye Problemy Tolerantnosti*, edited by Natalia Kupina
and Maxim Khomiakov, 15–29. Moscow: INO-Tsentr.

Kirill, Patriarkh. 2005. Interview in *Diplomatie*, September–October. www.orthodoxytoday.org.

– 2012. "Gender – eto otkaz ot ponyatiya biologicheskogo pola [The Idea of Gender – This Is a Disavowal of the Concept of Biological Sex]'. *Russkiy Narodnyy Sobor*, 30 March. http://www.narodsobor.ru/events/society/8485-patriarx-kirill-gender-eto-otkaz-ot-ponyatiya-biologicheskogo-pola.

– 2013. 'Nash Ideal – Obshchestvo Sotsialnoi Simphonii'. *Vzgliad*, 1 November.

Kiselev, Dmitry, Natalya Narochnitskaya, and Vitaly Tretyakov. 2009. 'Rossiya i Russkie v 2008 godu'. In *Natsionalnyi Interes, Russia 1*, 7 February. http://www.youtube.com/watch?v=gjjdOoJPNDY.

Kissinger, Henry. 2014. *World Order: Reflections on the Character of Nations and the Course of History*. London: Penguin Books.

Kline, George. 1968. *Religious and Anti-Religious Thought in Russia*. Chicago and London: University of Chicago Press.

– 1985. 'Russian Religious Thought'. In *Nineteenth Century Religious Thought in the West, vol. 2*, edited by Ninian Smart, John Clayton, Patrick Sherry, Stephen Katz, 179–231. Cambridge: Cambridge University Press.

Kohn, Hans. 1958. *The Idea of Nationalism: A Study in Its Origins and Background*. New York: Macmillan.

Kolakowski, Leszek. 2005. *Main Currents of Marxism*. New York: W.W. Norton.

Kollontai, Alexandra. 1923. *Polozhenie Zhenshchiny v Evoliutsii Khoziaistva*. Moscow: GIz.

Kommersant Daily. 2001. 'Generala Vlasova Povesili Pravilno'. 2 November.

Kon, Igor, and Olga Iusupova. 2009. 'Materinstvo i Otsovstvo: Sotsiologicheskii Ocherk'. In *Gender Dlia 'Chainikov' 1*, edited by Igor Kon and Olga Iusupova, 113–37. Moscow: Heinrich Bulle Foundation.

Kon, Igor, and Anna Temkina. 2009. 'Homo Sexualis i Sovremennost: Zakonchilas li Seksualnaia Revolutsia?' In *Gender Dlia 'Chainikov' 2*, edited by Irina Tartakovskaya, 138–62. Moscow: Heinrich Bulle Foundation.

Konchalovskiy, Andrey. 2012. 'Rossiya zhivet v feodalizme [Russia Lives in Feudalism]'. *Vzglyad*, 13 March.

– 2017. 'Delo ne v Svobode, a v Talante'. *Rossiiskaya Gazeta*, 12 June.

– 2019. 'Rad otstavaniyu Rossii ot Zapada. [Glad that Russia Lags Behind the West]'. *ria.ru*, 14 November.

Kontseptsiya natsional'noi bezopasnosti rossiiskoi federatsii. 1998. *Diplomaticheskii Vestnik*, no. 2, February: 3–18.

Kotsonis, Yanni. 1999. 'The Ideology of Martin Malia'. *The Russian Review* 58, no. 1: 124–30.

Krauthammer, Charles. 1991. 'The Unipolar Moment'. *Foreign Affairs*, 1 February.

Krechetnikov, Artem. 2007 'Yedinaya Rossiya zanialas natsional'nym voprosom [United Russia Takes Up the Nationality Question]'. BBC *Russian Service*, 7 February. http://news.bbc.co.uk/hi/russian/russia/newsid_6339000/6339465.stm.

Krug, Barbara, and Alexandr Libman. 2015. 'Commitment to Local Autonomy in Non-democracies: Russia and China Compared'. *Constitutional Political Economy* 26, no. 2: 221–45.

Kruglyi stol. 2012. 'Kruglyi stol. Otvetstvennost' za zashchiti [Roundtable. Responsibility to Protect]'. *Dipolmaticheskaya Akademiya MID Rossii*, 12 April. Accessed 15 December 2019. https://www.youtube.com/watch?v=VEudCoIfpt8.

Krylov, Konstantin, and Maxim Kalashnikov. 2013. 'Pochemu Rossiya Intellektualnaya Kolonia'. *kombta.tv*, 31 May 2013. Accessed 25 May 2017. https://www.youtube.com/watch?v=-Y5nb9IC-XQ.

Kryshtanovskaya, Olga. 2005. *Anatomiia Rossiiskoi Elity*. Moscow: Zakharov.

Kukhterin, Sergey. 2000. 'Fathers and Patriarchs in Communist and Post-Communist Russia'. In *Gender, State, and Society in Soviet and Post-Soviet Russia*, edited by Sarah Ashwin, 71–89. London: Routledge.

Kulikov, Alexandr. 2016. 'Eltsin-Tsentr o Vlasovtsakh: Poniat i Prostit'. *Pravda*, 11 August.

Kurayev, Andrey, and Lolita Milyavskaya. 2012. 'Surogatnoye Materinstvo'. *Poyedinok s Vladimirom Solovyovym*, 26 April. https://www.youtube.com/watch?v=WadotXVvr8Q.

Kurginyan, Sergey. 2009. *Isav i Yakov: Sud'ba razvitiya v Rossii i mire [Isav and Yakov: The Fate of Development in Russia and the World]*. Moscow: ETTs.

– 2011. 'Khvatit Kormit Kavkaz: Sergey Kurginyan ob Etoi Idee'. *Sut Igry*. Accessed 1 April 2019. https://www.youtube.com/watch?v=tUfBSi86Xa4

– 2015. 'SShA – Novyi Karfagen, Ustraivayushchii Khaos po Vsemu Miru [The USA Is a New Carthage that Creates Chaos around the Globe]'. *regnum.ru*, 30 September 2015. http://regnum.ru/news/polit/1982223.html.

– 2017a. 'Solzhenitsyn – ne Istorik. On ne Rabotal v Arkhivakh. [Solzhenitsyn Is Not an Historian. He Did Not Work in the Archives]'. 30 September. Accessed 12 December 2019. https://rossaprimavera.ru/news/1d8c6b51.

– 2017b. 'Desovetizatsiya Pogubit Rossiyu. [Desovietization Will Ruin Russia]'. *Krasnaya Vesna*, 27 May. Accessed 30 November 2019. https://rossaprimavera.ru/news/kurginyan-desovetizaciya-pogubit-rossiyu.

– 2017c. 'Ravenstvo Vozmozhnostey, Sotsialnaya Dinamika – Lozungi Budushchsego'. *rosprimavera.ru*, November 1. Accessed 12 December 2019. https://rossaprimavera.ru/news/6b001e38.

– 2017d. 'Demonizatsiya Sovetskogo Proshlogo Privedet k Katastrophe'. *regnum.ru*, 28 May 2017.

– 2018. 'Godovshchina Oktyabrskoy Revolyutsii 1917 Goda'. *Vecher s Vladimirov Solovyovym*, 7 November. Accessed 12 December 2019. https://www.youtube.com/watch?v=GRZcajerQXU&t=1225s.

– 2018. 'Lish By Voskhodil Chelovek'. *Krasnaya Vesna*, 21 December 2018. Accessed 5 November 2019. https://rossaprimavera.ru/article/81002373.

– 2019a. 'Russkie Dolzhny Skazat Perestroike: "Nikogda Bolshe" [Russians Must Say Never Again to Perestroika]'. *Krasnaya Vesna*, 18 March. Accessed 5 November 2019. https://rossaprimavera.ru/news/27ea724a.

– 2019b. 'Liberalnaya Merzost Privela Evropu k Natsizmu'. *regnum.ru*, 1 February. Accessed 12 December 2019. https://regnum.ru/news/2563917.html.

Kushanashvili, Otar. 2012. 'Discussion on Political Situation'. *russia.ru*, 6 October. http://tv.russia.ru/video/online_93/. Accessed 10 December 2019.

Kuttner, Robert. 2018. *Can Democracy Survive Global Capitalism?* New York: W.W. Norton.

Kuzmin, Nikolay. 1928. 'O Rabochem Zhilishchnom Stroitelstve'. *Sovremennaiaya Arkhitektura*, no. 3: 82–3.

Kymlicka, Will. 1995. *Multicultural Citizenship*. Oxford: Oxford University Press.

– 1997. *Multiculturalism: States, Nations, and Cultures*. Spinoza Lectures. Amsterdam: Van Gorcum.

– 2002. *Contemporary Political Philosophy. An Introduction*. Oxford: Oxford University Press.

– 2004. 'Dworkin on Freedom and Culture'. In *Dworkin and His Critics*, edited by Justine Burley, 113–33. Oxford: Blackwell.

– 2007. 'The New Debate on Minority Rights (and Postscript)'. In *Multiculturalism and Political Theory*, edited by Anthony Laden and David Owen, 25–60. Cambridge, UK: Cambridge University Press, 2007.

Laclau, Ernesto, and Chantal Mouffe. 1985. *Hegemony and Socialist Strategy: Towards a Radical Democratic Politics*. London: Verso.

Laing, R.D. 1960. *The Divided Self*. London: Penguin Classics.

Lane, David. 2008. 'The Orange Revolution: "People's Revolution" or Revolutionary Coup?' *The British Journal of Politics and International Relations* 10, no. 4: 525–49.

Lang, Anthony, Jr. 2007. 'Morgenthau, Agency, and Aristotle'. In *Realism Reconsidered*, edited by M. Williams, 18–41. Oxford: Oxford University Press.

Lankina, Tomila, Alexandr Libman, and Anastassia Obydenkova. 2016. 'Authoritarian and Democratic Diffusion in Post-Communist Regions'. *Comparative Political Studies* 49, no.12: 1599–629.

Lapina, Natalya. 2007. *Uroki Sotsial'nykh Reform v Rossii. Regional'nyi Aspekt*. Moscow: INION RAN.

Laqueur, Walter. 1993. *Black Hundred: The Rise of the Extreme Right in Russia*. New York: Harper Collins.

Laruelle, Marlene. 2007. 'The Orient in Russian Thought at the Turn of the Century'. In D. Shlapentokh, *Russia between East and West: Scholarly Debates on Eurasiansim*, 9–36. Leiden and Boston: Brill.

– 2008. *Russian Eurasianism: An Ideology of Empire*. Baltimore: Johns Hopkins University Press.

– 2014. 'Alexey Navalny and Challenges in Reconciling "Nationalism" and "Liberalism"'. *Post-Soviet Affairs* 30, no. 4: 276–97.

– 2018. 'Is Russia Really "Fascist"? A Comment on Timothy Snyder'. *PONARS*, Policy Memo 539, (September). Accessed 14 November 2019. http://www.ponarseurasia.org/sites/default/files/policy-memos-pdf/Pepm539_Laruelle_Sept2018_4.pdf.

Lasch, Christopher. 1979. *The Culture of Narcissism: American Life in an Age of Diminishing Expectations*. New York and London, W.W. Norton.

– 1994. *The Revolt of the Elites and the Betrayal of Democracy*. New York: W.W. Norton.

Latynina, Yulya, 2011. 'Mul'tikul'turalizm kak raznovidnost' sotsializma [Multiculturalism as a Variety of Socialism]'. *Yezhednevnyy Zhurnal*, 22 February.

Lavelle, Peter. 2013. 'What's Not to Like about Putin?' *Voice of Russia*, 4 May.

Lavrov, Sergey. 2015. Vystuplenie Lavrova v Gosdume [Address to the Russian State Duma], 14 October. https://russian.rt.com/article/123511.

– 2018. 'Remarks at the Opening Ceremony of the 26th International Educational Christmas Readings'. Moscow, 24 January. http://www.mid.ru/en/press_service/video//asset_publisher/i6t41cq3VWP6/content/id/3033884.

Le Bon, Gustav. 2002. The Crowd: A Study of the Popular Mind. New York: Dover Publications.

Lebow, Richard. 2003. The Tragic Vision of Politics: Ethics, Interests, and Orders. Cambridge: Cambridge University Press.

Lecky, William. 1868. A History of European Morals from Augustus to Charlemagne, 2 vols. London: Longman, Green and Co.

Leontyev, Mikhail. 2004. 'Soyuz mecha i orala [The Union of the Sword and the Plough]'. Izvestiya, 25 February.

– 2008. 'Yedinaya tserkov – sil'naya Rossiya. Master klass [Unified Churches – a Strong Russian Master Class]'. http://tomsk.fm/watch/21477?noredir=1.

– 2010. 'Vechnye Tsennosti Konservatizma'. Tsentr Konservativnykh Issledovaniy, 18 February.

– 2011. 'Kak SSSR Stal Truboi'. russia.ru, 16 March.

– 2012. 'Religiya vypolnyaet sterzhnevuyu funktsiyu dlya strany [Religion Performs a Pivotal Function for the Country]'. russia.ru, 13 September. http://actualcomments.ru/news/37404.

– 2015. 'V Nachale'. RadioVesti.ru, 10 August. Accessed 12 December 2019. https://www.youtube.com/watch?v=ku6FNIybN78.

Leontyev, Mikhail, and Yuliy Gusman. 2010. 'Nuzhny li Nam Migranty? [Do We Need Migrants?]' Poyedinok, 25 November. http://poedinoktv.net/mixail-leontev-i-yulij-gusman/.

Lévi-Strauss, Claude. 1963. Structural Anthropology. New York: Basic Books.

– 1966. The Savage Mind. Chicago: Chicago University Press.

Levitsky, Stephen, and Way, Lucan A. 2002. 'Elections Without Democracy: The Rise of Competitive Authoritarianism'. Journal of Democracy 13, no. 2: 51–65.

Lewis, Paul. G. 1992. 'Introduction'. In Democracy and Civil Society in Eastern Europe, edited by Paul Lewis, 1–16. London: St Martin's Press.

Lieven, Anatol, and John Hulsman. 2007. Ethical Realism: A Vision for America's Role in the World. New York: Pantheon Books.

Limonov, Eduard. 2016. 'Prizrak, Brodivshii po Rossii Materializovalsia'. Svobodnaya Pressa, 4 February.

Linklater, Andrew. 1982. Men and Citizens in the Theory of International Relations. London: Macmillan.

Linz, Juan, and Alfred Stepan. 1996. *Problems of Democratic Transition and Consolidation*. Baltimore and London: Johns Hopkins University Press.

Lipset, Seymour Martin. 1960. *Political Man*. Garden City, NY: Doubleday and Company.

Lister, Ruth. 2003. *Citizenship: Feminist Perspectives*. Basingstoke, UK: Macmillan.

Locke, John. 1996. 'Second Treatise of Civil Government'. In *Western Philosophy*, edited by John Cottingham, 486–92. Oxford: Blackwell Publishing.

Lossky, Nikolai. 1952. *History of Russian Philosophy*. London: George Allen and Unwin.

Lukes, Stephen. 1978. *Power: A Radical View*. London: Macmillan.

Lukin, Alexander. 2000. *The Political Culture of Russian 'Democrats'*. Oxford: Oxford University Press.

Lyotard, Jean. 1979. *The Post-Modern Condition: A Report on Knowledge*. Manchester: Manchester University Press.

MacCallum, Gerlad. 1967. 'Negative and Positive Freedom'. *The Philosophical Review* 76, no. 3 (July): 312–34.

MacIntyre, Alasdair. 1971. *Against the Self-Images of the Age*. London: Notre Dame Press.

– 1988. *Whose Justice? Which Rationality?* London: Duckworth.

MacKinnon, Sophie. 1987. *Feminism Unmodified: Discourses on Life and Law*. Cambridge, MA: Harvard University Press.

Macmillan, John. 1995. 'A Kantian Protest Against the Peculiar Discourse of Inter-Liberal State Peace'. *Millenium* 24, no. 3: 549–62.

Makarychev, Andrey, and Viatcheslav Morozov. 2011. 'Multilateralism, Multipolarity, and Beyond: A Menu of Russia's Policy Strategies'. *Global Governance* 17, no. 3: 353–73.

Malia, Martin. 1994. *The Soviet Tragedy: A History of Socialism in Russia, 1917–1991*. London: The Free Press.

– 2006. *History's Locomotives: Revolutions and the Making of the Modern World*. New Haven: Yale University Press.

Maltseva, Irina, and Sergey Roshchin. 2006. *Gendernaia Segregatsiia i Mobilnost na Rossiiskom Rynke Truda*. Moscow: Higher School of Economics.

Mamontov, Arkady. 2012. 'Provokatory-3 [Provocateurs-3]'. *Spetsial'nyy Korrespondent*. 16 October. http://www.youtube.com/watch?v=K4ryu-MHs6s.

Mannheim, Karl. 1936. *Ideology and Utopia. An Introduction to the Sociology of Knowledge*. New York: Harvest Books.

Manning, Charles. 1975. *The Nature of International Society* (reissue). London: Macmillan.

Marcuse, Herbert. 1969. *One-Dimensional Man: Studies in the Ideology of Advanced Industrial Society*. London: Routledge Classics.

Marshall, T.H. 1949. *Citizenship and Social Class*. London: Pluto.

Maslin, Mikhail. 2008. *Istoriya Russkoi Filosophii*. Moscow: KDU.

Mason, Andrew. 2007. 'Multiculturalism and the Critique of Essentialism'. In *Multiculturalism and Political Theory*, edited by Anthony Laden and David Owen, 221–43. Cambridge: Cambridge University Press.

Matthews, Thomas. 2010. *Byzantium: From Antiquity to Renaissance*. New Haven: Yale University Press.

May, Simon. 2011. 'Nihilism and the Free Self'. In *Nietzsche on Freedom and Authority*, edited by Ken Gemes and Simon May, 89–107. Oxford: Oxford University Press.

McCormick, John. 1997. *Carl Schmitt's Critique of Liberalism: Against Politics as Technology*. Cambridge: Cambridge University Press.

Mchedlova, Marina. 2012. Lecture given at the VTSIOM Academic Staff meeting at RGGU (Institutue of Humanities, Moscow), 20 June. Author's notes.

McIntyre, Kenneth. 2010. '"What's Gone and What's Past Help…": Oakeshott and Strauss on Historical Explanation'. *Journal of the Philosophy of History* 4, no. 1: 65–101.

McMahon, Charlie. 1999. 'Marxism and Culture'. In *Marxism and Social Science*, edited by Andrew Gamble, David Marsh, and Tony Tant, 195–217. London: Macmillan.

Mead, Georg. 1967. *Mind, Self, and Society from the Standpoint of Social Behaviourist*. Chicago: University of Chicago Press.

Medvedev, Andrey. 2016. 'Rossiya ne Prervala Preemstvennost s Vizantiyey'. *RadioVesti*, 17 June.

Medvedev, Roy. 1988. 'Nash Isk K Stalinu'. *Moskovskie Novosti*, 27 November.

Meier, Heinrich. 1995. *Carl Schmitt and Leo Strauss: The Hidden Dialogue*. Chicago: University of Chicago Press.

Melman, Alexander. 2019. 'Liberaly, Vy Soshli s Uma'. *Moskovskiy Komsomoletz*, 17 January.

Mendietta, Eduardo, and Jonathan Vanantwerpen. 2011. 'The Power of Religion in the Public Sphere'. In *The Power of Religion in the Public Sphere*, edited by Eduardo Mendietta and Jonathan VanAntwerpen, 1–15. New York: Columbia University Press.

Meyendorff, John. 1974. *Byzantine Theology: Historical Trends and Doctrinal Themes*. New York: Fordham University Press.

- 1975. *Christ in Eastern Christian Thought*. New York: Crestwood.
- 1980. *Living Tradition: Orthodox Witness in the Contemporary World*. Crestwood, NY: St Vladimir's Seminary Press.
- 1981. *Byzantium and the Rise of Russia*. Cambridge: Cambridge University Press.

Mezentseva, Elena. 2000. 'Gendernaia Ekonomika: Teoreticheskie Podkhody'. *Voprosy Ekonomiki* 3, no. 1: 54–65.
- 2003. 'Muzhchiny i Zhenshchiny v Sphere Domashnego Truda: Logika Ekonomicheskoi Ratsionalnosti Protiv Logiki Gendernoi Identichnosti'. In *Gendernoe Ravenstvo: Poiski Resheniia Starykh Problem [Gender Equality: Searching Solutions to Old Problems]*, edited by Elena Mezentseva, 50–71, Moscow: MOT.

Mezhuyev, Boris. 2012. 'SSHA khotyat ostanovit' progress [The USA Wants to Stop Progress]'. 4 April, *russia.ru*. http://russia.ru/video/diskurs_13072/.
- 2016. 'Suverennoe Bessoznatelnoe'. *Tetradi Po Konservatizmu*, ISEPI RAN 3, no. 1: 29–38.

Mezhuyev, Vadim. 2005. 'Chto takoe post-modernizm'. In Tretyakov, Vitaly, *Chto Delat?* 27 February. http://www.youtube.com/watch?v=O5byQgLB3Zs, Accessed 11 December 2019.

Mikhalkov, Nikita. 2011. 'Nuzhno li Spasat' Russkikh? [Do the Russians Need To Be Saved?]' *Poyedinok*, 21 January.
- 2015. 'Pogovorim o Kulture'. *Besogon*, 28 May. https://www.youtube.com/watch?v=GK7Mjk6xwKg.

Mill, John Stuart. 1973. *Auguste Comte and Positivism*. Ann Arbor: University of Michigan Press.

Miller, Karyn. 2004. 'British Spy Fired the Shot that Finished Rasputin'. *The Telegraph*, 19 September.

Milov, Vladimir. 2016. 'Diskussiya o Russkom Natzionalizme'. *Milov.org*, 22 January. http://milov.org/entry/1628.

Miscevic, Nenad. 2008. 'Philosophy and Nationalism'. In *Nations and Nationalism: A Global Historical Overview. 1770–1880*, vol. 1, edited by Guntram Herb and David Kaplan, 85–98. Santa Barbara, CA: ABC-CLIO.

Mizulina, Elena. 2013. 'Lyudey razdrazhyut ne gey, a propaganda [People Are Not Annoyed with Gays but with Propaganda]'. *gazeta.ru*, 10 June. http://www.gazeta.ru/politics/2013/06/10_a_5375845.shtml.

Mommsen, Wolfgang. 1984. *Max Weber and German Politics, 1890–1920*. Chicago: University of Chicago Press.

Morgenthau, Hans. 1945. 'The Evil of Politics and the Ethics of Evil'. *Ethics* 56, no. 1: 1–18.

- 1948a. *Politics Among Nations: The Struggle for Power and Peace.* New York: Alfred Knopf.
- 1948b. 'The Twilight of International Morality'. *Ethics* 58, no. 2: 79–99.
- 1970. *Truth and Power: Essays of a Decade, 1960–70.* London: Pall Mall Press.
Morrow, John. 2005. *History of Western Political Thought: A Thematic Introduction.* London: Palgrave.
Motyl, Alexander. 2015. 'Is Putin's Russia Fascist?' *Atlantic Council,* 23 April. Accessed 14 November 19. https://www.atlanticcouncil.org/blogs/ukrainealert/is-putin-s-russia-fascist/.
Mouffe, Chantal. 1988. 'Radical Democracy: Modern or Post-modern?' In *Universal Abandon: The Politics of Post-Modernism,* edited by Andrew Ross, 31–45. Minneapolis: University of Minnesota Press.
- 2005. *On the Political: Thinking in Action.* London: Routledge.
- 2007. 'Carl Schmitt's Warning on the Dangers of a Unipolar World'. In *The International Political Thought of Carl Schmitt: A New Global Nomos?* edited by Louiza Odysseos and Fabio Petito, 147–53. London: Routledge.
Mundlak, Guy. 2007. 'Industrial Citizenship, Social Citizenship, Corporate Citizenship: I Just Want My Wages'. *Theoretical Inquiries in Law* 8, no. 2 (July): 720–48.
Narochnitskaya, Natalya. 2010. 'Rossia – eto Model Mira. [Russia Is a Model of a World]'. *Nevskoe Vremya,* 19 November.
- 2011. *Budushchee Rossii – Budushchee Evropy,* 18 August. Accessed 25 November 2018. http://newsland.com/news/detail/id/761881/.
- 2012. 'V Obstanovke Neponimaniya. [In the Environment of Misunderstanding]'. *Narochnitskaya's Publications,* 2 March. Accessed 22 March 2019. http://narochnitskaya.com/in-archive/v-obstanovke-neponimaniya.html/.
- 2014. 'Nelzya Obyasnit Slepomu, Chto Zdes Temno'. *Vzglyad,* 16 January.
- 2017. 'Chem Grozit Rossii Demonizatsiya Sovetskogo Gosudarstva. [How Demonization of the Soviet State Threatens Russia]'. 10 November. Accessed 10 January 2018. http://narotchnitskaya.com/interviews/nataliya-narochnitskaya-chem-grozit-rossii-demonizatsiya-sovetskogo-gosudarstva.html?view=full.
Neifeld, Galina. 1998. 'Zhenshiny v Rossii v Kavychkakh i Bez'. *Itogi* 83, no. 1: 46–9.
Newsru. 2001. 'Glavnaya Voennaya Prokuratura Otkazalas Reabilitirovat Generala Vlasova'. 6 July 2001. www.newsru.com/russia/06jul2001/general_vlasov.html.

Nietzsche, Friedrich. 1990. *Beyond Good and Evil*. London: Penguin.

Nikonov, Vyacheslav. 2017a. *Kod Tsivilizatsii. Chto Zhdet Rossiyu v Mire Budushchego?* Moscow: Eksmo.

– 2017b. 'Nazad k Kontsertu [Back to the Concert]'. *Global Affairs*, no. 6 (7 December). Accessed 22 October 2019. https://globalaffairs.ru/number/Nazad-k-Kontcertu-19191.

Nikulina, Tatyana, and Kharlamenkova Natalya. 1998. 'Polovozrastnye Razlichiya v Stremlenii Lichnosti k Utverzhdeniyu i Zachshite "Ya"'. In *Rossiiskii Mentalitet: Voporsy Psikhologicheskoi Teorii i Praktiki*, edited by Ksenia Abulkhanova, Andrey Brushlinskii, and Margarita Volovikova, 224–40. Moscow: IP RAN.

Nimni, Ephraim. 1985. 'Marxism and Nationalism'. In *Marxist Sociology Revisited. Critical Assessments*, edited by Martin Shaw, 99–142. London: Macmillan.

Nino, Carlos. 1996. *The Constitution of Deliberative Democracy*. New Haven, CT: Yale University Press.

Nolte, Ernst. 1965. *Three Faces of Fascism: Action Française, Italian Fascism, National Socialism*. London: Weidenfeld and Nicolson.

Novodvorskaya, Valeriya. 2012. 'Takoi Narod Pust Vymirayet, ne zhalko'. *newsland*, 18 October. http://newsland.com/news/detail/id/1058648/.

'Number of Househusbands Triples in the Last Fifteen Years, as the Number of Women Who Are Family's Main Breadwinner Soars." *Daily Mail*, 26 January 2012.

Ogloblin, Constantin. 1999. 'The Gender Earnings Differential in the Russian Transition Economy'. *Industrial and Labour Relations Review* 52, no. 4: 602–27.

Okin, Susan. 2002. 'Mistresses of Their Own Destiny? Group Rights, Gender, and Realistic Rights of Exit'. *Ethics* 112, no. 2: 205–30.

Oppenheim, Felix. 1970. *Dimensions of Freedom*. New York: St Martin's Press.

Oren, Ido. 1994. 'The Subjectivity of the "Democratic Peace"'. *International Security* 20, no. 2: 147–84.

Oss, Natalya. 2013. 'Budte Romantikami, Potrebuite Vozmozhnogo'. *Izvestiya*, 28 October.

Otkrytiye. 2012. 'Otkrytiye novogo politicheskogo sezona [The Opening of a New Political Season]'. *Voskresnyy Vecher s Vladimirom Solov'yevym*, 9 September. http://rutv.ru/brand/show/episode/153821/viewtype/picture.

Outhwaite, William. 1996. *The Habermas Reader*. Cambridge: Polity Press.

Owen, David, and James Tully. 2007. 'Redistribution and Recognition'. In *Multiculturalism and Political Theory*, edited by Anthony Laden and David Owen, 265–91. Cambridge: Cambridge University Press.

Owen, John. 1994. 'How Liberalism Produces the Democratic Peace'. *International Security* 19, no. 2: 87–125.

Ozkirimli, Umit. 2010. *Theories of Nationalism: A Critical Introduction*. London: Palgrave Macmillan.

Panarin, Alexandr. 2001. 'Narod Bez Elity: Mezhdu Otchayaniem i Nadezhdoi'. *Nash Sovremennik*, no. 11. http://www.nash-sovremennik. ru/p.php?y=2001&n=11&id=5.

Panyushkin, Valery. 2005. 'Logika Beshennoi Sobaki. Bez Natsionalnoi Idei Nam Budet Legche Zhit. Eshche Legche – bez Gosudarstva'. *GQ*, no. 2.

Parekh, Bhikhu. 2006. *Rethinking Multiculturalism: Cultural Diversity and Political Theory*. London: Palgrave Macmillan.

Pateman, Carole. 1988. *The Sexual Contract*. Cambridge, UK: Polity Press.

– 1989. *The Disorder of Women*. Cambridge, UK: Polity Press.

Payne, Stanley. 1980. *Fascism: Comparison and Definition*. Madison, WI: University of Wisconsin Press.

Pazuchin, Dmitry. 1885. 'Sovremennoe sostojanie Rossii i soslovnyj vopros'. *Russkij Vestnik* 1, no. 1: 5–58.

Pelczynski, Z.A., ed. 2009. *The State and Civil Society: Studies in Hegel's Political Philosophy*. Cambridge: Cambridge University Press.

Pelikan, Jaroslav. 1974. *The Christian Tradition: A History of the Development of Doctrine*. Vol. 2: *The Spirit of Eastern Christendom*. Chicago and London: University of Chicago Press.

– 1993. *Christianity and Classical Culture*. New Haven, CT: Yale University Press.

Pertsev, Andrei. 2005. 'Sovremennyi Poriadok i Filosofiia Tolerantnosti'. In *Filisofskie I Lingvokulturnye Problemy Tolerantnosti*, edited by Natalia Kupina and Maxim Khomiakov, 29–51. Moscow: INO-Tsentr.

Petro, Nicolai. 1995. *The Rebirth of Russian Democracy*. Cambridge, MA: Harvard University Press.

Petukhov, Vladimir. 2008. 'Dinamika Mirovozzrencheskikh I Ideo-logicheskikh Ustanovok Rossiian'. *Gosudarstvo i Obshchestvo* 85, no. 1 (January-March): 48–62.

Pichler, Hans. 1998. 'The Godfathers of "Truth": Max Weber and Carl Schmitt in Morgenthau's Theory of Power Politics'. *Review of International Studies* 24, no. 2: 185–200.

Piketti, Thomas. 2013. *Capital in the Twenty-first Century*. Cambridge, MA: Harvard University Press.

Pinkard, Terry. 2002. *German Philosophy, 1760–1860: The Legacy of Idealism*. Cambridge, MA: Cambridge University Press.

Pobedonostsev, Konstantin. 2011. *Moskovskii Sbornik*. San Bernardino, CA: Ulan Press.

Polanyi, Karl. 1944. *The Great Transformation*. Boston: Beacon Press.

Polyakov, Leonid. 2004. 'Pyat' paradoksov Rossiyskogo konservatizma. [Five Paradoxes of Russian Conservatism]'. *Otechestvennyye Zapiski*, no. 2 (17).

Porter, Thomas, and William Gleason. 1998. 'The Zemstvo and the Transformation of Russian Society'. In *Emerging Democracy in Imperial Russia*, edited by Mary Conroy, 60–82. Louisville, CO: University of Colorado Press.

Poulantzas, Nicos. 1978. *State, Power, Socialism*. London: New Left Books.

Pozniakov, Vladimir. 2005. 'Konkurentnye i Partnerskie Otnosheniia Rossiiskikh Predprinimatelei: Regionalnye i Gendernye Osobennosti'. In *Problemy Ekonomicheskoi Psikhologii*, edited by Anatoly Zhuravlev, 181–204. Moscow: Institut Psikhologii .

– 2006. 'Gendernye Osobennosti Sotsialno-psikhologicheskikh Kharakteristik Rossiiskikh Predprinimatelei'. Institut Psikhologii RAN, Moscow. University for the Humanities, Accessed 25 May 2018. http://www.ipras.ru/cntnt/rus/media/on-layn-bibliote/otdelnie-statis/publikacii/rossijskie4/n4_poznyako.html.

Pozniakov, Vladimir, and Olga Titova. 2002. 'Psikhologicheskie Otnosheniia Rossiiskikh Predprinimatelei: Gendernye Osobennosti'. *Vestnik RGNF* 3, no. 1: 162–73.

Preston, Paul. 1985. 'Reading History: Fascism'. *History Today* 35, no. 9 (September): 46–9.

Pribylovsky, Vladimir. 2015. *Avtoritety i Vozhdi Russkogo Natsionalizma i Rossiskogo Natsional-Imperializma*. Moscow: Panorama.

Primakov, Yevgenyi. 2003. 'A World Without Superpowers'. *Global Affairs*, 2 September. Accessed 22 October 2019. http://www.globalaffairs.ru/number/n_1560.

Prokhanov, Aleksandr. 2012. 'Putin – Strategiya Ryvka'. *Zavtra*, 19 December.

– 2014. 'Putinu – Orden Nakhimova'. *Izvestiya*, 10 March.

– 2016. 'Na Putina Napravleny Sily Tmy'. *Znak*, 31 August.

– 2019. 'S Raspadom SSSR Rossiya Poteryala Svyaz s Tsarstviem Nebesnym'. *Krasnaya Vesna*, 6 October. Accessed 5 November 2019. https://rossaprimavera.ru/news/ad6fo12e.

Prokhanov, Aleksandr, Aleksander Dugin, Sergey Kurginyan, Maksim Shevchenko, and Mikhail Leontyev. 'Zasedaniye anti-Oranzhevogo Komiteta [A Session of the Anti-Orange Committee]'. *Zavtra*, 21 February 21.

Prokhorov, Mikhail. 2012. *Programma Kandidata v Prezidenty. Mikhail Prokhorov: Nastoyashchee i Budushcheei*, Chapter 'Mir'. http://mdp2012.ru/program/world.html.

Prosvirnin, Egor. 2014. 'Zasnovik Natsionalistichnogo Rossiiskogo Resursu Sputnik & Pogrom na Hromadske.TV'. *Hrmoadske Telebachenie*, 3 February. Accessed 25 May 2017. https://www.youtube.com/watch?v=DRDTfNkKsWw&feature=youtu.be.

Pugh, Jonathan. 2009. *What Is Radical Politics Today?* London: Palgrave Macmillan.

Putin, Vladimir. 2005. Interview to German Television. 5 May. http://kremlin.ru/events/president/transcripts/22948.

– 2012a. 'Rossiya: Natsionalnyi Vopros: Samoopredelenie russkogo naroda – eto polietnicheskaya tsivilizatsiya skreplennaya russkim kulturnym yadrom'. *Nezavisimaya Gazeta*, 23 January.

– 2012b. Address to the Federal Assembly, 12 December. http://en.kremlin.ru/events/president/news/17118.

– 2013. Address to the Valdai Expert Club, 19 September. http://en.kremlin.ru/events/president/news/19243.

– 2015. Address to the 70 UN General Assembly, 28 September. Accessed 11 November 2019. http://kremlin.ru/events/president/news/50385.

– 2016. 'The Future in Progress: Shaping the World of Tomorrow'. Address to the Valdai Expert Club, 27 October.

Pyzhikov, Alexander. 2017. 'Prezentatsiya Knigi "Korni Stalinskogo Bolshevizma"', *Den.TV*, 1 February. https://www.youtube.com/watch?v=7GkNo6y3YB8.

– 2017. *Korni Stalinskogo Bolshevizma*. Moscow: Argumenty Nedeli.

Radcliffe-Richards, Janet. 1980. *The Sceptical Feminist: A Philosophical Enquiry*. London: Routledge and Kegan Paul.

Radio Free Europe, Radio Liberty. 2011. 'Vozmozhen li Feminizm v Rossii?' 16 September 2011.

Radio Liberty. 2015. '8 Marta – prazdnik dlia kogo?' 8 March.

Rand, Ayn. 2007. *Atlas Shrugged*. London: Penguin Classics.

Rangsimaporn, Paradorn. 2006. 'Interpretations of Eurasianism: Justifying Russia's Role in East-Asia'. *Europe-Asia Studies* 58, no. 2: 371–89.

Rawls, John. 1971. *A Theory of Justice*. London: Oxford University Press.

– 1993. *Political Liberalism*. New York: Columbia University Press.

Raz, Joseph. 1986. *The Morality of Freedom.* Oxford: Oxford University Press.

RBC. 2012. 'Putin Snova Nazval Raspad sssr Bezuslovnoi Tragediei'. 22 October. https://www.rbc.ru/rbcfreenews/562913189a79477c0bb9d 78a.

Remchukov, Konstantin. 2008. 'Liberalizm kak politika v Rossii [Liberalism as Policy in Russia]'. In Vitaly Tretyakov, Alexey Kara-Murza, Boris Titov, and Igor Bunin. 2008. 'Liberalizm kak politika v Rossii [Liberalism as Policy in Russia]'. *Chto Delat,* no. 224 (14 December). Accessed 11 December 2019. http://www.youtube.com/watch?v=eKOfpWPZicw.

Remizov, Mikhail. 2010. 'Koservatizm i sovremennost [Conservatism and Modernity]'. In Konservatism/traditsionalizm: Teoriya, formy realizatsii, perspektiva. Materialy postoyanno deystvuyushego nauchnogo seminara, edited by A. Neklessa, 15–23. Moscow: Nauchnyy Ekspert.

– 2017. 'Chto Meshaet Rossii Uiti ot Kolonialnoi Ekonomiki'. *Komsomolskaya Pravda,* 9 June.

RIA Novosti. 2014. 'spch Prosit Putina Podderzhat Zakon o Profilaktike Domashnego Nasiliya'. 29 July.

Ricoeur, Paul. 1981. *Hermeneutics and the Human Sciences.* Trans. by John Thompson, Cambridge: Cambridge University Press.

Risse-Kapen, Thomas. 1995. 'Democratic Peace – Warlike Democracies? A Social Constructivist Interpretation of the Liberal Argument'. *European Journal of International Relations* 1, no. 4: 491–517.

Robbins, Richard, Jr. 1987. *The Tsar's Viceroys. Russian Provincial Governors in the Last Years of the Empire.* Ithaca, NY, and London: Cornell University Press.

Robinson, Paul. 2019. *Russian Conservatism.* Ithaca, NY: Cornell University Press.

Rogger, Hans. 1966. 'Reflections on Russian Conservatism: 1861–1905." *Jahrbucher fur Geschichte Osteuropas,* Neue Folge, 14, no. 2 (June): 195–212.

Rogozin, Dmitry. 2013. 'Interview with Rain TV'. *Dozhd TV,* 29 January. http://tvrain.ru/articles/dmitrij_rogozin_o_vragah_i_predateljah_serdjukove_navalnom_i_biznese_svoego_syna-336002/.

– 2014. 'Rossiya Nachala Osvaivat Arktiku s Pomoshyu Podvodnykh Robotov'. *Vzgliad,* 14 March.

Romanova, Olga. 2013. 'Zhurnalistka Romanova zayavlyaet, chto ne oskorblyala pamyat veteranov'. *RIA Novosti,* 9 July. http://ria.ru/society/20130709/948607182.html.

Rorty, Richard. 1983. 'Postmodernist Bourgeois Liberalism'. *Journal of Philosophy* 80, no.10: 583–9.

Roshchin, Sergey. 1996. *Zaniatost Zhenshchin v Perekhodnoi Ekonomike Rossii*. Moscow: Ekonomicheskii Fakultet MGU TEIS.

Rosman, Abraham, and Paula Rubel. 2009. 'Structure and Exchange'. *The Cambridge Companion to Levi-Strauss*, edited by Boris Wiseman, 59–80. Cambridge: Cambridge University Press.

Rossiiskaya Gazeta. 2014. 'Gosduma Mozhet Rassmotret Zakon o Profilaktike Domashnego Nasiliya'. *Rossiiskaya Gazeta*, 8 July.

Rottenberg, Dan. 1980. 'About That Urban Renaissance ... There Will Be a Slight Delay." *Chicago Magazine*, May.

Rousseau, Jean Jacques. 2016. *Discourse on the Origins of Inequality*. New York: P.F. Collier.

Rowe, Elana Wilson, and Stilana Trojessen. 2009. *Multilateral Dimensions in Russian Foreign Policy*. London: Routledge.

Russell, Bertrand. 1946. *History of Western Philosophy*. London: George Allen and Unwin.

Ryazanovsky, Nicholas. 1993. *Collected Writings*. Los Angeles, CA: Charles Schlacks.

– 2005. *Russian Identities: A Historical Survey*. Oxford: Oxford University Press.

Rynska, Bozhena. 2013. 'Iz-za etogo nevymershego pokoleniya stradaet ashi pokolenie'. *nakanune.ru*, 9 September. http://www.nakanune.tv/news/2013/09/09/bozhena_rinska_pro_pensionerov_iz_za_etogo_nevimershego_pokoleniya_stradaet_nashe_pokolenie/.

Ryzhkov, Vladimir. 2011. 'Sut Putinskoi Ideologii – Ideya Nepolnotsennogo Naroda'. *politsovet.ru*, 18 October. http://politsovet.ru/35546-.html.

– 2013. 'Lider RPR-Parnass Schitaet, chto Prishel na Vstrechu Putina s Neparlamentskimi Partiyami ne Naprasno'. *Izvestiya*, 22 November.

Sakwa, Richard. 2008. *Russian Politics and Society*. 4th ed. London: Routledge.

– 2015. 'The Death of Europe? Continental Fates after Ukraine'. *International Affairs* 91, no. 3: 553–79.

– 2016. 'Barkhatnye Perchatki Zapadnoi Gegemonii'. *Valdai Club*, 12 October. Accessed 21 October 2016. http://ru.valdaiclub.com/a/highlights/barkhatnye-perchatki-zapadnoy-gegemonii/.

Satanovsky, Yevgeny. 2014. 'Vse Tolko Nachinaetsia'. *Vzgliad*, 18 March.

Savitsky, Peter. 1997. *Geographicheskiy Obzor Rossii – Evrazii*. Moscow: Kontinent Evrazia.

Scheuerman, William. 2007. 'Carl Schmitt and Hans Morgenthau: Realism and Beyond'. In *Realism Reconsidered: The Legacy of Hans J. Morgenthau in International Relations*, edited by Michael Williams, 62–92. Oxford: Oxford University Press.

Schmemann, Alexander. 1979. *Ultimate Questions*. London and Oxford: Mowbrays.

Schmitt, Carl. 1963. *Theorie des Partisanen: Zwischenbemerkung zum Begriff des Politischen* [*Theory of the Partisan: A Commentary on the Concept of the Political*]. Berlin: Dunker and Humblot.

– 1985. *Political Theology: Four Chapters on the Concept of Sovereignty.* Trans. by George Schwab. Cambridge, MA: MIT Press.

– 2003. *The Nomos of the Earth in the International Law of Jus Publicum*. Berlin: Dunker and Humblot.

Schmitter, Philippe. 1985. 'Still the Century of Corporatism?' In *Private Interest Government: Beyond Market and State*, edited by Wolfgang Streeck and Philippe Schmitter, 7–52. Beverly Hills, CA: Sage Publications.

Scholte, Jan Aart. 2004. 'Globalization and Governance: From Statism to Polycentrism'. CSGR Working Paper No. 130/04. Warwick: University of Warwick, Centre for the Study of Globalisation and Regionalisation.

Seliger, Martin. 1976. *Ideology and Politics*. London: George Allen and Unwin.

– 1992. *The Idea of Civil Society*. Princeton: Princeton University Press.

Seliktar, Ofira. 2004. *Politics, Paradigms, and Intelligence Failures: Why So Few Predicted the Collapse of the Soviet Union*. Armonk, NY, and London: M.E. Sharpe.

Seltser, Dmitry. 2003. 'Transformatsiia Zhenskoi Politicheskoi Elity: iz SSSR V RF'. In *Zhenskaia Povsednevnost v Rossii v XVIII-XX vv. Materialy Mezhdunarodnoi Nauchnoi Konferentsii 25 Sentiabria 2003 goda*, edited by Pavel Shcherbinin, 219–27. Tambov: TGU im. Derzhavina.

Sennet, Richard. 1978. *The Fall of the Public Man: On the Social Psychology of Capitalism*. New York: Random House.

Sergeyev, Sergey. 2017. *Russkaya Natsiya. Natsionalizm i ego Vragi*. Moscow: Tsentrpoligraph.

Shchedrovitskiy, Pyotr. 2000a. 'Chto stoit za doktrinoy Russkogo Mira? [What Stands behind the Doctrine of the Russian World]'. *Russkiy Arkhipelag*. http://www.archipelag.ru/ru_mir/history/history9900/shedrovicky-doctrina/.

– 2000b. 'Russkiy Mir i Transnatsional'noye Russkoye [The Russian World and the Transnational Russian]'. *Russkiy Zhurnal*, 2 March.

– 2000c. 'Kto i Chto Stoit za Doktrinoy Russkogo Mira? [Who and What Stands Behind the Doctrine of the Russian World?]' *Shkola Kulturnoy Politiki*, 8 November.

– 2006a. 'Kul'turnaya Politika: Predposylki Peremen [Cultural Policy: Prerequisites for Changes]'. *Rossiyskoye Ekspertnoye Obozreniye*, no. 3.

– 2006b. "Kul'turnoye Mnogoobraziye – Resurs Postindustrial'nogo Razvitiya (Cultural Diversity – A Resource for PostIndustrial Development)." *Tsentr Gumanitarnykh Tekhnologii*, September 2.

Shchipkov, Alexander. 2016. 'Russko-Vizantiiskaia Tsivilizatsiia i Ideologiia Neokolonializma'. *Tetradi Po Konservatizmu*, ISEPI RAN 3, no. 1: 23–7.

– 2017. "O Russko-rossiiskom Voprose." *UM Plus*, 15 February. Accessed 27 February 2018. https://um.plus/2017/02/14/vopros/.

Shevchenko, Maxim. 1997. 'Bessmyslennyi i Besposhchadnyi'. *NG Religii*, 30 January.

– 2004. 'Kontury Obshchei Sudby'. *Musulmanskie Zametki*, 5 November.

– 2008. 'Trikolor s Krestom'. *Vedomosti*, 25 August.

– 2009. 'Gomoseksualizm ne poridet'. *russia.ru*, 21 August. http://tv.russia.ru/video/diskursshevgay/. Accessed 27 November 2019.

– 2010. 'Osoboye Mneniye'. *Ekho Moskvy*, 21 January.

– 2011. 'Multikulturalizm: Realnost ili Utopiia'. *Pryamaya* Rech, 11 February.

– 2012a. 'V Evrope Budet Revolyutsiia'. *russia.ru*, 29 May. Accessed 27 November 2019. http://tv.russia.ru/video/diskurs_13205/.

– 2012b. 'Mezhdu Dengami i Svobodoi'. *russia.ru*, 30 July. Accessed 27 November 2019. http://tv.russia.ru/video/diskurs_13371/.

– 2014. 'O liberealnom totalitarizme'. *Kto Protiv Maxima Shevchenko?* 10 February. http://www.onlinetv.ru/video/1393/?autostart=1.

– 2016. 'Elita Khochet Steret iz Pamyati Uroki Russkoi Revolyutsii 1917 goda'. *Nakanune.ru*, 30 October.

– 2017a. 'Pervyi Poshel: Sud nad Ulyukaevym – eto tolko Nachalo'. *Ekspert*, 7 December.

– 2017b. 'Chto Privelo k Revoliutsii [What Caused Revolution]'. *Interview*, 28 October. https://www.youtube.com/watch?v=Yl39m1mYYNo.

Shevchenko, Maksim, Aleksandr Dugin, Alexey Venediktov, Nikolay Svanidze, and Stanislav Govorukhin. 2012. 'Natsional'nyy Vopros [The National Question]'. *V Kontekste*, 26 January.

Shevchenko, Maxim, and Aleksandr Dugin. 2012. 'Otets teorii passionarnosti [Father of the Theory of *Passionarnost*]'. *russia.ru*, 8 October 8. www.russia.ru/news/politics/2012/1018/2216.html.

Shevchenko, Maxim, and Andrey Kurayev. 2012. 'Tserkov obyavila voinu miru [The Church Declares War on the World]'. *russia.ru*, 20 October. http://www.russia.ru/news/society/2012/10/19/2998.html.

Shevchenko, Maxim, and Boris Nemtsov. 2012. 'Ostraya Diskussiya o Politicheskoi Situatsii'. *russia.ru*, 20 March.

Shevchenko, Maxim, and Nikolay Svanidze. 2012. *Poyedinok with Vladimir Solovyov*, 27 September. https://www.youtube.com/watch?v=v8WHfB8qFII.

Shevtsova, Lilia. 2008. *Russia: Lost in Transition*. Washington, DC: Carnegie Endowment for International Peace.

– 2013. 'Valdaiskaya Doktrina Putina'. *Ezhednevnyi Zhurnal*, 24 September.

Shilliam, Robbie. 2009. *German Thought and International Relations: The Rise and Fall of a Liberal Project*. Basingstoke, UK: Palgrave Macmillan.

Shisheliakina, Alena. 2015. 'Feminnost v Diskursivnom Prostranstve Rossiiskogo Establishmenta'. *Zhenshchina v Rossiiskom Obshchestve* 74, no. 1: 62–70.

Shlapentokh, Dmitry, ed. 2007. *Russia Between East and West: Scholarly Debates on Eurasianism*. Leiden and Boston: Brill.

Shlapentokh, Vladimir. 1998. *Rethinking the Soviet Collapse: Sovietology, the Death of Communism, and the New Russia*. Edited by Michael Cox. London, Pinter.

Shull, Joseph. 1992. 'What Is Ideology? Theoretical Problems and Lessons from Soviet-Type Societies'. *Political Studies* 40: 728–41.

Shvydkoy, Mikhail, Mikhail Veller, and Oksana Gaman-Golutvina. 2011. 'Tolerant-nost' – Udel slabykh [Tolerance – Fate of the Weak]'. *Rossiya Kultura*, 27 April.

Simmel, Georg. 1971. *On Individuality and Social Forms*. Chicago: The University of Chicago Press.

Sitton, John. 2003. *Habermas and Contemporary Society*. London: Palgrave Macmillan.

Skinner, Quentin, ed. 1985. *The Return of Grand Theory in Human Sciences*. Cambridge: Cambridge University Press.

– 2002. *Vision of Politics*. Vol. 1: *Regarding Method*. Cambridge: Cambridge University Press.

– 2002. *Vision of Politics*. Vol. 2: *Renaissance Virtues*. Cambridge: Cambridge University Press.

– 2002. *Vision of Politics*. Vol. 3: *Hobbes and Civil Science*. Cambridge: Cambridge University Press.

Sleboda, Mark, and Aleksandr Dugin. 2012. Lecture to visiting LSE students at Moscow State University, 20 April.

Sliger, Martin. 1979. *The Marxist Conception of Ideology*. Cambridge: Cambridge University Press.

Slobodchikova, Olga. 2014. 'Zhenshchiny v Rossii: Mezhdu Feminizmom i Patriarkhatom'. *BBC Russian Service*, 27 October.

Smirnov, Ilya. 2014. 'Narodnyy Front [National Front]'. Izvestiya, 10 March.

Smith, Anthony D. 1986. *The Ethnic Origins of Nations*. Oxford: Blackwell.

– 1991. *National Identity*. London: Penguin.

Smith, Michael. 1990. *Realist Thought from Weber to Kissinger*. Louisiana: Louisiana State University Press.

Smith, Nicholas. 2002. *Charles Taylor: Meaning, Morals, and Modernity*. Cambridge, UK: Polity Press.

Snyder, Timothy. 2018. 'Ivan Ilyin, Putin's Philosopher of Russian Fascism'. *New York Review*, 5 April.

Solovey, Valery. 2016. 'Bol', Gnev i Nenavist. Tri Uroka Russikim Natsionalistam iz Ukrainskogo Krizisa'. *Slon*, 21 March. https://slon.ru/posts/65611. Accessed 5 November 2019.

Solovey, Valery, and Tatyana Solovey. 2009. *Nesostoyavshayasya Revolyutsiya*. Moscow: Fevoriya.

Solov'yov, Vladimir. 1891. 'Russkiy Natsionalnyi Ideal'. *Novosti i Birzhevaya Gazeta*, no. 23 (26 January).

– 2011a. *Vragi Rossii*. Moscow: Eksmo.

– 2011b. 'O Granitsakh Tolerantnosti [On the Limits of Tolerance]'. *radio-vesti.ru*, 27 April. http://www.radiovesti.ru/articles/2011-04-27/fm/577.

Solzhenisyn, Alexander. 1973. *Arkhipelag Gulag*. Paris: YMCA Press.

– 1990. 'Kak nam Obustroit Rossiyu'. *Komsomolskaya Pravda*, 18 September.

– 1991. 'Razmyshleniya po Povodu Dvukh Grazhdnskikh Voin. Interview A.I. Solzhenitsyna Ispanskomu Televideniyu v 1976 godu'. *Komsomolksaya Pravda*, 4 June.

– 1995. 'Razmyshleniya nad Fevralskoy Revolyutsiey'. *Moskva*, no. 2 (February): 146–62.

– 1999. 'Ugodilo Zernyshko Promezh Dvukh Zhernovov. Ocherki Izgnaniya'. *Novyi Mir*, no. 2.

Sorel, Georges. 1999. *Reflections on Violence*. Cambridge: Cambridge University Press.

Sorokin, Pitirim. 2010. *Social and Cultural Dynamics*. New Brunswick, NJ: Transaction Publishers.

Spengler, Oswald. 2013. *The Decline of the West*. USA: Stellar Classics.

Sperling, Valerie. 2006. 'Women's Organizations: Institutionalized Interest Groups or Vulnerable Dissidents?' In *Russian Civil Society: A Critical Assessment*, edited by Alfred Evans, Laura Henry, and Lisa Sundstrom, 161–78. New York: Sharpe Inc.

– 2012. 'Nashi Devushki: Gender and Political Youth Activism in Putin's and Medvedev's Russia'. *Post-Soviet Affairs* 28, no. 2: 232–61.

Squires, Judith. 1999. *Gender in Political Theory*. Cambridge, UK: Polity Press.

Starikov, Nikolay. 2011. *Kak Predavali Rossiyu?* St Petersburg: Piter.

– 2012. 'Politika i patriotizm [Politics and Patriotism]'. *russia.ru*. http://tv.russia.ru/video/online_105/.

– 2013. 'Zapad Unichtozhaet Institut Semyi u Sebia zhe'. *Nikolay Starikov's Blog*, 20 April.

– 2014. *Razgadka Russkoy Revolyutsii*. St Petersburg: Piter.

Starr, Frederick. 1982. 'Local Initiative in Russia before the Zemstvo'. In *The Zemstvo in Russia: An Experience of Local Self-governance*, edited by Terrence Emmons and Wayne Vucinich, 5–31. Cambridge, London, New York: Cambridge University Press.

Sternhell, Zeev. 1978. 'Fascist Ideology'. In *Fascism: A Reader's Guide*, edited by Walter Laqueur, 315–79. Berkley: University of California Press.

Strakhov, Nikolay. 2010. *Bor'ba s Zapadom*. Moscow: Institute of Russian Civilization.

Strauss, Leo. 1953. *Natural Right and History*. Chicago: University of Chicago Press.

– 1959. *What Is Political Philosophy?* Glencoe, IL: The Free Press of Glencoe.

Strelkov, Igor. 2016a. 'Dlia Spaseniya Rossii My Sozdaem Tretyu Silu'. *Dvizhenie Novorossiya*, 31 January. http://novorossia.pro/strelkov/1552-igor-strelkov-dlya-spaseniya-rossii-my-sozdaem-tretyu-silu.html.

– 2016b. 'My Protivostoim Liberalnomu Revanshu'. *Kolokol Rossii*, 29 January. http://kolokolrussia.ru/russkiy-mir/igor-strelkov-m-protivostoim-liberalnomu-revanshu?_utl_t=fb#.

Strizhak, Veronika, Sergey Kurginyan, Yurii Pivovarov, Vladimir Medinskiy, and Alexey Simonov. 2011. 'Operatsiya desovetizatsiya [Operation De-Sovietization]'. In *Otkrytaya Studiya, 5 Kanal St*

Petersburg, 24 April. Accessed 11 December 2019. http://www.youtube. com/watch?v=3EFd31huf3c.

Suganami, Hidemi. 2010. 'The English School in a Nutshell'. *Ritsumeikan Review of International Studies*, no. 9: 15–28.

Suslov, Mikhail. 2012. 'Geographical Metanarratives in Russia and the European East: Contemporary Pan-Slavism'. *Eurasian Geography and Economics* 53, no. 5: 575–95.

Swift, Adam. 2001. *Political Philosophy: A Beginners' Guide for Students and Politicians*. Cambridge, UK: Polity Press.

Syomin, Konstantin. 2015a. *Agitprop: Ideologiya Pobedy*. Moscow: Algoritm.

– 2015b. 'Resovetizatsiya ili nas Somnut. [Resovietization or We Will Be Crushed.) *km.ru*, 24 April. Accessed 12 December 2019. https://www. km.ru/v-rossii/2015/04/24/istoriya-khkh-veka/757952-resovetizatsiya-ili-nas-somnut.

– 2016a. '"Posledniy Zvonok" Dolzhen Stat Nabatom'. *dentv.ru*, 27 September. Accessed 12 December 2019. https://www.youtube.com/ watch?v=FPxoDrrwR68.

– 2016b. 'Komitet 25 Yanvarya'. *Agitprop*, 14 February.

Talmon, Jacob. 1952. *The Origins of Totalitarian Democracy*. London: Secker and Warburg.

Tarlo, Yevgeniy. 2015. 'Rossiya Vozvrashchyaetsya v Krug Velikikh Gosudarstv [Russia Returns to the Club of Great Powers]', *Struktura Momenta*, 29 September.

Taylor, C.C.W. 1995. 'Politics'. In *Cambridge Companion to Aristotle*, edited by Jonathan Barnes, 233–59. Cambridge: Cambridge University Press.

Taylor, Charles. 1979. 'What's Wrong with Negative Liberty'. In *The Idea of Freedom: Essays in Honour of Isaiah Berlin*, edited by Alan Ryan, 175–95. Oxford: Oxford University Press.

– 1994. 'The Politics of Recognition'. In *Multiculturalism*, edited by Amy Gutman, 25–75. Princeton: Princeton University Press.

– 1995. 'Invoking Civil Society'. In *Philosophical Arguments*, edited by Charles Taylor, 204–25. Cambridge MA: Harvard University Press.

– 2011. 'Why We Need a Radical Redefinition of Secularism'. In *The Power of Religion in the Public Sphere*, edited by Eduardo Medieta and Jonathan VanAntwerpen, 34–59. New York: Columbia University Press.

Taylor, George. 1967. 'Noncapitalist Wealth and the Origins of the French Revolution'. *American Historical Review* 72, no. 2: 469–96.

Temkina, Anna, and Elena Zdravomyslova. 2009a. 'Ushel li V Proshloe Patriarkhat? Spetsificheslaia Vlast Slabogo Pola'. In *Gender Dlia Chainikov*, edited by Igor Kon and Olga Iusupova, 25–43. Moscow: Heinrich Bulle Foundation.

– 2009b. *Gendernyi Podkhod v Issledovanii Reproduktivnykh Praktik. Preodolenie Nedoveriya k Reproduktivnoi Meditsine.* St. Petersburg: European University of St Petersburg Press.

Temkina, Anna, Elena Zdravomyslova, and Anna Rotkirkh. 2009. *Sozdanie Privatnosti kak Sfery Zaboty, Luibvi I Naemnogo Truda. Novyi Byt v Sovremennoi Rossii: Gendernye Isseldovaniya Povsednevnosti.* St Petersburg: European University of St Petersburg.

Teubner, Gunther. 1987. *Juridification of Social Spheres: A Comparative Analysis in Labour, Corporate, Social, and Antitrust Law.* New York, Berlin: Walter de Gruyter.

Thaden, Edward. 1964. *Conservative Nationalism in Nineteenth-Century Russia.* Seattle: University of Washington Press.

Thomson, John, and David Held. 1982. 'Editor's Introduction'. In Thomson, J., and Held, D. *Habermas: Critical Debates.* London: Macmillan.

Thurston, Robert. 1996. *Life and Terror in Stalin's Russia, 1934–1941.* New Haven, CT: Yale.

Timofeyev, Igor. 2004. 'The Development of Russian Liberal Thought since 1985'. In *The Demise of Marxism-Leninism in Russia*, edited by Archie Brown, 51–119. Basingstoke, UK: Palgrave Macmillan.

Tishkov, Valery, 2008. 'The Russian People and National Identity: Ways to Form a Civic Nation'. *Russia in Global Affairs* 6, no. 3 (July-Sept.): 172–180.

Tolstoy, Peter, Natalya Narochnitskaya, Sergey Dorenko, and Sergey Kurginyan. 2014. *Politika*, 18 March, Russia Channel 1.

Tolz, Vera. 2001. *Russia: Inventing the Nation.* London: Arnold.

Tourinho, Marcos, Oliver Stuenkel, and Stephen Brockmeier. 2016. 'Responsibility while Protecting: Reforming R2P Implementation'. *Global Society* 30, no. 1: 134–50.

Toynbee, Arnold J. 1939. *A Study of History.* Oxford: Oxford University Press.

Tretyakov, Vitaly. 2019. 'Sovetskiy Soyuz Prityagivaet Luidei Svoim Velichiem'. *Krasnaya Vesna*, 28 December 2018. Accessed 5 November 2019. https://rossaprimavera.ru/news/fdb3b701.

Tretyakov, Vitaly, Valery Fadeyev, Yurii Pivovarov, Igor Yurgens, and Vladimir Pligin. 2013b. 'Kto diskreditiruyet liberalizm v Rossii? [Who Is

Discrediting Liberalism in Russia?]'. *Chto Delat?* no. 346 (24 February). Accessed 11 December 2019. http://www.youtube.com/watch?v=t6xX2-BivWg.

Tretyakov, Vitaly, Alexey Kara-Murza, Yurii Pivovarov, Iosif Diskin, Andrey Fursov, and Leonid Yakobson. 2007. 'Kak modernizirovat Rossiyu? [How to Modernize Russia?]'. *Chto Delat?* 25 March. Accessed 11 December 2019. http://www.youtube.com/watch?v=WdhmfRCUlnU.

Tretyakov, Vitaly, Alexey Kara-Murza, Boris Titov, and Igor Bunin. 2008. 'Liberalizm kak politika v Rossii [Liberalism as Policy in Russia]'. *Chto Delat*, no. 224 (14 December). Accessed 11 December 2019. http://www.youtube.com/watch?v=eKOfpWPZicw.

Tretyakov, Vitaly, Sergey Kurginyan, Alexandr Dugin, Mikhail Leontyev, and Alex Nagornyi. 2007. 'Konspirologiya: Nauka ili Mifologiya'. *Chto Delat?* 23 December. https://www.youtube.com/watch?v=kOu-dWlzX1 E&list=PLC25C62E68E48A261.

Tretyakov, Vitaly, Konstantin Malofeyev, Alexey Chesnakov, Vladimir Kantor, Sergey Markov, Boris Mezhuyev, and Mikhail Remezov. 2010. 'Rossiiskiy Konservatizm-2'. *Chto Dealt?* 24 January. https://www.youtube.com/watch?v=DqxdG6gbxKQ.

Tretyakov, Vitaly, Vadim Mezhuyev, Sergey Kurginyan, Vladimir Neklessa, Oleg Kildyushov, and Alexandr Militarev. 2009a. 'Postmodern: Raspad tsivilizatsii i politiki? [Post-Modernity: Disintegration of Civilization and Politics?]'. Chto Delat? 24 May. http://www.youtube.com/watch?v1/4tkQLiGGHxYA.

Tretyakov, Vitaly, Vadim Mezhuyev, Sergey Kurginyan, Alexandr Neklessa, Oleg Kildyushov, Viktor Militarev. 2009b. 'Postmodern: Raspad Tsivilzatsii i Politiki? [Post-modernity: Disintegration of Civilization and Politics?]' *Chto Delat?* 25 May. http://www.youtube.com/watch?v=Ni8s5yIBQoA.

Tretyakov, Vitaly, Yurii Pivovarov, Alexey Kara-Murza, Iosif Diskin, and Boris Makarenko. 2011. 'Rossiya i liberalizm. Vechnyy mezal'yans? [Russia and Liberalism. An Eternal Misalliance]'. *Chto Delat?* April 3. Accessed 11 December 2019. http://www.youtube.com/watch?v=b4u9sSG_5Xo.

Tretyakov, Vitaly, Mikhail Remizov, Alexey Chesnakov, Boris Mezhuyev, Sergey Markov, and Maxim Kantor. 2013a. 'Rossiyskiy konservatizm [Russian Conservatism]'. *Chto Delat?* 21 December. Accessed 22 January 2019. http://www.youtube.com/watch?v1/4q-WVy7s6S6o.

Tretyakov, Vitaly, Tatyana Shishova, Anatoly Antonov, Olga Karabanova, Vladimir Khomyakov. 2013c. 'Smert Semyi. Diagnoz Okonchatelnyi?'

Chto Delat?, 14 February. Accessed 27 November 2019. http://www.
youtube.com/watch?v=P5v-s__AuSQ.

Trevor-Roper, Hugh. 1968. 'The Phenomenon of Fascism'. In *European
Fascism*, edited by Stuart Joseph Wolf, 19–39. London: Weidenfeld and
Nicolson.

Tribuna. 1998. "Reabilitatsii ne Podlezhit." 3 (1 February).

Troitsky, Artemyi. 2010. 'Ya schitayu, chto nastoyashchiy russkiy muzhik
dolzhen vymeret'. *Slon*, 15 January.

Trotsky, Leo. 2004. *The Revolution Betrayed*. Mineola, NY: Dover
Publications.

Tsipko, Alexandr. 2010. 'Dvoystvennost Russkoy Intelligentsii. [The
Duality of the Russian Intelligentsia]'. *Filosofskie Chteniia*, 28 January
2010. http://www.evrazia.tv/content/dvoystvennost-russkoy-
intelligencii.

Tsygankov, Andrey. 2016. 'Crafting the State-Civilization: Vladimir
Putin's Turn to Distinct Values'. *Problems of Post-Communism* 68,
no. 2: 1–13.

Tsymbursky, Vadim. 2007. *Ostrov Rossiya. Geopoliticheskie I
Khronopoliticheskie Raboty: 1993–2006*. Moscow: Evropa.

– 2008. 'Shelf Ostrova Rossiya: Geopolitika prostranstva i geopolitika
granits [The Shelf of Island Russia: The Geopolitics of Space and the
Geopolitics of Boundaries]'. Agency for Political News, 18 September.
http://www.archipelag.ru/ authors/cimbursky/?library1/42783.

Tully, James. 1988. 'The Pen Is a Mighty Sword'. In *Meaning and Context.
Quentin Skinner and his Critics*, edited by James Tully, 7–25. Princeton:
Princeton University Press.

– 1995. *Strange Multiplicity: Constitutionalism in an Age of Diversity*.
Cambridge: Cambridge University Press.

Turner, Stephen, and George Mazur. 2009. 'Morgenthau as a Weberian
Methodologist'. *European Journal of International Relations* 15, no. 3:
477–504.

Tweedy, John, and Alan Hunt. 1994. 'The Future of the Welfare State and
Social Rights: Reflections on Habermas'. *Journal of Law and Society* 21,
no. 3 (September): 288–316.

Umland, Andreas. 2005. 'Concepts of Fascism in Contemporary Russia'.
Political Studies Review 3, no. 1: 34–49.

– 2008. 'Is Putin's Russia Really Fascist? A Response to Alexander Motyl'.
History News Network, 26 March. Accessed 15 November 2019.
https://historynewsnetwork.org/article/49022.

Vanchugov, Vasiliy. 2014. 'Dukhovnaya Glubina Konservatizma'.
Izvestiya, 19 March.

Vayrynen, Raimo. 1995. 'Bipolarity, Multipolarity, and Domestic Political Systems'. *Journal of Peace Research* 32, no. 3 (August): 361–71.

Vedeneev, Evgeniy, and Sergey Kurginyan. 2013. *Sut Vremeni Sergeya Kurginyana*. Moscow: Algoritm.

Vernadsky, Georgy. 1926. *Nachertaniya Russkoi Istorii*. Prague: Evraziiskoe Knigoizdatelstvo.

Voegelin, Eric. 2000. *Modernity Without Restraint: The Political Religions; The New Science of Politics and Science; Politics and Gnosticism.* Columbia, MO: University of Missouri Press.

Vogel, Ursula. 1991. 'Is Citizenship Gender-Specific?' In *The Frontiers of Citizenship*, edited by Ursula Vogel and Mike Moran, 58–85. Basingstoke, UK: Macmillan.

Von Laue, Theodore. 1958. 'Sergei Witte and the Industrialization of Russia'. *American Slavic and East European Review* 17, no. 1 (February): 25–46.

Voronina, Olga. 2004. *Feminizm i Gendernoe Ravensto*. Moscow: Editorial URSS.

Voskresnyy vecher. 2012. 'Voskresnyy vecher s Vladimirom Solov'yevym – svoboda [Sunday Evening with Vladimir Solov'yev – Freedom]'. 7 October. http://www.youtube.com/watch?v=N9eu_du3Hig.

VTSIOM. 2017. 'Zhenshchina – president Rossii: Byt ili ne Byt'. *VTSIOM*, 17 October. Accessed 15 December 2019. https://infographics.wciom.ru/theme-archive/politics/internal-policy/political-ideology/article/zhenshchina-prezident-v-rossii-byt-ili-ne-byt.html.

Wagner, Peter. 1994. *A Sociology of Modernity: Liberty and Discipline.* London: Routledge.

– 2012. *Modernity: Understanding the Present*. Cambridge, UK: Polity.

Waldron, Peter. 2002. 'P.A. Stolypin: The Search for Stability in Imperial Russia'. *Slavic Review* 61, no. 3 (Autumn): 620–1.

Walicki, Andrzej. 1979. *A History of Russian Thought from the Enlightenment to Marxism*. Stanford University Press: Stanford, California.

Waltz, Kenneth. 1979. *Theory of International Politics*. Reading, MA: Addison-Wesley.

Walzer, Michael. 1994. 'Comment'. In *Multiculturalism*, edited by Amy Gutman, 99–105. Princeton: Princeton University Press.

Ward, Ian. 2009. 'Helping the Dead Speak: Leo Strauss, Quentin Skinner, and the Art of Interpretation in Political Thought'. *Polity* 41, no. 2 (April): 235–55.

Ware, Timothy. 1997. *The Orthodox Church*. London: Penguin Books.

Weber, Eugen. 1964. *Varieties of Fascism*. New York: Van Nostrand.

Weber, Max. 1971. *The Sociology of Religion*. London: Routledge.

– 2004. *The Vocation Lectures: 'Science as a Vocation'; 'Politics as a Vocation'*. Indiana: Hackett Publishing Company.

Weinstock, Daniel. 2007. 'Liberalism, Multiculturalism, and the Problem of Internal Minorities'. In *Multiculturalism and Political Theory*, edited by Anthony Laden and David Owen, 244–64. Cambridge: Cambridge University Press.

Wendt, Alexander. 1992. 'Anarchy Is What the State Makes of It: The Social Construction of Power Politics'. *International Organization* 46, no. 2 (Spring): 391–425.

Westphal, Merold. 1984. 'Hegel's Radical Idealism: Family and State as Ethical Communities'. In *The State and Civil Society: Studies in Hegel's Political Philosophy*, edited by Z.A. Pelczynski, 77–93. Cambridge: Cambridge University Press.

White, Stephen. 2011. *Understanding Russian Politics*. Cambridge: Cambridge University Press.

Willems, Joachim. 2006. 'The Religio-political Strategies of the Russian Orthodox Church as a "Politics of Discourse"'. *Religion, State, and Society* 34, no. 3: 287–98.

Williams, Bernard. 1972. *Morality: An Introduction to Ethics*. Cambridge: Cambridge University Press.

– 1979. 'Conflicts of Values'. In *The Idea of Freedom: Essays in Honour of Isaiah Berlin*, edited by Alan Ryan, 221–33. Oxford: Oxford University Press.

– 1993. *Morality: An Introduction to Ethics*. Cambridge: Cambridge University Press.

– 2005. 'In the Beginning Was the Deed'. In *In the Beginning was the Deed: Realism and Moralism in Political Argument*, edited by Bernard Williams, 18–28. Princeton: Princeton University Press.

– 2006. *The Sense of the Past: Essays in the History of Philosophy*. Princeton: Princeton University Press.

Williams, Michael. 2001. 'The Discipline of the Democratic Peace: Kant, Liberalism, and the Social Construction of Security Communities'. *European Journal of International Relations* 7, no. 4: 525–53.

– 2005. *The Realist Tradition and the Limits of International Relations*. Cambridge: Cambridge University Press.

– 2007. *Realism Reconsidered: The Legacy of Morgenthau in International Relations*. Oxford: Oxford University Press.

Williams, Stephen. 2006. *Liberal Reform in an Illiberal Regime: The Creation of Private Property in Russia, 1906–1915*. Stanford, CA: Hoover Institution Press Publication.

Wilson, Jonathan, and James Monten. 2011. 'Does Kant Justify Liberal Intervention?' *The Review of Politics* 73, no. 4 (Fall): 633–47.

Yakunin, Vladimir. 2014. 'Yakunin Predlozhil Plan Vykhoda iz Krizisa'. *Obshchaya Gazeta*, 13 March.

– 2017. 'The World after 2016: Imagining Possible Futures'. Lecture at Peking University, 21 March. https://doc-research.org/2017/06/world-2016-imagining-future-development/.

Yanov, Alexandr. 2003. 'Ideinaya Voina. Epigony, Liberaly, Rossiiya i Evropa'. *Polis*.

Yashin, Ilya. 2013. 'Ne Khodite k Nemu, Banderlogi. O tslesoobraznosti Dialoga s Vlastyu'. *Svobodnaya Pressa*, 22 November.

Yeatman, Anna. 1997. 'Feminism and Power'. In *Reconstructing Political Theory: Feminist Perspectives*, edited by Mary Lindon Shanley and Uma Narayan, 144–57. Cambridge, UK: Polity Press.

Yurgens, Igor, and Evgeniy Gontmakher. 2011. 'Rossiya XXI Veka: Obraz Zhelaemogo Zavtra'. Biblioteka Instituta Sovremennogo Razvitiya, 3 March. *gazeta.ru*. www.gazeta.ru/politics/2010/02/02_a_3319216.shtml?incut1.

Zadornov, Mikhail. 2017. 'Posledneye Interview'. 10 November. https://www.youtube.com/watch?v=evvP_OhaoRQ.

Zakamskaya, Evelina, Boris Mezhuyev, Natalya Narochnitskaya, and Leonid Polyakov. 2014. 'Referendum v Krymu'. *Meninie Rossiya* 24 (17 March). https://www.youtube.com/watch?v=YL-9A3B-Mtg.

Zakharova, Mariya. 2015. 'Kak Slushali Obamu I Uslyshat li Putina?' In *Spetsialnyi Korrespondent with Evgeniy Popov*, 29 September. https://www.youtube.com/watch?v=l6I5cZD4Eyw.

'Zakon o lishenii svobody za oskorbleniye chuvstv veruyushchikh vnesen v GD [Law on deprivation of freedom for insulting religious feelings is introduced in the State Duma]'. *RIA Novosti*, 26 September.

Zalewski, Marysia. 1995. 'Well, What Is the Feminist Perspective on Bosnia?' *International Affairs* 71, no. 2: 339–56.

Zaslavskaia, Tatyana. 2006a. 'Avangard Rossiskogo Delovogo Soobshchestva: Gendernsyi Aspekt'. *SotIs*, no. 4: 3–17.

– 2006b. 'Avangard Rossiiskogo Delovogo Soobshchestva. Statia 2'. *SotsIs*, no. 5: 3–15.

Zdravomyslova, Olga. 2001. *Na Puti k Novomu Etapu Ponimaniia. Gendernye Issledovaniia v Rossii: Sostoianie i Perspektivy*. Moscow: Gorbachev Fond.

Zemskov, Viktor. 2012. 'Masshtab Politicheskikh Repressii V SSSR. Pravad i Domysly'. *Trudy Instituta Rossiiskoi Istorii* 10, no. 1: 303–18.

Zhirinovskiy, Vladimir, and Leonid Gozman, *Poyedinok s Vladimirom Solovyovym*, 20 January 2011.

Zinoviev, Alexandr. 2001. *Gibel Russkogo Kommunizma*. Moscow: TsentrPoligraph.

Zolo, Danilo. 2007. 'The Re-emerging Notion of Empire and the Influence of Carl Schmitt's Thought'. In *The International Political Thought of Carl Schmitt: A New Global Nomos?* edited by Louiza Odysseos and Fabio Petito, 154–66. London: Routledge.

Zubov, Alexey, ed. 2017. *Istoriya Rossii XX Vek. Degradatsiya Gosudarstva i Dvizhenie k Novoi Rossii (1953–2008)*. Vol. 3. Moscow: Eksmo.

Zudin, Alexei. 1995. 'Fashizm v Rossii: obrazy i real'nosti novoi opasnosti'. *Politicheskie Issledovaniya* 26, no. 2: 41–3.

Zyuganov, Gennady. 2015. 'Otkrytoye Pismo Grazhdanam Strany'. *KPRF*, 9 February.

– 2016. 'Ideologiya Predateley'. *Krasnaya Liniya*, 8 June. Accessed 5 November 2019. https://www.rline.tv/news/2016-06-08-gennadiy-zyuganov-predsedatel-tsk-kprf-statya-ideologiya-predateley/.

– 2017. 'Gennadyi Zuiganov Nazval Navalnogo Popom Gaponom'. *Krasnaya Liniya*, 30 March. Accessed 30 January 2019. www.rline.tv.news/2017-03-30-gennadiy-zyuganov-nazval-navalnogo-popom-gaponom/.

– 2019. 'My Vozrodim Tebya, Sovetskiy Soyuz!' *KPRF*, 19 August 2019. Accessed 5 November 2019. https://kprf.ru/international/95882.html.

Index

171–2, 184; Western, 153, 161–2, 168, 272

nationalists, 16, 26, 57, 126, 141, 143–4, 163–5, 167–74, 211

nationhood, 215, 294

nations, 22–3, 68–70, 76, 78–80, 144–5, 162, 167, 170, 264, 267, 299, 301, 306–7, 317, 320; non-historical, 144; political, 153, 215

nation-state, 15, 22, 36, 106, 108, 137, 139, 143, 162–3, 170, 204

nature, human, 95, 101, 116, 139

Nazism, 25, 130

neo-liberalism, 11, 75–6, 98

neutralization, political, 275–6

Nietzsche, Friedrich, 66, 99–100, 296, 305, 308

nihilism, 102

non-interference, 209, 246, 254

norms: ethical, 72, 79; political, 34, 189; social, 232, 253

North Caucasus, 35, 154, 167, 173, 220–1

ontology, 14, 233

opposition: radical, 141, 172; radical-liberal, 29

order: republican, 22, 170; universal, 23, 170

Palamas, Gregory, 155

paradigm, 22, 57–8, 118, 140, 262; ideological, 16, 59; liberal, 118, 261–2; political, 34, 153; social, 46, 89–90; socio-cultural, 5–6

particularities, cultural, 147, 181–2, 184, 206–7

parties, political, 8–9, 111, 201, 228, 262

patriarch, 158–9, 300

Patriarch Kirill, 94, 101, 107, 111, 160–1

patriarchy, 231–3, 237, 240, 242–3, 250, 252, 259

patriotism, civic, 35, 213

perestroika, 13, 132, 301

periphery, 198, 200; societal, 45, 51

philosophy: German, 136, 310; political, 7, 179, 260, 309, 318–19; Western, 44, 52, 99, 123, 139, 178, 181, 197, 203, 230, 258

Platonism, 103, 116, 135, 155

pluralism: civilizational, 189; normative, 176, 190, 192, 198; paradigmatic, 16, 22, 24, 174, 211, 262–3, 266; religious, 211; tradition of, 30; value, 30, 32, 38, 70, 95, 109–10, 209

policies, foreign, 5, 112, 147–8, 228

politics: anti-political, 294; illiberal, 113; world, 177, 201, 274, 285, 294

polycentrism, 185–6, 314

polygyny, 165, 221

positivism, 157, 306

post-capitalism, 137

post-Marxism, 3, 97, 109

postmodernity, 14, 46, 59–60, 79, 85, 91, 99–102, 110–11, 287, 290, 321

post-society, 103, 287

poststructuralism, 179, 234

power: economic, 131; global, 128, 176; models of, 236, 242, 254–6

practices: cultural, 212; liberal, 29, 42, 206, 216, 225, 229; political, 33, 197, 210, 222, 228

privatization, 119, 132

progress, 22, 31, 42, 49, 54, 83, 96, 98, 101, 178, 185

314; classless, 42, 122, 127;
economic, 51; liberal, 206, 208;
modern, 98, 102, 223; patriarchal, 240, 252; post-industrial,
217; socialist, 114, 116, 247;
Soviet, 12, 98; Western, 56, 97–8,
102, 145, 272
solidarity, social, 75, 77, 137, 161
Solzhenitsyn, Alexander, 123–4,
171, 301
South Ossetia, 192, 195
sovereignty, 108, 174, 187–91, 193,
219, 314; civilizational, 108,
187–8; state, 139–40, 187–92,
201
Soviet Union, 4, 10–11, 13–15, 36,
59–60, 111, 119–21, 125–31,
147–8, 166–8, 170–1, 237,
240–1, 243, 280
Spain, 125, 220
spirituality, 69, 103, 150, 227
stability, social, 31, 44, 48
state: apparatus, 9, 11, 128; civilization, 15, 261, 322; fascist,
24–5; liberal, 47, 279; modern,
145, 230; power, 12, 120, 184;
Russian, 11–12, 14, 19–20, 62,
65, 140–1, 163, 165–7, 171, 173,
177, 215, 220; sovereign, 188–9;
Soviet, 11, 19–20, 114–15, 128,
130–1, 136, 239, 261
State Duma, 160, 218, 225, 246,
272, 325
statehood, 66, 69, 140
Stolypin, Peter, 42, 84
Strakhov, Nikolay, 182, 274, 281
structure, political, 25, 197, 249
Struve, Peter, 50, 281, 283
style, political, 25, 37
suffrage, universal, 45, 117
superpower, 65, 79, 310

symphony, 104, 158–9
system: financial, 191, 193; institutional, 80, 93, 161; political, 9,
16, 50, 53, 78–9, 81, 137–8, 140,
159, 164, 198, 239, 242; social,
89, 95, 271; Westphalian, 189,
191

taxonomy, 97, 185
technology, political, 78, 223
telos, 114–15
theology, 69, 156; political, 76,
293, 314
theory, multipolar-world-order,
187, 198
thinkers: conservative, 60, 73,
81–2, 104, 108, 170; Eurasian,
270; left-wing, 123–4, 129, 131,
138; liberal, 46, 216, 272, 276;
Russian, 211–12, 227, 229, 268,
281; Western, 95, 189
Third Rome, concept of, 71, 151,
154, 288
Third World, 180, 183
tolerance, 70, 191, 200, 223, 256,
316–17
toleration, 203, 209–10, 222–6,
233; conflict model of, 222–3,
225; practice of, 209, 223–4
Tolstoy, Leo, 171, 320
totalitarianism, 113, 292
Toynbee, Arnold, 96, 154, 320
traditionalism, 13, 142, 177, 230,
263
traditionalists, 15–16, 117–18, 140,
142, 146, 212, 214, 218–21,
226, 229, 261–4, 266, 269
traditions: cultural, 150; historic, 58,
78; neo-liberal, 203–4; political,
14, 66, 80, 158; religious, 103–4,
212; socio-political, 38, 208